Dalton Trumbo, Hollywood Rebel

Dalton Trumbo, Hollywood Rebel

A Critical Survey and Filmography

by
Peter Hanson

McFarland & Company, Inc., Publishers
Jefferson, North Carolina, and London

Library of Congress Cataloguing-in-Publication Data

Hanson, Peter, 1969–
Dalton Trumbo, Hollywood rebel : a critical survey and filmography /
by Peter Hanson.
p.   cm.
Includes bibliographical references and index.
ISBN 0-7864-0872-3 (illustrated case binding : 50# alkaline paper) ∞
1. Trumbo, Dalton, 1905–1976—Criticism and interpretation.
2. Motion picture plays—History and criticism.
I. Title.
PS3539.R928Z69   2001
818'.5209—dc21   00-53719

British Library cataloguing data are available

On the cover: Dalton Trumbo, 1941.
(Photograph by Harry Baskerville)

Manufactured in the United States of America

*McFarland & Company, Inc., Publishers
Box 611, Jefferson, North Carolina 28640
www.mcfarlandpub.com*

Contents

Acknowledgments

My main accomplice in this project was Leslie S. Connor, to whom this book is dedicated. She provided insight and guidance during every stage of research and writing, reviewed numerous passages in rough form, and helped streamline the final manuscript. Her intelligence, patience, and support are reflected on every page.

Christopher Trumbo's comments about his father's character and career were vital to this book, and I am deeply grateful for his reactions to the completed manuscript. Mitzi Trumbo provided photographs of her father that convey a great deal about the life he lived.

I am indebted to my predecessors, Bruce Cook, author of the biography *Dalton Trumbo*, and Helen Manfull, editor of *Additional Dialogue: Letters of Dalton Trumbo 1942–1962*, and also to Matti Salo, author of the important history *The Silent Heroes (The Brave Ones): Screenwriters on the Hollywood Blacklist*.

He was gracious about sharing his research with me, as was Jeff Blitz of the Writers Guild of America's Blacklist Credits Committee.

Others who provided invaluable assistance include Bill Evans, Jim Folts, and the staff of the New York State Archives' Manuscripts and Special Collections Department; Jill A. Rydberg and the New York State Archives Partnership Trust, a grant from which facilitated much of my research into Trumbo's obscure films; Anna C. Connor of the New York State Library; John Brent (and his trusty VCR); Justin Pettigrew of Turner Classic Movies; Greg Goutos of Karner Video; Kristine Krueger and the staff of the National Film Information Service; the library staff at the American Film Institute; Angelique C. Bovee of WXXA-TV (Albany, New York); and Harold L. Miller of the State Historical Society of Wisconsin. Thanks are also due to Publisher's Studio, Bruce G. Hallenbeck, and John Bracchi.

Introduction

Dalton Trumbo fought the good fight. A gifted artist, a fervent activist, and a true American, Trumbo used his position as one of Hollywood's most prominent screenwriters of the 1940s to portray idealistic characters who stood fast to their beliefs. And when standing fast to one of his own beliefs lost Trumbo his place in the limelight, he reinvented himself and shouted his messages about free speech and independent thought louder than ever until his death in 1976.

In a singular movie career that spanned over four decades, Trumbo crafted stories that ranged from intimate character studies to sweeping myths, yet one common thread connects the best of Trumbo's screenplays: honor. In the dozens of movies he wrote and the one he directed, Trumbo exemplified honor as he saw it. Consider the two aspects of his life with which Trumbo is still most closely identified, more than two decades after his death: the Hollywood blacklist and *Johnny Got His Gun*. Now regarded as one of the darkest chapters in America's history, the blacklist represented institutionalized ignorance and

paranoia, and it was the inclusion of Trumbo's name in the credits of *Spartacus* and *Exodus*, following 13 years during which political persecution prevented him from taking screen credit for his work, that broke the blacklist in 1960. Similarly, *Johnny Got His Gun*—both Trumbo's 1939 novel and his 1971 film—have earned venerable reputations among the canons of antiwar literature and cinema, respectively.

But what made Trumbo an exemplary talent among Hollywood screenwriters—and what makes him relevant for study years after his heyday—is how deeply his ideals permeated his work. Nearly all of Trumbo's scripts have aspects of social consciousness, because Trumbo never stopped observing the world around him. Trumbo didn't just make honor a theme in epics such as *Spartacus* and *Exodus*; he also made it a theme in light romances and dark dramas. Even the obsessed missionary played by Max Von Sydow in *Hawaii* adheres to a code of honor; although a callous zealot insensitive to the history and character of Hawaii's native people, he is relentless in pursuit of what he believes to be a higher goal. This reveals another aspect of Trumbo's screenplays: At his best, he didn't paint simple heroes or villains. Good guys in his scripts often used devious means to achieve noble goals; monsters were often honest or brilliant.

Trumbo saw honor as a way to view the human condition. By discovering what meant the most to each character he created or adapted, Trumbo found a way to reveal that character to audiences. Whether he was trying to make viewers sympathize with the rampaging crooks in *Gun Crazy*, revealing why a jaded American reporter fell for a privileged European princess in *Roman Holiday*, or taking us inside the minds of debauched Roman noblemen in *Spartacus*, Trumbo treated nearly all of his characters fairly. By understanding characters as people instead of archetypes, Trumbo fashioned dialogue and action that made characters in his scripts vibrant, real, and sometimes unforgettable. (That Trumbo occasionally slipped from these lofty ideals is an acknowledgment not only of his humanity but of the troubled times in which he worked.)

Consider the manner in which Trumbo introduced Jack W. Burns, played by Kirk Douglas in *Lonely Are the Brave*. The picture opens with a steady tracking shot of a cowboy's campsite—steaming embers, a saddle, chapped boots—and reveals Jack resting against a rock in a barren field in the American West. As Jack nurses a cigarette under the shade of his cowboy hat, a strange noise encroaches on the bucolic scene—that of airplane engines roaring overhead. Jack looks up and sees them, three jets zipping across the sky and leaving white smoke trails behind them. With

this simple juxtaposition, Trumbo shows viewers how odd a fit Jack's cowboy lifestyle is with modern existence.

Trumbo continues establishing Jack's world as the cowboy trots his horse, Whiskey, through rural Duke City, New Mexico. Jack and Whiskey encounter a barbed-wire fence, so Jack discreetly unsheathes a pair of wire cutters, scans the scene, and cuts his way through the fence. In just two scenes, Trumbo and director David Miller establish that Jack will find his way in this world that is not his own with the force of a square peg entering a round hole.

In the film's third scene, Jack reaches a busy rural highway and has to coax Whiskey into crossing through traffic. In addition to foreshadowing a significant run-in that Jack will have later in the movie, Trumbo makes us feel for Jack's losing battle to keep the western lifestyle alive. These cars, like the Industrial Age, aren't stopping for anybody, least of all a lone cowpoke on horseback. Finally, Jack reaches the other side of the road, and Miller frames the cowboy and his horse against a junkyard where hundreds of compacted cars are stacked. This easy, poetic image tells us the movie's viewpoint: Jack's lifestyle is something real, whereas rushed modern life, epitomized by cars, is junk.

Expressive sequences such as the opening of *Lonely Are the Brave* appear throughout Trumbo's scripts. The rugged, unforgiving landscapes of the American West told viewers what kind of man Jack W. Burns was, just as the twinkling fountains and welcoming piazzas in *Roman Holiday* made viewers believe Rome existed only to stimulate romance. As a master craftsman, Trumbo had myriad tools with which he communicated motivations, emotions, and conflicts. And like any craftsman, Trumbo had specialties. In the first half of his career, Trumbo distinguished himself as a master of story structure, often providing detailed frameworks upon which other writers layered dialogue and visual details. But in his later years, Trumbo asserted his gift for language by crafting eloquent interplay between characters. Some of the sharpest moments in Trumbo's scripts are quiet scenes in which characters dance around the issues connecting them. A vivid example of the dry wit Trumbo brought to his latter-day pictures is found in *Exodus*, producer-director Otto Preminger's colossal drama about the formation of Israel.

In the picture, Paul Newman plays Ari Ben Canaan, a Jewish freedom fighter who travels to the island of Cyprus intent on liberating 30,000 European Jews interred there. Partially to extricate a large number of the internees at once and partially to send a message to the world, Ari decides to free 611 Jews who just arrived on a steamship, the *Star of David*. To do so, he must move them past the British army, which occupies Cyprus and polices the camps. So, in a brazen scheme straight out of a pulp novel, Ari acquires a British uniform and falsified orders. Affecting a British accent and an officer's intimidating manners, Ari convinces the British to release the prisoners, provide trucks in which to move them, and even supply a military escort.

Once the procession of refugees reaches the dock where they are to board a ship bound for Palestine, Ari crosses paths with Major Fred Caldwell (Peter Lawford), a fatuous underling of the British commanding officer. An enlisted man calls Fred because he's not sure about Ari's credentials, but once the two officers—one real, one a disguised Jew—exchange niceties, Fred tells the enlisted man to expedite Ari's project.

"I don't care about the Jews one way or the other," Fred bleats to Ari, "but they are troublesome, aren't they?"

"Oh, no question about it," Ari replies. "You get two of them together, you've got a debate on your hands. Three, you're putting on a revolution."

"Half of them are communists anyway," Fred says.

"The other half, pawnbrokers," Ari responds.

"They look funny, too..." Before Fred's words have time to hang in the air, Ari shoots him a vicious glance, and in playing the scene, Newman lets indignation flare in his eyes for a split-second before regaining his poise. Oblivious to Ari's response, Fred finishes his thought. "I can spot one a mile away."

His anger quickly turning to mischief, Ari leans close to Fred and says, "Would you mind looking in my eye, sir? It feels like a cinder." Ari lifts his right hand to indicate his right eye, then Fred puts both of his hands onto the Jewish man's face, gently pulling back Ari's eyelids and peering into his right eye with little more than a few inches of space between them.

"You know," Fred continues, "A lot of them try to hide under Gentile names, but one look in their face, and you just know."

"With a little experience, you can even smell them out," Ari adds, barely hiding a grin.

"Sorry ... I can't find a thing," Fred says, pulling his hands away from Ari's face.

Trumbo fills this scene with anger but turns it comical and even subversive.

In the space of a few short lines of dialogue and a simple action between two people, Trumbo reveals, ridicules, and taunts Fred's anti–Semitism without letting him in on the joke. But the scene has deeper meaning, too. In addition to satirizing the ignorance of anti–Semitism, the scene slaps prejudice in the face. This may be the undercurrent of the scene that mattered most to Trumbo, because he was a victim of prejudice.

In 1947, Trumbo became one of the Hollywood Ten, a group of movie writers and directors whose refusal to name names before Senator J. Parnell Thomas's anticommunist House Committee on Un-American Activities (HUAC)[1] won them jail sentences. Trumbo, Ring Lardner, Jr., Edward Dmytryk, and seven others all stood on their First Amendment rights to free speech and assembly, and in so doing, thumbed their noses at Thomas's witch hunt. Trumbo, whose name would later be inextricably linked with the Hollywood blacklist that resulted from the committee's hearings, was sent to prison for nearly a year. He went from being one of the industry's highest-paid writers to an unemployed convict.

But prison wasn't enough to prevent Trumbo from earning a living—or practicing his own brand of civil disobedience. Trumbo spent 13 years writing screenplays for the Hollywood black market, during which time other writers' names appeared on the credits of his screenplays—which ranged from atrocious B movies (*They Were So Young*) to award-winning classics (*Roman Holiday*). Sometimes Trumbo used "fronts," writers who risked their reputations for idealistic or financial reasons, and sometimes the names on Trumbo's blacklist-era screenplays were pseudonyms. The

climax of this period came on March 27, 1957, when a man named Robert L. Rich won an Oscar for writing the story of the offbeat family drama *The Brave One*. Much to the embarrassment of the Academy of Motion Picture Arts and Sciences—which had gone to great lengths to disqualify blacklisted writer Michael Wilson, nominated the same year for the adapted screenplay of *Friendly Persuasion*—"Robert L. Rich" turned out to be a pen name for Trumbo. This event splashed the open secret that blacklisted writers were working underground onto front pages across the country.

And four years later, Trumbo emerged from the underground when his credits appeared on the adaptations of Howard Fast's *Spartacus* and Leon Uris's *Exodus*. Producer-star Kirk Douglas had planned for nearly two years to reveal that "Sam Jackson," the screenwriter of *Spartacus*, was actually Trumbo. But Otto Preminger stole Douglas's thunder—and surprised the movie industry—by announcing in January 1960 that Trumbo was writing *Exodus* for him. Preminger's announcement gave Douglas the momentum to get Trumbo credited on *Spartacus*. Douglas's and Preminger's willingness to defy the paranoid status quo of the day effectively broke the blacklist, but the blacklist's spirit lived on for many years afterward.

One place the blacklist haunted was Trumbo's writing. Always an independent thinker unafraid to buck convention for the sake of a story, Trumbo became a genuine rebel in the years following the blacklist. The characters about whom he wrote battled everything from the Establishment to fate itself, and they often did it with a smile and, most damning, a lack of remorse.

Nearly 20 years after he wrote the story for *The Brave One* under a pseudonym, Trumbo (seated) accepts his Oscar from Academy of Motion Pictures Arts and Sciences President Walter Mirisch. (AMPAS)

Just as Trumbo got sent to jail by refusing to cave to HUAC, so too did many of his latter-day characters seal their fates by refusing to abide by laws other men wrote.

Jack W. Burns in *Lonely Are the Brave* is typical of these latter-day Trumbo protagonists. After the opening sequence, he arrives at the home of his close friends Jerri and Paul Bondi. There's a hot romantic spark between Jack and Jerri (played by Gena Rowlands), which gives an edge to the scene that follows. Over coffee, Jack learns that Paul was jailed for helping illegal immigrants. He asks Jerri to explain her husband's crime, which, in her telling, sounds more like compassion.

"What's wrong with that?" Jack asks her, genuinely confused.

"Nothing," she responds. "It's just a crime, that's all." The bitter insinuation of that line—that lawmakers are at best erratic and at worst foolish—is illustrative of the nearly anarchistic politics that Trumbo brought to his post-blacklist films.

After this exchange, Jack launches into a monologue about a resentment against laws and borders that he shares with Paul. "The more fences there are, the more he hates them," Jack says in a line that could just as easily be descriptive of himself, and perhaps even of Trumbo.

"Jack, I'm gonna tell you something," Jerri responds, the easygoing conversation turning serious. "The world that you and Paul live in doesn't exist. Maybe it never did. Out there is a real world and it's got real borders and real fences, real laws and real trouble. And either you go by the rules or you lose ... you lose everything."

Jack barely lets Jerri's words settle

before saying she's right to think that Paul is irresponsible. In fact, Jack says, Paul is probably having one last fling with a woman before settling down for the rest of his life. Jerri freezes, hearing a nightmare she never had, but then Jack identifies Paul's mistress: "Her name is, 'Do what you want to do and the hell with everyone else.'"

With brittle exchanges such as this one—in which machismo and righteous indignation blend into something undefinable—Trumbo showed his true colors. He spoke as only a man who has made sacrifices to defend his ideals has the right to speak: from moral higher ground. Whether the sentiment illustrated in the dialogue is defensible is, of course, subject to the interpretation of individual viewers. But perhaps more significant than whether Jack's freewheeling attitude is defensible is the fact that Trumbo had a right to question the law. He obeyed it by serving ten months in prison, and he paid a price for his idealism by spending more than a decade working in anonymity. Trumbo walked it like he talked it.

And perhaps most important of all, Trumbo usually didn't let his politics get in the way of a good yarn. More than dialogue, character, and nuance, Trumbo crafted compelling stories, whether they were for the page or the screen. He gravitated toward underdog protagonists, from grand martyrs such as Spartacus to average Joes such as the reporter in *Roman Holiday*, who discovers that he possesses more dignity than he ever suspected. These underdogs rebelled against their constraints and often roused the audience through their actions. By establishing a bond between viewers and his freethinking heroes, Trumbo spread the gospel of civil disobedience and gave eloquent voice to people who, like himself, fought the good fight. Intentionally or not, Trumbo created a cinema of rebellion.

Interestingly, the emotion his rebel characters expressed most often wasn't anger, but sadness. There was a weariness hanging over some of Trumbo's most enduring protagonists, and it wasn't coincidental that Kirk Douglas, with his blazing eyes and raging angst, employed Trumbo as his interpreter on *Spartacus*, *The Last Sunset*, and *Lonely Are the Brave*. In these films, Douglas played a mythic hero, a brazen villain, and a rugged antihero, respectively, but what connects all three characters is a deep sadness at the price they paid for their individualism. By capturing that mixture of anger and angst, Douglas may also have personified an essential facet of Trumbo's character, and it's a shame that the fruitful partnership between Trumbo and Douglas ended almost as quickly as it began.

The mix of anger and sadness that distinguished the Trumbo-Douglas films can also be seen in *Johnny Got His Gun*, the defining work of Trumbo's career. Published in 1939, when Trumbo was still flitting between the highbrow world of magazine short stories and the populist craft of screenwriting, *Johnny* used the fictional story of a World War I soldier to deliver a searing antiwar message on the eve of World War II, although the timing was more coincidental than prescient. *Johnny Got His Gun*—the story of an innocent who suffers unimaginable torment because of his participation in war—is filled with both anger and pain, and that mixture of emotions surfaced again when Trumbo made his lone directorial effort, the 1971 adaptation of *Johnny Got His Gun*. A brutal, often depressing movie, *Johnny* never panders or condescends; instead, it delivers its theme with almost childlike simplicity. As Trumbo did throughout his career, he wore his heart on his sleeve while directing the film.

But, finally, it isn't his emotions for which most people remember Trumbo, if they remember him at all in these days of disposable heroes and short attention spans. When Trumbo is mentioned, it's usually in the context of the Hollywood Ten. Yes, Trumbo was a member of the Communist Party. Yes, he defied a committee of the U.S. House of Representatives. Yes, he was an unabashed lefty in an era when America loomed large after the victories of World War II and a handful of right-wing politicians tried to increase their profiles by demonizing those "filthy Reds." Yes, Dalton Trumbo was a Red.

But he was also a humanist, and a gifted technician whose craft often rose to the level of poetry. These two parts of Trumbo's soul, his politics and his art, can never be severed, and that's another reason why he's more relevant than ever. Today, artists—and politicians—tread so softly as not to be heard for fear of offending special-interest groups, niche demographics, and the fickle public. But for the four decades during which he worked in the movie industry, Trumbo stood his ground and spoke his mind. We need artists like Trumbo today, and that's why we need to look back and appreciate what he accomplished. By infusing popular entertainment with idealism and radical politics, Trumbo listened to his conscience instead of the prevailing opinions of the day. His cinema of rebellion is a quintessentially American body of work.

This book is not a comprehensive overview of Dalton Trumbo's creative output; instead, it explores themes that permeate films produced from his screenplays. Trumbo was incredibly prolific, and, because of certain odd characteristics of his blacklist-era career, a definitive list of films to which he contributed is evasive. For instance, when he became the *de facto* leader of a group of writers working in the film industry's black market, Trumbo guaranteed the work of anyone he recommended to an employer. This often meant that he was called to rewrite other people's scripts at the last minute, and his rewrites ranged from minor polishes to heavy restructurings. When added to the conundrum of discerning which blacklist-era scripts bearing pseudonyms or front names were actually written by Trumbo, his guarantees blur an already muddy period in his career.

Making matters even more complicated, Trumbo did vaguely defined consulting work on various films, and traded ideas back and forth with colleagues. Therefore, numerous movies have invisible Trumbo contributions.

In this book, I use themes as a window onto Trumbo's creative impulses. Certain themes—relating to work, social injustice, rebellion, and collectivism—recurred throughout his screenwriting career. And because these themes also recur in his novels, political writing, and correspondence, I believe they were among the topics that mattered most to him. That makes their presence in particular films relevant when appraising what he accomplished as a screenwriter.

One factor informing this study is that Trumbo was, on most of his movie projects, a hired hand; even on projects he originated, Trumbo's work was col-ored by the demands of the marketplace. Also, most of his film projects were adaptations of stories created by other writers. But because of the creativity that Trumbo brought to the adaptation process, Trumbo often made other people's stories his own.

By this I mean that he was more than just the last person through whose typewriter a story passed before it was filmed. Trumbo injected something of his distinct viewpoint into the stories he told. When he arrived in Hollywood, he was idealistic and given to writing in the era's most popular, escapist tone: naive romanticism. But when adverse experiences started to affect Trumbo's personal life, the tone of his work changed. As the blacklist era progressed, antiestablishment rancor colored his screenwriting more than it had before. By the 1960s, Trumbo wrote like a full-on radical. I have identified what I believe to be the important points along this progression to illustrate an extraordinary creative journey.

I also have identified as clearly as possible the nature of Trumbo's work on particular films, but some guesswork is involved. Therefore, in certain instances Trumbo's name is representative of a creative collective. When discussing the skill with which Trumbo wrote *Spartacus*, for instance, I am, by inference, talking about the skill with which Trumbo, producers Kirk Douglas and Edward Lewis, director Stanley Kubrick, and a cast of highly assertive actors adapted their story from a novel by Howard Fast. Wherever possible, credit has been given to individuals responsible for particular ideas. The intent of this book is not to put forth Trumbo as the author of films bearing his name, but rather to identify his contributions to those films.

Finally, here is a brief explanation of this book's components. The main body of the book is a chronological narrative including critical examinations of more than three dozen films along with biographical facts that illuminate Trumbo's creative process. An extensive filmography—which I believe to be the most accurate and inclusive representation of Trumbo's screenwriting career to date—follows. Together, I hope these components convey the breadth, variety, and importance of Dalton Trumbo's screenwriting career.

1

From Colorado to Hollywood
(1905–1938)

One of the most common analogies used to describe screenwriting is that it's like carpentry—a craft in which practitioners use accepted tools and techniques, along with their own ingenuity, to build structures. And like carpenters, the best screenwriters are those whose structures last. By that analogy, Dalton Trumbo stands high among screenwriters because, although some of his work seems rudimentary in its ornamentation—stock characters, familiar dialogue, a reliance on cuteness to wriggle out of complicated situations—there is an underlying craft that distinguishes Trumbo from his peers. His structures last.

Trumbo saw screenwriting more as a job than an art, and approached it as such. With one notable exception—his ambitious but flawed screenplay for the one film he directed, *Johnny Got His Gun*—Trumbo wrote scripts with a detached craftsmanship that allowed him to avoid pretentious narrative devices, indulgent peripheral scenes and, in most

cases, inordinate verbosity. He crafted structures that adhered to known narrative conventions, so his screen stories flowed in the comfortable way good short stories and novels flow. Trumbo devoted much of his screenwriting energies to finding the "line" of stories, whether they were his own or another writer's, and once he identified that line, he used it as the framework upon which every other element of the screenplay was laid.

In his least distinguished efforts—particularly some of the B movies on which he collaborated before he made his name in Hollywood and, later, the quickie films he banged out during the nadir of his blacklist period—Trumbo merely established a structure and offered hints of where embellishment could be added. *Road Gang*, the first picture to bear his name, is a prime example of Trumbo at his least ambitious. The parameters of the First National Pictures production unit by which the film was made prevented anyone from contributing truly original ideas. As did so many of the production entities for which Trumbo worked, the focus at First National was on grinding out pulp. Nonetheless, the film has a clearly delineated protagonist-antagonist relationship and a full complement of effectively used narrative conventions. That these conventions are never elevated from their clichéd nature and that they never coalesce into convincing drama is the failure of the film, but the picture's minor success—the presence of a coherent, propulsive story—is perhaps Trumbo's signature.

❖ ❖ ❖

James Dalton Trumbo was born on December 9, 1905, in Montrose, Colorado.[1] His father, Orus Bonham Trumbo, was an unlucky but intelligent man who worked at various times as a teacher, a beekeeper, a farmer and, for the better part of Trumbo's youth, a store clerk. Trumbo's mother, Maud Tillery, came from a colorful background because her father was a frontier sheriff named Millard Tillery; he had a reputation as a hard-driving lawman who never lost a prisoner. Trumbo's parents shared a love of literature, so even when the Depression-era economy forced Trumbo to spend most of his 20s working menial jobs, he had a base in the arts that inspired him to keep writing despite few prospects of making a living as an artist.

Trumbo's family moved to Grand Junction, Colorado, in 1908, and the rural town would figure prominently in Trumbo's work as the thinly disguised setting of novels, screenplays, and other fiction. Trumbo clearly felt rooted in his provincial background, because during the prime of his career, he re-created a

facet of it by purchasing and renovating a Ventura County, California, ranch that he dubbed the Lazy-T. Trumbo never installed a phone at the ranch, which was located approximately 85 miles north of Hollywood, and it became something of a fortress of solitude at which he churned out a remarkable amount of work. Many of Trumbo's most vibrant screenplays involve men and their relationship with nature; in such pictures as *Cowboy* and *Lonely Are the Brave*, there is a palpable longing for the hard, simple pleasures of the Old West.

When World War I ended, Trumbo met wounded veterans whom he later said were among the inspirations for *Johnny Got His Gun*. Another hard lesson came when Trumbo started doing part-time jobs for pocket money, because, as he said, "I was actually making more money than my father."[2] Trumbo split his time among a handful of jobs, the most important of which was cub reporter at the *Grand Junction Sentinel*, a daily newspaper. And while his journalistic work helped him learn skills including reportage and research, Trumbo began to display his legendary eloquence—and, most likely, his obstinacy—as a member of his high school's debate team. Together, these activities formed an important phase of Trumbo's apprenticeship.

Schoolmate Hubert Gallagher describes Dalton Trumbo in his senior year in high school as the one "who always looked like a man in a hurry, churning along with that thin trench coat he wore flapping in the breeze behind him. He was always trying to make a deadline at the *Sentinel*, or rushing because he was late for school. Always in a hurry." He was "an amazing guy," Gallagher adds. "He never did much homework—he never had the time—but he got by on pure genius."[3]

Trumbo quickly became a larger-than-life figure. The combination of a quick wit, fierce temper, and ferocious work habits stayed with him throughout his life, and Trumbo rarely toiled on any one project very long before growing restless to work on another. (Later in life, he admitted that he shortchanged himself by working so hard to maintain the lifestyle to which he grew accustomed once he became a success, and many argue that he sacrificed a promising career as a novelist to pursue the fast, easy paychecks available in Hollywood.)

In Grand Junction, the Trumbo family grew to include Trumbo's two sisters, Catherine and Elizabeth. The children were raised as Christian Scientists, although none of them continued practicing the religion as adults. Trumbo exhibited a mischievous streak in his youth that manifested in disciplinary problems at elementary school. After slacking through several years of classes, however, Trumbo made an academic recovery when he was an upperclassman.

Trumbo attended the University of Colorado at Boulder, beginning in the fall 1924 semester, but soon after his arrival at college, problems arose at home. In November 1924, Trumbo's father lost his job at the Grand Junction shoe store where he had worked for several years, and moved the family to Los Angeles while Trumbo was away at school.

At the University of Colorado, Trumbo dove deeper into writing, working on the student paper, the yearbook, and a student humor magazine; during his second semester he also scored a job with a newspaper, the *Boulder Daily*

Camera. But whatever inroads Trumbo was making toward his writing career were put on hold at the end of his first school year, because his family's situation in Los Angeles was too financially precarious to pay for another.

Forced to move from Colorado to California, Trumbo intended to continue his studies at the University of Southern California, but his father's deteriorating health meant that he had to get a job to help support the family. Fatefully, Trumbo started working at the Davis Perfection Bakery, and what was intended as a temporary position stretched into an eight-year tenure that he often described as the bleakest period in his life. Yet the long period that he spent doing overnight shifts of blue-collar labor deeply informed Trumbo's work— he used the bakery as the setting for part of his most important work, the novel *Johnny Got His Gun*, and, as biographer Bruce Cook argued, the experience of working in the bakery helped Trumbo discover values that would define him. "A fundamental change was worked in his thinking during those years in the bakery," Cook wrote. "He began to split the world in two: them and us. On the other side were 'the bosses,' whom he soon grew to hate; and on his side were the boys at the bakery."[4]

Because his Christian Scientist beliefs made him refuse medical help until it was too late to treat his illness, Orus Trumbo died of pernicious anemia in 1925. Maud Trumbo's clerical work did not bring in enough money to support herself, her son, and her two daughters, 17-year-old Dalton Trumbo took a second job and began his studies at USC. By this time, he was determined to pursue a writing career, and during his tenure at the bakery, Trumbo wrote six novel-length manuscripts, in which he dealt variously with his youth in Grand Junction and his father's death, subject matter that later figured heavily in Trumbo's first published novel, *Eclipse*, as well as in *Johnny Got His Gun*. Yet while he was revisiting past events in his fiction, Trumbo was also taking in the harsh realities of life during the Depression. As Trumbo put it:

> The atmosphere at the bakery was remarkable. This was during Prohibition, and there was a very corrupt police force. Cops used to constantly come in there, and we'd give them bread and cakes to keep them happy and they gave us whiskey.... The despair of that particular area—honky-tonks, whorehouses, everyone scrounging, scrambling—well, it was just beyond belief. There was *real* Depression there. We would give away our hard, two-day-old bread. Two or three men would stand on the ramp, handing the stuff out, and there would be a line three wide—for a block and a half. Kind of a hopeless state.[5]

The lawlessness of the time rubbed off on Trumbo; at the nadir of his bakery period, Trumbo had a short career as a bootlegger, but quit after two other bootleggers in his part of town were killed by competitors; he also got a hint of later problems when he angered his bakery employers by organizing a labor strike there.

Trumbo's salvation from the bakery came in June 1932, when he sold a piece about bootlegging to *Vanity Fair* magazine. This led to one of the most fortuitous meetings in Trumbo's career— a lunch date with legendary writer-editor Clare Booth Luce, who at the time was known as Clare Booth Brokaw. Based on Trumbo's bootlegging piece,

she hired him as *Vanity Fair*'s Hollywood correspondent. As Trumbo recalled: "[She] assumed I knew something about movies, and I had never been inside a studio.... To fake it for an hour and a half ... was an appalling task. But somehow I pulled it off, or I tried, because it meant to me that I might do more articles for them."[6]

Trumbo did freelance writing assignments for various magazines and, at one point, ghost-wrote the autobiography of Austrian nobleman Baron Friedrich von Reichenberg. Although there was a certain chaos to his career, Trumbo was quickly proving his proficiency and speed; this ability to churn out voluminous numbers of pages on tight schedules eventually helped him survive the blacklist better than most of his contemporaries. Because Trumbo was no stranger to hard, thankless work, when the time came in the 1950s for him to accept insulting paychecks to write insignificant movies, he did so unblinkingly. After spending nearly a decade in the bakery, he wanted never to be poor again. "I never considered the working class anything other than something to get out of," he once quipped.[7]

As much as he was influenced by his workplace experiences and by the ignominy of his father's passing, however, Trumbo was perhaps most deeply affected by his mother's personality. Maud Trumbo was, by all accounts, as fierce, intelligent, and socially conscious as her son; that she survived her husband by 44 years was a measure of her tenacity.[8] After Orus Trumbo died, clashes arose between Maud Trumbo and the new man of the house. Trumbo's sister Catherine recalled that her brother's heavy smoking and drinking were particularly contentious issues, and that mother and son fought bitterly about politics, each as intractable as the other. Maud voted Republican from the World War I era to the Vietnam era, while her son was, of course, a diehard Democrat.[9] Later in life, Trumbo wrote:

> When I look back on my own convictions and rebellion, I find nothing remarkable in it. For I am reminded that at a younger age than I my mother, too, rebelled, left her church [and] joined an unpopular and ridiculed faith.... How, then, could a rebellious mother produce anything but a rebellious son?[10]

Trumbo's entrance into the film industry was humble and haphazard. After working for about a year as an editor, writer, and critic for *The Hollywood Spectator*, Trumbo sold several short stories to magazines. By this point, he had quit the bakery, but he still needed steady work. He found it in the summer of 1934, when writer Frank Daugherty—who had worked with Trumbo at the *Spectator*—helped Trumbo get a job as a reader in the Warner Bros. story department. The work gave him a crash course in movie writing, but Trumbo still didn't aspire to a screenwriting career: he considered himself a novelist, and spent much of 1934 writing *Eclipse*, a dark story based in a fictionalized version of Grand Junction. Trumbo used the book to purge his frustration at what he perceived to be the town's mistreatment of his father, and in so doing burned bridges with several old acquaintances. *Eclipse* was not the last time Trumbo got into trouble for expressing himself in print, because his later decision to write pamphlets for labor groups and the Communist Party cost him dearly.

Eclipse was published in England and given limited distribution in the States, but it gave Trumbo's name some much-needed weight. He sold more short stories, eventually getting one called "Darling Bill—" published in the venerable *Saturday Evening Post*. This sale spurred Trumbo to get his first agent and explore the possibility of selling "Darling Bill—" to the movies. Trumbo was quickly yielding to Hollywood's siren call, although he thought otherwise at the time:

> I wanted a place in which to hibernate, safe from the ballyhoo and the pressure to which the highly paid movie writer invariably succumbs. In a word, I want[ed] the movies to subsidize me for a while, until I establish[ed] myself as a legitimate writer.[11]

Trumbo signed a seven-year contract with Warner Bros. as a junior writer in October 1935. His ambitions reached so far past the movies, however, that he used some sleight of hand while negotiating his contract with the studio. Trumbo demanded permission to write three novels for his British publisher and, "In addition, he appended a list of titles—two novels and 41 short stories—which he declared he had written before the drawing up of [the] contract, but which he really had not." Showing the same ingenuity with which he would later subvert the Hollywood blacklist, Trumbo also made an arrangement by which he could change the titles of the unwritten stories and still retain rights to them—meaning that Trumbo could pick and choose which of his literary properties he would give to Warner Bros. He happily termed the scheme "deliberate fraud."[12]

Trumbo was barely in the door of

the movie industry, and he was already setting up ways by which he could leave it. More importantly, he was trying to protect his "real" stories from Hollywood. Trumbo's early disgust for Hollywood never really faded, as seen in a letter he wrote to novelist Nelson Algren in 1951:

> I am obliged to warn you in advance that an original story, designed for sale on the local market [Hollywood], involves a combination of prose and construction and sentimentality and vulgarity that appalls even me, who am used to it, and would appall you even more. The only thing which makes it possible for a self-respecting writer to engage in such an enterprise is that the story is never published, and is read only by Hollywood.[13]

❖   ❖   ❖

Trumbo worked in Warner Bros.' B-picture unit under producer Brian Foy, described by film historian Rudy Behlmer as a "spectacular corner cutter."[14] The unit's job was to recycle elements of successful films for quickie potboilers, so the first film project to bear Trumbo's name is *Road Gang*,[15] a minor crime picture modeled after the hit drama, *I Am a Fugitive from a Chain Gang* (1932, Warner Bros.). *Road Gang*, for which Trumbo wrote the screenplay from a story by Harold Buckley and Abem Finkel, is a tough, quick picture that employs several interesting elements. It opens briskly in the offices of the *Chicago Sun*, where the daily newspaper's senior editor, Shields (Joseph Crehan), reviews a submission with his city editor. The article, written by a man named Jim Larrabie, is a tough exposé about the political machine of Southern

power broker J.W. Metcalfe; Shields says that he'd like to see Metcalfe's rise to power thwarted. Although the name Huey Long is never used in the scene, clear allusions are made to the infamous Louisiana senator, a likely model for Metcalfe's character.[16] In classic potboiler fashion, when we meet Jim (Donald Woods), we discover that his life is entwined with Metcalfe's—he is engaged to Barbara Winston (Kay Linaker), whose stepfather, entrepreneur George Winston (Henry O'Neill), is a spineless toadie in Metcalfe's thrall. Jim explains that based on the response to his Metcalfe article, he's been offered a job with the *Sun* and wants Barbara to travel with him to Illinois. When Metcalfe (Joseph King) finally makes his entrance, he is incensed that the *Sun* ran Jim's piece. A confrontation soon arises among Jim, Metcalfe, and Winston, in which Metcalfe tries to bribe Jim by offering him a job managing Metcalfe's campaign publicity. Jim's charged response is naive but telling:

"There's nothing more to be said, gentlemen. I may sell out when I'm so old I can't make a living any other way. In the meantime, I've at least got to keep clean enough to live with myself and Barbara!"

It's not difficult to hear echoes of Trumbo's stubbornly idealistic personality in Jim's refusal to compromise his beliefs. Resonating with the us-and-them attitude that Trumbo developed in his years at the bakery, Jim's social consciousness is important because it set a tone that continued through Trumbo's screenwriting career. Although not every Trumbo protagonist was an idealist, virtually all of them subscribed to some deeply held belief that motivated their every action, whether it was a political,

Although he considered movie writing a way to support his serious work, Trumbo thrived in the B movie unit of Warner Bros. The legendary Bette Davis, with whom he never made a picture, poses with Trumbo in this studio publicity shot on the occasion of the publication of his story "Darling Bill—" in the *Saturday Evening Post*. (Warner Bros.)

moral, or spiritual one. So it's heartening to see that even in his first produced screenplay, Trumbo was already giving voice to the underdog. It should be noted, however, that Trumbo's choice of subject matter at this point in his career was not his own. Until his stature rose during the war era, Trumbo had to make the best of the assignments offered him; therefore, parallels between his ideals and the content of his early films are somewhat coincidental. Nonetheless, *Road Gang* is a good example of an early picture falling in line with his beliefs.

After turning down Metcalfe's offer, Jim receives a second blow when

Winston forbids Barbara to marry him. In a saccharine good-bye scene, the lovers promise to keep believing in each other, but it's unclear whether they'll be able to restart their engagement while Barbara lives in Winston's home. Thus are the predictable elements of the script—a man endangered by his ideals and the woman from whom he is separated—put in place.

Jim and his roommate, Bob Gordon (Carlyle Moore, Jr.), drive toward Chicago, but are stopped by a patrol cop before leaving their home state. The policeman tells Jim and Bob that they're wanted for grand larceny. The scene is filled with portent and menace, because it's clear that Metcalfe is using his political power to frame Jim. The friends are thrown in jail and soon get embroiled in a jailbreak that results in the death of a policeman. Although really victims of circumstance, Jim and Bob are held responsible for the trouble once recaptured.

Barbara, horrified at these new developments, confronts her stepfather and says she's going to hire a lawyer named Dudley (Edward Van Sloan) to get Jim and Bob out of trouble, but Dudley is in cahoots with Winston—so the two innocent men get sentenced to five years each.

The picture's intensity increases when the men are moved from jail to prison; the latter is portrayed as a brutal, inhumane place where inmates are lashed, worked near to death and, if they're foolish enough to attempt an escape, sent to the nearby Blackfoot mines, which the inmates talk about as if it was a death chamber. During his time at the prison, Jim concocts a plan to write an exposé of the conditions there, which reiterates the film's theme of the power of words to affect social change, a theme that had major ramifications in Trumbo's life.

After the picture's early climax—Bob's death during an escape attempt—the picture becomes pure hyperbole, because Winston gets appointed as the director of the state's prison board and Barbara leaves home to devote her time to getting Jim out of prison. During a visit in which Barbara attempts to smuggle out an article that Jim has written, she implausibly stands up to the prison's brutal warden, Parmenter (Addison Richards), who confiscates the article and hints that Barbara shouldn't come around anymore. In a melodramatic speech, Barbara tells Parmenter that she can't be intimidated:

> I've talked to men who've come from here. I know how you treat them. You torture, beat, and brutalize them until they're half-mad. I've seen it. Seen it in their eyes!... If anything happens to Jim because of this, I'll expose you and your rotten prison if it takes me the rest of my life!

There are a couple of interesting aspects to this speech. First is its place in *Road Gang*'s long string of activist sentiments, and second is the baldness of its language. Although Trumbo wrote many speeches for movie characters that hit "on the nose"—which is to say that the words and the intent were identical, as opposed to more graceful screenwriting, in which characters talk around subjects—his dialogue generally was not as graceless as Barbara's rant would suggest. It's therefore entertaining to note the flat, expository nature of Barbara's speech in context of Trumbo's attitude toward Hollywood—at this point in his career, he treated screenwriting as slumming, and it wasn't until several years later that Trumbo's movie dialogue started to contain echoes of his offscreen eloquence.

After Barbara's showdown with Parmenter, *Road Gang* gets meaner still when Jim is sent to the Blackfoot mines, which turn out to be as rough as expected—he's set to work 14 hours a day in a black, claustrophobic pit. Meanwhile, Barbara goes over Winston's head to speak with District Attorney Marsden (William B. Davidson), hoping to gain his assistance in freeing Jim from Blackfoot. Prison officials, fearing what Jim might reveal, in turn contrive a plan to kill him in a staged "accident." Jim gets wind of his impending murder, though, and starts a riot in the mine. Although such incredible plot developments were the norm of 1930s programmers, Trumbo showed real gusto for crafting oversized narrative. This ability to contrive grandiose solutions for story problems served him well throughout his career, and even when he later earned the liberty to tell stories in a more conscientious fashion, he often relied on plot developments as ludicrous as those in *Road Gang*. Excepting a handful of projects, Trumbo wrote for the marketplace when he wrote for movies, so it's often more illuminating to explore the subtexts or themes of his films than to simply examine the mechanics of their stories. This is especially true when considering the blacklist era, during which his work situation forced him to rush through screen projects as quickly as he did in the 1930s, focusing on quantity instead of quality.

The story of *Road Gang* gets even more extreme when Jim's *Chicago Sun* editor, Shields, arrives at the prison. His appearance makes sense for no reason except that he has a role in the film's conclusion: Shields and District Attorney Marsden demand to see the prison's records. And because no potboiler is complete until the villain arrives for his comeuppance, Metcalfe joins the scene and vainly tries to use Winston, now the state's top prison man, to defuse the situation. Predictably, the good guys triumph and the riot is settled without loss of life. Jim is freed, reunited with Barbara, told he will be exonerated, and told that his prison exposé will be published.

Road Gang contains topics that recur throughout in Trumbo's scripts—journalism, activism, the push for social change, a corrupt power structure—but these themes are handled in such a derivative way that they don't feel powerful or original. All told, Trumbo's film debut was an inauspicious one—but it was enough to begin his invaluable apprenticeship in B pictures.

❖ ❖ ❖

Trumbo's relationship with Warner Bros. produced only one more screenplay before he jumped ship to Columbia Pictures. Adapted from Martin Flavin's play *Broken Dishes*, the whimsical *Love Begins at Twenty* was scripted by Trumbo and Tom Reed. Although the picture moves at a breezy pace and has an engagingly screwball mentality, it's ultimately just a trifle with a few clever, if terribly forced, twists.

The reasons why Trumbo left Warner Bros. eerily presage his blacklisting in 1947. While working at Warner Bros., Trumbo joined the Screen Writers Guild, a labor union formed in 1933 and led by future Hollywood Ten member John Howard Lawson, a left-leaning writer who angered movie-industry executives when he appeared before the House of Representatives' Patents Committee in early 1936 and argued that screenwriters' material should be afforded the same copyright protection as that of other writers. This and other events caused a left-right rift in the Guild and led two conservative-leaning writers, Rupert Hughes and James K. McGuinness, to form a new trade union, the Screen Playwrights. Trumbo was told that in order to continue working at Warner Bros., he had to change his allegiance to the new union. He refused, and his seven-year contract was voided after less than a year of work.[17] This incident is significant because it reasserts how central Trumbo's us-and-them attitude was to his personality—and it shows an early example of Trumbo making a principled stand by aligning himself with an unpopular political group. Moreover, Trumbo's brazen departure from Warner Bros. helped shape his attitude toward the studios, which he generally regarded as money troughs run by idiots.

In the fall of 1936, after only a few weeks of being "blacklisted" for refusing to join the Screen Playwrights, Columbia Pictures executive Harry Cohn put Trumbo under contract. Trumbo's time at the studio was brief, resulting in only a handful of realized projects. The first of them, a Shirley Temple–style confection called *Tugboat Princess*, is a minor example of the frothy escapism that was so popular during the Depression. Trumbo cowrote the picture's fanciful, inconsequential story with Isadore Bernstein, and Robert Watson wrote the screenplay. *Tugboat Princess* is an ultimately harmless fluff, but as he later proved with *Roman Holiday*, Trumbo had it in him to craft transcendent fluff— so the comparison quickly puts *Tugboat Princess* into perspective.

The picture concerns a soft-hearted seaman, Captain Zack Livermore (Walter C. Kelly), whose small crew includes a stalwart first mate, Bob Norfolk (Lester Matthews), and a preadolescent charge, "Princess" Judy (Emily Booth). Zack, who adopted Judy after she was orphaned, is almost saintly—and this one-sided portrayal makes him typical of the protagonists in Trumbo's early films. The leading characters in these films are mostly devoid of shadings, a contrast to Trumbo's later practice of looking for the complexities in the people whose ex-ploits he was dramatizing. In *Tugboat Princess* and other pictures of its substandard ilk, Trumbo merely plugs stock characters into formulaic stories. It should be reiterated, though, that at this point, Trumbo had none of the autonomy he enjoyed later in his career. His job was to generate the product ordered by his employers and then relinquish ownership of that product so it could be reshaped by studio executives, directors, and, in some cases, other writers brought in to polish his work. Screenwriting scholar Tom Stempel described the dispiriting atmosphere at the studio:

> Screenwriters at Columbia began … their careers by being directly intimidated by Harry Cohn. After the writer had been working at the studio for two weeks, Cohn's office called and asked the writer to send over the work he had been doing. The next day the writer was sent into Harry Cohn's imperial office and heard Cohn tear the script apart. If the writer caved in to Cohn and began to grovel, he was soon fired. If the writer fought back, he stayed. The writer would make additional points with Cohn if he could prove that Cohn had in fact not read the script at all.[18]

Early in *Tugboat Princess*, young Judy breaks her leg and is sent to a local hospital, but Zack discovers that it will cost nearly $1,000 to keep her there as long as the doctors recommend. Zack is forced to ask an old adversary, Captain Fred Darling (Reginald Hincks), for a loan. Clumsily expositional dialogue is used to explain that the two sailors once had a boat race in which Zack's tugboat, *The Princess Judy*, beat Fred's craft. Fred never forgave Zack the humiliation, and now that Zack has fallen onto hard times—his boat is in disrepair and business is slow—it's time for payback. Fred is unsavory from his first scene: He commits the cardinal sin of urchin movies by referring to Judy as a "brat," and then preys upon Zack's vulnerability by loaning him the $1,000 with Zack's invaluable 99-year dock lease as collateral. This linchpin moment is dull and predictable, because viewers don't expect a film with such a cuddly narrative to truly endanger the welfare of likable Zack. Instead of creating tension, the moment merely sets the stage for Zack to risk his welfare in Judy's name and lets viewers know that Fred's comeuppance is forthcoming.

The picture gets even more contrived a few scenes later, when Judy is removed from the boat by a social-services matron (Ethel Reese-Burns) and put into a children's home. Judy longs to return home, however, which leads to several scenes filled with treacly dialogue. Trumbo was not averse to plucking heartstrings in his film work—sentimentality is the dominant tone of such films as *A Guy Named Joe* and *The Brave One*—but he rarely trafficked in such low, populist junk as *Tugboat Princess*. With its manipulative theme of the lengths to which a surrogate father will go to ensure the welfare and happiness of his diminutive charge, the film is as deep as a greeting card. It also relies heavily on sleight of hand, because several pivotal moments are staged with an overflow of coincidence and convenience.

A day before Fred's loan comes due, for instance, Zack realizes that he doesn't have enough money. Fred gives Zack a one-day extension, and Zack conveniently overhears a phone call during which Fred refuses a tug job because a dense fog is coming into town. Zack tricks a secretary into giving him the name of the client so he can take the job for himself.

Piling contrivance upon contrivance, a homesick Judy runs away from the hospital and returns to the dock, only to find the *Princess Judy* gone because Zack is out trying to earn money to repay the loan that covered her hospital bill. A longshoreman recognizes Judy and offers her shelter while Zack is away. At sea, Zack sees that one of Darling's boats, the *Georgiana*, is lost in the fog and headed straight for the shore. Despite the objections of his crew, Zack charges the *Princess Judy* in front of the *Georgiana*'s bow. Zack saves Fred's boat, but the *Princess Judy* gets damaged and sinks.

The next day, Fred visits Zack, but instead of trying to collect on the $1,000 loan, Fred gives Zack $11,000 and explains that, according to maritime law, Zack is entitled to salvage fees for the boat and cargo he saved. Zack's first reaction is to exclaim that now he can buy Judy a real home, a selfless statement that implausibly melts the ice around Fred's heart. He offers Zack a job running one of his boats—despite the fact that, moments before, Zack called him a "liver-faced son of a chimpanzee."

Tugboat Princess was followed by another painfully predictable Columbia B picture, the submarine-themed *The Devil's Playground*. A symphony of unlikely coincidences, the picture was created by a cabal of writers of whom Trumbo was just one member, and although it desperately wants for originality and credibility, the picture moves at a speedy clip. The plot is melodramatic silliness about two friends, a champion diver and a submarine captain, who feud over the affections of a loose woman. The picture's dramatic high point, such as it is, occurs when the submarine captain's boat sinks and the diver nearly refuses to perform a rescue because he thinks his imperiled friend has betrayed him. (Never mind that the diver seems willing to let his friend and other crew members die just to save his wounded pride—and never mind that the U.S. Navy has neither another diver able to perform the task nor the gumption to commandeer the diver's services while he's in a romantic funk.) Pulp through and through, *The Devil's Playground* is cheap nonsense.

❖   ❖   ❖

As if to underscore the mediocrity of his early films, Trumbo's screenwriting career soon took a backseat to his private life. Since the spring of 1936, he had been courting Cleo Fincher, a delicately beautiful but tenacious Californian who quickly became Trumbo's soul mate. The couple were introduced by screenwriter Earl Felton, who was a Warner Bros. script reader at the same time as Trumbo and had become a contract writer at Metro-Goldwyn-Mayer.[19] By 1937, the couple's convoluted romance dominated Trumbo's life so completely that he left Columbia and briefly worked at MGM, but none of his screenplays written for the latter studio were produced. True to his various proclamations that he wanted to exploit the industry while devoting himself to more important matters, Trumbo let his screenwriting career falter while chasing the woman who changed his life.[20]

Trumbo and Fincher married on March 13, 1938. Later that year, the couple took up residence at a 320-acre ranch in Ventura County, California, the Lazy-T. The ranch, which was lo-cated nearly two hours by car from Los Angeles, was a fitting representation of Trumbo's iconoclastic personality. Even though he had yet to establish himself in the movies, Trumbo withdrew from Hollywood to build a family and work on serious writing. The move proved fortuitous, because during the decade that he lived at the Lazy-T, Trumbo's family grew to include three children— Nikola (b. January 1939), Christopher (b. September 1940), and Melissa, a.k.a. "Mitzi" (b. October 1945)—and his *oeuvre* increased with the publication of two novels, the timeless *Johnny Got His Gun* and the minor *The Remarkable Andrew*. Despite his plan to escape Hollywood and become a "real" writer, Trumbo's profile as a screenwriter grew immensely during his Ventura County years, so much so that his movie work eventually eclipsed his fiction writing. Furthermore, it is one of the richest contradictions of Trumbo's career that even though he didn't play by Hollywood's rules, he nonetheless developed a quintessentially Hollywood style of writing. In his quest to master his new trade, Trumbo turned into a paragon of professionalism and efficiency, ironically rising to the top of an industry he disdained.

Trumbo's success in the late 1930s and thereafter coincided with the maturation of his screenwriting. Working in the RKO Radio Pictures B-movie unit beginning in April 1938, primarily with producer Robert Sisk,[21] Trumbo spent two years proving himself on such a variety of projects that by the end of 1939, movies based on his stories were produced by studios including 20th Century-Fox—and even Trumbo's former employer, Warner Bros.

❖   ❖   ❖

Given Trumbo's penchant for exploring sweeping themes in his work, it's amusing that his first effective screenplay was a superficial bit of entertainment. Adapted from Richard Wormser's original screen story, Trumbo's first RKO movie, *Fugitives for a Night*, has some of the choicest dialogue of his early career, and stands alongside *Roman Holiday* as one of his few truly endearing trifles. *Half a Sinner*, a 1941 Trumbo picture with some of the same story elements as *Fugitives*, comes close to the same kind of brisk entertainment, but is too feather-light and inconsequential; similarly, Trumbo's 1941 romance *You Belong to Me* has charms but is hampered by presenting a backwards view of women in the workplace, albeit one germane to the picture's time. So *Fugitives*, otherwise anything but unique, is unique among Trumbo's pictures for its breezy, well-told story and flashes of romance, violence, and satire.[22]

The story's protagonist, Matt Ryan (Frank Albertson), is a gofer for frustrated movie star John Nelson (Allan Lane) at a time when John is convinced that his employer, Apollo Studios boss Maurice Tenwright (Russell Hicks), isn't doing enough to advance his career. After John threatens to break his Apollo contract, Maurice fires several underlings involved with steering John's career, but before he fires Matt, Matt's services are requested by another Apollo star, aging Dennis Poole (Bradley Page). During his first scene with Dennis, Maurice feeds him a line of nonsense meant to placate the actor's fragile ego, but Dennis interjects: "I suppose you have to be more or less of a liar, Maurice, but I can't understand why you like it so well." Lines such as these, which express character details, skewer the entertainment industry, and provide a slight chuckle, permeate the witty, fast-moving *Fugitives* and hint at the wit that Trumbo would unleash toward the latter part of the blacklist era—and especially after that era was over.

Trumbo's sense of humor manifests itself in broad comedic touches. For instance, during a scene in which Matt asks his best friend at the studio, publicity writer Ann Wray (Eleanor Lynn), out on a date, she is supervising a publicity photo shoot with an action star. The star is known for Tarzan-style jungle adventures, so he's posing dramatically—and precariously—in a jungle set. After several false alarms throughout the scene, he falls down and gets tangled in the set dressings. Such slapstick complements the more sophisticated tone of the movie's best lines, lending its comedic aspect an egalitarian appeal.

A run of enjoyable dialogue occurs when Matt and Ann discuss Eileen Baker (Adrienne Ames), a vapid starlet with whom Matt is enchanted. Ann tolerates Matt's infatuation, but repeatedly warns him that Eileen will only use him. Matt's response: "I know she's nothing but a chiseling little dame, and I know she's been kicking me around ever since she came out here, and she'll keep right on kicking me around, and I'll keep right on taking it, and I can't tell you why."

The self-awareness in Matt's flip line is charming, but it also gives us essential information about his character. He's infatuated with a starlet, and by extension we realize that he's also infatuated with Hollywood—he's working as a lackey for other actors because he thinks doing so might win him a chance to act in a movie himself. The tenacity that Matt expresses in his line about

Eileen is also important, because it foreshadows that he's a man who doesn't give up, which proves to be a life-saving attribute when the story's stakes are raised to life or death. Finally, there's the confusion that Matt expresses about his own actions ("I can't tell you why"); although he superficially knows the reasons why he puts up with Eileen (her beauty) and Hollywood (his dreams of stardom), the line about his confusion suggests that on some level, he knows these reasons are false ones and that if he truly looked inside himself, he wouldn't be able to come up with a compelling reason for his behavior. This ambivalence proves important later in the picture, because it helps us believe the transition in Matt's character that prompts him to give up his Hollywood dreams.

This telling bit is followed by a tart exchange between Eileen and Dennis. After watching him film a scene, Eileen drifts over to Dennis and oozes fatuous praise. "You had a certain quality about your work there. Repression, restraint. You know what I mean," she says. Unimpressed by puffery, Dennis responds: "Critics' phrases, my dear—they sound good but they mean nothing."

The plot event that sets the movie in motion is a party at Dennis's house, during which most of the central relationships are clarified. Maurice and John are both widely disliked; Eileen is an opportunist; and Ann is the film's voice of reason. For his part, Dennis is a gentleman weary of the lies and cheap relationships associated with his business. And stuck in the middle of these characters is Matt, a comparative innocent. The party is held at an illegal gambling club, and when the crowd hears that police are on their way to raid the place, tempers flare and a fistfight erupts between Matt and John. Their fight is interrupted by a power failure, and during the confusion created by the sudden darkness, someone shoots and kills Maurice.

The police arrive soon after the murder, and the police captain (Jonathan Hale) is an amusing character so infatuated with movie stars that he draws out his interrogation. "It's very seldom I have the opportunity of moving in such exalted company," he says in appropriately bloated, self-important words. "Forgive me if it goes to my head occasionally." During the interrogation, Matt's enemies try to frame him for killing Maurice, so Ann creates a distraction and leads Matt outside. They steal a car to evade capture, becoming the titular fugitives for a night.

After a brisk chase scene during which Matt convinces Ann of his innocence, they reach an impasse because Matt decides to turn himself in. What follows is the toughest exchange of dialogue in the picture, and one of the sharpest exchanges in Trumbo's early films.

> MATT: I'm going to let them arrest me.
> ANN: I was afraid you would. I would have bet two to one you would.
> MATT: What made you think that?
> ANN: Because you're weak. You've been a stooge for so long, you can't get out of the habit. You were swell for a while, but I knew it couldn't last. For just a little while, you were being Matt Ryan.
> MATT: You're pretty sure of yourself, aren't you? The girl who never made a mistake.
> ANN: You can bet your life I never made the same one twice.

The fugitives soon reconcile their differences, partly because Matt impresses Ann by attacking and tying up a shopkeeper who refuses to rent them a car. The inference of this scene, that Ann is aroused by Matt's criminal activity, is a provocative theme that Trumbo later returned to in pictures including *Half a Sinner* and *Gun Crazy*, and it meshes with the rebel iconography that permeates Trumbo's films. In Trumbo's universe, refusing to abide by the rules is a virtue so long as a greater good is being served; in this case, the greater good is proving Matt's innocence. By breaking laws to prove that he didn't break laws, Matt shows Ann that he's his own man. Interestingly, accountability—a theme explored at some length in other Trumbo pictures—is glossed over here. The movie ends without any mention of whether Matt experienced repercussions for assaulting the shopkeeper or, for that matter, resisting arrest and fleeing the police.

After a reconciliation so complete that they share their first kiss, Matt and Ann head to Dennis's house because Matt thinks Dennis will help him out of trouble. The story resolves itself efficiently and with a satisfying surprise, because Matt confronts the movie-mad police captain with information that incriminates John in Maurice's murder—only to be told that the evidence isn't enough. But just as the captain is about to arrest Matt, Ann makes a speech about how the suspects gathered before the police captain are willing to let Matt take the fall for their misdeeds just as thoughtlessly as they'd been willing to use him as a stooge for years. Her argument convinces the captain to try a paraffin test, which prompts Dennis to confess that he killed Maurice.

The movie ends with Matt finally renouncing Hollywood and, upon Ann's good counsel, buying a hamburger stand at which he hopes to make an honest living. (One final jab at Hollywood is that the proprietor of the stand says he's happy to sell his business, because he wants to start a movie career.) As Ann and Matt marvel at the events of the long evening, Matt proposes a salute to their purchase of the hamburger stand. "Let me make the toast," Ann says. "Let's drink to the young man who died tonight."

"Young man?" Matt asks.

"Quite young, quite good-looking, quite dead," Ann responds. "He was quite a stooge."

2

The Part-Time Screenwriter (1938–1940)

Fugitives for a Night paved the way for Trumbo to work on *A Man to Remember*, the myriad virtues of which are only slightly undercut by the knowledge that the film's story was recycled from a novel and a previous film. Katherine Havilland-Taylor's short story, "Failure," was first put on screen as *One Man's Journey* (1933, RKO), but the Trumbo-scripted version has proven far more enduring. Because Havilland-Taylor's story about a small-town doctor who endeavors to comport himself with integrity amid apathy and greed is moralistic without being mawkish, *A Man to Remember* is touching even from a modern perspective. Trumbo's treatment of the story is rich with believable dialogue, a clever story structure, and a minimum of opportune coincidences.

Directed by Garson Kanin,[1] the picture opens with a large, somber funeral procession moving through the small town of Westport. Most in the town are observing the procession, and offhand comments made by a pair of onlookers set the tone of the screenplay.

"Of course he was a good man, and he did a fine work here, but this seems just a bit showy to me," the first woman says.

"Not for him, it ain't," the second woman responds. "If they got the biggest band in the state and had the Archangel Gabriel leading it, it wouldn't be too big for him."

These lines accomplish a great deal of expositional business, establishing that opinions in town about the deceased are split, and also establishing the character of the townsfolk; the presence of the word "ain't" in one of the picture's first lines correctly suggests that the film will be populated with salt-of-the-earth types. Also significant is the on-the-nose specificity of the lines—consider the phrase "a fine work," for instance. Trumbo tells viewers what the scene is about in its first few seconds. Although he was capable of stretching scenes past their dramatic value—witness the puffery

26

in his *Sorority House*, released seven months later—Trumbo generally placed economy high on his list of priorities.

In his best scripts, of which *A Man to Remember* is one, events unfold quickly and their significance is not hidden. Put simply, Trumbo played fair.

The film cuts from the funeral procession to three town leaders gathered in an office for a reading of the deceased's will. They are George Sykes (Gravine Bates), owner of the town hospital; Homer Ramsey (Harlan Briggs), owner of the town's general store; and Jode Harkness (Frank M. Thomas), who publishes the town's paper. The fourth man in the room is a lawyer named Perkins (Charles Halton). In this quick scene, we learn not only the identities of these characters but also that of the deceased, one Doctor John Abbott.[2] While waiting for Perkins to read the will, the men marvel that despite their own accomplishments, Abbott's funeral is probably bigger than any ceremony the town would give any of them. They sound bitter that their efforts haven't been appreciated.

As Perkins begins going through the papers of Abbott's estate, the film dissolves to its first flashback, which portrays Abbott's return to Westport after years spent living in Chicago. This transition establishes the main device of the film: Abbott's funeral causes the town leaders to reflect on their experiences with Abbott. This simple conceit pays off handsomely, if a bit predictably, at the end of the picture.[3]

In the first flashback, Abbott (Edward Ellis), accompanied by his young son Dick (Dickie Jones), announces his plan of starting a general practice in Westport. Abbott visits Sykes to borrow start-up money, but says that his only collateral is 17 years of medical experience. This quick scene has some edge, because Sykes and Abbott were competitive with each other in high school. Sykes reveals old jealousy that Abbott was chosen "most likely to succeed," by smugly commenting that Abbott hasn't made good on that promise, at least not in financial terms. Nonetheless, he loans Abbott the money.

The next scene sets several plot elements in motion when Abbott, now established in his practice, visits the house of a poor man named Johnson (John Wray) because Johnson's wife is in labor. After the delivery, Abbott speaks with Johnson, who offers to pay for the medical service in potatoes because he doesn't have money.

"Mr. Johnson, you have a fine baby girl," Abbott says.

"Girl, huh," Johnson responds.

"And a healthy one, too."

"Girls ain't no good on a farm. I wanted a boy.... Girls are for people that can afford them."

This exchange, coming as it does so early in the film, clues viewers into the film's lack of excessive sentimentality. Johnson's crude but pragmatic reaction to the news of his child's gender tells viewers a great deal about the social strata to which Abbott's clients belong—they are rural, hard people for whom life is about work, not luxury. As the film progresses, we see that despite his education and skills, Abbott is very much of these people. Therefore, what happens next is significant above and beyond its important function in the plot. After discussing the baby's gender, Abbott tactfully reveals that Johnson's wife died in labor.

"There's only one thing I can say, Johnson," Abbott offers. "I know how you feel because that's the way I lost my wife."

"She never had nothin' while she lived," the farmer says. "Bad crops, bad times. Crops were going to be good this year. I was gonna buy her something."

After uttering these bleak words, Johnson attacks Abbott, who flees. And in the following scene, Abbott answers a knock at his door to discover that Johnson's little girl has been left in a box at the door with a note asking Abbott to find a home for her. The doctor adopts the girl.

The Johnson sequence mixes tragedy and sentiment, two qualities that epitomize the tone of the picture. One could argue that this makes the picture a masculinized version of what is stereotypically considered a feminine genre, but it is perhaps more apt to say that the script—unlike those of quintessential tearjerkers along the lines of *Stella Dallas* (1937, United Artists), which aim for cheap emotional payoffs through heavy-handed audience manipulation—tries to earn its emotional payoff through the hard work of thoughtfully constructed and depicted story events. In that sense, the difference between *A Man to Remember* and lesser films of its ilk is less about gender than integrity, a quality befitting its protagonist.

The picture quickly eases into a series of vignettes depicting the way that Abbott develops his practice. In one, he answers an emergency call to operate on Ramsey's wife, only to have Ramsey haggle over the cost of the operation. "Now look, Doc," Ramsey says. "All of you fellows have two prices, one for people who have money and one for people who are broke." Quickly sensing Ramsey's intent, Abbott asks if Ramsey wants to pay the lower price despite being able to pay

the higher one. The end result of their debate is that Abbott settles his $100 bill for $2, thereby making a statement that embarrasses Ramsey but stays on Abbott's books. In other vignettes, Abbott accepts bartered food and services instead of pay.

As Abbott's practice grows more popular, the doctor becomes impassioned about his patients' welfare even though they're barely paying him enough to survive. In a significant, albeit didactic, scene, Abbott petitions Westport's board of supervisors for money with which to build a hospital. They refuse, and Abbott counters that the board just spent $18,000 to prevent an outbreak of hog cholera. He further notes that building the hospital would save money, because the town is currently paying a steady stream of money to the local mortician, Hank, who buries local poor folk at the town's expense. This launches Abbott on a monologue that bears Trumbo's signature of righteous indignation, wit, and meticulousness:

> ABBOTT: Sorry I can't spend any more time with you boys, but I've got work to do. There's a fellow over on the other side of town by the name of Lubinovsky. He's foreman in the flour mill. They say his crew turns out more flour than any other outfit in the mill. He's a good man. Almost as good as a hog. I had to operate on him yesterday in his own kitchen. I think in about three hours from now, he'll be dead. A case for you, Hank. But that man would have lived if I had had a decent operating room and an experienced assistant. Well, you boys take care of the hogs, and I'll take care of the people. Someday, we'll all meet at Hank's place.

Although the monologue courts stridency with its cry for more sensitivity on the part of government, the bulk of the speech stays on track; it doesn't sacrifice the momentum of the scene for the gain of making a pedantic point. Trumbo had a taste for monologues, and this Abbott speech is a good early example of his soliloquy style. Whereas in later pictures, particularly verbose ones such as *Exodus* and *The Sandpiper*, Trumbo succumbed to the lure of words and drifted away from plots to wax poetic on various points, his best monologues used poetic rhythms, fanciful imagery, and emotional passion.

Amid the charged material pertaining to Abbott's conflicts with the town leaders, several other plot points fall into place in the first hour of *A Man to Remember*. In the most important of them, Abbott's son Dick, now a young adult (played by Lee Bowman), graduates college and goes to Paris to study neurology at the National University. We learn that Abbott long dreamed of taking this educational adventure, but he happily sacrifices his dream with the understanding that Dick will return to practice medicine in Westport and eventually take over the family business.

In another plot strand, Abbott's adopted daughter, Jean (played as an adult by RKO stalwart Anne Shirley), is courted by Howard (William Henry), son of Abbott's longtime adversary, John Sykes. While on a date, Howard gets drunk and accidentally fires a gun, shooting Jean in the arm. After ensuring that she's not badly hurt, Abbott calls Sykes and cheerfully blackmails him: If Sykes will fund a hospital, Abbott won't tell the authorities about the incident.

The scheme works, but Sykes gets his revenge. When Abbott visits the new hospital to establish his credentials there, he's told that he can't, because the hospital requires its doctors to have done postgraduate work within the last 20 years. Undefeated, Abbott gets the rule put down in writing and then tells the hospital superintendent that Dick is on his way back from Paris. "I just wanted to make sure there wasn't any stipulation against all doctors named Abbott," he comments.

But when Dick returns, he announces that he won't join his father's practice, explaining that he doesn't have the heart to work for meager financial rewards. Dick then sets his attention on courting Jean.

Plot developments pile on quickly, because by this point, the film has departed from the framing device of the town leaders reviewing Abbott's will and is following a straight narrative. The events in the latter part of the picture are so interrelated that were they constantly interrupted by cuts to the town leaders, the momentum of the scenes would be lost, and this deviance from the film's narrative mode reflects a growing confidence on the part of Trumbo the screenwriter. He used the framing device to intrigue viewers, then maintained it because it allowed him to collapse several years of time into a few minutes of screen action. But when he reached the pivotal moment of Abbott's career, Trumbo set aside the framing device. After the final transition into the past, the story stays there until its conclusion, when the framing device briefly resurfaces to provide dramatic closure.

When a screenwriter uses a structural device such as consecutive flashbacks well, watching the film containing that device unreel is as comforting as listening to music, because patterns and rhythms reveal themselves at a comfortable pace. When such a device is used poorly, though, the result is incoherence. So for Trumbo to pull off such a tricky balancing act this early in his career reflects his natural aptitude for the craft.

Abbott is dealt another blow when Dick accepts a job in New York, dashing his father's hope of having a "Doctor Abbott" in Westport after his retirement. Jean, sharing Abbott's disappointment at Dick's apparent greed, snuffs her blossoming romance with Dick by announcing that Howard proposed to her.

The bad news about Dick's plans is ameliorated by an unexpected visitor to Abbott's home—Johnson, the man who left Jean at Abbott's doorstep, arrives and apologizes for his actions years earlier. Explaining that he has no designs on reclaiming his daughter, Johnson gives Abbott $3,000, which he says he saved to help pay for her upbringing. This scene, although important for plot purposes, stretches credibility more than almost anything else in the film. Despite a couple of unbelievable coincidences during the picture's denouement, Johnson's return is among the only real fallacies in this script; even though the picture takes place on an elevated fictional level in which events occur solely to propel the narrative toward a foregone conclusion, Trumbo—and the other writer whose voice is audible here, Havilland-Taylor—generally avoid obvious contrivances. Yet in the scene of Johnson's return and the picture's dramatic climax, they stop playing fair for a moment and "cheat" to expedite the story.

Jean encourages Abbott to spend the $3,000 on the studies at the National University in Paris that he's always wanted to take. Accepting the almost karmic appearance of the money, Abbott fills out an application.

But then the most significant crisis of the film arises. Abbott discovers a potential outbreak of infantile paralysis and asks the town leaders to cancel an upcoming fair. Perceiving him as a bumpkin GP crying wolf, the town leaders dismiss Abbott's warnings. Undaunted, Abbott posts flyers about the possible epidemic and then goes door-to-door administering preventive medicine. This is depicted in an intense montage sequence that shows Abbott working himself into exhaustion with Jean's assistance. At the end of the sequence, Dick, not yet moved to New York and presently a member of the County Medical Association, tells his father that Abbott is in trouble for treating other doctors' patients. In a change from his previous self-centerdness, Dick promises to stand by his father.

The association suspends Abbott's license, because they feel he acted without proof. Finally worn down by adversity, Abbott sheepishly accepts his punishment and walks away. Dick, true to his word, makes a speech defending his father—and then resigns from the association on principle. But before Dick can leave, word arrives of several cases of infantile paralysis: Abbott was right after all. The association quickly rescinds Abbott's suspension and his son's resignation, then gets to work treating the epidemic.

The epidemic is never shown, but its sweep is implied in a scene depicting a nurse pushing pins into a map wherever cases are reported. Viewers are told that more than one hundred children are stricken, and during the entire epidemic sequence—which spans more than ten minutes of screen time—Trumbo

Soon after he joined the movie industry, Trumbo became involved in labor issues and associated with members of the American Communist Party. Known for his acidic wit and sharp mind, Trumbo struck most as a suave, larger-than-life figure. (Harry Baskerville)

suddenly transforms *A Man to Remember* from a drama to a medical thriller. As with his masterful use of the framing device, this sudden and beautifully executed shift in tone proves that Trumbo's skill at screenwriting was far in advance of his time spent in the movie industry. In fact, the natural affinity for dramatic storytelling that Trumbo exhibited in his novels and short stories prior to joining the industry served him well in his movie work; *A Man to Remember* is, then, just the moment at which Trumbo either achieved mastery over the technical aspects of screenwriting or was given enough leeway to exhibit that mastery.[4]

After the epidemic passes, however, Abbott receives a rejection letter from the National University in Paris, making the significance of Havilland-Taylor's title, "Failure," fully evident. At the end of his life, Abbott seems a failure because he "wasted" his life doing what amounted to charity work—only to be shunned by medical professionals and town leaders. The unsubtle irony, of course, is that Abbott's spiritual success was as complete as his financial failure. This climactic point is illustrated by a scene in which Jean tells Abbott that someone is at the door to see him. Now old and exhausted from his marathon of immunizations, Abbott walks to his porch and discovers a huge crowd of townsfolk, who burst into applause when they see him. Abbott is handed a thank-you letter signed by Westport's 4,000 residents. As Abbott weeps, the scene is capped by Dick's arrival. Dick says that he'll join his father's practice after all.

This scene evokes similar moments in other films about men and women who sacrifice their dreams to serve their communities, films ranging from such classic fare as *Goodbye Mr. Chips* (1939, MGM) to more recent efforts including *Mr. Holland's Opus* (1996, Touchstone)— to say nothing of the quintessential movie of this genre, Frank Capra's *It's a Wonderful Life*.[5] In *It's a Wonderful Life* and *Mr. Holland's Opus*, the lead characters resent giving up their dreams; in *Goodbye Mr. Chips* and *A Man to Remember*, the heroes understand and believe in their life choices. Heroes like Abbott, then, are the least complex and most profound of this batch: they personify selflessness. Putting the weight of such an idealized concept onto the shoulders of a character often crushes the humanity right out of him, and that nearly happens during the last stretch of *A Man to Remember*. The more Trumbo skews the story toward sanctifying Abbott, the less believable Abbott becomes. Therefore the film's title makes more sense than Havilland-Taylor's title; as the muscle and edge of the movie's early sequences gives way to something softer and less credible at the denouement, Abbott becomes an abstraction of human goodness, hence the reverent past tense of the title.

The last scene in the long flashback begins simply enough, when the phone rings in the Abbott household after the townsfolk drift away. Dick takes the call, then tells his father: "That was Mrs. Harmon. She thinks Joe's broken his arm." Abbott starts to rise from his chair, but Dick gently stops him.

"I'll go," Dick says.

"But she expects me," Abbott interjects.

"I told her Dr. Abbott would be right over," Dick replies.

Jean, moved to see her adoptive brother finally accepting his role in the family practice, says she'll accompany Dick, and as the couple walk to Dick's car, Jean hints that their courtship will resume. Inside, Abbott sits in his chair with a newspaper, grinning happily. "Dr. Abbott 'll be right over," he says before dropping his paper and dying peacefully in his own home.

The picture then cuts back to the three men waiting to hear Abbott's will. Perkins, the lawyer, opens an envelope and finds the $3,000 that Johnson had given Abbott, then reads a frosty note from Abbott explaining that $2,526.37 of the money will cover Abbott's debts to Ramsey, Sykes, and Harkness, with the remaining amount going to Dick and Jean. With a pith suiting both Abbott and Trumbo, the note ends in these words: "Until I see you all in eternity, I am your humble servant—John Abbott, MD." Shaken by their memories and the acid in Abbott's tone, the three men fumble for something to say:

"Well, that's that," Harkness says.

"He was a good man," Sykes offers. "Yes, yes. He paid every cent he owed."

"I suppose the service is just about over by now," Ramsey says. "Kinda wish I went."

Ramsey's line is fitting final note for the film. With succinct language and the kind of veiled sentiment that Trumbo used throughout the movie, the line shows us one more aspect of the impact that Abbott's life had on the people of Westport. If only for a moment, his charity caused the town's greediest men to look inside themselves and see how badly they compare to Abbott.

Although *A Man to Remember* is mostly significant as a display of Trumbo's blossoming craft, it is also notable for the inclusion of a theme that connects his most important films: honor. While Trumbo was able to hint at this theme in *Fugitives for a Night* by showing the price Matt paid for betraying his true self, *A Man to Remember* is the first instance in Trumbo's *oeuvre* of life-or-death stakes riding on how well an individual stands his ground. Abbott is thought by his peers to be a small man until he surprises them by discovering the epidemic; thereafter, all around him glimpse the integrity in his soul. That he dies soon after his finest hour underlines how Abbott didn't expose the epidemic for personal aggrandizement or any other dubious reason. Instead, Abbott did the right thing because he felt compelled to do so. This simple idea—of individuals living up to moral obligations—became crucially important later in Trumbo's career. In pre-blacklist films such as *Kitty Foyle*, *The Remarkable Andrew*, and *A Guy Named Joe*, Trumbo depicts characters torn between their weaknesses and the need to live righteously. As noted in the introduction of this book, the parallel between these characters and Trumbo is inescapable. So John Abbott forms the first important link in a chain that includes the most haunting characters in any of Trumbo's films, notably Princess Ann in *Roman Holiday*, Spartacus, Yakov Bok in *The Fixer*, and Henri "Papillon" Charrière.

❖ ❖ ❖

Following *A Man to Remember*, Trumbo split his time between writing *Johnny Got His Gun* and churning out more screenplays for RKO. Trumbo's ascendance in the movie industry, which continued through World War II and ended with his blacklisting, was among his most prolific periods and also a time in which he did much of his best work. But there was a compromise for that productivity, and that was Trumbo's apparent willingness to pass off work that was at times merely satisfactory. He was using the movie industry to support his novel writing, and because this tradeoff produced *Johnny Got His Gun*, it seems disingenuous to quibble with the wisdom of his plan.

In addition to his work at RKO, he sold several stories to other studios by, as his biographer cryptically put it, "the usual slightly devious means."[6] Many of these pictures were junky entertainments, but it's interesting to examine the tricks that Trumbo developed to keep up his productivity. Intentionally or not, he skimped on characterization: The protagonist in the 1940 drama *We Who Are Young*, for instance, is a cipher more representative of economic trends than personality traits. He let plots steamroller over anything that might be time-consuming to write. His least conscientious trick was recycling scenes. In the 1939 drama *The Flying Irishman*, a character attempts a wing-walking stunt and falls, but is saved by a parachute; later that same year, in *Five Came Back*, a pilot delivers a monologue about his days as a barnstormer and describes the tragic day when his girlfriend died in a wing-walking stunt. Many of Trumbo's late-1930s screenplays apparently were written on autopilot.

One such script was *The Flying Irishman*, which was written by Trumbo and rewritten by Ernest Pagano. The picture tells the real-life story of Douglas "Wrong Way" Corrigan, an aviator whose oddball feat was a humorous footnote to the era in which Charles Lindbergh and Howard Hughes redefined the parameters of air travel.[7] Although there are traces of the quintessential rebel hero in the character of Douglas Corrigan, his pervasive ineptitude and lack of any agenda other than a vague desire to fly make it difficult to extract anything of thematic importance from *The Flying Irishman*. Instead, the picture is proof of Hollywood's strange aptitude for flattening real-life narratives into generic potboilers. Generated by RKO to exploit Corrigan's short-lived notoriety—the aviator gives a lifeless performance as himself—the picture is unrelentingly dull and insipid, making it one of the worst on Trumbo's résumé.

Released by RKO in May 1939, *Sorority House* is a trifle with little content of note save for the oddly political bent of its denouement. Adapted from Mary Coyle Chase's story "Chi House," the film tells the breezy story of a young woman named Alice Fisher (Anne Shirley), who comes from a struggling family. Her big-hearted father, Lew Fisher (J.M. Kerrigan), surprises Alice after her high school graduation by revealing that he's saved $1,500 to send Alice to college for two years. (The scene in which Alice is moved to tears by her father's selfless act must have come easily to Trumbo, as he wrote a nearly identical one for *A Man to Remember*.) While traveling to college, Alice overhears women talking about the joys of sororities, then meets her roommate Merle (Pamela Blake) who is obsessed with getting into a sorority. Alice also meets Bill Loomis (James Ellison), who quickly devotes his energies to courting Alice.

Viewers have to trudge through almost 15 minutes of bland exposition and endless niceties before discovering the first entertaining scene in *Sorority House*. Alice and the rest of the freshmen women gather for their physicals, and one of the men administering the tests is Bill, a medical student. He sweet-talks Alice while taking her blood pressure, and though she protests that he's not getting to her, he observes that her blood pressure jumps every time he says something like, "I think you're the sweetest girl in the world." That this faintly charming scene feels outstanding is an appropriate measure of *Sorority House*'s stature.

The film trudges through predictable plot elements centering around Alice's quest to join a sorority, and it's sufficient to say that Alice loses sight of her values along the way, eventually hurting the feelings of her father, who comes to visit her on campus. The fluffy events come to a head when Lew sits down with Alice and Merle, who is devastated after learning she didn't get into a sorority. Lew offers the girls an inane homily:

> LEW: Now there was a young fellow not so long ago. He never had a chance to go to college the way we figure college these days. Never cared much about clubs. Well, I guess he hadn't time for them, had to work too hard. Never had much money and folks begin to figure out that he was a queer kind of duck, but in the long run, Abe Lincoln turned out pretty well.

Pure fluff meant to float by on the charm of star Anne Shirley and the pretty surroundings of the college milieu, *Sorority House* is the opposite number of Trumbo's best lightweight films. Whereas he was able to invest such pictures as

Fugitives for a Night and *Roman Holiday* with heart—and even some subtle commentary—*Sorority House* is painfully obvious and painfully ineffective. Following the bizarre Lincoln speech, Alice and Merle decide that they don't care about getting into sororities after all, and propose to start a house on campus for women who aren't in sororities. In short order, though, this plan spurs Lew to deliver another salt-of-the-earth oratory. "Surely you don't think you're the only nice girls in the whole school," he asks. "It strikes me that most of the grief in the world is caused by people acting just like you youngsters, forming cliques and hating everybody else."

Although an argument could be made that the philosophy projected by Lew in his monologues falls in line with Trumbo's beliefs, the slipshod nature of the screenplay containing these speeches suggests that *Sorority House* represented nothing more to Trumbo than a paycheck, so dredging for personal nuances within the screenplay seems more indulgent than worthwhile.

Trumbo's next credit was actually written two years prior to its release. Trumbo's screen story, "Broadway Cavalier," was sold to Warner Bros. in 1937 but not released into theaters until late in May 1939. Retitled *The Kid from Kokomo*, the picture is another of Trumbo's frivolous early efforts as are *Road Gang* and *The Flying Irishman*, a minor and derivative entry into a popular genre—in this case, the boxing movie. Whereas previous boxing stories had either been topical (Clifford Odets's influential leftist stage play *Golden Boy* was made as a Columbia film the same year that *Kokomo* was released) or at least glossy and well-produced (such as the 1937 Warner Bros. drama *Kid Galahad*, the success of which

likely prompted production of *Kokomo*), *Kokomo* is farcical and entertaining but neither credible enough to have much impact nor original enough to mean much in posterity. The picture boasts one of Trumbo's more absurd plots and features not only the kind of frenetic comedy plotting Trumbo would later put to good use in pictures ranging from *A Guy Named Joe* to *Roman Holiday*, but also a misanthropic protagonist. As Trumbo was something of a misanthrope himself, it's significant to note the echoes of Trumbo's own manner in the persona of crooked fight promoter William Jennings Murphy (Pat O'Brien)—whose nickname, "Square-Shooting" Murphy, is about as disingenuous a moniker as one might ever encounter.

Borrowing from the great screwball comedies of the 1930s, *Kokomo* is peopled with characters who exist merely to facilitate gags, particularly peripheral figures such as Judge Bronson (Sidney Toler), whose connections to the story include his paternity of the girl who courts the title character, his having nearly incarcerated the petty thief who poses as the title character's mother, and his having once run with the small-time hood who poses as the title character's father. Such tenuous connections are complemented by even less credible connections to create a sense of inevitability in the story, which is to say that every character exists as a necessary piece of a larger puzzle.

The picture, which enjoyed some popularity during its original release, has a couple of fundamental problems that make it seem negligible to modern eyes. Trumbo relies too heavily on coincidence and double-talk, and he cheats his way out of the plot's trickiest predicaments. The story also lacks a real central character. At the outset, we think the protagonist is Murphy, whose brazen dishonesty makes him an appropriate figure around which to build a farce, but then the titular character, whom one might have expected to be something of a red herring, becomes the center of the action. When the picture finally lurches toward its tiresome, sunny ending, it leaves in its wake a few chuckles but not much more.

❖ ❖ ❖

Although Trumbo was not the principal screenwriter of *Five Came Back*—that honor belongs to Nathanael West[8]—the picture remains one of the best credits of his early career. A pulpy adventure story that relies somewhat on stock characterizations, *Five Came Back* is mightily entertaining and significant as an early model of what later came to be termed the "disaster flick." As in modern entries into the genre—notably producer Irwin Allen's hit spectacles *The Poseidon Adventure* (1972, 20th Century–Fox) and *The Towering Inferno* (1974, 20th Century–Fox)—a group of characters from varied walks of life embark on a doomed journey that reveals their mettle, with dabs of romance, humor, and social commentary thrown in for good measure.

The picture opens at a Los Angeles airport, where the movie's characters gather for a flight to Panama City. Among the passengers are a mysterious fallen woman named Peggy Nolan (played by comedienne Lucille Ball, relatively early in her screen career) and a private detective named Crimp (John Carradine). Crimp is the gun-toting escort of the film's most intriguing character, an anarchist named Vasquez (Joseph Calleia),

who is being extradited to Panama to face execution for committing a politically charged murder. Although several of the characters follow predictable paths once they encounter adversity—privileged millionaire Judson Ellis (Patrick Knowles), for instance, is revealed as a drunken coward—Nolan defies everyone's condescension and proves a capable surrogate mother for young Tommy (Casey Johnson), who becomes an orphan in the course of the film. It is the change in Vasquez's character that is most interesting, however; introduced as a shifty criminal who nearly escapes by stealing Crimp's gun, Vasquez emerges as the strongest and noblest character in the picture.[9]

The film progresses with a steady but not terrific momentum until the plane crashes in South American headhunter territory, where the characters spend 18 days repairing the plane and forging a community built on necessity. Crimp and Ellis crumble under the pressure, somewhat predictably sealing their eventual fates.

Directed by John Farrow,[10] the picture includes a thread of sociopolitical commentary courtesy of Vasquez. In a deceptively casual scene that occurs about halfway through the picture, Vasquez chats with Professor Henry Spengler (C. Aubrey Smith) and Spengler's wife, Martha (Elisabeth Risdon). The professor asks if Vasquez would repeat his crime if he had the chance to do things over.

> VASQUEZ: I don't know. My experiences here have made me think. Now look at this camp. We have chosen a leader in whom we have supreme confidence and whom we respect completely. We have plenty to eat.... We are well-sheltered, we

are in good health. By all theories, ours is an ideal community. And yet, everyone here except myself is living for the day when all this will come to an end. That is how tightly modern living has become wrapped up in nonessentials. Personally, I should be happy to spend all my life here. So you see, even in the jungle I'm antisocial.

The virtues of this speech are somewhat self-explanatory, in that Vasquez is commenting on how adverse circumstances have democratized the characters and removed them from the pressures of a materialistic society, but the expositional purpose of the speech is invaluable. With a handful of simple words, Vasquez reveals that he's a natural outsider, and in so doing casts an interesting light on the rest of his speech. In effect, Vasquez is saying that he's not an anarchist for anarchy's sake but rather out of discontent with a social model—capitalism, presumably—with which he doesn't agree. This nuance is magnified later in the script, when Spengler makes a noble sacrifice. "If there were more men like you, professor, there would be fewer men like me," Vasquez comments. This deeply resonant line augments Vasquez's earlier assertions and clarifies his stance—he's not opposed to capitalism or any other social model per se, but with men who abuse such social models. This is an essential distinction, because it takes the often strident political posturing present in Trumbo's films and gives it a human element that transcends political fashion and says something timeless. Although it is difficult to discern Trumbo's involvement in the screenplay, the import of Vasquez's commentary is nonetheless significant because through Vasquez, the filmmakers behind *Five*

Came Back took ideology off its pedestal and put it back on the ground, where it belongs.

This idea of humanizing ideology and putting a real face on abstract concepts of social order is picked up again at the end of the picture, when the passengers prepare their escape from the jungle. By this point in the story, two characters—Crimp and likable gangster Pete Casey (Allen Jenkins)—have been killed by headhunters, and the pilots have just learned the plane can only carry five of the nine people left alive. With the pressure on because a headhunter attack seems imminent, Vasquez steals a gun and addresses the others.

> VASQUEZ: Now some of you want to live, others deserve to. But the question cannot be decided emotionally. It has to be decided by cold, hard logic. And since I am to have my neck cut by one kind of savage or stretched by another, I have nothing to gain either way. I am the only one you can depend on to decide things logically.... I am the law now.

The irony that an anarchist has become the personification of social order is the richest of *Five Came Back*'s many interesting elements, and the parallel that one might draw between the way Vasquez chooses the survivors and the process of natural selection is a valid one. At their request, Vasquez determines that the professor and his wife will stay behind, because most of their lives are behind them, but Vasquez asserts his power by deciding that Ellis will stay behind as well. "You're not worth saving!" Vasquez barks. This decision plays like a fierce condemnation of a "have" by a "have-not," which falls right in line with Trumbo's lifelong distaste for the idle rich. With its provocative subtexts, brisk drama and intense cinematography by RKO stalwart Nicholas Musuraca—who, among other touches, lights the scene in which Vasquez takes control from the ground so that all the characters look haunted—*Five Came Back* is among the most effective of Trumbo's B pictures.

The origin of the film's political bent, however, is unclear. While Vasquez's rebel politics and his emergence as the film's most honorable character mark him as a typical Trumbo protagonist, the character was created by Nathanael West, who wrote the first treatment and screenplay of the film. And while Trumbo's sympathy for the character led him to reconfigure Vasquez as a hero, Trumbo's son, Christopher, cautioned against reading too much into the political aspects of his father's early films.

> The oddity is, if you go through the '30s and '40s and look for progressive content, people who weren't [subsequently] blacklisted were putting that content in.... I don't know any of the left-wing writers who were doing that. [As a screenwriter], you put in whatever you want, knowing that people are going to say, "I don't think we can get away with that." Making movies and writing scripts, there's a lot of peer review.[11]

The question of how much progressive content Hollywood's left-leaning writers were able to put into their movies—and, moreover, how much content they wanted to put into their movies—has been the subject of intense debate for decades. While certain figures on the left trumpeted their ability to put political subject matter into mainstream

films, Trumbo often commented that the greater and more useful challenge was to keep negative content out. As will be seen throughout the remainder of this book, though, Trumbo left himself open to scrutiny by continually writing about social causes: Kitty Foyle's difficulties in crossing caste lines, the political corruption exposed by the hero of *The Remarkable Andrew*, and so on.

Christopher Trumbo's argument that his father did not intentionally lace his prewar and war-era films with political content is interesting when contrasted with the apparent political naiveté of his father's pre-blacklist films. Was Trumbo working within the parameters of the studio system and trying not to rock the boat? Or did Trumbo, as his behavior in other areas of his life might suggest, test the limits on political content in mainstream films? Because so much of the sociopolitical subject matter in Trumbo's pre-blacklist films can be read innocently or "subversively," these are questions without definitive answers. What is inarguable, though, is that in exploring the themes that Trumbo definitely laced into his films, notably personal honor, Trumbo often depicted characters caught in conflict with the Establishment—even if, until the HUAC hearings in 1947, he himself was not such a person.

❖ ❖ ❖

Released a handful of days after *Five Came Back*, *Career* is one of the few pictures on Trumbo's résumé with a truly chaotic narrative. Adapted from Philip Strong's novel by Trumbo (who did the final screenplay) and Bert Granet, the film tells a cautionary tale involving jealousy, careerism, and, through the use of an awkward metaphor, isolationism. These themes are addressed in a roundabout, pretentious fashion—and they're muddied by the inclusion of several distracting subplots and a generally overworked story.

The film concerns an adversarial relationship between Pittsville, Iowa, shopkeeper Stephen Cruthers (Edward Ellis[12]) and banker Clem Bartholomew (Samuel E. Hinds). When they were younger, the two men competed for the affections of a woman named Adele. Stephen resents that Clem married Adele and had a daughter with her, Sylvia (Anne Shirley), while Stephen married a plain woman named Amy (Janet Beecher) and had a son, Ray (John Archer). Stephen's resentment is compounded by the fact that Adele died years ago. When the Depression rolls around and Clem's bank starts to go under, Stephen exacts revenge on his rival by extracting his abundant savings from Clem's bank, thereby sparking paranoia among Pittsville residents that the bank will close and people will lose their deposits. These events coincide with a subplot involving the romance between Sylvia and Ray.

Following Stephen's bank withdrawal, Pittsville residents entreat him to restore their confidence in Clem's bank by redepositing his money, but he refuses. These factors lead to a peculiar scene set on the porch of Stephen's house, which recalls the climax in *A Man to Remember*. In the earlier film, townsfolk gathered outside John Abbott's home to show their appreciation for his efforts; in *Career*, townsfolk gather outside Stephen's house like an angry mob, ready to lynch Stephen for what they see as his betrayal of the town. In a moment that stretches credibility—and viewers' patience—to the breaking point, Stephen walks onto his porch and addresses the throng:

> STEPHEN: If I have committed a crime, you can prosecute me according to the law. Heaven knows there's enough of them in this country. [But] remember this. The minute it becomes unsafe for me to step out onto the front porch, that very minute it becomes unsafe for you. If the liberty of a single man in this country is illegally threatened, then the liberty of us all is threatened. The very thing that's happening to me now, once started, can happen to any of you tomorrow. Liberty and justice are not things to be tampered with. They are not things to be qualified. They are absolute. Either they exist or they don't. There is no compromise. If you carry through what you planned to do tonight, not one living soul of you can ever again, with a clear conscience, claim justice for himself. Remember that. I'm not defending myself now, I'm defending you. The only thing I'm wondering is whether or not you're worth it. I'm disgusted with you. You're a disgrace to the state of Iowa. Now go on, get out of here. Go on home. Get off my tulip bed.

Although it pales next to more efficient monologues that appear in later Trumbo movies, this speech is the high point of *Career* because it reiterates the theme that Trumbo explored so effectively in *A Man to Remember*, that of personal honor. By telling his neighbors to leave him be, Stephen is telling them to comport themselves honorably and respect his freedom to do with his money as he chooses. The patriotic bent of the speech meshes with similar sentiments expressed throughout Trumbo's correspondence to illuminate that Stephen is, at least for the duration of the speech, espousing Trumbo's ideas about what it means to be American. That Stephen later becomes a hero by protecting the welfare of various neighbors—and that he sets aside petty jealousies to protect his town by taking control of Clem's bank—entwines the idea of nobility with Stephen's Americanism. This sanctification of a patriotic character is a precursor of the kind of flag-waving that Trumbo did in his wartime films.

That mob hysteria is the element threatening Stephen's personal liberty is resonant because of how anti–Communist hysteria affected Trumbo just a few years after *Career* was released, but the speech is also interesting for technical reasons. At first glance, it seems to have a repetitious rhythm closely resembling speech—note the emphatic use of phrases with roughly the same intent ("not to be tampered with" and "not to be qualified"; "remember this" and "remember that"). The almost musical way in which Trumbo stacks bits of repetitive language upon each other creates the kind of sing-song momentum a preacher conjures on a particularly impassioned Sunday morning.

❖ ❖ ❖

The last of Trumbo's six 1939 credits was, like *The Kid from Kokomo*, a film based on a story that Trumbo sold to another studio while he was working at RKO. Released by 20th Century–Fox in early November, *Heaven with a Barbed Wire Fence* is a straightforward road movie set in the world of hobo rail-riders. At the outset of the picture, we meet Joe Riley (Glenn Ford) at his job in a New York City department store, where he announces to a coworker that he has bought a plot of land in Arizona and intends to become a rancher. Joe meets Tony Caselli (Nicholas Conte), a likable hobo who suggests that Joe should to ride the rails to Arizona, thereby avoiding costly train fare. Shortly afterward, Joe meets Anita Santos (Jean Rogers), a kind but somewhat hapless character who latches onto Joe as a possible benefactor. Joe brushes her off and makes the first of many proclamations about how women are nothing but trouble.

Predictably, the three set off together, proving that Joe's protestations are mostly hot air. The fourth member of this intrepid crew is Professor Townsend Thayer (Raymond Walburn)—known to his traveling companions only as "the Professor"—an oddly articulate older hobo who we later learn once taught paleontology but got lost in a haze of alcohol.

Although the movie's cross-section of characters seems interesting at first, *Barbed Wire Fence* quickly devolves into a series of clichéd altercations with a few melodramatic twists thrown in for good measure; instead of offering an instructive look at life on the rails or even an intimate examination of the lives that led these characters to this point, Trumbo and his collaborators stir the plot elements into a pulpy drama that is entertaining but incurably superficial. We are told a few facts about Thayer's past, for example, but for the most part, the characters are exactly as they seem—so the story is less about revelation and more about momentum, a word with incredible significance when the subject is Trumbo's early screenplays. With pictures such as *Barbed Wire Fence*, Trumbo does what was quickly becoming his magic act—he fills the screen with enough events that a story unfolds without anything really happening. Characters face simple crises that force them to better themselves, and once their predictable arcs are completed, the story is over with few loose ends left dangling. In this kind of screenwriting, the priorities are slickness, speed, and dexterity, with substance an afterthought.

Barbed Wire Fence is ultimately most interesting for its links to a far superior Trumbo film, *Cowboy*. Actor Glenn Ford's performance as Joe Riley was his screen debut, but by the time he costarred in *Cowboy* nearly 20 years later, he was an established name. A more significant connection between the two pictures is the similarity of Joe to Frank Harris, the character played by Jack Lemmon in *Cowboy*. Both are clerks who seek their destiny in archetypal Western milieus. Frank's journey, based on the experiences of a real person, is more complex and credible, but is similar to Joe's in that both men are changed by cross-country treks fueled by the ambition to become a rancher. It is therefore instructive to note how much sleight of hand Trumbo used to portray this journey in *Barbed Wire Fence*—and then look at the careful craftsmanship with which he told a similar story later in his career.

❖ ❖ ❖

Trumbo began 1940 with two more pictures based on stories that he sold to outside studios while still under contract at RKO. The first of them, Columbia's *The Lone Wolf Strikes*, was an entry into the popular series depicting the exploits of Michael Lanyard, a reformed jewel thief working as a private detective. Introduced by novelist Louis Joseph Vance

in 1914, Lanyard had already appeared in 11 films before a mystery story by Trumbo was used as the basis for *The Lone Wolf Strikes*: The clichéd and silly thriller is as minor an entry on Trumbo's résumé as it as a chapter in Lanyard's exploits.

Trumbo's second 1940 credit, the Universal release *Half a Sinner*, is half a success. Based on Trumbo's story "Lady Takes a Chance," the picture is filled with potential—a young teacher longing for adventure embarks on a petty-crime spree—but the potential is not realized. A frothy romp in the spirit of *Fugitives for a Night* that lacks the earlier picture's solid construction, *Half a Sinner* relies heavily on coincidence and the convenient stupidity of minor characters, so it never develops much credibility. There's entertainment value in the spectacle of a pretty, 25-year-old teacher and her mysterious, handsome paramour evading a motorcycle policeman by racing their stolen limousine through rural terrain, but there's not much substance.

Instead of exploring what drives Anne Gladden (Heather Angel) to run away from her ordered life, the story slides by on momentum and whimsy, never giving Anne an opportunity to reflect on her actions. *Half a Sinner* also has a passing similarity to *Fugitives for a Night*; recalling the way that an idea from *The Flying Irishman* showed up in *Five Came Back*, Trumbo might have borrowed the concept of *Fugitives* as the basis for *Half a Sinner*. Whatever the case, *Half a Sinner* is one of his shoddiest efforts.

❖ ❖ ❖

The first RKO film to bear Trumbo's name in 1940 is as lightweight as *Half a*

In 1938, Trumbo married beautiful Californian Cleo Fincher. The couple (above) lived in California and Mexico, raised three children, and survived the endless difficulties of the blacklist era. Their marriage lasted the rest of Dalton Trumbo's life. (AMPAS)

Sinner but far more rewarding. Adapted from Howard J. Green's competent but predictable story about how a neophyte playwright gets enmeshed in the backstage drama at an ego-driven New York theater company, Trumbo's screenplay for *Curtain Call* is slick, witty, and fast. The picture has to recommend it several entertaining plot twists, a broadly satirical character whose rampant egotism plays like a softened version of the narcissism exhibited years later by Norma Desmond in Billy Wilder's *Sunset Boulevard* (1950, Paramount), and, as with the best of Trumbo's second-rate movies, an intoxicating pace. *Curtain Call* is also notable in that, along with *Fugitives for*

a Night and *A Man to Remember*, it offers early evidence that Trumbo's greatest gift as a screenwriter was his ability to streamline other writers' stories into crisp movie scenarios.

Curtain Call begins is the small town of Medbury, New Jersey, where young Helen Middleton (Barbara Read) is so obsessed with becoming a playwright that she barely notices her paramour, Ted Palmer (Frank Faylen). When celebrated New York theater director Donald Avery (Alan Mowbray) visits Medbury on a hunting trip, Helen asks Don to read her play but is told to send it to his New York office. Shortly thereafter, Don phones his business partner, producer Geoffrey Crandall (Donald MacBride), and learns that the diva who has starred in their productions for 15 stormy years, Charlotte Morley (Helen Vinson), wants to quit the company. Don reluctantly cuts his vacation short to negotiate with Charlotte.

Back in New York, the diva throws a tantrum in which she says she's sick of "carrying" Don and that she's not growing as an artist—then acknowledges that she's contractually obligated to do one more play for Don and Jeff. After she leaves, Jeff hatches a plan to offer Charlotte the worst play imaginable, the idea being that she will submit to renewing her contract rather than appear in a sure-fire flop. Predictably enough, the play the partners choose is Helen's submission, *The End of Everything*. At this point, the character of the film is already clear: It's got a locomotive of a plot, a steady stream of cheap shots at the pretensions and egos of show business, and precious little introspection. Because Trumbo was at this stage of his career a theatrical neophyte—he didn't write his only produced play, *The Biggest Thief in Town*, until 1948—it's likely that much of the inside humor in *Curtain Call* was transposed directly from Green's story, even though Trumbo's *Fugitives for a Night* screenplay featured several tart entertainment-industry barbs. Given the acidity of much of the dialogue and Don's misanthropic nature, though, it's easy to see what made Trumbo the right man for this job.

The story gets interesting when Charlotte receives a copy of *The End of Everything*, because she likes the play. "Here and there some of the scenes need a few more words for me, and things like that, but that will be simple," she says in one of Trumbo's many tangy one-liners.

Don and Jeff scramble to escape their own trap by convincing Charlotte that she really doesn't want to do the play, but she reminds them of a clause in her contract—if they renege on their offer to stage the play, they'll owe Charlotte a $50,000 settlement. Don then tries to seduce Helen into rewriting the play, but Charlotte gets wise to the scheme, and informs Helen of her contractual right to refuse rewrite requests. Thus emboldened, Helen has an entertaining and revealing chat with Don during one of their dates.

> HELEN: Before you became interested in the commercial theater—in money—didn't you have ideals?
> DON: Oh, but my dear child, I learned long ago that ideals never pan out. Somewhere along the line, one is forced to compromise, and that's why I've been thinking of again asking you if I can make just a few changes in that lovely play of yours.
> HELEN: Do you really want to, Don?
> DON: Darling, I've never wanted to change anything so much in all my life.
> HELEN: I'm not going to let you change one word of my play because of you and all the ideals you've had to compromise. This is one dream that will come true.

Don eventually realizes that his seduction plan isn't working, so he reveals to Helen that his affection is fake. She storms away, thinking that she'll protect her play by doing so, but an underling reminds Don and Jeff that when playwrights are unavailable for rewrites, producers have the right to make whatever text changes they deem necessary.

Three weeks later, Helen and her long-suffering paramour, Ted, attend the premiere of *The End of Everything*, and she is devastated to discover that Don has transformed her tragedy into a farce. This development meshes well with the dialogue about ideals and compromise, because Don's flagrant destruction of Helen's art defines him a lost soul, and Helen's overwhelmed reaction defines her a victim. This puts viewers firmly in Helen's camp, so even though she's a neophyte who wrote a rotten play, we sympathize with the way she was abused, and our sympathy becomes part of the film's message.

Backstage after the play, a critic tries to ingratiate himself to Don by saying that he got a great performance out of Charlotte, who is in earshot. Charlotte's indignant response sparks a funny exchange:

> CHARLOTTE: I played comedy long before I ever met Don Avery.
> DON: Yes, but *how* you played comedy, darling.
> CHARLOTTE: Very much better than at present, I dare say. There was a little nuance in my work then.
> DON: Yes, there's little of that left over in your performance this evening.

The picture ends in a flurry of slapstick comedy highlighted by Don's inevitable comeuppance, and the comic sequence is one of the many whipped-cream pleasures of *Curtain Call*.

❖ ❖ ❖

Trumbo's next important credit bridged the two studios with which he was most closely associated during his pre-blacklist years. *We Who Are Young* was released by MGM, the studio from which Trumbo had been dismissed for lack of productivity in the mid–1930s,

but which would soon come to rely on Trumbo as a top writer. *We Who Are Young* also forms the bridge between Trumbo's apprenticeship and his most successful streak. Given this context, it's highly ironic that *We Who Are Young* is on almost every level an atrocious movie. The story about a young couple's monetary woes deals with real-life issues in such an undramatic fashion that it's akin to a pedantic documentary about financial prudence; that it was the first film both conceived and written by Trumbo offered a depressing omen about the nature of Trumbo's purely original screen work.[13]

The picture opens with odd images of New York City and narration promising a story about "one of the least of the creatures called men." This line has a certain humor in retrospect; although it was intended to position *We Who Are Young* as a story of humble people, it now functions as a warning that the picture is trivial. When we first meet them, young lovers William Brooks (John Shelton) and Marjorie White (Lana Turner) are getting married in night court and discussing their dreams of a life together. From the first scenes, the dialogue in the picture is painfully bland, as when we hear the lovers' thoughts: "Gosh, she's beautiful!" William exclaims in voice-over. "Her hair is so soft and shiny— smells just like flowers." After an expositional scene of the couple hiding their relationship at their workplace, a company called Accountrex, we see the couple spend more than they should on furniture for their apartment, and the portent afforded the seemingly innocuous scene is a hint of how little is yet to come. Back at work, the couple's marriage is discovered, and their supervisor—unctuous C.B. Beamis (Gene

Lockhart)—fires Marjorie because of Accountrex's policy against employing married women at a time when single men are having difficulty finding work. Undaunted, William tells Marjorie that he's drafted a reorganization plan for Accountrex, which he believes will earn him a promotion.

Complications soon pile up: Marjorie becomes pregnant, Beamis rejects William's reorganization plan, and the couple has to take a loan to pay Marjorie's medical bills. The couple reaches their nadir when William defaults on his loan, forcing William's creditor to garnishee his wages. This violates another Accountrex rule, so Beamis fires William, who leaves a few stormy words in his wake. The couple's last hope is William's upcoming examination for certification as an accountant, so Marjorie hocks her wedding ring to keep them afloat until he becomes a CPA, but once he does, he discovers that the job market is flooded. Because he can't find work, the couple's furniture is repossessed and they're forced to sign up for government relief payments. After three months of living off the government, William goes crazy with desperation at not being able to find work, so he sneaks onto a construction site, picks up a shovel, and starts working until he's arrested for trespassing.

The film's only interesting moment occurs when William gets thrown in jail. Although previous scenes are so perfunctory and graceless that the picture is a chore to sit through, the film suddenly becomes sociopolitical propaganda with the introduction of Braddock (Jonathan Hale). Braddock, owner of the construction site, visits William in jail and explains that because he too was once broke, he empathizes with

William's plight. "I'm your friend," he tells William. "And a lot of people you've never heard of yet will be your friends. We'll help you and you can help somebody else sometime. Pass it along—that's the only important rule."

In light of Trumbo's left-wing sensibility, this dialogue seems to have a vaguely communistic bent, inferring that a citizen can rely on the collective to carry him through bad times so long as he's willing to help the collective in good times. Significantly, the dialogue comes without warning, because there were several other directions in which Trumbo could have taken the scene—he could have made Braddock a father who understands William's need to feed his growing family; he could have made Braddock an altruist who conveniently stumbles upon William's plight; he could have simply made Braddock a hard worker impressed by William's willingness to work. But, knowingly or not, Trumbo made Braddock a figurehead for collectivism, and in so doing inserted a surprising political edge to an otherwise toothless film.

It's important to note, though, that the dialogue could be read as being about democracy, not communism. The two political systems were seen by many leftists of the period as being close cousins, so it's possible to interpret the dialogue as advocating either system and still be on fairly solid ground. That Trumbo's politics were proudly American but deeply influenced by what many leftists believed to be the positive model of communist Russia is one of the reasons behind Trumbo's political troubles of the late 1940s. Witnesses told HUAC that Trumbo's films contained communist propaganda disguised as pro-democracy sentiment, and *We Who Are Young* contains some of the earliest examples of dialogue that can be read innocently or "subversively."

The film gets even more political when William, freed from jail after Braddock drops the trespassing charge, confronts Beamis to recover the reorganization plan, which William wants to sell to another company. The men get into an argument as ideological as it is personal. "You're a wrong guy, Mr. Beamis," William barks. "You've got the soul of an adding machine." Beamis retorts by saying that William's a weakling. This accusation launches William on a tirade that feels like a *non sequitur* but actually advances ideas that Trumbo had expressed in previous pictures, especially *Career*.

> WILLIAM: Our homes, our churches, our schools and what they stand for. Nobody could build those alone. We did it together. All of us, the people, helping each other.... If any man says that he made his money, or built his life, without the help of anybody else, he's a fool! He's worse than a fool! He's a liar!

Picking up on the theme of collectivism featured in Braddock's jail house dialogue, William's spiel suggests that the arc of the entire picture has been William's slow discovery that, as the cliché goes, no man is an island. This contrasts him with Beamis, who considers himself a self-made man with no time for charity.

After William leaves Beamis's office, Beamis decides to seek some perspective on his management style. He asks his secretary, Miss Anderson (Shirley Worde) why a woman named Tillery left Accountrex for a lower-paying job elsewhere.[14] Anderson's meekly uttered

answer: "Money isn't everything." That line is a loaded one, because it can easily be read as an anticapitalism snipe, which, in tandem with the pro-communism stance that runs through *We Who Are Young*, gives the picture an even more radical quality.

Despite such potentially charged material, the picture's conclusion is as drab as its early sequences. Marjorie delivers a daughter, and she and William—his confidence restored because Braddock has offered him a job—are sitting with the newborn when a letter from Beamis arrives. In the letter, Beamis invites William back to Accountrex. "You said rules were like machines that need oil, and that oil was kindness," Beamis writes in noxious simile. "Perhaps our machine would work better if it had more oil." Because maudlin plot developments such as this one dull the impact of the provocative, albeit murky, political posturing in the film, *We Who Are Young* has a place among, to paraphrase the picture's opening narration, the least of these screenplays by Dalton Trumbo.

As did *Five Came Back*, *We Who Are Young* raises the thorny issue of how—or whether—political content got onscreen in the prewar era. While it is inarguable that enough sociopolitical content got into the picture to spark discussions, it is also inarguable that the picture is not fundamentally a political film. This second fact lends credence to Christopher Trumbo's assertion that his father was not filling his movies with left-wing slogans, but screenwriting historian Tom Stempel had this to say on the subject:

> While studio heads were willing to hire writers they knew were communists, they were not about to allow them to put any obvious propaganda

in their films. MGM and Fox softened potentially pro–Communist material in Dalton Trumbo's 1940 script for *We Who Are Young* and John Howard Lawson's 1939 script for *Four Sons*, respectively.[15]

While devoting surprisingly little attention to Trumbo's screen work, Larry Ceplair and Steven Englund, two of the most astute students of the blacklist era, explored the concept of whether left-wing writers could get political content into their movies and drew several thought-provoking conclusions. They generally found that while radical writers tried to get films made about social issues, the studios were cool to such films; for instance, Ceplair and Englund note that six scripts were written about the Spanish Civil War but shelved because no approach to the material could be found that didn't run the risk of offending right-wing interests. Ceplair and Englund determined that many Hollywood radicals settled for advancing humanist themes, and their assertion parallels Trumbo's argument that the best left-leaning writers could do was prevent ignorance from permeating popular movies.[16]

Incidentally, Christopher Trumbo had a great deal to say when presented with the preceding analysis of *We Who Are Young*. In a February 2000 letter to this author, he argued that true radical content didn't appear in his father's films prior to the blacklist era, and cautioned against looking at his father's early films through the prism of his father's political sensibilities. Christopher Trumbo took particular issue with this book's sections on *We Who Are Young* and *Tender Comrade*, stating that this book propagates decades-old fallacies about radical content. While a son is in a unique position to comment on a father's work, the preponderance of radical and/or pseudo-radical symbols and language is the justification for this book's analysis about the pictures that Christopher Trumbo feels are nonradical. The only person who could truly resolve this disagreement of interpretation, of course, is Dalton Trumbo—and, as seen in the interviews and correspondence quoted in this book's test and notes, Trumbo rarely gave simple and clear answers about subjects as importatnt as the content of his most controversial films.

3

The Path to Glory
(1940–1942)

Trumbo eventually found a way out of B movies by, appropriately, writing one that was received like an A-list feature. Best-known as legendary dancer Ginger Rogers's first foray into straight drama, *Kitty Foyle: The Natural History of a Woman*[1] was based on Christopher Morley's best-selling novel, which had become controversial because of its depiction of premarital sex and an abortion. The picture—which Trumbo rewrote from an early draft by fellow leftist Donald Ogden Stewart, enough of whose work was retained that he got an "additional dialogue" credit—represents the zenith of Trumbo's early attempts at portraying complex cinematic women. Excepting rebellious characters in *Fugitives for a Night* and *Half a Sinner*, nearly all of the women in Trumbo's early movies were one-dimensional characters who let men run their lives; therefore, the independence shown by the title character in *Kitty Foyle* is notable. Furthermore, the movie falls in line with a provocative, and probably unin-

tentional, theme that runs throughout Trumbo's films: one suggesting that women who defy old-fashioned gender roles are punished for doing so.

For instance, there's Doctor Helen Hunt in *You Belong to Me*. A competent professional who gets involved with a rich playboy, Helen suffers her husband's endless suspicion because she has male patients. Despite her many proclamations that her husband should learn to trust her, Helen shockingly closes her practice toward the end of the movie so she can spend more time with the playboy. Aside from the hostile inference that Helen is manipulative, there is a more damning subtext to this plot—that Helen's career was merely a hobby and that what she really wanted was an opportunity to conform to a traditional gender role. The price for Hunt's happiness: her independence.

Then there's Jo Jones, the lead character in *Tender Comrade*, who defies not only her traditional gender role but the American system of government by founding a collective of women whose husbands are at war. The price Jones pays for her defiance: her husband is killed in action. Although the death of Jo's husband is a germane development in a war story, it can be seen as another example of a woman in a Trumbo movie suffering for overstepping her bounds.

And then there's Princess Ann in *Roman Holiday*. A free spirit who flees her life as a European royal to experience life among commoners, she falls in love with an American journalist, yet neither member of the couple ever truly believes they can have a life together. Instead, the only question between them is when their happiness will be sacrificed on the altar of duty. Although it may be dubious to describe Ann's acceptance of a life of privilege as a true sacrifice, it's inescapable that the price she pays for her future as a royal is to surrender her chance at happiness with a commoner. In this case, Ann is punished not for escaping a gender role but rather an archaic societal obligation.

There are other examples of women in Trumbo movies suffering sad fates because of their rebelliousness—Annie Laurie Starr in *Gun Crazy* rebels and dies violently; the slave Varinia in *Spartacus* rebels and wins freedom for herself and her child but loses her husband to crucifixion. And though the trend of women suffering for independence is prevalent in Trumbo's pictures, he was capable of writing from a more progressive stance. Dorinda Durston, the female lead in *A Guy Named Joe*, rebels and wins not only a kind new lover but a blessing from the ghost of her previous paramour; Kitty Fremont, the bereaved widow-turned–freedom fighter in *Exodus*, rebels and wins perhaps the most precious of prizes, a proud new identity.

Importantly, it is not just women in Trumbo's movies who suffer for rebelling—considering the fates of the characters played by Kirk Douglas in *Spartacus*, *The Last Sunset*, and *Lonely Are the Brave* is proof of that.

Nonetheless, certain examples suggest that the very quality Trumbo found heroic in screen men—independence—was one that he disliked in screen women, whether consciously or not. And while it is certainly true that Trumbo's view of women was consistent with the tenor of his time, it's valid to criticize his apparent lack of tolerance, much less enthusiasm, for female independence given that Trumbo was such an ardent supporter of other progressive causes, including the organization of labor in the movie industry, the fight to protect civil rights, and various campaigns to free unjustly jailed individuals.[2]

The first troubling material in *Kitty Foyle* appears after the credit sequence, when a title card flashes: "This is the story of a white-collar girl. Because she is a comparative newcomer to the American scene, it is fitting that we briefly consider her as she was in 1900."

Next comes a brief vignette in which a woman boards a trolley and sees every man aboard stand to offer his seat. In the next vignette, the woman is sweetly courted by a man; in a third, she enjoys idyllic married life. Then another title flashes: "But this was not enough." Next we see the woman engaged in a pro-suffrage demonstration. The demonstration is followed by another title: "And so ... the battle was won. Women got their equal rights." The woman is again shown on a trolley car, but this time she's holding a ceiling strap. When a man gets up from his seat, another man butts in front of the woman to take the

Trumbo earned an Academy Award nomination for the script of *Kitty Foyle*, a social drama that featured dancer Ginger Rogers's first major dramatic performance. Here, Kitty (Rogers, center) realizes that her blueblood husband Wyn (Dennis Morgan, right) and Wyn's mother (Gladys Cooper) have a plan for smoothing her rough edges. (RKO)

seat. The prologue concludes with a final title card, part of which reads as follows: "Thus woman climbed down from her pedestal and worked shoulder-to-shoulder with men."

Although the entire prologue is presented in light, comical vignettes suggesting that the sequence was meant to gently satirize the suffrage movement and, by extension, women's entrance into the workplace, five words in the prologue put a dark edge onto the entire sequence: "But this was not enough." There's a hard, disapproving quality to these words. One is reminded of a harried parent indulging the whims of a whiny child—as if women demanding equal rights is just a phase to be tolerated until women come to their collective senses. Seen through this prism, the prologue isn't so much about women claiming what's rightfully theirs as it is about women growing "uppity" and demanding rights they don't deserve and, more importantly, don't really want.

After the crude sexism of the prologue, however, the film becomes a celebration of one woman's independence. A snapshot of a time when women began to juggle romantic choices more complex than those available to their ancestors, the film is on its surface about a woman learning from her mistakes and discovering a way to make the most of her life. That the woman eventually sets aside blind passion and chooses a course likely to give her years of happiness is the ultimate victory of the character—and the best argument against reading *Kitty Foyle* as a sexist tract.

The story proper begins with perfume saleswoman Kitty Foyle (Ginger Rogers) riding in a cab with straight-talking doctor Mark Eisen (James Craig). After a quick expositional scene in which Kitty assures Mark that she's over her old flame, Mark proposes marriage and Kitty accepts. They arrange to meet several hours later, at midnight.

But Kitty returns to her hotel and finds her old flame waiting in her room. A rich, handsome, Philadelphia blueblood, Wynnewood Strafford VI (Dennis Morgan) reports that Kitty recently mailed him a ring that he had given to her years ago. She clarifies that she sent the ring as a good-bye gesture, not an invitation, but "Wyn," as he is nicknamed, won't be deterred. He invites her to move with him to South America, and the discreet, economical dialogue that follows is among the best in the picture.

"You're going to be divorced?" Kitty asks.

"No," Wyn says. "I'm afraid I can't even promise you that."

"Then we'd...."

"That's it. I wish it were different, but that's the way it is."

"I see," Kitty concludes.

Undaunted, she accepts Wyn's offer, so he sets off to make arrangements. Alone in her room, Kitty picks up a snow globe and turns it upside down to dream as the flakes drift down onto the figurine of a girl on a sleigh. Her reverie is interrupted when she hears her own voice say: "You're making a mistake, you know." Kitty turns and sees her own reflection—her conscience personified. This entertaining device allows Trumbo to verbalize Kitty's interior thoughts, and it is intertwined with the film's other principal structural device: flashbacks. After each scene of Kitty chatting with her conscience, the camera pushes in to the snow globe and then dissolves to a flashback, making the globe the picture's recurring transition image.[3] Kitty's conscience scolds her for choosing Wyn over Mark, arguing that if she heads to Buenos Aires with her rich Philadelphian, she'll get a reputation as "that woman Wyn's mixed up with." It's in scenes such as this one, which address adult-themed subject matter directly, that *Kitty Foyle* is its most potent—even though the filmmakers softened or extracted the material that made Morley's book controversial.

Kitty says her conscience is wrong about Wyn; her conscience then reminds Kitty of everything that's led up to this point, ostensibly so Kitty can make an informed decision, but really to justify the flashbacks. The straightforward manner in which the flashback device is set up has Trumbo's fingerprints all over it, not only because it reflects his craftsmanship but because it casts the story as a moral homily.

In the first flashback, 15-year-old Kitty (portrayed, rather ridiculously, by nearly 30-year-old Rogers) rushes home after gawking at Philadelphia's rich and famous at the city's biggest social event of the year, the Assembly. Kitty tries to sneak into her house, but her blusteringly Irish father, Tom Foyle (Ernest Cossart), confronts her. Speaking with as much affection as concern, he says he wants her to attend Sunday School in order to develop values with which to balance her daydreaming about wealth and luxury. In a memorable line that echoes the repressive aspect of the movie's prologue, Tom explains his reasoning: "It may not keep you from sinning, but by Judas Priest, it'll keep you from getting any fun out of it!"

Undeterred, Kitty starts talking dreamily about Cinderella, clearly imagining herself as the fairy-tale character. Tom launches into the picture's funniest—and, in light of the picture's attitude toward female liberation, most telling—monologue:

> TOM: Judas Priest, if ever a man deserved to be hung, it's the fellow who started that Cinderella stuff. Writing claptrap stories about Cinderella and princes, poisoning the minds of innocent children, putting crazy ideas into girls' heads, making 'em dissatisfied with honest shoe clerks and bookkeepers—why, they're the ruination of more girls than— 40 actors!

In ensuing flashbacks, we see Kitty get a business-college degree and then meet Wyn, an ambitious young man just starting a magazine called *Philly*. Wyn hires Kitty as a secretary and then courts her, eventually squiring her on a romantic getaway to New York City. Once there, Kitty realizes he doesn't want to be seen with her in Philadelphia; his reluctance to "go public" with her is the demon of their relationship. In all of the Kitty-Wyn scenes, Trumbo adeptly balances the two elements: the couple's voracious love for each other and their knowledge that, like Romeo and Juliet and countless other lovers before them, their heredity is an obstacle.

Despite her father's warnings that Wyn will use her, Kitty pursues the relationship until Wyn announces that *Philly* is folding. In an important and touching scene, he whines that his family has cut off funding for the magazine and that he's not strong enough to fight the family's wishes. Kitty says he's strong enough to do anything he wants, and her feisty manner almost persuades him to break free of his passive nature. But Wyn goes wrong when he offers to keep Kitty on the payroll until she can get another job. Trumbo stages this moment masterfully: In the preceding scene, Kitty announced to her father that she expected Wyn to propose, so as Wyn struggles through a monologue about the plans he has for Kitty, she tries to hide a smile that shows what she's expecting to hear. When the dialogue turns, Kitty's face turns incredulous, as if she can't believe that Wyn is as shallow as her father warned. When Wyn drops the bombshell about "keeping" her, Kitty's shocked expression and Trumbo's deft screenwriting is sufficient to infer that Wyn has, in essence, just called her a whore. As with the best moments in the picture, this scene confronts provocative subject matter with restraint, but not so much restraint that the impact of the scene is dulled.

Kitty's response to Wyn's bombshell is melodramatic but filled with important thematic material: "You needn't worry about me.... I'll go on loving you from here on out.... But nobody owes anything to Kitty Foyle except Kitty Foyle!" Kitty's assertion that her love is hers to give is the most truly independent sentiment she expresses in the entire film, and it starts establishing the connection *Kitty Foyle* has to other Trumbo films concerned with personal honor. By taking possession of her emotions, Wyn and everyone else be damned, Kitty says she's her own person and will comport herself as her own morals and beliefs demand. The short speech also connects her to the various rebellious characters in Trumbo's films; just as Kitty defied her father's advice by pursuing Wyn, she's not going to let his disappointing aspects change her way of thinking.

Shortly after Wyn makes his distasteful offer, Kitty's father dies, and, with no ties left to Philadelphia, Kitty moves to New York. She soon meets Mark, her other suitor, and the sequence depicting their courtship is dull and awkward, because the filmmakers struggle against credibility to portray Mark as Wyn's opposite. Blunt where Wyn is eloquent, cool where Wyn is romantic, Mark is portrayed as an eminently "practical" suitor for Kitty—in other words, a huge comedown from her Prince Charming. Mark's biggest selling points are his independence and his unmistakable affection for Kitty, but his advances are tart compared to the sugar of Wyn's courtship.

As if on cue, Wyn arrives to sweep Kitty off her feet with a whirlwind night of drinking, dancing, and extravagant spending. Still believing in the fairy tales her father warned her about, Kitty accepts Wyn's lovemaking, and there's a surprisingly erotic exchange during a scene of Wyn and Kitty dancing in a posh ballroom.

"You like to dance, don't you?" Wyn asks.

"All women do," Kitty responds. "It's good training."

"How do you mean?"

"It's the first way a woman learns what a man is going to do before he does it."

The huge grin on Morgan's face after Rogers delivers that last line leaves no doubt as to whether the performers knew exactly what was being inferred by the dialogue.

Wyn ends the romantic evening at six the next morning, when he proposes to Kitty. She refuses him with a long speech about how they'll never be comfortable in Philadelphia society because she's from the wrong side of the tracks, and he says the answer is for them to live in New York, away from the old class issues. She accepts.

But when Wyn takes Kitty home as his bride, Wyn's family informs the couple that if Wyn moves to New York, he'll lose his inheritance. The cold drawing room conversation among Wyn's aunts and uncles chills Kitty, because she discovers that Wyn and his family had made plans to send Kitty to finishing school prior to her marriage to Wyn. Emboldened by the fact that Wyn defied the plan and married her anyway, Kitty tells her new family just what she thinks of them:

> KITTY: Let's get a few things straight around here. I didn't ask to marry a Strafford, a Strafford asked to marry me. I married a man, not an institution or a trust fund. Oh, I've got a fine picture of your family conference here—all the Straffords trying to figure out to take the curse off Kitty Foyle. Buy the girl a phony education and polish off the rough edges and make a mainline doll out of her. Oh, you oughtta know better than that—it takes six generations to make a bunch of people like you! And, by Judas Priest, I haven't got that much time!

At this point in the movie, it becomes clear that the filmmakers are drawing Wyn as the villain of the piece—even though his love for Kitty is genuine—because he's a spineless playboy driven more by impetuousness than true passion. By pulling Kitty to and fro with his mixed signals, he's the cause of Kitty's troubles. She's complicit, of course, but at several junctures, Wyn makes exactly the wrong choice with regard to Kitty's welfare and happiness. By presenting Wyn as an anti–Prince Charming who inadvertently demonizes the woman he loves, *Kitty Foyle* functions as an anti–fairy tale.

Following the drawing room confrontation, Kitty leaves Wyn again, because she doesn't believe him strong enough to defy his family. Back in New York some time later, Kitty runs into Mark on the day her divorce from Wyn becomes final. Mark says he's still available, but Kitty says her heart belongs to Wyn. She then discovers she's pregnant, and before she's even had time to process the news of her condition, she gets a call from Wyn saying he wants to meet her for dinner. While waiting for Wyn at a restaurant, Kitty glances at the social section of the newspaper, in which she learns that Wyn is engaged to Philadelphia blueblood Veronica Brook Gladwyn (Kay Linaker).

Heartbroken but still defiant, Kitty decides to have the baby alone. But, in the picture's harshest plot twist, the baby is stillborn.[4] Five years after the death of her baby, Kitty is transferred to Philadelphia, where she supervises the opening of a new department store. Despite her anxiety about returning to her hometown, nothing adverse happens until her last day in Philadelphia, when she discovers that her last customer is Wyn's wife. Kitty is forced to listen as Veronica speaks with Wyn on the phone, and is then confronted with a vision of the child she should have had: Wyn's young son (Richard Nichols).

After Veronica and the boy leave, Kitty discovers that he left his stuffed teddy bear behind. The boy returns to fetch it, and Kitty chats with the boy in a pointed but maudlin scene. Looking at the child longingly, Kitty removes Wyn's ring from her finger and hands it to the boy, asking him to give it to his father but keep the exchange secret from his mother.

The film then makes one last transition to the "present." Kitty's conscience declares that it's time for Kitty to choose between her two loves. Smiling contentedly, Kitty chooses Mark. The choice is more than just Kitty's romantic triumph; it is a comeuppance for Wyn, who tried to use Kitty's independence to his advantage.

With its mixture of intricate structural devices, sly wordplay, and charged subject matter, *Kitty Foyle* was just what Trumbo needed to put him over the top in Hollywood—but it also set the tone for his most successful pre-blacklist films. Although its melancholy storyline made the picture a major success at the time of its release, *Kitty Foyle* has aged poorly because it dances around subject matter that was taboo before the war but is commonplace in modern popular entertainment. In writing the picture, Trumbo was charged with making Kitty's sexual adventures palatable to mainstream audiences, and one tool he and the other filmmakers used to accomplish this trick was to make Kitty as sympathetic as possible. They stopped short of depicting Kitty as a pawn manipulated by sophisticated Wyn, which is to their credit; their portrayal of Kitty left room for her charged speeches about personal integrity, and those speeches link Kitty to some of the other noble characters in Trumbo films.

But by softening the edges of Morley's novel, the filmmakers diminished the film's potential to become an important historical artifact. As it is, the picture says more about Hollywood's reluctance to explore sexuality onscreen than it does about the role of sexuality in American culture of the 1930s and early 1940s, the periods in which the picture is set. Finally, the film's mixed messages about women's liberation—the hostility of the opening sequence and the dear price Kitty pays for her relationship with Wyn clash with the idea that she takes charge of her own life by choosing Mark—muddy the film's subtext so greatly that it's difficult to determine where on the spectrum of tolerance the filmmakers fell. When all of these mitigating factors are considered, *Kitty Foyle* is seen as timid mainstream entertainment largely devoid of anything provocative or "distasteful." That the same description could be used to describe Trumbo's big 1940s hits (*A Guy Named Joe, Thirty Seconds Over Tokyo, Our Vines Have Tender Grapes*) offers a picture of his career in this period. By playing it safe, Trumbo secured his place at the top of the movie industry—while producing some of the most banal screenwriting of his career.

❖   ❖   ❖

Trumbo received an Academy Award nomination for the adapted screenplay of *Kitty Foyle*, but while Rogers took home an Oscar for her leading performance, Trumbo lost—ironically, to his friend Donald Ogden Stewart.[5] The timing of Trumbo's Oscar nomination was perfect, because he fulfilled his RKO contract with *Kitty Foyle*. This enabled him to use the nomination as a bargaining chip while arranging free-agent deals with 20th Century–Fox, Columbia, and Paramount (all of which released Trumbo pictures in 1941 and 1942) before signing a lucrative, long-term contract at MGM (which released all of his films from 1943 to the beginning of the blacklist). Trumbo's work in 1941 and 1942 is generally unimpressive, because the pictures he wrote in this period were among his lightest efforts. Still, the issues that Trumbo addressed in these movies spoke to themes that recurred throughout his career.

Written by John Larkin from Trumbo's story, the nonsensically titled *Accent on Love* traffics in the same topics of work and privilege that Trumbo explored in *We Who Are Young*. And in another instance of Trumbo borrowing from himself, the picture's plot—an idly rich businessman walks away from his pampered life to find meaning in hard work—mirrors certain elements of Trumbo's other 1941 picture, *You Belong to Me*. While this subject matter feels awkwardly shoehorned into the frothy romanticism of *You Belong to Me*, it is germane to *Accent on Love* even though it's not much more credible.

In *Accent on Love*, John Worth Hyndman (George Montgomery) is an executive married to the boss's daughter. The boss in this case is tycoon T.J. Triton (Thurston Hall), whose various holdings include a real estate firm that, John says, operates inhumane tenements. John's distaste for his father-in-law's business practices is compounded by his disillusionment in his status-obsessed wife, Linda Hyndman (Cobina Wright, Jr.). In a prophetic early scene

During the most prosperous years of his pre-blacklist career, Trumbo lived with his wife, Cleo (seen here with Trumbo in 1939), on a Ventura County, California, ranch that Trumbo called the Lazy-T. He wrote dozens of scripts there, as well as novels including *Johnny Got His Gun*. (Earl Felton)

typical of the picture's heavy-handed methodology, Linda chides John's restlessness and tells him to be happy he's not digging ditches for a living. Sure enough, John walks out of Triton's office building one day and tries to join a ditch-digging crew. In so doing, John ingratiates himself to a group of Mexican-American workers led by Manuel Lombroso (J. Carrol Naish), and catches the eye of a pretty young Mexican girl who is seeking American citizenship, Osa (Osa Massen). Partly by misunderstanding and partly because of John's desire to reinvent himself, the Mexicans mistake John for an immigrant from Europe.

Respecting the work habits he has exhibited, they offer him a place to stay.

Following a few cuts back to John's old world—in which it is revealed that Linda wants John to return not because she misses him but because she doesn't want to be publicly embarrassed—the picture gets down to business when the Mexicans ask John to be their representative in talks with the owner of their unsafe tenements. The owner is, of course, Triton.

John storms into Triton's office and threatens that the Mexicans will march on City Hall if their living conditions are not improved. Triton responds by calling the police. In a far-fetched and almost comical scene, John and Triton argue so violently in the presence of a police officer that both men are arrested. To wriggle free of legal troubles, Triton agrees to look at the condition of the tenements, so John disguises Triton as a bum. John and Triton visit Manuel's house, and at this point in the story, the falsehoods are almost farcical in their number—John is pretending to be an immigrant, Triton is pretending to be destitute, and so on. At the end of his time in the tenement, Triton is unmoved by the suffering of the workers and infuriated at having had to endure life on the other side of the economic fence, even if only for a few hours.

Adding a final insult to the picture's credibility, the plot turns when Manuel and Osa visit Triton in his office and discover that their seemingly destitute house guest was actually Triton. Seeing an opportunity to gain revenge on John, Triton reveals that his son-in-law has misrepresented his economic and marital status to the Mexicans. The Mexicans are predictably appalled, so when John returns to their tenement and tries to explain his actions, they won't listen to him. Just when it seems that John's hopes are dashed, Triton inexplicably shows up at the tenement and defies every previously defined aspect of his character by saying that John opened his eyes to the suffering of the poor. Triton gives John control of the real estate firm and permission to divorce Linda, thereby facilitating a wholly implausible happy ending.

Although it began as a promising, albeit clunky, rant about work and privilege, *Accent on Love* is quickly revealed as another cheap Trumbo potboiler. *Accent on Love* is less characteristic of

Trumbo's social consciousness than it is of one of his lesser traits: a willingness to sacrifice provocative ideas for a condescending ending.

Trumbo's next credit, *You Belong to Me*—which Columbia Pictures threw together as a quick follow-up to the Henry Fonda–Barbara Stanwyck hit *The Lady Eve* (Paramount, 1941)—is one of his more sprightly trifles. Written by Claude Binyon from Trumbo's original story "The Doctor's Husband," the picture is a romantic comedy about an idly rich heir who learns there's more to life than luxury (shades of Triton's comeuppance in *Accent on Love*) and a willful woman who teaches her husband to rise above his natural inclination toward jealousy (shades of Kitty's attempts to reform Wyn in *Kitty Foyle*).

The film's story—about how the marriage of physician Helen Hunt (Barbara Stanwyck) and millionaire Peter Kirk (Henry Fonda) is threatened when Peter becomes convinced that Helen is romantically involved with her male patients—is interesting for its dated commentary on gender roles. For instance, after Peter proposes to Helen, she comments that she's wed to her career:

"Marriage is for women who can create homes for their men and devote their lives to them. I can't do that. I've already signed over my future. I have to continue in practice."

The prison-sentence tone in Helen's words—"I've already signed over my future"—may not have come from Trumbo's pen, but the spirit of the speech probably did. The idea that career and marriage are either-or propositions for women can also be found, for example, in *We Who Are Young*; Trumbo didn't truly acknowledge the validity of women working until *Tender Comrade*, but even that script subscribed to the "Rosie the Riveter" stereotype of women keeping the home fires burning while their men were away at war. The characters in *Tender Comrade* seem ready and even willing to give up their jobs when their men return, and that fits with the decision that Helen eventually makes to give up her medical practice.[6]

The tension between Peter and Helen comes to a head when Peter first suggests that Helen close her practice to become a housewife. She's deeply offended, so Peter proves that he doesn't think himself above work by getting a job at a department store under an assumed name. Once she learns what Peter has done, Helen suddenly betrays her every declaration of independence by quitting her job. This flip-flop is one of the most appalling turnarounds by a protagonist in any Trumbo story, and the possible reasons for it range from Trumbo's pre-blacklist devotion to happy endings to his ideas about women in the workplace to interference by those who expanded his story into a full screenplay. Whatever the reason, Helen's flip-flop badly undermines *You Belong to Me*'s charm.

When Peter's coworkers discover his identity, they declare it unfair for a millionaire to occupy a position that could otherwise be filled by someone in need of work, and get him fired. After unexpectedly losing his job, Peter becomes desperate to prove to Helen that he's not just a loafer, so he spends most of his fortune buying a hospital, then installs himself as director and Helen as chief of staff. That both of *You Belong to Me*'s protagonists eventually find fulfilling work is perhaps the saving grace of a picture that, by its very structure, demeans Helen.

The film's conclusion suggests that *You Belong to Me* is fundamentally about Peter discovering that a life spent in service is a life worthwhile. The idea that work is fulfilling because it allows individuals to serve their communities (or, as the case may be, collectives) might suggest a leftist reading of the film, but because the picture seems utterly apolitical, *You Belong to Me* is a perfect illustration how "subversive" subject matter in some of Trumbo's movies exists only in the eye of the beholder. If *You Belong to Me* means anything in the context of Trumbo's films, it is proof that his desire to depict characters acting honorably was rooted so deeply in his stories that even when they were fleshed out by other writers, the theme of honor survived. Because even though the arc of Peter discovering the value of work may not lend itself to a sociopolitical interpretation, it does fit with the idea that runs through many of Trumbo's pictures: that of characters adhering to, or discovering, their integrity.

❖ ❖ ❖

Reasons are numerous why *The Remarkable Andrew* is as important among Trumbo's early credits as *A Man to Remember* and *Kitty Foyle*, but none of them stem from the picture's nature as a memorable entertainment, because it is instead turgid, didactic, and silly. Trumbo wrote the story upon which the film is based, titled "The General Came to Stay," in 1938, and then shopped it to movie producers. Paramount producer Richard Blumenthal wanted the story, but suggested that were Trumbo to write it as a novel first, he could sell it to two mediums instead of one. So in 1940, Trumbo's fourth novel, *The Remarkable*

Andrew: Being the Chronicle of a Literal Man, was published. The film adaptation, with a screenplay by Trumbo, followed in 1942, so *Andrew* and *Johnny Got His Gun* share the distinction of being the only films that Trumbo based on his own novels.

The story of how *Andrew* got to the screen represents how deeply Trumbo was enmeshed in the movie industry by the early 1940s. By the time *Andrew* was released in March 1942, 36-year-old Trumbo had four published novels to his credit—and almost five times that many produced screenplays. That he cheapened the "serious" side of his work by writing the *Andrew* novel as a rough draft for a movie reveals that the line Trumbo had drawn between his film work and his serious writing was starting to blur. Despite his promises to do the opposite, Trumbo devoted far more of his life to movies than to novels. Although this may seem to be an area in which Trumbo made himself vulnerable to charges of hypocrisy, it actually is proof that Trumbo's pragmatic plan of using Hollywood to support his novel-writing went to hell after his Oscar nomination for *Kitty Foyle*.

With a growing family to support, Trumbo was disinclined to refuse the money that Hollywood was offering—but before he knew it, of course, the money dried up when Trumbo got blacklisted. After HUAC, Trumbo's plan to support himself on movie writing became a necessity, where before it had been a luxury. Although Trumbo continued working on novels throughout the blacklist era, a staggering 32 years elapsed between the publication of *The Remarkable Andrew* in 1940 and the publication of Trumbo's fifth and final completed novel, *The Time of the Toad*, in 1972.

Although its connection to Trumbo's career as a novelist is by far the most important aspect of *The Remarkable Andrew*, that connection is not the film's only significance. The picture is the first film of Trumbo's impressive war-era run, during which he was paid princely sums for his screenwriting talents, and it also is one of his most overtly political films. The disappointing addendum to all of these points is that for all of its significance in the context of Trumbo's career, *The Remarkable Andrew* is insignificant in almost any other context.[7]

Directed by Stuart Heisler,[8] *The Remarkable Andrew* concerns a Shale City, Colorado,[9] bookkeeper named Andrew Long (William Holden). Perpetually upbeat and full of vigor for what others might regard as a tedious job, Andrew is engaged to pretty Peggy Tobin (Ellen Drew) and seems utterly content. But when he sits down to balance Shale City's books for the year, he discovers what he believes to be embezzlement. When he confronts the city officials whom he suspects were involved in the crime, he is suspended from his job.

A dejected Andrew returns to his apartment, and is shocked when the ghost of President Andrew Jackson (Brian Donlevy) materializes. Jackson, portrayed as hard-drinking, tough-talking bear of a man, explains that he plans to help Andrew through his crisis.

The Remarkable Andrew chugs along at a leaden pace through several plot developments that result in Andrew getting framed for the embezzlement he tried to expose. Once Andrew is incarcerated, Jackson conjures the ghosts of towering American figures including George Washington (Montagu Love), Thomas Jefferson (Gilbert Emery), Benjamin Franklin (George Watts), and

Supreme Court Chief Justice John Marshall (Brandon Hurst). For comic relief, the group of spirits also includes legendary robber Jesse James (Rod Cameron), and an innocuous American private from the Revolutionary War, Henry Bartholomew Smith (Jimmy Conlin); Smith spends most of his screen time sniping at Washington and the other great men. Once the great men and their hangers-on are gathered in Andrew's jail cell for an initial consultation about his case, he irritates the great men by saying that all he wants to do is clear his name.

> ANDREW: Well, my job is to keep books. That's what I'm hired for. I do an honest job, and that's as far as it goes.
> JEFFERSON: I fail to see your reasoning. Dishonesty in government is the business of every citizen.
> MARSHALL: Did it ever occur to you that knowledge of a crime constituted complicity?
> JEFFERSON: It is not enough to do your own job. There's no particular virtue in that. Democracy isn't a gift—it's a responsibility.

And so it goes for the remainder of the movie, which alternates between lackluster comedy and heavy-handed speeches about democracy. Although the dialogue is generally brisk and articulate, the sentiments expressed in it are so pedantic that it's difficult to enjoy the film's meager virtues. Trumbo's critics often accuse him of using sledgehammer metaphors, and that accusation never has more weight than when one is considering a work along the lines of *The Remarkable Andrew*.

That said, one of the film's subplots is notable for its coincidental relation to Trumbo's HUAC ordeal. As Jackson and the other great men try to convince Andrew that he should expose Shale City's corrupt politicians, Marshall makes a comment that could easily have been spoken by one of the "unfriendly" witnesses at HUAC's hearings:

> MARSHALL: The chief internal enemies of any state are those public officials who betray the trust imposed upon them by the people.... You have a job laid out for you, young man—every true American has—and by the great Jehovah, I envy you and them!

The most charged of the picture's accidental allusions to HUAC occurs during Andrew's trial, when Shale City District Attorney Orville Beamish (Minor Watson) presents the case against Andrew. Just as Marshall's line about "internal enemies" could have been spoken by a member of the Hollywood Ten, Beamish's speech could have spilled from the lips of one of HUAC's rabid members:

> BEAMISH: What can more quickly undermine the confidence in American government than to have a city employee steal from the people, thereby violating the most sacred trust under heaven? Look at him! Sullen, morose, of questionable sanity—given to furtive reading instead of that red-blooded exercise which has made our youth the envy of the civilized world!... Mark you well, this constant reading is the sign of the radical, the agitator, the spy, the thief! Shall this country become like those countries which did not discover their weaknesses until too late—or shall it remain a democracy?... Shall we become a nation of shifty, sniveling cowards?

By the early 1940s, Trumbo (left) was quickly becoming one of Hollywood's top writers because of his facility with language and astounding speed. One of his important 1940s films was *The Remarkable Andrew*, adapted from his own novel. Here, he discusses the film with star William Holden on the Paramount lot. (Paramount Pictures)

The slanderous tone of Beamish's comments ("furtive," "shifty") is almost as inflammatory as the comments themselves, and the inferences contained in the lines—a link between intellectualism and radicalism, a link between radicalism and cowardice—prove that Trumbo was aware of the price of political activism well before HUAC descended upon Hollywood. And though Beamish's tone is probably so extreme because he's a character in a fantasy, there's an aspect of cynicism underlying both the character and the content of his speech. A fascist who regards ignorance a virtue and free thought a crime, Beamish could be seen as a product of Trumbo's lifelong mistrust of authority—presuming, of course, that Trumbo held such a mistrust. It's therefore poignant that the resolution of *The Remarkable Andrew* involves Shale City's corrupt politicians getting their comeuppance. Because the picture is idyllic, one ventures that there might have been an element of wish fulfillment in Trumbo's writing, the wish at hand being the desire to see bastards get theirs. In Trumbo's life, of course, such comeuppance was usually not so forthcoming.[10]

Possibly the most scurrilous of Beamish's assertions is his criticism of Andrew's reading habits. Andrew's fiancée, Peggy, retorts this assertion when she appears on his behalf as a character witness: "The books he reads are fine books!" she says. "They're about the men who made this country, and the things America stands for." Peggy's heart is in the right place, but her argument doesn't get at what made Beamish's insinuations so dangerous. He never actually accused Andrew of reading radical books—instead, he argued that Andrew was a radical simply because he likes to read. Be-

cause it's not much of a leap from this position to outright censorship, it's inevitable that ardent civil-rights advocate Trumbo has a character refute Beamish's fascist perspective. It's also inevitable that the character is Trumbo's proxy, Andrew.

> ANDREW: Thomas Jefferson once said, "Our first object should be to leave open all avenues of truth. The most effectual hitherto found is freedom of the press. It is, therefore, the first shut up by those who fear investigations of their actions." I think that ought to answer Mr. Beamish's criticism of what I read.

Andrew goes on to explain that he thinks his effort to expose embezzlement was a manifestation of his own personal democracy, and then adds his explanation of democracy. As with so much of the material in this picture, the following dialogue could easily have been uttered by Trumbo himself in a speech, letter, or pamphlet. Throughout his warera films, Trumbo visits and revisits the theme of democracy as an ideal; in fact, one of the first phrases to appear in Andrew's below dialogue ("flag-waving") is a phrase often used by critics seeking to dismiss Trumbo's patriotic films.

> ANDREW: I hope that what I'm trying to say doesn't sound like flag-waving, because I always felt that flag-waving was something sacred and quiet, and not to be done for any selfish motive.... Mr. Beamish has told you what democracy means to him. I think I ought to tell you what it means to me. Democracy means that people can say what they want to—all the people. It means that they can do what they wish—all the people. It means that they can worship God in any way that they feel right—and that includes Christians

and Jews and voodoo doctors as well. It means that everybody should have a job if he's willing to work; and an education; and the right to bring up his children without fear of the future…. It means: "Do unto others as you would have them do unto you."[11]

Following this rousing but self-explanatory speech, the picture lurches toward its resolution as clumsily as it approached every previous juncture. The great men help Andrew prove his innocence and incriminate the corrupt politicians; the bad guys are sent to jail; Andrew gets rehired and promoted; and his relationship with Peggy is repaired following some rough patches stemming from his preoccupation with Jackson and the court case. The picture ends on an light note when Jackson thanks Andrew for the "fun" of fighting corrupt politicians. Jackson's ghost fades away, and seeing Jackson become translucent is an appropriate final image for the film, because Trumbo's intentions are as transparent as Jackson's ghost.

Despite some entertaining moments—and despite the window it offers on Trumbo's politics—*The Remarkable Andrew* is best appreciated as either an exercise in didactic storytelling or as a strangely prescient tract about issues that would later figure so prominently in Trumbo's life. Because it contains such charged material, *The Remarkable Andrew* naturally fits into discussions that permeate this book: Trumbo's portrayal of personal honor and the presence, or lack thereof, of radical politics in his films. The theme of personal honor is present in every frame of *The Remarkable Andrew*, from the way that Andrew innocently discovers a mistake and then explores its causes to the way that Jack-

son and his undead cronies impress upon Andrew the importance of his patriotic duty. As with several previous Trumbo films, *The Remarkable Andrew* is on its surface a simple story about integrity and responsibility.

The presence of political discussions in the film is a more difficult issue. Christopher Trumbo said he considers the film a whistle-blower story and nothing more,[12] but the content of the speeches made before and during Andrew's trial suggests that Dalton Trumbo conceived *The Remarkable Andrew* as a patriotic tract. And because patriotism is necessarily entwined with politics, that makes the film a political tract. Christopher Trumbo's point is well taken insomuch as the politics expressed in the film are not obviously radical—it is ultimately the embezzlers who are acting contrary to the law, not Andrew, and Andrew seeks his recourse through the courts, not through civil disobedience—but there is a political edge to the way Andrew topples an ingrained power structure. Perhaps the most valid reading of *The Remarkable Andrew*'s place in Dalton Trumbo's cinematic politics, then, is that it offers a sanitized version of the political insurgency that figures prominently in *Spartacus*, *Exodus*, and *The Fixer*. This reading fits with the whitewashed quality that connects all of Trumbo's pre-blacklist films, and, if nothing else, reiterates that he was exploring the possibility of inserting politics into his movies even if he wasn't yet able to delve very deeply into the idea of radicalism. In fact, the idea is quickly introduced and dismissed when Beamish uses "radical" as a dirty word during his prosecution of Andrew, echoing the distaste the Hollywood studios had for anything left-wing.

4

The "Good" War
(1943–1946)

Trumbo nearly followed *The Remarkable Andrew* with another comedy for Paramount, but he discovered that writing by committee didn't suit his taste. Comedy titan Preston Sturges—whose *The Lady Eve* was the precedent for teaming Barbara Stanwyck and Henry Fonda in Trumbo's *You Belong to Me*—was looking for a project with which to launch French director René Clair in America. Sturges picked a Thorne Smith novel titled *The Passionate Witch* and recruited Trumbo to help develop a screenplay. After several conferences with Clair and Sturges, however, Trumbo dropped out of the project; using a script credited to Robert Pirosh and Marc Connelly, Clair eventually turned Smith's novel into the Veronica Lake-Frederic March comedy *I Married a Witch*.[1] That Trumbo was working with filmmakers of Sturges's caliber was indicative of how quickly he ascended to the top of the industry. By 1942, he settled into a cozy relationship with MGM, and on Christmas Eve 1943,

the first of his big-budget MGM films was released.

A Guy Named Joe is proof of the collaborative nature of commercial filmmaking—although Trumbo's work on the picture justifiably contributes to his reputation, he was far from the only cook in the kitchen. The picture was based on an original story by Chandler Sprague and David Boehm (whose work merited an Academy Award nomination) that had been stuck in MGM's development department for some time before it entered production. Frederick Hazlitt Brennan (who receives credit for adapting the story) had taken a pass at the screenplay before it was assigned to Trumbo.[2] The director on the project was the venerable Victor Fleming, a versatile journeyman with arguably the single most impressive one-two punch in cinema history—although he didn't entirely helm either film, he was the credited director on *The Wizard of Oz* and *Gone With the Wind*, both released by MGM in 1939.

The sweetness and optimism evident throughout *A Guy Named Joe* indicates how chameleon-like Trumbo was as a writer, because very little of his anxiety about battle shows in his World War II movies. This raises a question, though: Why did the author of an anti-war classic write pro-war movies? The best answer is probably that Trumbo, like so many in the world, saw World War II as a "good" war because the Axis powers were such a clear enemy. It is a measure of Trumbo's complexity that he quickly shifted from demonizing war in *Johnny Got His Gun* to "celebrating" one specific war in *A Guy Named Joe* and *Thirty Seconds Over Tokyo*; it is a measure of his integrity that he never backed away from the films.[3]

A Guy Named Joe opens with the kind of patriotic flourish that was common in mainstream American films of the World War II era: Warplanes rush overhead while the soundtrack swells with the song, "Off We Go Into the Wild Blue Yonder." As the planes arrive at a British airfield, English children gather at a fence on the perimeter of the field.[4] One of the children harps, "It's Pete Sandige's squadron," to which another child responds, "I'll bet you he's the best flyer in the world." The blunt exposition continues with the introduction of Pete's commander, Lieutenant Colonel "Nails" Kirkpatrick (James Gleason), who chides Pete's show-off attitude. Validating Nails's concerns, the lead plane in Pete's squadron crash lands—albeit without injury to any of its crew—and Pete (Spencer Tracy) pops out of the cockpit with the flip aside, "Any bloody noses down there?" The brisk sequence tells viewers that Pete's cavalier but supremely competent attitude will dominate the story. After the landing, Pete visits the children by the fence, and one of them asks Pete what flying is like. The ensuing speech is often cited in reference books as the most memorable aspect of the picture, and with good reason—although it suffers for the inclusion of the kind of sentimentality that permeated many of Trumbo's pre-blacklist films, it also has a measure of blue-collar poetry. The monologue also is interesting in how it differs from other Trumbo movie speeches. Usually, his long dialogue passages were constructed with mathematical precision, but this oratory is a loosely constructed flight of fancy. Tracy's inherent sweetness sells the speech on film, but its excesses are immediately visible on paper.

PETE: When you're up there, you're—you're all alone, see? Just you and the ship and the sky, and you don't want anybody up there with you. You don't want anybody to spoil it. Everything's kinda still, and you've got a feeling that you're ... halfway to heaven. You don't even seem to hear the sound of your own motor—just a kind of buzz, like the sky was callin' you. Like the sky was singin' you a song.... You feel like nudging it and saying, "Hiya sky, how are you today? And how was the old moon the last time you saw him?" The wind drift comes straight off the morning star, and beautiful white clouds drift toward you, and they're like old friends.... And you see a patch of clean air in between, and you duck in and out like a porpoise rollin' in the ocean. And then you say to yourself, "Boy, oh boy. *This* is the only time a man is ever really alive. It's the only time he's ever really free."

Because freedom—of speech, of action, of thought—was so important to

Trumbo, it's possible that the sentiment behind this speech was his way into Pete's character. Like Pete, Trumbo was a cantankerous freethinker whose competence won him the equivalent of an officer's rank in his field. And like Pete, Trumbo's maverick attitude got him in trouble on a regular basis.

After the speech scene, viewers meet Pete's girlfriend, flyer Dorinda Durston (Irene Dunne), and best friend, Al Yackey (Ward Bond). Trumbo takes great care with the romantic scenes in the early part of the picture, conveying several facets of the love shared by Pete and Dorinda. The romantic sequence culminates in an intimate dancing scene set in a quiet Scottish inn, during which Pete and Dorinda exchange insults the way others exchange niceties. "You're such a fool and you've no right to be," Dorinda says to Pete. "But just the same, you're kind of cute."

Following a moody good-bye scene during which Dorinda explains that she's got a bad premonition—a weak device with which Trumbo braces the audience for what's coming—Pete is killed during a valiant attack on a German destroyer. Following the model set by previous afterlife films including *Here Comes Mr. Jordan* (1941, Columbia)[5] and *Heaven Can Wait* (1943, 20th Century–Fox), Pete's spirit arrives in a gossamer-looking heaven and runs into the spirit of a deceased buddy, Dick Rumney (Barry Nelson). Dick introduces Pete to the film's proxy for the Creator—who, in keeping with the picture's military milieu, is portrayed as Pete's celestial commanding officer. The General (Lionel Barrymore) leads a cadre of ghostly pilots who shepherd earthly charges through battle. The brisk sequence involving Pete, Dick, and the General sets up the

film's central device quickly, which is a testament to both Trumbo's economy and Fleming's eminently watchable style. Giving Pete a spiritual mentor facilitates speedy exposition, because Dick spends the movie reminding Pete that he can't be seen by the living; Nelson also functions as Tracy's straight man.

By this point in the story, all that remains is to introduce Ted Randall (Van Johnson), the rich kid-turned-pilot whom Pete is assigned to shepherd. The scenes establishing Pete's cranky tutelage of Ted are brisk and enjoyable, but the plot proper doesn't kick in until the picture cuts to Pete's friend, Al, at his new post in New Guinea. Dorinda arrives in New Guinea on military business, and she and Al speak cordially until they're alone. Then Al tears into Dorinda for wasting her life by mourning. He convinces her to join him at the officer's club that night, where they meet the base's latest recruits—including, predictably, Ted. The scene in which Ted meets Dorinda is played for laughs, because Ted's come-on to Dorinda interrupts a sweet homily that Pete delivers upon seeing Dorinda for the first time in his afterlife.

This cute scene, though, contains a contradiction that would have been characteristic in one of Trumbo's knocked-off RKO screenplays but is unusual in his glossy MGM scripts. In one of his first scenes, Ted is depicted as a wallflower who needs prodding to approach a woman—but just a few moments later, we see him woo Dorinda with the confidence of Casanova.[6] Similarly, Trumbo's script plays fast and loose when developing the relationship between Ted and Dorinda. Because the relationship is necessitated by the plot, Trumbo glosses over their courtship and presumes that the audience will suspend their disbelief that Dorinda would just happen to fall for the pilot being "mentored" by Pete. There is a valid argument why these characters might bond, however: Dorinda somehow senses Pete's presence and therefore associates Ted with Pete. Nonetheless, these slippery plot developments cheapen the screenplay.

The picture gets a shade darker when Dorinda gets a premonition that Ted will be killed just as Pete was—and when Pete lets jealousy color his work with Ted. This is one of the most effective stretches of the film, because it portrays Dorinda and Pete as wounded souls who haven't moved into the next stage of their lives (a neat depiction of what psychologist Elizabeth Kübler-Ross defined, years later, as the denial step of the grieving process). Trumbo rises to this dark material, filling it with wit and edge, and his own, somewhat misanthropic personality shines through in the way that characters repeatedly use the word "idiot" as an affectionate reference.

For instance, when Nails—reintroduced into the story as Ted's commander—watches Ted pull a stupid airborne stunt, Nails asks to speak with him privately. During the conversation, however, Nails reveals that he was not appalled by Ted's flying, but impressed. He offers Ted a dangerous bombing mission, and Ted accepts. What could have been a dryly expositional scene is made brightly entertaining, because Pete makes commentary revealing his hope that Ted will be chastised for his daredevil flying. When Nails commends Ted, Pete whines: "What, are you going soft? This guy should be busted!" The undercurrent of the scene—and of all the scenes depicting Pete's spirit visiting

Dorinda—is that Pete is using his otherworldly powers to break up Ted and Dorinda. If Pete can't be with Dorinda, he doesn't want any man to be with her.

The scene with Nails is paralleled by the following sequence, in which Pete is disciplined by the General. The long exchange between them contains some of the best dialogue—and most touching sentiment—in *A Guy Named Joe*. The General explains that his command serves "every man who ever flew" (notwithstanding, apparently, the Japanese and German pilots killed throughout the movie) and that Pete should have as his inspiration the freedom of flying—an allusion to the speech that Pete made to the English children at the beginning of the picture.

> THE GENERAL: That's what we're fighting for: the freedom of the very air we breathe. The freedom of man rushing to greet the future on wings.... No man is really dead unless he breaks his faith with the future. And no man is really alive unless he accepts his responsibility to it. That's the opportunity we're offering you here. The chance to pay off to the future what you owe for having been part of the past.

Responsibility is a topic that recurs throughout Trumbo's screenplays and his celebrated correspondence. He invokes the golden rule repeatedly; in fact, the rule even concludes Andrew Long's climactic speech in *The Remarkable Andrew*. For Trumbo, doing right wasn't a higher calling; it was a moral imperative. Examining how he tried to hold people, whether real or fictional, accountable, it becomes immediately clear that Trumbo held himself to high standards and demanded nothing less of his characters and peers. Trumbo was willing to catalog his own transgressions—his letters are peppered with apologizes to people he felt he wronged—but more often he used his acidic wit to skewer those he felt had wronged him. Whether addressing the mighty (the movie-studio executives, bureaucrats, and lawyers who participated in the persecution of communists) or the insignificant (retailers and contractors who invoked his ire by selling shoddy products or failing to provide services), Trumbo used his record of integrity as reason to speak from "on high."[7]

At worst, Trumbo's attitude was condescending. He was often pedantic, and some of his films are structured as simplistic homilies. But at best, Trumbo was a voice of reason and authority. *A Guy Named Joe* is one of innumerable films in which both sides of Trumbo's presumed moral superiority are visible. In the film's most effective passages, particularly those in which Pete's good deeds are complemented by his abrasive manner, Trumbo used his tools the best way he knew how. But in the picture's cheapest moments, including, to some degree, its ending, Trumbo sets aside his unpretentious approach and becomes a preacher from on high. When Trumbo spoke of the people, he was magnificent; when Trumbo spoke to the people, he could be insufferable.

After having his head put straight by the General, Pete returns to Earth and tries to convince Dorinda to forget him and move on, beginning the film's final push toward its cathartic resolution. But Dorinda's devotion to Pete runs deep; the next time she sees Ted, she says she can't marry him because all she can offer him is a "cheap imitation" of love. A heartbroken Ted leaves Do-

rinda's quarters without informing her about the danger of his imminent bombing mission.

Dorinda learns about Ted's mission from Al, however, and Al's ominous words give her a flashback to the dread she felt before Pete died. So she hurries to the airfield, hoping to stop Ted from risking his life. She rashly jumps into the cockpit of Ted's plane and takes off, intending to fly Ted's mission for him rather than lose another lover. A dumbfounded Ted reaches the airfield too late to stop her.

In the plane, Pete's spirit materializes and, charged with fear for Dorinda's safety, rages in words she can't hear: "You're throwing your life away because … you're afraid of life! And that's double-crossing a lot of guys who are out there fighting for it." When it becomes clear that she won't give up, Pete talks Dorinda through the mission, which ends successfully despite heavy antiaircraft fire. As in all the scenes between Pete and living characters, the filmmakers suggest that although Pete can neither be seen nor heard, echoes of his comments enter the minds of the living like stray thoughts. Trumbo finds poignancy in this haphazard method of communication during the scene immediately following the bombing run.

As Dorinda pulls away from the target area, Pete urges her to "Pull your nose up into the air and climb straight to heaven." This line hits on several levels, the most touching of them being Pete's impossible wish to have Dorinda visit his new home. Once she rises above the clouds, Dorinda starts to hear an angelic choir that both Pete and the General have described as the "song" of the sky—an anthem of the freedom only flyers know. Trumbo puts all his skills to

Although he wrote a famous antiwar novel, *Johnny Got His Gun*, Trumbo was an ardent supporter of America's involvement in World War II. The enduring wartime fantasy *A Guy Named Joe*—starring Spencer Tracy as a pilot who returns to earth as a ghost—was one of the roaringly patriotic films that Trumbo wrote during the 1940s. Pictured, left to right, are Barry Nelson, Tracy, Van Johnson, Irene Dunne, and Ward Bond. (MGM)

bear on this scene, finding a sweet pitch of sentimentality that stays consistent with the tone of the movie but also wrings intense emotion from the long, prosaic speech that Pete's spirit makes to his earthly lover. The tear-jerking monologue, which compares badly to Pete's earlier speech about flying, says a great deal about Trumbo's pre-blacklist storytelling: Trumbo was something of a softy, for only a man with a mile-wide soft side could write a speech like this one.

> PETE: I can tell you now, Dorinda. I can tell you everything I've ever wanted to tell you.... You know, the only decent thing I ever did in my life was to love you, Dorinda. But if the memory of that love is going to make you unhappy all the rest of your life, Dorinda, there must have been something wrong with it. It should have been the kind that filled your heart so full of love that—that you just had to go out and find someone to give it to. That's the only real kind, isn't it, Dorinda? That's the only kind that ever lives.

Dorinda returns to the airfield, and a tense moment ensues during which neither Dorinda, in the cockpit, nor Ted, on the field, knows whether to approach the other. Pete gives closure to the film's story by saying: "Go on. I'm setting you free, Dorinda. I'm moving out of your heart." Like much of the dialogue in the picture, this line is loaded with components, any one of which would have sufficed to convey the necessary information but which, together, maximize emotional impact. Thus liberated, Dorinda runs to Ted, and Pete smiles with bittersweet happiness, declaring proudly: "That's my girl. And that's my boy." Having grown, against his own worst impulses, into his new role as a mentor to living pilots, Pete walks off to the horizon as a reprise of "Off We Go Into the Wild Blue Yonder" swells on the soundtrack.

Continuing the pattern of *A Man to Remember*, *Kitty Foyle*, *The Remarkable Andrew*, and other pictures, *A Guy Named Joe* is about honor and integrity as much as it is about love and the supernatural. There is honor among fighting comrades, a theme that Trumbo explored to strong effect in another World War II movie, *Thirty Seconds Over Tokyo*; there is the honor among lovers, as seen in Pete's grudging respect for Ted and in Pete's decision to relinquish his hold on Dorinda's heart; and there is, most importantly, the honor of living a worthy life. Even though Trumbo was not the architect of *A Guy Named Joe*'s story, the elements in the narrative blended with his own attitudes about righteousness and dignity to produce a coherent statement. They also, conveniently, fit with the maturation of how Trumbo told stories about honor. In early pictures such as *Road Gang* and even *A Man to Remember*, characters are noble from the moment we meet them, so even though those characters suffer for their ideals,

viewers don't see the characters evolve. But in later films such as *A Guy Named Joe*, viewers watch as characters discover their principles. The latter model is far more effective, because by showing what characters cast aside in order to pursue honorable lives, Trumbo presents parables about people rising beyond their limitations.

❖ ❖ ❖

Trumbo's reunion with his *Kitty Foyle* star, Ginger Rogers, was a freelance job done for RKO. *Tender Comrade* became a notorious footnote to the blacklist era because Rogers's mother, Lela Rogers, told HUAC that Trumbo made her daughter unknowingly spread communist propaganda with dialogue such as the film's call to "share and share alike." Moreover, the film's story about a group of American wives forming a "collective" while their husbands are at war was characterized as leftist subversion.

When clearer heads set to the task of analyzing *Tender Comrade* years later, though, the picture was generally determined to be reprehensible not for any subversive material, but for its cloyingly melodramatic story and simplistic patriotism. Despite this revisionist take on the film, *Tender Comrade* does contain fairly radical, if mixed, messages. The story has unmistakably communistic overtones and presents a dramatic conflict between the collective and the individual, as personified by a character willing to sacrifice for the greater good and a character blinded by selfish desires. Although the picture's main story is decidedly unradical (none of the characters ever question either America's participation in World War II or the need to make war at all), the almost subconscious manner in which a dialogue about collectivism seeps into the picture's narrative makes *Tender Comrade* fascinating several decades after its release.

The picture is also interesting for its portrayal of women. Although Trumbo is closely associated with such quintessentially macho outings as *Spartacus*, *Lonely Are the Brave*, and *Papillon*, his breakthrough success was a classic "women's picture," *Kitty Foyle*, and that film has several sisters among Trumbo's scripts: *Half a Sinner*, *You Belong to Me*, *Roman Holiday*, *The Sandpiper*, and so on. *Tender Comrade* is so female-driven that the picture's top-billed male actor, Robert Ryan, appears primarily in flashbacks designed to bring out aspects of Ginger Rogers's character. As does *Kitty Foyle*, *Tender Comrade* shows Trumbo's ability to explore women's issues with a measure of sensitivity, even though the limiting vision of womanhood that he puts across in the picture is defined by the era in which it was made.

The picture, which draws its title from a Robert Lewis Stevenson poem describing his wife as a "tender comrade," opens with a passionate reunion between Jo Jones (Rogers) and her soldier husband, Chris Jones (Ryan), home on a furlough. The couple live in Los Angeles, but talk frequently of life in their rural hometown, Shale City[8]; they also recall the classroom flirtation with which their relationship began. The main imagery in this scene—a buzzing fly that makes Chris remember a fly that was buzzing in the classroom when he wrote a note to Jo expressing his love— is forced but sweetly effective. Associating something so significant as the early days of a long love affair with something

so insignificant as a nettlesome insect is such an odd touch that it feels lifelike. Yet while the imagery of the scene works, the mechanism of the scene is forced; because the story proper hasn't either begun or been hinted at, diving right into such flowery exposition suggests (rightly) that *Tender Comrade* will unfold at a slow pace.

It's tempting to guess why Trumbo chose to write so deliberately, because one outlandish possibility is that he was "conspiring" to lure viewers with innocent romance before hitting them with radical propaganda. More likely is the possibility that Trumbo was establishing the couple's "normal" lifestyle to contrast Jo's unusual wartime living arrangement.

The reunion scene ends when the lovers part in a tearful farewell, then we're shown Jo's workplace: a Douglas Aircraft factory in Los Angeles in which women are assembling airplanes because the factory's male employees are away at war. Several of the film's principal characters are introduced during a chatty lunch time scene, as are some of the film's main themes. For instance, after Jo and Barbara Thomas (Ruth Hussey) chat vaguely about where Barbara's husband is stationed, meek Doris Dumbrowski (Kim Hunter) says: "You shouldn't have said that, Jo—that's talking about troop movements, and we're not supposed to." This line is significant on a couple of levels. First, it indicates the ubiquity of war in these women's lives by showing that they monitor each other's speech, and second, it indicates that *Tender Comrade* is, at least in part, a mechanism for spreading "positive" propaganda. Both overtones hold true throughout the picture. The connection between the women at the lunch table is quickly identified:

Jo, Barbara, Doris, and Helen Stacey (Patricia Collinge) are all married to soldiers. Relations among the women are generally harmonious, but Jo, Doris, and Helen all cast a disapproving eye on Barbara's flirtations with men at the factory. Barbara contends that her infidelity is justifiable because her husband, Pete Thomas, is also a cheat.

Barbara's argument reeks of the moral relativism that Trumbo attacked in pictures including *The Remarkable Andrew* and *Exodus*, so the pattern of dubious characters getting criticized for making their own rules offers an interesting contrast to the generally favorable light in which rebellion is cast throughout Trumbo's *oeuvre*. It seems that Trumbo drew a distinction between righteous rebellion—exemplified at its most extreme by the slave Spartacus's revolt against his captors—and the actions of characters such as Barbara, who simply ignore moral or legal codes they find bothersome. Interestingly, the characters in Trumbo's movies whose employment of moral relativism is most provocative are those who teeter between righteousness and lawlessness. For instance, Jack W. Burns in *Lonely Are the Brave* breaks laws that annoy him (he surreptitiously cuts a gap in a barbed-wire fence that's impeding his path), but he also defies rules on moral grounds (as when he tries to free his friend Paul from jail because he feels Paul's infraction of helping illegal immigrants was not wrong).

At the outset of his career, Trumbo was capable of, if not inclined toward, oversimplifying moral issues to make statements. Later in life, he was more willing to allow for moral gray areas. The evolving maturity of Trumbo's outlook is seen in the above cinematic ex-

amples, but also in his life—what is the infamous "only victims"[9] speech that Trumbo made about the blacklist if not a desire to put old recriminations to rest and write off past transgressions as ugly proof of human frailty? Still, such a forgiving attitude was far in the future when Trumbo wrote *Tender Comrade*.[10]

Trumbo's blunt approach to complicated issues is evident at the end of the lunchtime scene, when the women discuss how much rent each is paying for a place to live. Jo suggests pooling their resources by moving in together.

> JO: It might work. But it's only fair to point out that we're all different people, and there might be a clash of personalities occasionally. We'd have to find some way of adjusting any disputes that might come up.... We could run the joint like a democracy! And if anything comes up, we'll just call a meeting. Oh, jeez, kids—that'd be wonderful! For instance, now, the four of us have two cars—two sets of tires wearing out. We could sell one car and use the other on a share-and-share-alike basis.[11]

This monologue has often been used as "proof" that Hollywood communists were slipping subversive messages into mainstream entertainment films, but it is provocative for numerous reasons. First, there's the thread of Jo asking people to participate in her new organizational system of their own free will, which, combined with the deliberate use of the word "democracy," is fodder for the argument that the monologue is nothing more than it appears to be on the surface—an American gal telling other American gals to get together in an American way. Because there exists the possibility that Trumbo and director Edward Dmytryk did not use *Tender Comrade* as a venue for exploring leftist ideas, it needs to be said that virtually every clue hinting at leftist content can be interpreted as innocuous or "devious." The language of the monologue is a perfect example of how easy it is to paint the movie in either light.[12]

Look at the most potent clue in Jo's monologue, the oft-cited phrase "share-and-share-alike." In the context of several members of the working class (read: proletariat) discussing how best to surmount the obstacles facing them, Jo's suggestion that they give up individual possessions and pool their resources into a collective is a radical thought. It suggests a willingness to ignore the social status quo and establish a new, more efficient social system in which individual property ownership and, as seen later, certain personal freedoms, are subjugated beneath the needs and will of the collective.

That Jo lays out the possible downside of her plan ("clashes of personalities") and then asks her friends to base their decisions upon knowledge not only of the good in her plan, but also the bad, is perhaps the most radical concept in Jo's monologue: the idea that Americans would choose, by democratic vote, to become communists or at the very least something like socialists.

Even with all of these charged political undertones, however, the picture is deadly dull. As was proven by *We Who Are Young* and *The Remarkable Andrew*, Trumbo became something of a stuffed shirt whenever he attacked social issues head-on.

After the women pick a house and move in, the film cuts to first of Jo's flashbacks to life with Chris before the war. The flashback is a cutesy, brief scene depicting the argumentative way in which Jo accepted Chris's marriage proposal. Jo's garrulous manner muddies the waters by suggesting that she's not a freethinker, as previous scenes imply, but rather a shrew.

Back in the "present," the four women decide they don't want to spend their free time doing housework and advertise for a housekeeper. This plot development says two things: That the women are more bourgeoisie than proletariat (the class distinction of the various characters wavers throughout the picture as the mettle of each is tested) and that they are more American than their "radical" lifestyle might suggest.

The servant, who is not treated like one, is German immigrant Manya Lodge (Mady Christians). In applying for the job, she makes a bizarre speech declaring that even though she's not yet a citizen, the fact that her husband is fighting alongside the Allies makes her a sister to the other women. Or, as she puts it, "That makes us one." This line makes the clearest allusion yet to the household-as-collective, and the allusion is amplified when Barbara proposes a novel mode of paying Manya: "Why don't we take our cash, after the rent and groceries are paid, and split it five ways?" Again comes the idea of sacrificing individual possessions for the good of the collective. After the women vote unanimously to enact Barbara's plan, Jo explains it to Manya with a reiteration of her earlier mantra: "You see, we're running this joint like a democracy." Manya's unexpected reply stops the other women cold.

"That's good," Manya says. "Once, in Germany, we had a democracy, but we..."

"You lost it," Helen interjects.

"Nein," Manya responds. "We did not lose it. We let it be murdered. Like a little child."

Manya's graphic simile is one of many lines of dialogue in *Tender Comrade* that make it difficult to ascribe to the picture any one political agenda; her line can be read to suggest that Trumbo was spouting communist ideals because of his love for democracy—and, by extension, because of his outrage that fascism had overpowered democracy in Germany. The complicity inferred by Manya's statement, "We let it be murdered," advances the idea that democracy is inherently dangerous because some people, when faced with the freedom to choose their course, will inevitably choose the path of least resistance. Therefore the line suggests that the true villain in Third Reich Germany was not fascism but apathy. Trumbo could, then, be saying that because democracy is susceptible to apathy, it is imperfect—and ready to be replaced by communism.

Despite the harmony created by Manya's arrival, Barbara's adherence to her prewar ways creates friction in the collective. When Barbara announces that she's going on a date, Doris and Jo express their disapproval. Barbara, usurping the system for her own needs—in a sense, acting as a political insurgent—calls for a vote asking everyone to mind their own business. Barbara's maneuver clashes with the precept of the collective, because Barbara is asking for permission to deny the will of the collective. This is an interesting point, because were Trumbo depicting a purely communist model, Barbara's individualism would have been suppressed. But because Trumbo is using the story to illustrate the gulf between two political sys-

tems, Barbara wins her vote. That this predictably leads to more friction may be Trumbo's way of asserting that pseudo-collectivism won't work.

The next challenge to the collective arises when Manya announces that she's upset at the local butcher, who gave her two pounds of bacon when she asked for only one. Infuriated that the butcher has defied rationing laws, Manya fumes until Doris, the innocent of the group, asserts: "But Manya, it's such a little thing." This comment spurs Manya into more dark speechifying:

> MANYA: When little things go, big things follow.... I have seen in Germany the little things and what happened afterwards.... Next time I report him. There's not going to be any hoarding of bacon in this house. There's not going to be any hoarding of anything in this house!

Manya's sudden emergence as the household's voice of communistic authority leads to Doris's line, "She makes you feel kind of like a spy or something." The inference that Doris is uncomfortable living with someone whose devotion to the collective ideal is so intense gets paid off in a funny but important scene proving that Barbara isn't the only member of the household whose materialism clashes with the household's pseudo-communist model. As the hoarding debate grows more intense, Barbara makes a comment that underlines how out-of-sync she is with the other women: "This joint's getting so moral we're all afraid to take a deep breath." Responding to Barbara's comment, Jo addresses Barbara with the condescension of a parent explaining something to a child for the hundredth time.

JO: I suppose you don't think hoarding is very important....

BARBARA: I've been listening to "We've gotta do this" and "We've gotta do that" for three weeks, and sisters, I'm plenty sick of it! Rationing? Sure. I'll hold still for it because I've got to. But I'm not going to run around like a moon-faced Pollyanna saying I like it.... While we're being pushed around at home, our guys are out fighting in countries they've never even heard of for a lot of foreigners who'll turn on us the minute it's over!

JO: You oughtta be ashamed of yourself. Do you know where that kind of talk comes from? It comes straight from Berlin. Every time you say it—every time you even think it—you're double-crossing your own husband.... Who wants to get slick and fat when half the people in the world are starving to death for things we can do without?

This exchange is the heart of *Tender Comrade* for many reasons. Functionally, it brings the idealistic conflict between Barbara and Jo to a head, thereby advancing the principal thrust of the story. Idealistically, though, the exchange covers a lot more ground than just identifying the positions of two characters. Barbara's dialogue reiterates her apathy and adds to it the idea of isolationism; her comment about "foreigners who'll turn on us" reveals that she is so far removed from the spirit of the collective, and that of the Allied war effort, that she feels everyone who isn't serving her materialistic needs is her enemy. In Barbara's mind, getting into World War II is a nuisance, not a necessity. Her refusal to acknowledge the importance of world events explains why she hasn't yet been able to accommodate herself to the lifestyle changes necessitated by the war. She is an island and wants everyone else to bow to her will or leave her alone; insomuch as the characters in the film represent political stances, Barbara's is probably the most troublesome, because were a country to act like Barbara, it would be everyone's enemy and no one's ally.

In contrast, Jo's bleeding-heart attitude ("half the people in the world are starving") might in fact be overly compassionate, notwithstanding the irony that she's preaching altruism in the same breath as defending her government's killing of German, Italian, and Japanese soldiers. Still, the basis of her argument ("Who wants to get slick and fat....") is Americanized communism at its most honorable. Jo imagines a political system that will alleviate suffering and hardship, whether by pooling the resources of four women or refusing to hoard during wartime. This scene, in which Trumbo virtually sanctifies Jo's approach, is the most "subversive" in *Tender Comrade*.

The idea of communism portrayed in the film has little to do with Moscow and Stalin, however, and everything to do with the "we're all in this together" doctrine of President Franklin Delano Roosevelt, whose New Deal many leftists adopted as a validation of their political leanings. This distinction, really, is what makes the leftist ideas put across in Trumbo's movies so interesting—instead of merely demonizing the American system of government or deifying the Soviet one, Trumbo suggests a compromise in which a measure of free will is retained but collectivism is the guiding ideal.

Perhaps sensing that the debate opened by the argument between Jo and Barbara is an endless one, Trumbo cuts the conversation short with a radio broadcast in which it's inferred that Barbara's husband has been killed in action. Barbara, every inch the grandly self-possessed American, takes the news as a cue for an actorly "moment" before withdrawing from the scene. Jo, meanwhile, is so distraught at the timing of her attack on Barbara that she flashes back again to her home life with Chris.

In the flashback, Jo is once again the shrew we saw in the marriage proposal scene. The setting is a quiet evening after dinner. Chris, a stereotypically aloof American male, wants to read a newspaper article about America's possible involvement in the war. Jo, a stereotypically decadent American female, wants some romance. The scene becomes an argument in which Chris complains that Jo doesn't do enough housework while she complains that he doesn't show her enough affection. "I'm just a cheap substitute for a housekeeper!" Jo barks. Chris explains that he's been putting in overtime because he anticipates having to join the military soon and wants Jo to have enough money to get her through the war. Jo counters that if the question is money, she'll get a job. Disgusted at the thought of his wife working, Chris relents and says he'll stop doing overtime.

This scene is peculiar in its relation to the rest of the movie. Although part of its function is comic relief—Jo makes a dramatic show of tossing all of Chris's shirts onto the living room floor and then sewing buttons on them, turning housework into hyperbole—the scene defines Jo's character as a frivolous woman more interested in sex than the realities of the day. In other words, the scene defines Jo as Barbara. This raises the inevitable question of how Jo evolved from a materialistic shrew into a freethinker with

strong ideas about work and collectivism, and the best answer the film offers is that Jo evolved out of necessity. With Chris gone, she needed to work, and once she joined the workplace, she was necessarily confronted with issues relating to the American economic system. The lack of any explanation for Jo's evolution is probably the shabbiest element of the movie, but unfortunately also one of the most important.[13] By failing to show how Jo became the woman who sets the plot of *Tender Comrade* into motion, Trumbo misses the opportunity to "sell" the picture on a human level. Without the explanation, the film is almost entirely an idealistic tract.

Back in the "present," the women find Manya crying with joy because she's just been sent a medal of valor received by her husband, who is still alive. Doris, having been turned into something of a monster by Jo's influence, grabs the medal from Manya with the intent of displaying it prominently. "You don't think we're gonna let Manya keep this all to herself, do you?" Doris blurts. "Share and share alike, isn't that right?" Manya, dejected at having her prized possession assumed into collective ownership, sadly comments: "Ja—democracy." Manya's lack of enthusiasm echoes Barbara's revolts against the collective and ties into the picture's recurring theme that Americans spoiled on democracy can't adjust themselves to communism.

After the medal scene, Jo announces that she's pregnant, and the film soon cuts to Jo in the hospital after delivering a son, whom she names after her husband. Jo drifts into the film's final flashback, a sentimental and rather needless scene in which Chris and Jo discuss parenthood. Chris explains that he worries

Although it was marketed as patriotic wartime propoganda, *Tender Comrade* was later branded as subversive by those who thought communist writer Trumbo used the picture to make collectivism sound appealing. In this flashback, Jo Jones (Ginger Rogers) shares a romantic moment with her future husband, Chris Jones (Robert Ryan). (RKO)

about leaving Jo alone with a baby, a bit of clunky foreshadowing for the tragedy looming just ahead.

After Jo comes home with her son, the collective is thrown into a tizzy by the homecoming of Doris's husband, Mike Dumbrowksi (Richard Martin). Following a long, uninspired comedy sequence of the women cooking food for Mike because they miss caring for their own men, Jo receives a telegram that, unsurprisingly, informs her of Chris's death in action. Keeping her bad news secret, Jo leaves the dinner party and heads upstairs for a quiet moment with her baby. The picture plunges straight into tearjerker territory as we hear voice-over echoes of happier times while a teary-eyed Jo cradles her son. Jo picks up Chris's picture as her way of introducing Chris, Sr., to Chris, Jr., then launches into a treacly monologue:

"Remember your dad, little guy. He never made speeches, but he went out and died so you could have a better break when you grow up than he ever had."

Jo puts her baby to bed and heads to the top of the stairs so she can rejoin the party, but nearly breaks down with emotion. She steels herself as a voice-over reveals her interior monologue:

"No matter how tough things are— no matter how bad they seem—think of him. You'll come through. Come on, Jo, head up. Take it on the chin, like a good guy. Like a soldier's wife should."[14]

Her identity, needs, and emotions now fully sublimated beneath those of the collective, Jo forces a smile and sets her tragedy aside to ensure that her "comrades" enjoy their dinner party. As she heads downstairs, the film dissolves to an image of Jo and Chris walking toward the horizon, which has been used throughout the picture to link present day scenes and flashbacks. The dissolve makes sense, because Jo's comparatively carefree life with Chris is now a thing of yesterday, while today is about confronting hardship with strength and not letting trivial things such as pain and happiness interfere with the workings of the collective. This mixed message—in which collectivism can be seen as either a tremendous source of emotional support or an equally tremendous oppressive force—is a fittingly ambiguous way to end a film so loaded with political signs, symbols, and rhetoric that its content is still being dissected nearly six decades after it was released.

The political content—or lack thereof—in *Tender Comrade* is such a point of contention, in fact, that Christopher Trumbo argued that his father intended the movie as just what it purports to be, a movie about wartime living arrangements.[15] Because Edward Dmytryk echoed this line of thinking,[16] the possibility that *Tender Comrade* was not in any way a leftist tract needs to be reiterated. What makes it difficult to accept this possibility is the thread of sociopolitical discourse that runs through the movie. Intentionally or not, Dalton Trumbo filled *Tender Comrade* with provocative conversations about the possibility of American women assuming a

collective lifestyle. The claim that Ginger Rogers's mother made to HUAC about Trumbo and others corrupting her daughter was ridiculous, but Lela Rogers was not totally unfounded in seeing a communist interpretation of *Tender Comrade*.

So once again, the question arises of whether that interpretation is valid or simply a game of imposing the historical facts of Trumbo's politics onto one of his movies. For their part, blacklist scholars Larry Ceplair and Steven Englund argued that the communist content of movies made by the Hollywood Ten was illusory, even in light of the Ten's attempts at inserting progressive content:

> In short, communist screenwriters did not revolutionize, Stalinize, communize, Sovietize, or subvert the output of the film industry. They did try to approach their subject matter more objectively and straightforwardly than was the norm; they endeavored to add realism and delete racial distortions and ethnic stereotypes; they aimed to accentuate any real elements or story material they found within their assignments. If the majority of the films made from their scripts seem politically indistinguishable from the films made from the scripts of non-radical screenwriters, it is not necessarily because they lacked skill or determination, but because the studio executives were more skilled and determined— and by far more powerful.[17]

Although the question of radical content will arise again later in this book—particularly after the blacklist, by which time Trumbo gained the freedom to openly express radical themes in pictures such as *Spartacus*, *Exodus*, and *The Fixer*—for now the last word on the subject of whether Trumbo's films were political comes from Trumbo himself:

> Every screen writer worth his salt wages the battle in his own way—a kind of literary guerilla warfare.... There are, of course, those who declare that because of the enormous capital agglomeration invested in motion pictures, the medium itself is hopeless, and can never be employed for progressive purposes. To accept this view is tantamount to abandoning the struggle altogether.[18]

Trumbo's screenwriting blossomed during his wartime tenure at MGM, perhaps because the inherent qualities of war stories—life-or-death stakes, fast-moving action—finally gave him enough ink for his brisk quill. (It's not at all coincidental that Trumbo's defining achievement as a writer, *Johnny Got His Gun*, is set in wartime.) When Trumbo wrote war stories, the obstacles that caged his other types of screenplays weren't present. He could be as dramatic as he wanted to be, because war is by definition a matter of life and death; he could attack every big issue he wanted to, because war is by definition an arena in which man confronts big issues. And just as these factors liberated Trumbo to write his greatest novel, they liberated him to write one of his greatest screenplays, *Thirty Seconds Over Tokyo*.

Here are a few qualifications for framing *Thirty Seconds* in such grandiose terms. *Thirty Seconds* is a movie as notable for its visual appeal as its scenario. The picture, which won an Academy Award for special effects, is filled with lush flying scenes and impressive production design. Director Mervyn LeRoy

and his cinematographers, Harold Rossen and Robert Surtees, give early scenes a glossy, romantic feel, and latter scenes sufficient grit that viewers can almost feel the foreign environments through which downed American soldiers travel.

The picture's intoxicating visual splendor is one factor that makes it easy to overlook the screenplay's minor shortcomings, and another is the pervasively upbeat mood of the film. Because the picture was conceived as propaganda, the soldiers whose story it tells are never shown cracking under pressure. Even in the most extreme scene, during which Van Johnson's character experiences horrific pain, morale is implausibly high and the soldiers' sense of mission and duty is implausibly unchallenged. This second factor, which gives the story the veneer of a fairy tale, also distracts viewers from what's happening beneath the surface of the events.

These points are significant because, unlike Trumbo's other exemplary scripts, there's very little beneath the surface of *Thirty Seconds*. Many individual moments have gravity, but the tale as a whole is a shallow homily to patriotism. Because Trumbo never gives anything more than lip service to the issues that might believably be swirling inside the heads of the characters, seeing *Thirty Seconds* as much more than entertainment is difficult. That said, *Thirty Seconds* is marvelously entertaining, and also a terrific display of Trumbo's craftsmanship.

More specifically, *Thirty Seconds* shows how much Trumbo learned in less than a decade of screenwriting. Only five years before he wrote *Thirty Seconds*, Trumbo cowrote the miserable drama *The Flying Irishman*; both pictures were based on actual events and made with the cooperation of the individual upon whom the protagonist was based, but the films are dissimilar in every other respect. *The Flying Irishman* is static, dull, and laden with cumbersome narration while *Thirty Seconds* is fast, eventful, and filled with effective narrative devices; *The Flying Irishman* is awkward while *Thirty Seconds* is graceful.

Based on the memoir of Army Air Corps Captain Ted W. Lawson, *Thirty Seconds* tells the story of America's first air assault on Japan following the Japanese attack on Pearl Harbor. Much of the picture is spent detailing the practice sessions of the B-25 crews who volunteer for the air assault, and what makes these scenes interesting is that instead of depicting the growth of friendships that are then tested under fire, as is the war-picture norm, the expository sequences merely establish a mood and deliver interesting information. Although some routine war-movie stuff is presented — several scenes in which Ted (Van Johnson) tells his pregnant wife, Ellen Lawson (Phyllis Thaxter), that he'll survive the mission, for instance — scenes such as a moody one of B-25 pilots superstitiously visiting their planes at night are more characteristic of the film.

That scene, which is tremendously effective at communicating the way the pilots find comfort in the familiar while in foreign territory, contributes to the film on an almost subconscious level. Yet while such subtexts are commonplace in the film, they don't contribute to a larger theme. Instead, they inform and deepen the drama. The distinction speaks to how Trumbo was approaching his film work at this point in his career. During his busiest period (1938–1940) Trumbo used dramatic devices to put across thematic ideas, but by the time he wrote *Thirty*

Seconds, he had learned the far more difficult trick of using thematic devices to put across dramatic ideas. The risk in this method, of course, is that screenplays will comprise evocative moments that collectively signify very little, and that's just the problem with which *Thirty Seconds* is afflicted. In later films including *Roman Holiday*, *The Brave One*, and *Spartacus*, Trumbo married thematics and dramatics with consummate grace, and the first signs of his ability to so masterfully control his craft can be seen in *Thirty Seconds*.

One last thing worth considering is the inherently conventional style of Trumbo's *Thirty Seconds* screenplay. For example, he uses a commonplace device of having recurring dialogue suggest continuity. During their first scene together, Ted asks Ellen, "Tell me honey, how'd you get to be so cute?" She responds, "I had to be, if I was going to get such a good-looking fellow." These seemingly innocuous lines, perfectly believable dripping from the mouths of love-struck newlyweds, prove important when they are invoked later in the picture. As Ted ships off for Japan, these sweet nothings are his last words to Helen, and the lines recur at the conclusion of the picture in a different context. When Ted returns from the war missing a leg, he's petrified about Ellen's possible reactions to his injury. Within seconds of reuniting with her, however, he discovers that her love is still strong, so he asks the loaded question one more time: "How'd you get to be so cute?" By answering with words that have become familiar to the characters and the audience, Ellen provides closure when she says: "I had to, if was going to get such a good-looking fellow." This trick is among the most common in screenwriting, but because Trumbo used it so perfectly, the device feels as natural as a contrivance can.[19]

During the middle section of the film, which leads to and includes the titular raid on Tokyo, Trumbo methodically illustrates seemingly every minute aspect of the soldiers' preparation. Once given their orders, they fly from Florida to California, where their planes are loaded on the aircraft carrier *Hornet*. And once out to sea, the Army flyers overcome rivalries among the various armed forces and bond with their Navy counterparts.[20]

At regular intervals during the preparation sequences, the inspiring officer who authored the plan to assault Japan, Lieutenant Colonel James Dolittle (Spencer Tracy), addresses the pilots and reiterates the danger of the coming mission. Although Trumbo provides Dolittle with some marvelously authoritative dialogue, the stakes of the mission are stated so overtly that they reflect the literal nature of the film's first half. This is a picture with very little "cheating"—Trumbo and the other filmmakers present exhaustive detail so that the film is equal parts travelogue, propaganda, and narrative. Although this painstaking approach might strike some viewers as tedious, a more favorable reading characterizes the movie's many informational scenes as the equivalent of local color.

The picture's transition from preparation to action is foreshadowed during an effective scene involving Ted and fellow pilot Bob Gray (Robert Mitchum), who walk onto the *Hornet*'s deck at night for some fresh air.

> TED: My mother had a Jap gardener once. Seemed like a nice little guy.
> BOB: You know, I don't hate the Japs—yet. It's a funny thing. I don't like 'em, but I don't hate 'em.

> TED: I guess I don't either. You get kinda mixed up.
> BOB: Yeah.
> TED: It's hard to figure.... Here we are. All I ever wanted to be was an aeronautical engineer. I joined the Army in '40 because I figured it was the best way to learn, and I wasn't sore at anybody. But here you suddenly realize you're gonna drop a ton of high explosives on one of the biggest cities in the world.
> BOB: You're not getting squeamish, are you?
> TED: Aw, no, no—I don't pretend to like the idea of killing a bunch of people, but it's a case of drop a bomb on them or pretty soon they'll be dropping one on Helen.
> BOB: Yeah, you're right.[21]

The leisurely pace of the dialogue reflects the pace of the entire picture. Even in its high-action sequences, *Thirty Seconds* is meticulous and deliberate, as if Trumbo and the other filmmakers didn't want to leave any room for misunderstanding. In the dialogue scene, several "beats" happen around the central idea of Ted expressing ambivalence about his mission. First, there's the beat of the two men not hating the enemy; second, of Ted acknowledging the cost in human lives of his mission; and third, of Bob nudging Ted to say that misgivings won't prevent him from performing his duty. By taking this methodical approach, Trumbo ensures that viewers are constantly in step with him. Each leap from one concept to the next is cued in the dialogue and skewed toward one particular reading of the scene. The sum effect is that the scene is like a game of connect-the-dots, in which the elements, when placed in proper succession, can lead to only one result.

This ability to use organization,

reason, and patience to put across a point is typical of Trumbo, but because his method on *Thirty Seconds* is largely without passion—note how much more intimate the picture gets in the sequence of Ted losing his leg, during which Trumbo integrates ideas and emotions from *Johnny Got His Gun*—he doesn't run into the conundrum of overstating his points as he often did on other films. Instead of writing with hot passion, he writes with cold logic, and it suits him well.

Trumbo's organizational skills come into play again during the sequence of the pilots frantically taking off from the *Hornet* to begin their bombing runs. When enemy fire forces the planes to leave ahead of schedule, Trumbo fills Ted's bombing run with six possible crises before the real crisis occurs. In addition to filling the attack sequence with drama even though the real-life Ted entered and exited Japanese airspace unscathed, Trumbo ratchets the tension by crying wolf repeatedly before the wolf finally shows up. This device works beautifully, because by the fifth and sixth fake crises, viewers are likely convinced that Ted will get through—so when the seventh crisis proves real, it's more shocking than it would have been had it been telegraphed in a more conventional manner.

Director LeRoy stages one of his moodiest scenes after Ted crashes just short of the Chinese coast and then makes his way to the shore in the middle of a nighttime rainstorm. As fierce weather pounds the craggy rocks and meager beaches of the shoreline, Ted's wounded men slowly emerge from various directions like ghosts, and their moans of pain are almost lost in the din of the rainfall. As the men determine the severity of their situation, Chinese soldiers appear from behind a nearby hill and seem like otherworldly wraiths descending upon the Americans. This scene sticks out from the rest of the movie because it conveys a mood almost exclusively with visual information; although there is dialogue within it, the scene primarily communicates through surreal images and is therefore closer to expressionism than anything else in the evocative but mostly literal movie.

After an expositional sequence in which it's revealed that the Americans have been found by Chinese soldiers who are sympathetic to their cause and will help transport them through Japanese-occupied territory, the picture becomes almost purely procedural in its depiction of Ted's long, arduous journey through China. As various plot strands, particularly the fates of Ted's other crew members, are resolved, one subplot emerges as the focus of the last portion of the movie: the severity of a leg injury that Ted suffered during the plane crash. It soon becomes clear that amputation is required, and this revelation sparks some of the most vivid screenwriting of Trumbo's career.

During the amputation sequence, Trumbo was able to echo thematic and dramatic material about emasculation, male pride, helplessness, and the price of war that he explored so poignantly in *Johnny Got His Gun*. Trumbo also employs gallows humor throughout the amputation sequence; after learning that he might lose his leg, Ted laments that he and Helen will never ski again, which feels like just the kind of *non sequitur* that might pop into the delirious mind of someone facing a traumatic experience.

When the moment comes for Ted's

Trumbo started raising a family on his ranch in Ventura County, California, during the war years. The blacklist era was difficult for all of the Trumbos, including, from left, Christopher, Cleo, Mitzi, Dalton, and Nikola. They are pictured in 1949. (Courtesy Mitzi Trumbo)

leg to be removed, the horrific stakes of the scene are established methodically. The doctors have only enough medicine to administer a topical anesthetic, so Ted learns that he'll be awake during the operation. "Oh, swell," Ted responds. "I can watch and make sure you don't take off too much." LeRoy maximizes the vivid mood of Trumbo's writing by filming the procedure in harshly lit wide angles that put viewers close to Ted's panicked, sweating face (actor Van Johnson is positioned in the foreground of the scene's most intense shot) and imply, through dramatically large shadows cast on the ceiling over his head, how oppressed Ted feels.

Soon into the procedure, the anesthetic starts to wear off, and Johnson's fidgety, terrified line deliveries and body movements communicate Ted's fear that he may actually feel his leg being removed. "Hurry, Doc, hurry!" he barks while on the verge of blacking out. Just as the scene grows too painful to watch, Trumbo pulls away by having Ted drift into a hallucination.

This cut, from the operating table to the inside of Ted's mind, is one of the most significant of Trumbo's career because it was one of his first attempts at using the kind of stream-of-consciousness storytelling that permeates his film of *Johnny*. Also, the cut is either one of the most brilliant things that Trumbo ever did as a screenwriter or one of the worst, depending on the perspective of the viewer. Because the hallucination bluntly reflects the "real" action happening at that point in the story, those who find Trumbo's method heavy-handed can easily point to this scene as an example of his using metaphor as a sledgehammer. But another perspective on the hallucination reveals that the scene is as vivid a bit of expressionism as the plane-crash scene.

In the hallucination, a healthy and whole Ted rushes into a lodge to answer a phone call from Helen. It's Christmas, and Ted is away on work but checking in to see that Helen is enjoying her holiday. As Ted stands in the foreground and makes sweet conversation with the offscreen Helen, two workers are visible in the background through a lodge window. They are chopping down a tall tree. Because the two men are visible from the beginning of the long master shot that dominates the scene, it's easy to miss them at first, but once they're discovered, it's clear that their action is an unsubtle metaphor for the removal of Ted's leg. And when Ted hears the tree starting to fall, he turns to look at it—thereby cueing a dissolve back to "reality."

What makes this moment so vibrant—and what protects it from accusations of heavy-handedness—is that it speaks to how imagination works. Trumbo is saying that even though Ted imagined himself out of reality and into a happier time, he brought reality with him as a nagging echo. And when the pain of the procedure became overwhelming—presumably at the moment when his leg was fully separated from his body—Ted was shocked out of his reverie. This makes the scene work on two levels: On one, it's merely a colorful way of communicating information that viewers would not want to see depicted literally; on the other, it's a poetic device for illustrating the way Ted's mind works. That Trumbo was able to craft a scene that is effective both intellectually and viscerally is proof that his true talent was finally starting to manifest itself in his screenwriting.

The events following Ted's operation are anticlimactic, because the amputation marked the last of the real-life Lawson's trials before he returned to America. After some hard-edged scenes depicting Ted's fury at having lost his leg and his determination to get over his disability—and after some sweet moments of Ted saying good-bye to the Chinese citizens who saved his life— Ted is reunited first with Dolittle and then with Helen. As discussed earlier, the reunion scene between Ted and Helen reiterates the couple's trademark dialogue ("How'd you get to be so cute," et cetera) and therefore provides closure. But it is not the most poignant in the concluding sequence.

That distinction belongs to a quick scene depicting Dolittle's visit to Ted's hospital room. After boosting Ted's spirits by indicating that he'll still have a place in the Army, even with just one leg, Dolittle starts to leave—and then pauses at the door to offer some parting commentary.

> DOLITTLE: Your wife's gonna have a baby, isn't she?
> TED: Yes, sir.
> DOLITTLE: I've got a couple of kids myself—both in the service. You know, Lawson, if my kids and all the other kids who are in this thing could fix it so this would really be the last one, your kid would get quite a break, wouldn't he?
> TED: He sure would, sir.

In conjunction with the earlier scene of Ted and Bob discussing the impending assault on Tokyo, this scene arguably advances a pacifistic agenda in a film that is otherwise pro-war.[22] In the former scene, Ted expresses his ambivalence about killing Japanese civilians but adds that his urge to protect his wife will help him carry out his mission. In the latter, Dolittle infers that he has no stomach for war but sees a greater goal being served by World War II: the end of war itself. When these scenes are taken together, a philosophy emerges in which it's possible for pacifism and militarism to coexist, although not harmoniously.

In this philosophy, a "good" war such as World War II—in which the aggression of Axis powers against innocent victims created an almost black-and-white distinction between good and evil—is worth fighting because it is, in effect, a war against war. If communicating this essential idea was all that Trumbo did in writing *Thirty Seconds*, it would tower among his best screenplays, yet it also contains some of his finest craftsmanship.

❖ ❖ ❖

In a perverse way, it's fitting that the last major picture Trumbo wrote before getting blacklisted was an innocent family drama. Although Trumbo later returned to family-oriented subject matter in *The Brave One*, that picture has an antiestablishment edge consistent with Trumbo's perpetual theme of righteous rebellion. Therefore, *Our Vines Have Tender Grapes* can accurately be called the last truly innocent Trumbo movie. It appears that once he got blacklisted and saw the fates of others who, like him, were persecuted for their political beliefs, Trumbo lost some measure of his faith in the human spirit. Whereas he had previously written movies in which people helped each other in times of struggle, after his HUAC testimony, Trumbo tended to concentrate more heavily on rebellious individuals.

Our Vines begins with two youngsters, Arnold Hansen (Jackie "Butch" Jenkins) and Selma Jacobson (Margaret O'Brien), strolling through a remote part of Fuller Junction, Wisconsin. After an incident in which Selma impulsively kills a squirrel—echoing a similar scene in the beginning of a later Trumbo movie, *The Sandpiper*—the children encounter a seemingly disturbed young woman,

Ingeborg Jensen (Dorothy Morris). During a brief conversation with the children, Ingeborg reveals her trepidation about the family farm on which she works, so viewers immediately sense that *Our Vines* is going to be about children discovering the harsh realities of the world. That proves partly true. Although the children's adventures include a near-death experience, the death of an acquaintance, and a catastrophic fire, the resolution of the picture is presented with such naive optimism that it discounts the picture's attempts at realism. But the "inspiring" denouement probably also explains why *Our Vines* is one of the few pre-blacklist Trumbo films to enjoy true longevity. As a warm fable about the way a community nurtures its young, the picture is as comforting as a placebo.

Adapted from George Victor Martin's novel, the film is certainly not without its virtues, but coming as it does on the heels of such entertaining pictures as *A Guy Named Joe* and *Thirty Seconds Over Tokyo*, it is a disappointment. Also, as directed by Roy Rowland, the picture has a turgid pace that spotlights the weak, artificial acting of O'Brien and Jenkins. Even the generally colorful Edward G. Robinson[23] plays a comforting archetype. His character, farmer Martinius Jacobson, is strong enough to support his family and earn stature among proud working people, but such a softy that he's unwilling to discipline his daugther.

The picture's strengths include the steady flow of the story—which takes place over the course of a year and uses seasonal changes both as narrative devices and metaphors—and the sheer sincerity of the effort. That Trumbo was in private life an acid-tongued cynic might lead some to find the prosaic tone of *Our*

Vines disingenuous, but at least up to the beginning of the blacklist, Trumbo was a man who spoke two languages: the caustic, verbose diction of his private life and the succinct, rosy prose of his screenplays.

Still, it's interesting to note the moments during which familiar Trumbo themes emerge. As the story follows the progression of Selma and Arnold's friendship and the integration of jaded big-city teacher Viola Johnson (Frances Gifford) into the rural community, scenes arise in which characters articulate their feelings with the force of politicians making platform statements. The first such scene occurs when Martinius's wife, Bruna (Agnes Moorehead), discovers that he has given one of the family's calves to Selma as a pet. Bruna tries to explain that Selma doesn't really own the animal.

> BRUNA: Everything on the farm is all yours, Selma—yours and ours. The things that keep us warm, the food we have—it couldn't just belong to one of us any more than the—the sunshine.

Were these lines not so innocuous and treacly, they would provide another opportunity to note Trumbo's habitual insertion of themes relating to collectivism. As it stands, though, the lines seem less about asserting leftist ideas than they are about teaching a child her place in the world.[24] For plot reasons, it's necessary to note that Bruna backs away from her stance and tells Selma that she actually does own the calf, determining that Selma needs to start proving she's worthy of taking on such responsibilities. Discussions of property ownership recur throughout *Our Vines*, as in a scene of Bruna reacting to Martinius's announcement that he wants to build an expensive new barn. As Bruna explains to Selma:

> BRUNA: Well, what you'd like people to have and what people are able to have—those are two different things. Now, your pa's out in the barn mending a harness when he ought to be here with us, gettin' some rest. With the old barn, he works more than any man should. To pay for a new one, he'd be working longer—he'd never be able to stop a minute. He's growin' old and dreamin' at night of his debts. Oh, it's better, Selma—it's better never—

Bruna's homily trails off because her husband joins the scene, but the point about appreciating what you have is already well made, as is a secondary point about the gap between the haves and the have-nots, another favorite Trumbo theme. Although Bruna's dialogue doesn't specifically allude to any ill will held by rural people against those in higher social strata, the fact that Bruna sees her life as a compromise suggests that her contentment, while considerable, is not absolute. Were Bruna truly content living on a farm and avoiding extravagances, she wouldn't feel the need to explain her contentment to Selma in terms suggesting that it's "better" to have a little than a lot. Were Bruna truly content, she might have said so in simple, declarative terms, telling Selma that the family doesn't need a bigger barn. Instead, Bruna declares that a bigger barn would come at too high a price. Contented people live as they wish; malcontents live within their means and dream of more.

Exploring this subtext is worthwhile because *Our Vines* is one of the few Trumbo movies to deal with an un-derclass of people and not give voice to whatever resentments they might hold about the social order that defines them.

A notable scene occurs late in the picture, when the editor of Fuller Junction's newspaper, Nels Halverson (James Craig), announces that he's joined the Army. This upsets Viola, the big-city teacher, because she's developed feelings for Nels, and it upsets Arnold and Selma because Nels is a beloved member of their Fuller Junction "family." In a quiet, rainy day scene, Selma and Arnold question Martinius about why Nels—whom they simply call "Editor"—has to fight.

> MARTINIUS: These things are awful hard to explain. Now, uh—now, you take milk. It's a good thing, isn't it? Well, it's good for calves, for children, for grownups—for everybody.... Well, just because it's good, there's no reason it's free. We have to work for it. Now does that make any sense?
> SELMA: Yes.
> MARTINIUS: Well, uh, the way I look at it, it's the same thing with peace on earth and goodwill toward men. It's good for everybody, and it doesn't come free either. You have to work for it. And—somebody comes along, tries to take it away from us—well, we've gotta fight for it.[25]

Several interesting things happen in this exchange, which should be prefaced with an explanation that some of the specific wording—"peace on earth and goodwill toward men"—is inserted as a reference to an earlier scene in which Selma delivered a homily at a church service. Beyond that Christian allusion, though, the dialogue taps into several themes that appear throughout *Our Vines*, first among them the idea of property ownership.

As a way of beginning the discussion of an abstract concept, peace, Martinius grounds the children in their understanding of a concrete concept, milk. This device also works for the audience, because it provides context for Martinius's beliefs. For him, life is as simple as the understanding that to get things, one must work; therefore this dialogue harks back to Bruna's spiel about property ownership and reiterates the idea of collective responsibility.

This leads to the second interesting inference of the dialogue. Instead of talking about the enemy as an enemy—thereby opening up uncomfortable discussions of fascism, genocide, and religious intolerance—Martinius characterizes the enemy as an unseen force. He reduces a world conflict to terms that even children can understand: We have something that the enemy wants to take from us. Because Selma and Arnold have previously quarreled over possessions—specifically a pair of roller skates that Selma did not want to share with Arnold—these terms are familiar to them.

A final noteworthy aspect of the dialogue speaks to a technique that Trumbo frequently employed. In adapting the sentiment conveyed in Martinius's dialogue from the pages of Martin's book, Trumbo put himself inside Martinius's shoes and imagined how Martinius might best put forth his ideas to his listeners. And because Martinius's best tack was to speak as a child, Trumbo spoke as a child. This maneuver necessarily reduces the dialogue in the scene to simplistic terms, and necessarily precludes the insertion of the more complex ideas that the dialogue might have communicated were Martinius speaking to adults.

Trumbo often made similar maneuvers when looking for ways to make dialogue seem true not only to the person speaking it but germane to the life experience of the person(s) hearing it. This explains why some of the most sweeping social statements in Trumbo's movies are delivered in what might seem to be childlike language. There's virtually no difference between this screenwriting tack and the decision that Trumbo made to write *Johnny Got His Gun* in the unvarnished, stream-of-consciousness syntax of protagonist Joe Bonham. Trumbo used characters as the conduits through which he conveyed either his own ideas or those of the writers whose work he adapted, so those ideas were phrased in dialogue seemingly unrepresentative of the deep thought behind them.

All of the talk about possessions and their worth comes to a head when Martinius learns that the new barn owned by his neighbor, Bjorn Bjornson (Morris Carnovsky), is burning down. This development is significant, because it was the construction of Bjorn's barn that made Martinius dream of having a new one himself. After helping Bjorn's family during the fire, Martinius says to his wife that he'd like to make improvements to their house instead of buying a new barn. Taken aback, Bruna responds:

> BRUNA: Maybe if a man wants a barn as bad as you do—maybe he ought to have it.
> MARTINIUS: No. Not if it costs a price a man ain't willing to pay. I've got you. I've got Selma. Now if I had a barn, I'd have everything. There wouldn't be anything else to want…. Maybe it's a good thing for a man to want something, something he ain't ever gonna get. Just to

keep his interest up and help him take care of things he has.

Although Martinius's speech peters off into vagueness, suggesting that the thought behind it hadn't been followed through to a logical conclusion, the sentiment clearly articulated at the beginning of the dialogue completes the arc of Martinius's lust for material possessions, thereby punctuating the homily that is *Our Vines*. When we met him, Martinius was working himself to exhaustion in order to keep up with his neighbors' acquisition of possessions, but after being shown what really matters to him, Martinius determines that possessions aren't the reward that he thought them to be.

Just as Martinius's brief speech about why he doesn't want a new barn trails off into nothing, one of the picture's subplots is resolved in a blunt and didactic sequence. Ingeborg, the disturbed girl whom Arnold and Selma encountered in the film's opening scene, dies about halfway through the movie, prompting Viola to criticize Fuller Junction's citizenry. She argues that were the townsfolk truly decent, they would have been kind to Ingeborg while she was alive. Nels, the newspaper editor, tells Viola that she hasn't seen the best of Fuller Junction yet, and she gets to see just that during a church service at which Nels asks the townsfolk to contribute to a relief fund for Bjorn, who lost most of his livestock in the fire.

The townsfolk are initially meager in their charity, donating only pocket change. As Viola watches this scene, Nels worries that his neighbors aren't the people he thought them to be. Then, proving that Martinius is not the only character to have learned from recent events, Selma stands up and says she wants to give her prized calf to Bjorn. After being shamed by a child, the townsfolk follow her example and give generously, filling Martinius and Bruna with pride. The outpouring also moves Viola into declaring, somewhat suddenly, that she loves Fuller Junction after all and plans to stay there and marry Nels.

The picture's last scene hammers home the metaphor of the title, because as Martinius and Selma walk home from church through a field of blossoming trees, they make comments to each other about how all the flora are thriving with the new spring. In a blunt exchange consistent with the picture's technique of bringing everything down to a level that children can understand, Selma says, "I'm growing too," and her father proudly responds, "We're all growing."

❖ ❖ ❖

Despite its sickly sentimentality, *Our Vines Have Tender Grapes* offered further proof that Trumbo's tenure at MGM promised to be a long one. He wrote three hits in a row for the studio, so it took something as catastrophic as the blacklist to end Trumbo's relationship with MGM. And though *Our Vines* was his last MGM credit before the HUAC hearings, it was Republic Pictures that issued the last film to bear Trumbo's name until he emerged from the underground with the 1960 releases of *Spartacus* and *Exodus*.[26]

The Republic release, *Jealousy*, is rare among Trumbo's original stories in that it's a dark, lustful romance in the mold of books by Raymond Chandler and James M. Cain. During the 1940s, Trumbo generally trafficked in lighter fare, and *Jealousy* reveals several reasons why. Every single element of the picture feels borrowed from stories by other writers, and even though the opportunities for strident moralizing and metaphorical imagery should have made the genre a natural fit for Trumbo, thrillers simply didn't fit his pre-blacklist style. Also, Trumbo's pre-blacklist affinity for happy endings—admittedly, an outgrowth of his desire to craft marketable stories—blocked him from embracing the doom-and-gloom ethos of film noir.

While *Jealousy* is certainly the darkest of the five crime-related films that Trumbo wrote before the blacklist set in, the film's bleak subject matter is dulled by a bogus ending. This is especially bothersome because the denouement undoes the interesting work that Trumbo and screenwriters Gustav Machaty (who also produced and directed) and Arnold Phillips did in creating the character of expatriate writer Peter Urban (played by Nils Asther). Were the picture more in tune with Peter's fatalistic attitude and less with the cheeriness of Trumbo's early films, it might have been something provocative, instead of a near-miss.

The movie opens in Los Angeles, where Janet Urban (Jane Randolph) is working as a cab driver to support the writing career of her husband, Peter. Janet meets and nearly has a dalliance with self-possessed physician David Brent (John Loder), but returns to Peter. We soon learn that Peter is a famous European writer who can't get a foothold in America. A proud, cynical bastard who laments that the peons around him don't recognize his greatness, he is best characterized by the pretentious manner of his speech, as written by Machaty and Phillips: "I'm the only creature on earth miserable enough

to give you that feeling of superiority," Peter says to his wife.

Characters this morally destitute and dialogue this cutting are commonplace in blacklist-era Trumbo films such as *Gun Crazy*, *The Prowler*, and *He Ran All the Way*, but it's important to note that it wasn't Trumbo's typewriter from which the pages bearing these words issued. Trumbo hadn't yet explored on-screen darkness in any depth, so it's somewhat ironic that his last pre-blacklist credit presages the verbal and physical violence running through many of his blacklist-era pictures.

After the dispiriting confrontation with her husband, during which Janet learns that he owns a gun, Janet seeks comfort in David's arms. She also becomes friends with David's assistant, Doctor Monica Anderson (Karen Morley), whose relationship with him is platonic. Meanwhile, Peter slides further down the emotional ladder and begins stalking Janet because he suspects infidelity. Next comes some convoluted business involving Janet hiding Peter's gun in her purse and then losing the purse while on a shopping trip with Monica; shortly afterward, we see a shadowy scene in which someone uses the gun to kill Peter. After the police are persuaded that Peter killed himself, Monica is revealed—to the audience, not the other characters—as the murderer.

Skeptical that Peter killed himself, Peter's friend Hugo Kral (Hugo Haas) convinces the police to reopen their investigation. Janet is convicted of murdering her husband, at which point Monica makes her move on David. But the doctor shocks his assistant by revealing that he and Janet wed before she was incarcerated. Monica faints upon hearing the news, thereby setting in motion David's discovery of her crime. Eventually, Monica confesses with a particularly choice line: "Of the two women who wanted you, I loved you enough to kill." The picture ends with Janet and David reunited to face a presumably rosy future.

Because Trumbo explored the film's titular theme far more entertainingly in *You Belong to Me*—and far more provocatively in *The Prowler*—*Jealousy* is of little consequence in his *oeuvre*. Only the picture's portrayal of duplicity is interesting, because that theme recurs in Trumbo's movies. In *Accent on Love*, a tycoon masquerades as a member of the working class; in *Roman Holiday*, a reporter and a princess disguise their identities from each other. Still, there's not much to say about the theme because Trumbo generally used it the same way

every time—characters lied or misrepresented themselves to enter worlds or situations they couldn't enter honestly.

Almost to a one, these characters pay for their duplicity by losing everything they dishonestly gained. In some cases, the characters are rewarded for acknowledging their lies (as in *Accent on Love*), but in others, the characters simply get punished for lying (as in *Jealousy*). The only wrinkle in Trumbo's treatment of duplicity comes in *Roman Holiday*, in which liars are neither rewarded nor punished for their dishonesty. Although they don't get what they really want— each other—they do walk away with deeper understandings of their selves. The issue of duplicity naturally dovetails the dominant theme of Trumbo's best films, that of personal honor; just as Trumbo sanctified characters with integrity, he punished those without it.

5

Going Underground
(1947–1956)

Trumbo's leftist activities caught up with him in 1947, when he was among the first wave of "unfriendly" witnesses called to testify before HUAC. Trumbo and the other members of the Hollywood Ten used the First Amendment to explain why they felt the committee had no right to ask private citizens about private matters. When he appeared before the committee on October 28, Trumbo brought a characteristically detailed statement and reams of what he thought pertinent evidence: his screenplays. Because entertainment industry leftists were accused of putting pro-communist propaganda into their films, he came ready to prove that scripts such as *Thirty Seconds Over Tokyo* and *Our Vines Have Tender Grapes* were patriotic.

Trumbo's give-and-take with Chairman J. Parnell Thomas grew acrimonious when it became clear the committee's main interest was making him name other communists, but—using the debating skills he had been refining since

high school—Trumbo got in a few zingers. When pressed him to answer questions simply, Trumbo quipped: "Very many questions can be answered 'yes' or 'no' only by a moron or a slave." More pointedly, Trumbo closed his testimony with these charged words: "This is the beginning of an American concentration camp."[1]

The question of why show business professionals were summoned to Washington has been debated for decades by the various historians, apologists, and pundits who have written scores of books, essays, and diatribes about what was later termed the "McCarthy era," after notorious communist hunter Senator Joseph McCarthy. One of the most articulate interpreters of the period, Victor S. Navasky, noted the following:

> The actors, directors, writers, and publicity people called as witnesses before HUAC had no atomic secrets to steal, no vital war materials to leave unloaded on the docks, no opportunities to "poison" young minds in the

In November 1947, Trumbo and nine other movie-industry professionals were blacklisted for refusing to tell a Congressional committee whether they were communists. In this 1950 rally, Trumbo (standing beneath the sign for Alvah Bessie), his wife, Cleo, and their children gather with other members of the Hollywood Ten. (Courtesy Mitzi Trumbo)

classroom. It might be argued that Hollywood people were in the ideal spot to create and distribute communist propaganda to the American people. But, as the congressional hearings soon made clear ... the collective nature of work in the Hollywood studio system and on the broadcast networks precluded individual attempts at agitprop, and in any event the final products were available for inspection and criticism in motion-picture theaters and on television sets across the country.[2]

While Navasky's suggestion that leftists were unable to slip progressive

content into mainstream films is arguable, his assertion that Trumbo and his peers were not a threat to national security is a critically important one. Even the historians who argue that communists were conspiring to change popular culture agree that one of HUAC's goals was getting publicity. And because stars ranging from Humphrey Bogart to Robert Walker to Sterling Hayden appeared either in the audience at committee hearings or as witnesses, HUAC got all the publicity it could handle. For his part, Trumbo thought HUAC's motivation was multilayered. "I think it had three reasons," he wrote in 1953, "to destroy trade unions," "to paralyze anti-fascist politi-cal action," and "to remove progressive content from films."[3]

The Hollywood Ten and others called before HUAC were singled out for their offscreen activities as much as for anything they put into movies. Larry Ceplair and Steven Englund noted that one of the political groups to which Trumbo belonged, the Hollywood Writ-ers' Mobilization, organized events such as the Writers' Congress of 1943. The authors quoted Robert Gordon Sproul, who said the goals of the Congress were to "analyze propaganda techniques as weapons of victory," "investigate the most effective use of new media of ex-pression," and "to mobilize the entire writing profession in a freedom of action for the free world of tomorrow."[4]

Real evidence of seditious behavior by the Hollywood communists has yet to surface. While Trumbo and his con-temporaries likely spent many long eve-nings espousing views that could ar-guably be described as "antigovernment" or "anticapitalist," the fact is that none did anything traitorous. They were in-stead guilty of, in Orwellian terms, "thought crimes." Alvah Bessie, a friend of Trumbo's and a member of the Ten, described the activities of communist writers this way:

> When [communist labor leader] Wil-liam Z. Foster came out [to Holly-wood] one time, there was a Party section meeting with him, and I re-member something he said ... "The best you guys and girls can do here in this industry is what I would call, in military terms, 'a holding action.' You can't really do very good work in this industry because they won't let you. But you can prevent them, if you know how to do it, from making really anti-

black, anti-woman, anti–foreign-born, anti–foreign-country pictures. You can prevent them from making anti-human pictures, and that is a very worthy thing to be doing."[5]

Blacklisted actress Betty Blair Reicz declared: "Of course, there *was* a com-munist conspiracy in Hollywood.... It was a conspiracy to do good work and establish the movie unions."[6] Reicz said that while some observers dismissed Hollywood liberals as "champagne so-cialists," most of her peers were genu-inely devoted to their cause, and while the history of the Hollywood liberals may be filled with more rhetoric than action, it is also filled with speeches, ral-lies, pamphlets, and other means by which Trumbo and his "tender com-rades" fought for what they believed to be right. Even within the parameters defined by Navasky, Foster, Reicz, and the dozens of others who lived through or studied the HUAC era, Trumbo proved himself to be a committed radical, not just a "champagne socialist." His best pre-blacklist films are filled with hu-manistic ideals and portrayals of char-acters trying to live honorably, and when HUAC pressure made it dangerous for anyone in Hollywood to embrace left-wing ideas, he stood fast to the same principles that guided him during his first decade in the movie industry. He was guilty of all three things that he per-ceived HUAC as trying to destroy—he was a labor activist, an anti-fascist po-litical activist, and a progressive screen-writer. In that light, it's no wonder he was one of the first to fall victim to HUAC's persecution.

After the Ten's recalcitrance before Congress made them pariahs in Holly-wood, the heads of several studios met in New York for the infamous Waldorf

Conference, at which the executives agreed not to employ any of the Ten unless the defiant witness cleared himself before the committee. Pursuant to this decision, MGM "suspended" Trumbo in the fall of 1947, even though he was partway through a screenplay assignment. He spent 1948 and 1949 fighting his MGM suspension and his conviction for contempt of Congress, but when it became clear that jail time was inevitable unless he named names, he started writing at an obscene rate of speed to generate pseudonymous screenplay sales before his incarceration. After producing some of his best small-scale scripts—*Gun Crazy, The Prowler, Roman Holiday, Cowboy*, and others—he entered the Federal Correctional Institute in Ashland, Kentucky, in the summer of 1950.

Trumbo used his prison time to resume the "serious" writing he had put aside, and his correspondence from prison is filled with descriptions of an ambitious war novel that he never finished.

After completing his jail term, Trumbo moved his family to Mexico in November 1951, because he heard from friends including Hugo Butler that black market work was plentiful south of the border. That proved untrue, however, and by February 1954, the Trumbos—Dalton, Cleo, Nikola, Christopher, and Mitzi—were back in California. Trumbo went after black market work with a vengeance, and his efforts paid off handsomely when *The Brave One* earned him an Oscar, albeit under a pseudonym.

Trumbo's life in these years was not easy. He and his family were regularly harassed by those who considered him a traitor; at one point he was beaten by thugs outside of his home. Once again setting aside his dreams of writing great novels, Trumbo used his anger at the persecution and ignorance of this period as motivation for more frantic screenwriting—his way of giving as well as he got.[7]

It appears that over two years elapsed between the last pre-blacklist film to bear Trumbo's name, *Jealousy*, and the first credited to one of one of his fronts. Trumbo wrote an original screen story titled "The Lady From Laredo," and recruited Earl Felton, the friend who had introduced him to his wife Cleo, to provide a name to put on the project. The story sold to 20th Century–Fox, and studio chief Darryl F. Zanuck gave it to director Preston Sturges as a potential vehicle for star Betty Grable. Sturges threw out most of the elements of Trumbo's story and titled the resulting screenplay *The Beautiful Blonde from Bashful Bend*. Whereas Trumbo's story was a light romance involving duplicity, cutesy plot developments, and a rebellious heroine (somewhat in the spirit of *Roman Holiday*) Sturges created a farce so broad and insipid that despite his rarefied stature and Grable's impressive track record at the box office, *The Beautiful Blonde* flopped.[8] This was the second time a possible Sturges-Trumbo collaboration ended badly, the first being the project that became *I Married a Witch*, but it's probable that Sturges never even knew he had once again crossed paths with Trumbo.

❖ ❖ ❖

Although it's one of the most compelling pictures on his résumé, the endless appeal of *Gun Crazy* stems less from Trumbo's contributions than from those of director Joseph H. Lewis—whose startling camera angles, bold staging, and fierce mood setting earned the picture a reputation as one of the best B films ever made. The picture was based on a *Saturday Evening Post* story by MacKinlay Kantor, who contributed an unwieldy, 320-page first draft. Lewis told film historian Danny Peary that Kantor's draft was basically sound in terms of character and story, but unusably long. Peary described how Lewis and screenwriter Millard Kaufman rewrote Kantor's draft, and offered this pointed quote from Lewis: "I can honestly say that I made the film twice as good as the Kantor script. But he never spoke to me again."[9]

Peary, writing in 1981, did not know Kaufman was a front of Trumbo's which indicates how long a shadow the blacklist cast. It took more than 25 years, for instance, for Trumbo to be revealed as the author of *Roman Holiday*'s original story. And because the truth about blacklist-era credits remained evasive for so many years—some questions are still unanswered as of this writing—a great deal of misinformation has been disseminated. After it was determined that Kaufman fronted for Trumbo on *Gun Crazy*, for example, some began looking elsewhere on Kaufman's résumé and discerned that Trumbo had written the scripts for *Bad Day at Black Rock* (1955, MGM) and *Never So Few* (1959, MGM). In fact, he was involved in neither.

Gun Crazy occupies an important place in Trumbo's *oeuvre* because it was his first job for the King brothers—producers Frank, Herman, and Maurice King. The brothers were among the first independent filmmakers to recognize the opportunities created by the blacklist. From the late '40s to the late '60s, King Brothers Productions hired writers including Michael Wilson, John Howard Lawson, Lester Cole, and Ring Lardner, Jr., for a fraction of the rates those writers earned before the blacklist. "Politics didn't enter into it at all," Frank King told Bruce Cook. "We were just interested in making pictures." Generally described ruthlessly cost-efficient filmmakers—shades of the Warner Bros. and RKO B-picture units for which Trumbo worked in the '30s—the Kings had a mutually beneficial relationship with Trumbo that produced, among other movies, *The Brave One*. As Trumbo recalled:

> When I and others plummeted in value, we naturally found ourselves in this new market, and naturally these independent producers availed themselves of our services because they felt that for this money they could get better work. So there wasn't really this brutal exploitation of black-market writers that has sometimes been referred to.[10]

Gun Crazy also marks a transition from Trumbo's uplifting 1940s films to the brutal crime movies he wrote in the blacklist era, including *The Prowler*, *He Ran All the Way*, and *The Boss*. Although this transition was prophesied by Trumbo's original story for *Jealousy*, the bleak subject matter of *Gun Crazy* is notable because nearly all of Trumbo's blacklist-era films are touched by cynicism. He was certainly able to tap into optimism when needed, for pictures such as *Roman Holiday* and *The Brave One*, but from 1947 on, Trumbo largely set aside the sunniness that distinguished his pre-blacklist era films.

It may seem a knee-jerk response to say that the darkening of Trumbo's screen work was a reaction to political persecution, yet ample evidence supports such an assertion. Even if one sets aside Trumbo's blacklist-era output—to allow that Trumbo might not have associated himself with those projects had he more options—the pictures that he wrote between 1960 and 1973 are colored by cynicism and infused with rebellion. In the two 1960 epics with which he "broke" the blacklist, *Spartacus* and *Exodus*, Trumbo mythologized heroes fighting against corrupt systems, and in character-driven pictures such as *Lonely Are the Brave* and *The Sandpiper*, he portrayed characters who rebelled against society because their nature drove them to do so.

And in the last important statement of his film career, the movie version of *Johnny Got His Gun*, Trumbo portrayed a man literally destroyed because he went along, unquestioningly, with the status quo. Seen in the light of these later developments, the juncture represented by *Gun Crazy*—between Trumbo's wide eyed pre-blacklist idealism and his more eloquent, latter-day cynicism—is an important one.

The picture opens in the small town of Cashville, where young Barton Tare (Rusty Tamblyn) breaks into a store to steal a gun. Director Lewis stages this scene dramatically with torrential rain, throbbing camera movements, and histrionic energy, all of which sets a larger-than-life tone. Also, the lustful expression on Bart's face before he steals the gun cues viewers that Bart's relationship with guns is a dangerous one.

In family court, Bart is tried for his theft, and his older sister Ruby Tare (Anabel Shaw) tells a story, portrayed in flashback, indicating that Bart has been obsessed with guns for years but that he would never knowingly kill anything or anyone. Back in the present, Ruby offers a feeble explanation for Bart's behavior: "It's something else about guns that gets him—not killing." Two of Bart's young friends testify on his behalf, with their story also told in flashback. Finally, Bart's eighth grade teacher, Miss Wynn (Virginia Farmer), tells the most damning story: In a third flashback, Bart brings a gun into school, shows it off to other students, and then refuses to give it up until the superintendent gets involved. The sequence ends with stoic Judge Willoughby (Morris Carnovsky) asking for Bart's side of the story.

"I like shooting, judge," the boy says. "I don't know why, but I feel good inside when I'm shooting 'em. I feel awful good inside, like I'm somebody."

Willoughby calls Bart's fixation a "dangerous mania," and commits Bart to reform school. The intercutting of flashbacks during the courtroom testimony is a straightforward device used to maximize the exposition of the hearing scene, but the combination of courtroom dialogue and flashback vignettes lets us peek inside Bart's mind. We learn that he's an orphan being raised by his sister, so the assertion that Bart finds his identity in the thing he does best (shooting) suggests that he might be compensating for feelings of abandonment and alienation associated with the loss of his parents. Seen in this light, Bart's obsession is tied to his identity—if he doesn't "belong" to his talent, then he doesn't belong to anything. There is another possible interpretation, however. Freudians might argue the phallic significance of the device by which Bart identifies himself, and given the amount of defensive talk in the picture about Bart's confidence with a gun (read: potency), this interpretation is probably valid on some level.

In fact, a combination of both interpretations might be the most valid reading of the picture. Later in the story, when Bart finds his soul mate in a female sharpshooter, it's fair to say that he responds to her on a sexual level because she acknowledges his potency. But Bart's association with the lady gunslinger also relates to his parental issues. Because she, too, identifies herself by her ability to shoot—although, in her case, gunplay is more of a defense mechanism than an artistic expression, as it is for Bart—she represents an outgrowth of his identity. Like two Americans in a strange country who bond because of their common language, the way Bart and his inamorata understand each other is magnified by how completely they are misunderstood by others.

His reform school term and a tenure in the army behind him, the grown-up Bart (played by John Dall) returns to Cashville, where his sister Ruby has become a housewife with a passel of children, and his childhood friends, Dave Allister (Nedrick Young), and Clyde Boston (Harry Lewis), have settled into their respective professions. Dave is a reporter, and Clyde is Cashville's sheriff.

Bart and his friends visit a traveling carnival, where Bart meets sideshow sharpshooter Annie Laurie Starr (Peggy Cummins). Their flirtation is staged vividly, if incredibly; as part of her act, Laurie challenges audience members to a sharpshooting contest, and Bart volunteers. After passing the first round easily, Bart forces Laurie into a second round. She places a crown adorned with several unlit matches onto Bart's head, then has him stand against a wall. She lights the matches by shooting at them from across the room, but ignites only five of the six. Bart and Laurie switch places—and the sexual tension between them is evident in her utter confidence that he won't accidentally shoot her in the head. Bart hits all six matches, much to the chagrin of Laurie's blustery employer, Packett (Barry Kroeger). Infatuated, Laurie offers Bart a job in the carnival and he accepts, but Packett is visibly jealous.

The plot moves quickly after Bart joins the carnival. One night, Bart heads to Laurie's trailer and is confronted by Packett, who says he's got a "claim" on her. Thinking Bart sufficiently discouraged, Packett enters Laurie's trailer and tries to seduce her. She refuses, so he reminds her that he knows she killed a man in St. Louis. That knowledge, we suspect, is the extent of his "claim" on Laurie. Sensing that he's losing her to Bart despite his blackmail, Packett comments disgustedly: "I saw the way you were looking at each other tonight—like a couple of wild animals. It almost scared me."

"It should," Laurie responds.

As if on cue, Bart enters Laurie's trailer, and the combination of Packett's lust, Laurie's insolence, and Bart's jealousy leads to a heated moment in which Bart shoots a mirror situated just inches from Packett. Snarling with satisfaction, Packett fires Bart and Laurie.

Next comes one of the most pivotal scenes in the picture. As the couple drives away from the carnival, feeling liberated and ready for anything, Bart proposes and she accepts. But when they reach the office of an all-night justice of the peace, Bart pauses. Reverting to her natural state of defensive cynicism, Laurie asks: "Changed your mind?... You're signing up for an awfully long term." Bart reveals that he was in reform school, but she doesn't own up to her criminal past.

Instead, she alludes to it in one of the film's best speeches:

"Bart, I've never been much good—at least up to now I haven't. You aren't getting any bargain…. But I've got a funny feeling that I want to be good. I don't know, maybe I can't—but I'm going to try. I'll try hard, Bart."

Bart ignores the warning signs in Laurie's behavior, and the couple enjoys a quick honeymoon before Laurie, predictably, gets restless within the humble lifestyle of working-class newlyweds. She startles Bart by suggesting that they hold up a bank, and, reflecting the pacifism he exhibited as child, he refuses to go along with the idea.

His reluctance falters during a scene set in a cheap hotel room. Bart says that he can get a job demonstrating guns for Remington, but his wife says a salesman's salary can't buy the lifestyle she wants. She reiterates her desire to rob a bank, and Bart, quickly growing disillusioned with her, asks how long the idea has been brewing. She says she "always" had the idea, and, in a line that's at once perfunctory and poetic, he responds: "I didn't think we'd had it figured out that way." His line is perfect: The use of the "we" pronoun infers that even though Laurie is suggesting something he abhors, he's still committed to their relationship, and the use of the past tense ("had it figured") reveals that on some level, Bart suspected Laurie's true nature all along. Bart's complicity is an important point, because Kantor and Trumbo make utterly clear that Bart is not an unsuspecting victim of Laurie's wiles. This essential subtext—that Bart is doomed finally not by his obsession with guns but his love for Laurie—is what gives *Gun Crazy* its punch.

Laurie finally persuades Bart to become a criminal by threatening to leave him if he doesn't. The movie then cuts to a montage of holdups, which marks a notable transition; Bart previously was portrayed as a decent, misguided sort able to deal with other people until they pushed him into a corner. But now that he's part of Laurie's world, he is, in effect, always pushed into a corner. The lovers have proven Packett's description of them as "a couple of animals," and their world—symbolized by the steel box of their getaway car—is a cage.

After a few jobs, Bart tells Laurie that he's had enough, but in classic crime movie fashion, she convinces him to do "just one more" heist. During a dramatically staged robbery, Laurie, fearing capture, shoots two people. She and Bart escape with a heap of loot, and they seem ready to start a new life together until Bart reads a news report indicating that the two people Laurie shot are dead. "Two people dead—just so we can live without working!" he exclaims. Laurie tells Bart he's not complicit in the deaths, but he disagrees: "I'm as guilty as you are—I've just let you do my killing for me." Finally pushed to real honesty by extreme circumstances, Laurie confesses to the murder she committed in St. Louis. Offering Bart one more chance to escape her influence—and her likely fate—Laurie says he can leave. He refuses, adding sadly: "We go together, Laurie. I don't know why. Maybe like guns and ammunition go together."

Among the most stylized lines in the film, this is as introspective a statement as Bart ever makes about why he's so willing to accompany Laurie along the downward spiral. If the film has a glaring shortcoming, it's that it plays verbal games with explaining the characters' motivations but never offers concrete

During the blacklist era, Trumbo wrote an eclectic group of films using various pseudonyms. One of the best B movies to which he contributed during the 1950s was *Gun Crazy*, starring John Dall and Peggy Cummins as lovers on a crime spree. (United Artists)

explanations. In a less meticulously structured picture, leaving motivations unspoken could be written off as justifiable ambiguity, but because *Gun Crazy* is in every other way a well-oiled piece of machinery, the absence of explanation more concrete that "we go together" feels like superficiality. This superficiality, finally, is what defines *Gun Crazy* as a B movie even though so many of the picture's elements define it as something more.

After Bart declares that he's with Laurie for better or worse, the lovers embark on a night on the town that gets cut short when they realize the stolen money they're spending has put the police on their trail. They flee the city, hop onto a freight train, and ride to Bart's hometown, Cashville.

By the time the lovers arrive at Ruby's house, word of their exploits has reached Cashville, so the filmmakers get tremendous mileage out of the tension between Ruby and Laurie. Ruby represents Bart's old, lawful life, and Laurie represents his career in crime. The interplay between these two characters is one of the innumerable devices the filmmakers use to foreshadow Bart's fate—and to underline that he chose his fate because of his love for Laurie. The fugitives hide at Ruby's house until Dave and Clyde, suspecting Bart's plan, show up to confront him. Bart seals his fate by telling them he won't surrender.

After a hasty escape, during which Laurie disgusts Bart by proposing to take one of Ruby's toddlers as a hostage, Bart and Laurie speed into the mountains outside Cashville. Having Bart flee to a place that figured prominently in his childhood brings the story full circle and cues viewers that the end is near. Such obvious cues, which are inserted throughout the film, mark the confident handiwork of Trumbo the screenwriting veteran; he and Kantor structured the film's story so that viewers could be intimately involved in each new plot development. The hazard of this method, to which *Gun Crazy* occasionally succumbs, is that plot events too explicitly foreshadowed become predictable.

The film's last sequence begins when Laurie and Bart ditch their car and rush into the woods on foot with the barking of dogs, a distant reminder that their pursuers aren't far behind. Laurie and Bart, pushed beyond exhaustion, fall asleep on a mound of dirt in the middle of a fog-drenched swamp. After a dissolve conveys the passage of some time, the lovers wake to the splashing of feet in the marsh. At first, Laurie and Bart are unsure if they're hallucinating; they hear people approaching but, because of the thick fog, can't see them. Reality soon sets in, and Bart realizes it's time for whatever declaration he's going to make: "Laurie, no matter what happens, I wouldn't have it any other way," he says before kissing Laurie passionately. This line completes the arc that has been established by every line and action that illustrated Bart's complicity in Laurie's crime spree; it tells viewers that Bart is not a martyr to love but its willing victim.

Clyde's offscreen voice announces that Laurie and Bart are surrounded, and now we start seeing silhouettes of the figures approaching the fugitives. Laurie gets scared, and prepares to shoot, even hissing the line, "I'll kill you!" several times. To save his friends, Bart shoots Laurie, and the pursuers respond by riddling Bart with bullets. The film ends with Dave and Clyde standing over the lovers' bodies, wondering how fate brought them to this conclusion.

One last reason why *Gun Crazy* occupies a crucial place in Trumbo's *oeuvre* is that it shows how his depiction of personal honor changed in the blacklist era. In the last of his major pre-blacklist films, *Our Vines Have Tender Grapes*, honor is represented by a young girl selflessly giving her prized calf to a needy neighbor, and this representation is consistent with the straightforward parallel Trumbo drew throughout his early films between honor and self sacrifice. (He returned to this parallel in later films, of course, notably *Roman Holiday*.) But in his dark blacklist-era films, Trumbo treats honor differently.

The lovers in *Gun Crazy* are not honorable by moral standards—they lie, cheat, and steal—but they are honorable in that they're true to themselves. Even when he realizes staying with Laurie will get him killed, Bart doesn't give up on her. This manifestation of personal honor is a twisted relation of how personal honor is depicted in Trumbo's strongest post-blacklist films; in *Spartacus*, *Exodus*, *The Fixer*, and *Papillon*, rebellious characters defy governments and other ruling bodies to pursue higher callings. Characters such as Spartacus, Ari Ben Canaan in *Exodus*, Yakov Bok in *The Fixer*, and Papillon are at once lawless and righteous. *Gun Crazy*, then, is the juncture at which Trumbo's screenwriting started to acquire the complexity that distinguishes his latter-day writing from the rosy simplicity of his pre-blacklist films.

❖ ❖ ❖

The script for the next Trumbo film released during the blacklist era, *The Prowler*, was the last he wrote before entering jail. Trumbo's front on the picture was his good friend Hugo Butler (who also did rewrites), and the screenplay was based on a story by Robert Thoeren and Hans Wilhelm.[11] Like *Jealousy*, *Gun Crazy*, and Trumbo's other important noir, *He Ran All the Way*, *The Prowler* is a dark romance filled with jealousy, betrayal, and danger. Despite some offbeat elements and a generally compelling seediness, the film's story of a low-rent policeman driven to criminal acts by his obsessive love for a married woman has appeared, with its variables shifted, in virtually every memorable film noir, from black-and-white classics including *Double Indemnity* (1944, Paramount) and *Out of the Past* (1947, RKO) to modern, color thrillers such as *Body Heat* (1981, Warner Bros.) and *Basic Instinct* (1991, Caralco).

The wrinkle that gives *The Prowler* its tension is that the story's principal female character isn't a *femme fatale*; instead, she's relatively innocent whose only crime is letting loneliness drive her into the arms of a man who isn't her husband. Also, an intense twist at the end of the picture—in which the story's lovers run away to a ghost town to hide the birth of their child—is one of several touches that add to the picture's bleak mood of pervasive danger.

The Prowler was one of last American films made by noted director Joseph Losey,[12] who moved to Europe after getting blacklisted in the early 1950s. Although he earned his greatest acclaim for understated European films including *The Servant* (1963, Elstree) and *Accident* (1967, London Independent Producers), Losey won a fair amount of attention for his stylish direction of *The Prowler*, which accentuated the eerie mood of Trumbo's screenplay with devices including long takes and high-key lighting. Losey biographer David Caute noted the following about the picture:

> The original [Thoeren-Wilhem] story and script ... was "pretty awful," Losey recalled. [Producer Sam] Spiegel called in Dalton Trumbo ... who (Losey observed) "lived incredibly in a vast, incongruous place somewhere in the mountains outside Hollywood, where he'd built his own trout lake and imported Italian marble and French antique furnishings...." According to Trumbo, he wrote two drafts for Losey, for which he received $7,500.... Trumbo was paid a princely $35 for playing, uncredited, the radio voice of the cuckolded husband—a fine gesture of ironic bravado.[13]

The movie's setup is graceful and involving. Policeman Webb Garwood (Van Heflin) responds to a report of a prowler at the home of beautiful Susan Gilvray (Evelyn Keyes), accompanied by his somewhat thick partner, Bud Crocker (John Maxwell). There's an immediate attraction between Webb and Susan, so Webb ends his first visit to Susan's house with a promise to check in on her again. After an interlude that puts across expositional information about a remote ghost town at which Bud indulges his hobby of looking for rare mineral specimens, Webb visits Susan again.

In a deft, erotic scene, the two discover that they're both from the same region of Indiana—he was an East Indianapolis high school basketball star who played against Susan's school, Terre Haute, and she used to clip his pictures from the local paper. Webb and Susan also reveal that they both have unfulfilled dreams. His temper led to a disagreement with a coach that ruined his sports career; she wanted to become an actress. In one of the picture's most unusual devices, Susan reveals that she's married by indicating that the voice of the all-night deejay on the radio is that of her husband, John Gilvray.[14] This revelation adds a fine level of tension to the flirtation, because John is effectively "present" while his wife is being seduced by Webb.

When John comes home in the morning and learns of the prowler incident, he gives her a gun for protection. That this decision will later prove foolhardy would have been phenomenally predictable even if it wasn't nearly identical to a plot development in *Jealousy*.

The illicit romance between Webb and Susan grows more intense than either of them expected, and when a guilt-ridden Webb tries to break off the affair, Susan becomes the aggressor—despite Webb's warnings that he won't be able to give Susan the comfortable lifestyle to which she is accustomed. Webb eventually convinces Susan to give up the affair, but their parting leaves him in an inconsolable funk until there's another report of a prowler at the Gilvray house. He visits the house and encounters John, who is holding the gun he had given to Susan. Mistaking Webb for the prowler, John aims at Webb, but Webb shoots first, killing John.

By this point, the intense, seamy little film has developed a strong rhythm. Plot points are introduced rapidly, but before any one of them pays off, another has been introduced, so the picture is like a daisy chain of dramatic elements. For instance, the gun is introduced into the story, but before the gun element pays off with John's "accidental" death, the element of Webb and Susan's breakup is introduced. Then, after the gun element pays off, a new element—a court trial—is introduced before the breakup element climaxes in a reconciliation scene.

Even though *The Prowler* is ultimately a minor film because it traffics in familiar subject matter, the ingenuity with which dramatic tension is created makes the picture a fine display of Trumbo's craftsmanship, with an appropriate nod to Butler's contributions. At his best, Trumbo was able to marry well-oiled plots to witty dialogue and a strong theme; at his worst, he merely constructed plots by rote so that a semblance of drama was created even if it wasn't activated by the complementary elements of surprise, personality, and wit. More often than not, though, what Trumbo ended up doing was something halfway between these two extremes. *The Prowler* is an example of this middle ground: The picture has sparks of intensity, as in the scene of Webb seducing Susan in the "presence" of her husband, but it is often routine.

The plot's momentum takes over following John's death. In a far-fetched courtroom scene, Susan (who believes that Webb killed John intentionally) and Webb both lie by saying that they had never met before the night of John's death. Even after the prosecuting attorney proves that they met earlier by producing a police report of Webb's first visit to the Gilvray house, the lovers sway the court into ruling John's death an "accidental homicide."

After Webb convinces Susan of his innocence—and after enough time passes to avoid unwanted attention—they wed and use the money that Susan inherited from John to buy a motel outside of Las Vegas. Then Susan realizes she's pregnant. Because it was established earlier in the movie that John was incapable of impregnating her, the newlyweds realize they have to hide the birth of the baby from the eyes of the public, lest the timing reveal that they were lovers prior to John's death.

At this point the picture starts to get really interesting, if somewhat over baked. Susan's illegitimate pregnancy is dealt with in strong terms, given the conservative mores of the early 1950s; also, the couple's response to the pregnancy reeks of such desperation that it quickly raises the stakes of the movie. Webb and Susan leave Las Vegas for the ghost town that Bud mentioned earlier in the film, with the intention of having the baby there and then laying low until enough time has passed to create the illusion that the baby was conceived after John's death. What isn't said, but what clearly must be on the minds of the lovers, is that their child's age will always brand them as liars, so the birth of their baby signals the end of their freedom. This cynical twist, in which a joyous event becomes an ominous one, is what makes *The Prowler*, like *Gun Crazy*, true noir.

In a convenient plot development, Bud makes a trip to visit the newlyweds in Las Vegas, and discovers they've left their motel. He guesses that they've gone to the ghost town for some privacy, then heads to the ghost town to visit them, all the while ignorant of Webb's illicit activities.

Susan has difficulty during labor,

so Webb abducts a physician, Doctor James (Wheaton Chambers), and forces him, at gunpoint, to help Susan. Seeing Webb act like a brazen criminal, Susan realizes that he isn't the man she thought him to be, so she helps the doctor escape. This leads to a heated confrontation with Webb, during which he admits that he killed John on purpose because he wanted Susan and the $62,000 she stood to inherit.

Meanwhile, police summoned by the doctor converge on the ghost town, and Bud arrives in time to learn that his friend has become a criminal. Crazed with anger at Susan's "betrayal," Webb rushes from the building in which Susan is cradling her newborn and is confronted by Bud and the police. Like the lovers in *Gun Crazy* who choose their own fates, Webb pulls his gun and gets shot dead.

❖   ❖   ❖

He Ran All the Way is an intense but stagy drama that squeezes an impressive amount of character, pathos, and emotional violence into 77 minutes. The story of a small time crook who finds safe haven in the apartment of a working-class family that he subsequently terrorizes, the picture is by design intimate and short on explosive events. Instead of revealing the criminal's character by showing him tangling with police or other criminals, the picture offers dark satire by contrasting his twisted mindset with the warmth of a loving family. In a sense, the criminal becomes the family's surrogate black sheep, drawing out their prejudices and fears.

Using future blacklistee Guy Endore as a front, Trumbo adapted the screenplay from Sam Ross's novel, *He Ran All the Way*, and the project was helmed by John Berry, who was blacklisted shortly after the release of the film. Berry recalled the project's development:

> Hugo Butler, quite frankly, kept me from fucking up Dalton's script. Dalton did one script. Then Jack Moss went away with me, and we thought we'd fixed up Dalton's script. What we actually did was make some romantic piece of shit out of it, although we did find an ending that was quite extraordinary. When we came back, everybody was upset, so Hugo [Butler] was put on the script. Hugo hated our script, said it was all bullshit. So he fixed our script by going back to Dalton's, although Hugo got the credit.[15]

The most poignant of the picture's various blacklist connections involves star John Garfield, a sensitive actor who earned Oscar nominations for his performances in *Four Daughters* (1938, Warner Brothers) and *Body and Soul* (1947, Enterprise). Prior to making *He Ran All the Way*, Garfield was subpoenaed by HUAC—but not because of his own activities. Instead, the committee wanted him to name friends who were communists. Garfield's refusal got him blacklisted, and *He Ran All the Way* was his last picture. As writer-director Abraham Polonsky, himself a blacklistee, recalled:

> [Garfield] said that he hated communists, he hated communism, he was an American. He told the committee what it wanted to hear. But he wouldn't say the one thing that would keep him from walking down his old neighborhood block.... [I]n his mind he lives in the street where he comes from and in the street where he comes from,

you're not a stool pigeon. That's the ultimate horror.[16]

The picture is brutal from its first scene. Asleep in his mother's dingy New York apartment, lowlife Nick Robey (Garfield) is shocked awake when his mother, Mrs. Robey (Gladys George), snaps the blinds open and lets in the morning light. The animosity between them is revealed in a violent exchange. "If you were a man, you'd be out looking for a job," Mrs. Robey snarls.

"If you were a man, I'd kick your teeth in," Nick responds.

The argument escalates until Mrs. Robey slaps Nick and hisses, "I'll *kill* you for talkin' like that," to which Nick blithely retorts: "You're losin' your punch, Ma."

Nick hooks up with his hoodlum friend Al Molin (Norman Lloyd), who has convinced Nick to participate in a robbery. Validating Nick's bad premonition about the crime, he and Al steal $10,000 in payroll money, then run into a policeman. The cop shoots Al, then Nick shoots the cop. Now alone and panic stricken, Nick blends into the first crowd that he finds, a line of people waiting to get into a public pool. Once he gets into the pool's locker room, legendary cinematographer James Wong Howe provides one of the film's many startling compositions. With the camera positioned above a claustrophobic dressing room and angling down through the room's chicken wire ceiling, Nick is trapped in a corner of the room as he struggles with a stolen briefcase, trying to extract the $10,000 in cash. Echoing the vibrant imagery of *Gun Crazy*, this shot describes Nick as an animal who thinks himself free but is really just moving from cage to cage.

To wait out the police who are searching the area around the pool, Nick makes conversation with plain, gullible Peg Dobbs (Shelley Winters). Stupidly ignoring the flashes of violence she sees in Nick's manner, Peg invites Nick into the apartment she shares with her father, Fred (Wallace Ford); her mother, identified only as Mrs. Dobbs (Selena Royle); and her little brother, Tommy (Bob Hyatt). After the others depart for a movie, Nick tries to stay cool while Peg tries to accommodate her fidgety suitor. The tension between the couple surfaces in a moment featuring another of Howe's fantastic shots. Nick, framed in the foreground, looks out one of the apartment's windows while Peg, in the background, asks if he wants to go out. After hissing, "I don't want to go out," Nick pulls the curtain closed, providing a potent visual metaphor for his plans to hide in the apartment—and reiterating the cage imagery from the locker room scene.

When Peg's family returns, a misunderstanding trips Nick's nerves and leads him to not only reveal his identity but announce his plan of hiding in the apartment for the night. With the film's central device established, the picture goes through a few predictable developments in which Nick becomes more and more violent, Peg appeals to Nick's almost-nonexistent soft side, and Fred begins to see Nick's siege as an attack on his masculinity.

But not all that occurs during the siege is formulaic. In one of the picture's most creative scenes, Nick has Tommy fetch a lavish turkey dinner, but Fred—letting his feelings of emasculation manifest in a foolish act of defiance—refuses to eat the food, explaining that his family will tolerate Nick's presence but not indulge Nick's delusions of "belonging."

Nick spits out an indignant response: "You'll eat my dinner or one of you walks out of here with a bullet in his head!" The dinner scene has an unexpectedly touching denouement: After Nick uses his gun to make the Dobbs family eat his food, he loses his appetite and walks to another room to drink in solitude, having made himself unwelcome at the "family dinner" by his objectionable behavior. This sad image reiterates Nick's characterization as a black sheep.

It's in scenes such as this one that *He Ran All the Way* makes the most of its storyline by illustrating that Nick might have, on a subconscious level, gravitated toward the Dobbs household because he desired an environment as loving as his own home was hateful. A subsequent film with a similar plot, *The Desperate Hours* (1955, Paramount), added the useful element of contrasting the working-class nature of its villains with the suburban lifestyle of their hostages; this effectively made *The Desperate Hours* a comment on the gap between haves and have-nots, a theme with which Trumbo would likely have run wild were it integrated into *He Ran All the Way*. But because both Nick and Peg are working class, *He Ran All the Way* is less about Nick trying to appropriate Peg's life than it is about a personality clash between members of the same social class. Therefore, the portrayal of Peg, who apparently shunts from right to wrong—in so doing spurring her father's maddening rage—is the most provocative aspect of the picture.[17]

Peg's turnabout occurs late in the film, by which point it has been implied that she and Nick have had sex. She tells her father that she's running away with Nick, adding that she just spent $1,500 of Nick's stolen money on a getaway car.

An appalled Fred confronts his daughter with dialogue that reflects the unrelentingly harsh tone of the film: "Do you think he loves you? He doesn't know what the word means. When he has no more use for you, he'll leave you. Kill you—kill you and stuff your body in a culvert."

At the end of the argument, Fred storms out of the apartment and encounters Mrs. Dobbs and Tommy, who are returning from church. Fred leads the others out of the building, leaving Peg alone in the apartment with Nick as the "lovers" await delivery of their car. Although it seems a stretch of credibility that Nick would allow Fred to leave, the screenwriters clearly imply that Nick feels emboldened by Peg's show of faith. His confidence fades as hours pass and night falls, then dissipates when he hears a police siren approaching the building. He draws his gun and points it at Peg. The constant turnabouts in Nick's relationship with Peg underline that Nick can't escape his criminal nature, and that he's been treated so badly throughout his life that he can't even trust a woman who apparently loves him.

After the siren passes, a frenzied Nick grabs Peg and leads her out of the apartment and down several flights of stairs—a descent photographed so darkly and dramatically by Howe that the allusion to Dante's nine levels of hell is unmistakable. Falling apart as he hurtles down the stairs, Nick berates Peg with hard-hitting dialogue created by Butler during one of the script's many rewrites: "Nobody loves anybody! You, your old man, your family, the cops, my old lady—Al Molin—garbage. Garbage!"

The picture's ending is as bleak as its beginning. Nick and Peg reach the ground floor of her building and discover that Fred is waiting outside with a gun. Fred fires a warning shot that makes Nick drop his gun, which Peg picks up. After a wonderful exchange of tight, sweaty close-ups revealing Nick's terror and Peg's despair, Peg shoots Nick, prompting him to moan the unfinished line, "You've got as much love in you as..." In a metaphor that has appeared in various forms in countless films noir, Nick stumbles out into the street and falls into a gutter to die. But just before Nick expires, the car that Peg bought is delivered: Until the moment that he turned on her by threatening her with his gun, Peg hadn't betrayed Nick after all. His string of tragic mistakes now complete, Nick dies and the last cue of Franz Waxman's thunderous score signals the movie's conclusion.

In her second memoir, Winters described a haunting undertone to the conclusion of *He Ran All the Way*:

> When we got to that last scene, in which I was supposed to shoot [Garfield's character] because of what he had done to my family, John suddenly looked at me like an enemy. He flatly refused to let me do the scene. He wanted "the police" to kill him, which made no sense as far as the writer and director of the film were concerned. Now, in retrospect, I understand he didn't want *a friend* to kill him. (I think a friend had named him before HUAC.) He wanted a nameless force, a blur. "Let the police do it."[18]

Garfield died less than a year after making *He Ran All the Way*, and many of his associates suggest that the actor had something akin to a death wish following his HUAC ordeal. Looking at all of the blacklisted talent involved in the picture, it is wrenching to note the swath that HUAC cut through liberal

Hollywood—and inspiring to see that artists such as Garfield, Berry, Butler, and Trumbo responded to persecution by attacking social issues more vigorously than ever before.

So, even though it treads a path already well worn by *Gun Crazy*, *The Prowler*, and numerous other films, the taut and occasionally disquieting *He Ran All the Way* is among several films to indicate that when Trumbo let the darkest parts of his soul sing on screen, he was often at his most eloquent. Moreover, the picture underlines the way that Trumbo's depiction of personal honor changed in the blacklist era. In *Gun Crazy* and *He Ran All the Way*, disenfranchised characters use criminal means in their quest for belonging and validation. Bart and Laurie come to life when they use their guns to commit crimes; Nick sees flashes of love in his twisted relationship with Peg. All of these characters are torn, on some level, between doing right and succumbing to their weaknesses, and it's telling that the characters who die in these films—notwithstanding innocent victims caught in the crossfire—are those who cannot overcome their violent instincts. Bart, Laurie, and Nick all die because of who they are, victims of their own misguided integrity. That their stories were brought to the screen by a man who paid a high price for his own integrity underlines the poignancy of films such as *Gun Crazy* and *He Ran All the Way*.

❖ ❖ ❖

The authorship of *Roman Holiday* has been scrutinized more than that of any other picture in Trumbo's *oeuvre*. Trumbo put his original screenplay on the market under the name of his friend Ian McLellan Hunter,[19] and it was bought by Paramount. Drafts by Preston Sturges, Ben Hecht, and others were discarded; the draft that director William Wyler took with him to Rome was Hunter's rewrite of Trumbo's script. Wyler hired British writer John Dighton to polish the script and write new scenes during production, so Hunter and Dighton shared the screenplay credit on the film when it was released in 1953.

In recent years, however, it has come to light that enough of the ideas from Trumbo's original script—including, most importantly, his bittersweet ending—survived that *Roman Holiday* is generally conceded to be largely his creation.

Aside from the controversy surrounding its credits, *Roman Holiday* is notable in that its historical stature is inextricably linked to the enduring enigma of one of its stars. Although several of Trumbo's pictures are forever wed to their leading actors—*Kitty Foyle* and Ginger Rogers, *A Guy Named Joe* and Spencer Tracy, *Spartacus* and Kirk Douglas—virtually none of Trumbo's pictures are as closely associated with a particular performer as *Roman Holiday* is with Audrey Hepburn.

A former ballerina who honed her enchanting persona in minor European films prior to making a smash on Broadway as *Gigi* and then landing the lead role in *Roman Holiday*, Hepburn made a spectacular Hollywood debut as Princess Ann, instantly rising to the top echelon of movie stardom and winning an Academy Award for her performance. The character of the aristocrat with a playful spirit so fit Hepburn's demeanor—and the role's royal air, her unique beauty—that Ann set the tone for many of Hepburn's significant roles. The tension between duty and frivolity that she puts across is the movie's spirit.

Trumbo's vision of *Roman Holiday* is that rare thing, a modern fairy tale. The movie addresses themes that run through myriad Trumbo stories—duty, honor, honesty, rebellion, and individualism—yet it primarily entertains. Trumbo, Hunter, and Dighton achieved a near-perfect balance of thematics, dramatics, and pure enchantment, and their fine efforts were elevated to something timeless by Wyler's sure direction, costar Gregory Peck's rock of a performance, and, most of all, Hepburn's elusive magic.

The picture opens, à la *Citizen Kane*, with a faux newsreel about Princess Ann's goodwill trip through Europe. The clips in the newsreel show a robotic Ann waving to crowds and greeting dignitaries, and the newsreel's narrator hints at forthcoming events with his comment that Ann isn't showing signs of strain despite "continuous public appearances."

Next, the filmmakers stage a playful, almost dialogue-free entrance for Hepburn. During an official function, she stands uncomfortably on a platform while greeting dignitaries. Beneath her long gown, she kicks off one of her shoes. When her aides notice that she can't get the shoe back on, they scramble to cover for her, implying that Ann's impetuous behavior necessitates special handling and that her every move is scrutinized. Later, Ann laments that it is preposterous for her, a teenager, to spend her whole life following ancient traditions. "I'm not 200 years old!" she says. Her aides react by having a doctor give Ann a sedative, but before the drug kicks in, Ann slips out of an embassy window to explore Rome.

The film then cuts to a poker game at which American reporter Joe Bradley (Peck) and photographer Irving Radovich (Eddie Albert) are introduced. The jaded friends chat nonchalantly about Ann's forthcoming press conference, which they have to attend the next day. Strolling through Rome after the poker game, Joe discovers Ann, now woozy from the sedative and napping on a public bench. The filmmakers have fun with this scene, in which Ann recites polite babble in a drugged stream ("Thank you very much. Delighted. No thank you. Charmed.") while inadvertently revealing her breeding with a literary quote and articulate diction.

Joe hails a cab, intending to drop Ann at her home, but because of the sedative, she can't remember where she lives. He reluctantly decides to let her crash on his couch. When they retire for the evening, Joe is more amused by Ann than attracted to her, but a faint sexual connotation arises when she comments that she's never been alone with a man before. That the film doesn't make any overt references to the sexual undertones of the scene is reflective of the picture's intentions and methodology; although the sexual tension between the characters is addressed later in the story, the filmmakers avoid the ploy of suggesting that Joe is physically attracted to Ann from the moment they meet, because to do so would make his subsequent actions seem salacious.

The next morning, Joe wakes to discover that he's missed his appointment for Ann's press conference, still unaware that she's the woman sleeping in his apartment. He soon realizes her identity, however, and conjures a plan through which, he hopes, a newspaper story about Ann will earn him enough money to return to America. Joe visits the offices of the English language paper for which he writes, and tantalizes his editor, Hennessy (Hartley Power), by offering "the private and secret longings of a princess ... as revealed to your Rome correspondent in a private, personal, exclusive interview."

Hennessy's lust for an exploitative story has a certain poignancy for modern viewers, because it echoes the ravenous paparazzi mentality that contributed to the August 1997 car crash in which Diana Spencer, Princess of Wales, was killed. The parallels between Ann and Diana are numerous: Both are beautiful young royals idolized by a public eager to devour tales of their peccadilloes. In truth, though, the member of the Windsor family to whom Ann bears perhaps the strongest resemblance is Princess Margaret—whose various romantic entanglements won her a place in the gossip pages of the era in which *Roman Holiday* was made.

Within about 15 minutes, the film puts us inside the head of a restless royal, lays out the fanciful scenario by which Joe ends up in the catbird seat, and frames the moral parable of the film by establishing that Joe will pursue his interview under false pretenses. The decency he showed in getting Ann off the street hints that he'll eventually have qualms with his unethical plan, a necessary bit of foreshadowing. The portrayal of journalists as cynical opportunists is the only real concession to modern attitudes in the sequence, for in every other regard the story could as easily take place in the nineteenth century as the twentieth.

After getting authorization from Hennessy to pursue the interview, Joe persuades Ann to join him and Irving on a frolic through Rome because, as he says, "Today's a holiday." The picture then slips into a series of silly adventures that result in the couple's arrest. Joe talks them out of trouble by saying that they were rushing to their wedding, sparking a pointed exchange.

"Joe's a wonderful liar," Irving notes.

"I'm a good liar too, aren't I, Mr. Bradley?" Ann asks.

"The best I ever met," Joe says.

Reinforcing that Ann is lying about who she is takes the edge off of Joe's duplicity and also makes them seem two of a kind. Furthermore, the ease with which they fall into their pretense of being an engaged couple hints at the romantic spark between them.

The picture's most famous scene occurs at the tail end of the afternoon romp, when Joe and Ann visit a Roman tourist spot called the Mouth of Truth—a bas-relief stone sculpture of a foreboding face with a deep black hole for a mouth. Joe explains that according to myth, any liar's hand inserted into the sculpture's mouth will be bitten off. So, as composer Georges Auric provides suspenseful string music on the movie's underscore, Joe sticks his hand in, squeals with pain, and withdraws his arm—which is now missing a hand. Ann shrieks until he reveals that he merely pulled his hand into his sleeve. She collapses in relieved laughter and falls into her first embrace with Joe, thereby slyly advancing the romantic tension of the story.[20]

That night, Joe escorts Ann to a romantic dancing spot, and Joe is visibly uncomfortable when Ann compliments his kindness; this moment reveals not only that Joe is falling for Ann, but that her innocence is shaming him. Then, government agents from Ann's embassy catch up with her, and a comical brawl

The best-known film that Trumbo conceived under a pseudonym, *Roman Holiday* stars Audrey Hepburn as a European princess who tosses aside her royal obligations to enjoy a romantic adventure. (Paramount Pictures)

breaks out. Joe and Ann escape by jumping in a river and swimming away. They climb up the opposite shore and nestle against a tall tree, shivering and wet, and after some small talk, Joe suddenly kisses Ann. Wyler stages the moment wonderfully, conveying the combination of affection and attraction that led to the kiss but also, in the way the pair draw away from each other after the kiss, their knowledge that their situation is impossible. This ties into the film's well-structured pattern of overt foreshadowing, because the scene with which the couple's intimacy is turned back to polite distance functions as a clue to nature of the picture's conclusion.

The foreshadowing in *Roman Holiday* works on two levels: It provides necessary information so that plot developments seem credible when they occur, and it warms viewers what to expect so that their hopes for another conclusion are not too badly dashed. As with so many of Trumbo's pictures that employ foreshadowing, the manner in which events in *Roman Holiday* are "telegraphed" takes some of the surprise out of the story—one of its few shortcomings.

Following the kiss, the couple return to Joe's apartment and make strained small talk until an American radio broadcast interrupts them with a story about Ann's "illness"—explained in a previous scene as the cover story being used by her embassy. The radio announcer says that Ann's malady is "causing alarm and anxiety" among her countrymen; although one of the clumsiest devices used in the picture, the radio broadcast defines the presence that has come between Joe and Ann, even though neither has yet revealed his or her secret to the other. Ann turns off the radio,

commenting sadly that, "The news can wait till tomorrow."

Echoing the dancing scene, during which Ann's sweetness made Joe aware of his duplicity, her declaration that she doesn't want to hear the news shows that it's hard for her to shirk her duty. Ann announces her intention to head home and fusses at packing her things before happening into Joe's arms and bursting into tears. The staging of this moment is similar to the haphazard intimacy of the Mouth of Truth scene, and it's interesting to note that even though both scenes create the illusion of Ann bracing herself against Joe, they are instead instances in which Ann—first inadvertently and then intentionally—tastes the life she can't have, in the person of a commoner's loving embrace. After the first embrace, Ann pulled herself away and regained her royal composure; after the second, she pulls away to fulfill her royal duty. Seen this way, the embraces are less about Joe giving Ann strength than they are about her resting a moment before exerting her own strength.

Joe drives Ann to the embassy, and the filmmakers wring sweet emotion from the way that neither member of the couple addresses the secret revealed by her destination. Hepburn's performance reaches its emotional crescendo with her plaintive good-bye. "I have to leave you now," she says. "I'm going to go to that corner there and turn. You must stay in the car and drive away. Promise not to watch me go beyond the corner. Just drive away and leave me—as I leave you."

"All right," Joe weakly responds.

"I don't know how to say good-bye," Ann continues. "I can't think of any words."

"Don't try," Joe says.

The pained exchange concludes with the couple kissing for the second and final time before Ann leaves Joe's car and walks back to face her destiny. Joe, stunned, waits a long moment before realizing that she isn't coming back, then drives away. The grace note to this poignant good-bye is a scene set inside the embassy. As Ann returns "home," aides swarm around her and buzz with questions. Taking the emotionalism of the farewell scene to a new level, Hepburn delivers curt dialogue that, because it contains a gravity not visible elsewhere in her performance, reveals the maturity her character won by leaving Joe:

"Were I not completely aware of my duty to my family and my country. I would not have come back tonight— or indeed ever again. Now, since I understand we have a very full schedule today, you have my permission to withdraw."

This dialogue is among the most overt commentaries on duty and personal honor in all of Trumbo's films. It reflects ideas expressed by John Abbott in *A Man to Remember*, Andrew and his undead colleagues in *The Remarkable Andrew*, the General in *A Guy Named Joe*, and Martinius in *Our Vines Have Tender Grapes*. In all of these films, Trumbo expresses the idea that duty supersedes personal gratification; in all of these films save *The Remarkable Andrew*, characters sacrifice a cherished goal to do what they believe to be right. This noble sentiment permeates Trumbo's films, even the latter-day ones; characters in *Spartacus*, *The Fixer*, and *Papillon* also suffer for their beliefs. And while the point has already been made in this book that Trumbo echoed this noble sentiment in his private life, the parallel between Trumbo's principled characters and his principled behavior is perhaps the most import lesson gleaned from studying his cinematic output.

The morning after Joe returns Ann to the embassy, he informs Irving and Hennessy that he didn't get the exclusive interview he promised. Irving is bewildered by Joe's sudden attack of conscience, and Hennessy bellows that the interview was just one more of Joe's empty promises. Eager to discipline him but trapped by a tight schedule, Hennessy sends Joe, and Irving, to Ann's long-delayed press conference.

Once out of Hennessy's earshot, Irving tries to persuade Joe into writing about Ann. "She's fair game," Irving argues. "It's always open season on princesses." Seen through modern eyes, this line hammers the parallel between Ann and Princess Diana, particularly with the hunting allusion. This modern connotation makes the nobility of Joe's decision to protect Ann's secret seem all the more special. But even deprived of its relationship to a 1997 tragedy, the scene in which Joe honors Ann's privacy is rewarding. In its original context, Joe's sacrifice mirrors Ann's: She gave up freedom to fulfill her duty, so he gives up easy money to justify her love.

At the press conference, Ann reacts anxiously when she sees Joe and Irving among the press corps. The filmmakers give the never-to-be lovers a way to communicate secret messages, however, and the grace of this scene suggests that all concerned were operating at the height of their powers. When asked a question about the future of international peace, Ann says: "I have every faith in it—as I have faith in relations between people." Looking deep into Ann's eyes from across the room, Joe interjects: "May I say, speaking for my own press service, we believe that your highness's faith will not be unjustified." This eloquent line lets Joe simultaneously reveal his identity and tell Ann that her secrets are safe. Next, Ann is asked which of the stops on her European tour she most enjoyed. Wyler cuts between close-ups of Peck and Hepburn before Ann answers: "Each in its own way was unforgettable. It would be difficult to—Rome. By all means, Rome. I will cherish my visit here as long as I live."

The strength with which Hepburn's voice says "Rome" the first time is like a declaration of independence, and it shows how the princess has been changed by her experience: Now, instead of spewing puffery, she'll speak her mind. This final parallel between Ann and Diana, the outspoken "people's princess," offers an exclamation point to *Roman Holiday*'s enduring relevance. Following the question-and-answer session, Ann shakes hands with the members of the press corps. When Ann reaches Joe, they share a brief moment in which they aren't wearing masks. Ann departs the press conference and takes a sad, final look at Joe, but in the movie's last shot, he walks away with reflection, not sadness, playing on his features. The touching inference is that, for the first time in years, this jaded reporter has just experienced something he didn't anticipate. He was as revitalized by the adventure as Ann.

❖ ❖ ❖

Just months after the enchanting *Roman Holiday* was released, two pictures that collectively represent the nadir of Trumbo's blacklist-era output were unleashed upon an unsuspecting world.

Although Trumbo had, up to this point, subsisted on a diet of last-minute re-writes and stories sold via fronts, it was still rare for him to be intimately involved with each stage of a black-market screenplay's development. One reason for this was the drastic drop in Trumbo's asking price—whereas he earned $75,000 per script at the apex of his MGM period, Trumbo got just $1,000 per script during the bleakest of his underground years. Therefore Trumbo concentrated on quantity, not quality, returning to the enterprising, formulaic style of writing that he employed while cranking out routine B films at Warner Bros. and RKO.

The first of Trumbo's 1954 quickies was *They Were So Young*, produced and directed by Kurt Neumann. An exploitative and chaotic thriller about models lured to Rio de Janeiro and then forced into a prostitution ring, *They Were So Young* was written by Trumbo from a scenario by fellow blacklistee Michael Wilson.[21] A close friend of Trumbo's whose spectacular work on the scripts of *A Place in the Sun* (1951, Paramount), *Friendly Persuasion* (1956, Allied Artists), *The Bridge on the River Kwai* (1957, Columbia), and *Lawrence of Arabia* (1962, Columbia) was crucially important to undermining the blacklist, Wilson showed as much enterprise during his underground years as Trumbo did in his—often by joining forces with him. As Wilson recalled:

> We decided we couldn't work together in the same room. Not many can.... [S]o we decided that we'd rely on what we called the "pony express" method. I did an extended treatment which I sent off to him a few pages at a time. When he had knocked out about 20 or 30 pages of screenplay from those

pages of the treatment, he would mail them to me, so that we were mailing stuff back and forth every day.²²

Although they were two of the most talented writers in the movie industry, neither man brought his full talent to bear on their blacklist-era collaborations. *They Were So Young* has a narrative so pulpy and contrived that it's more a balancing act than a feat of storytelling: Wilson shot ludicrous plot developments to Trumbo, who then struggled to find words with which to energize the plot. What resulted was an ugly mess filled with beatings, inferences of rape, and insipid chase scenes. Likely the most exploitative thing that Trumbo ever wrote, the picture deserves its anonymous place in film history.

Trumbo wrote Neumann's follow-up to *They Were So Young*, *Carnival Story*, without Wilson. The over-plotted drama has a claim for the distinction of Trumbo's worst screenplay—if only because of the stupidity of its denouement. A fast-moving and sexually provocative movie about a German girl who becomes a circus performer and gets enmeshed in romances with two of her coworkers, the film is a tangle of stops and starts. Despite its turgid narrative, the picture earned respectable notices and regularly appears on television. One of the strange truths of Trumbo's career is that while some of his best "little" films (including *Fugitives for a Night* and *The Boss*) are rarely shown, the comparatively inferior *Carnival Story* is still in distribution. The film's longevity may stem from its exploitative aspects more than anything else, though; even given the chaste presentation of carnal subject matter in 1950s films, *Carnival Story* has more sexual content than any Trumbo film prior to *Spartacus*.

More than anything else, *Carnival Story* traffics in skin—specifically that of star Anne Baxter, who spends most of the film in the revealing swimsuits her character wears to perform diving stunts. While the story does have a few interesting elements, such as the culture clash between American circus folk and the Germans with whom they interact, these elements are largely ignored in favor of scenes about sex, jealousy, and murder.

As mentioned above, though, the most memorable aspect of the film is its ludicrous ending. After Neanderthal-like strongman Groppo (Adi Berber) witnesses a quarrel between Willie (Baxter) and her lowlife suitor, Joe (Steve Cochran), Groppo chases Joe to the top of a tall amusement park ride. In a wild and jarring change of pace from the seedy bedroom drama of the rest of the film, Groppo tosses Joe to the ground in the manner of King Kong dispatching nettlesome biplanes. The scene is unforgivably stupid, in part because Groppo plays only a peripheral role in the rest of the movie. Yet the filmmakers milk the scene for pathos when Willie, moved by Groppo's selfless act, convinces him to surrender to the police, then moans, "Poor Groppo!"

Although there were certainly more bad movies in Trumbo's future—the 1958 science fiction picture, *From the Earth to the Moon*, for which Trumbo did a quick screenplay polish, is every bit as insipid as the two Neumann pictures released in 1954—Trumbo's next two films were a world removed from the lurid milieu of *They Were So Young* and *Carnival Story*. His first 1956 credit, *The Boss*, was another hard-hitting crime film, and his second, *The Brave One*, unexpectedly began the chain of events leading to his emergence from the underground.

❖ ❖ ❖

Featuring one of Trumbo's best blacklist-era scripts, *The Boss* is part of a long tradition of films exploring the connection between urban politics and organized crime. Chronologically, it falls between the tough Warner Bros. gangster movies of the 1940s and Francis Ford Coppola's revisionist *Godfather* films, released by Paramount in the 1970s. Aspects of both types of films can be seen in *The Boss*. The picture has an old-fashioned, gritty feel and quick pace, but it also touches on larger themes of betrayal and redemption. The script, which bore frequent Trumbo front Ben L. Perry's name, was Trumbo's first job after returning from Mexico.

The Boss is distinguished by the kind of complex plotting at which Trumbo excelled, and it's interesting that he dove headlong into complex stories during the blacklist. Although in many cases he had less time than ever before to produce complete screenplays—he reputedly did a top-to-bottom rewrite of Perry's *Terror in a Texas Town* script in four days—Trumbo nonetheless made ambitious storytelling choices and stuck to them. One possible explanation for this choice is that by concentrating on complex structures that, by their nature, necessitate the use of short scenes, Trumbo avoided the greater challenge of scene work. This is to say that while conjuring plot event after plot event certainly requires talent and imagination, the real work of screenwriting is making individual scenes compelling and original.

Some proof of this theory can be found by comparing movies from the latter part of the blacklist era with their successors in the early 1960s. For instance, compare *The Boss* to *Spartacus*. In *The Boss*, scenes rarely last more than one or two minutes; in *Spartacus*, scenes lasting five minutes are not unusual. Admittedly, countless other factors affect this difference—particularly *Spartacus*'s three-hour running time—but the factor that appears most important is the luxury of time. When Trumbo was writing quickie pictures such as *The Boss*, he was, as the cliché goes, under the gun. He faced brutal deadlines and split his attention among various low-paying projects. But while writing latter-day films such as *Spartacus*, Trumbo was given sufficient time and support to spread his wings, as it were, and write the best scenes that he could.

The titular figure of *The Boss* is Matt Brady (John Payne), introduced as a decorated officer just back from World War I. Upon returning to his tough, inner-city neighborhood, Matt butts heads with the older brother who raised him, Alderman Tim Brady (Roy Roberts). Tim wants Matt to attend college and make something of himself, but Matt is a belligerent individualist with no interest in anyone's ambitions but his own. He soon encounters an old friend, Bob Herrick (William Bishop), who suggests that someone could consolidate power over the whole city from a base in their neighborhood, the Third Ward.

Matt's plans to marry his sweetheart, Elsie Reynolds (Doe Avedon), fall apart after a spat turns into a heated argument, so he gets drunk at a bar and impulsively proposes to barfly Lorry Reed (Gloria McGhee). A plain woman surprised by Matt's "affection," she accepts but warns Matt that no good will come of their union.

Shortly after Matt's impetuous marriage, Tim unexpectedly dies. Matt takes Tim's seat on the city council, and quickly discovers the lure of power. At Matt's swearing-in ceremony, he befriends Governor Beck (Harry Cheshire), a connection that will later prove important. Matt then offers to help his honest but down-on-his-luck friend Ernie Jackson (Joe Flynn) get a job; soon afterward, Matt makes his first foray into dirty politics. Upon discovering that a gangster with whom he is acquainted, Johnny Mazia (Robin Morse), is in trouble with the law, Matt gets the charges against Johnny dropped.

In his next illicit move, Matt strong-arms the proprietor of a local cement business, Roy Millard (Alex Frazer), by buying a half-interest in Roy's failing company and then promising to give Roy extensive city contracts. Matt has his old friend Bob, a lawyer, broker the deal and take a 10 percent interest in the company, thereby breaking a handful of laws in the space of a short conversation. Despite his quick slide down the moral ladder, Matt is humanized by his desire to seem pure in the eyes of his true love, Elsie, who is now Bob's girlfriend; after arranging the cement deal, Matt has Bob swear not to tell Elsie about the scheme.

A hint of the ugliness to come is seen when Bob and Elsie have dinner with Matt and Lorry. Lorry has grown bitter about her loveless marriage, so she's disturbed when she sees the love with which Matt still regards Elsie. After Bob and Elsie leave, a heartbroken Lorry asks Matt for a divorce, sparking one of the picture's most intense scenes.

MATT: I'm not gonna have a divorce. Every cheap reformer in this town's gunning for me. My private life is gonna stay clean.

LORRY: Why don't you tell the real truth? You told your brother you'd never divorce me.... You're still fighting his ghost.

[*He slaps her.*]

MATT: Who do you think you are?

LORRY: You've never asked before. My father was a bum. I never even saw him. My mother was what you thought I was. I'm your wife, and you'd be wise to try to get to know me, because I'm stronger than you'll ever be.

MATT: If you ever take one step toward a lawyer, or ever say that again, I'll have you committed to an insane asylum.

It's at this point, almost exactly halfway through the movie, that the first hints of Matt's inevitable downfall start to appear. Following a tradition reaching back to Eden, Trumbo sets up that Matt's greatest crime isn't corruption but hubris. It's one thing for Matt to exploit his job for political or financial gain, the film says, but quite another for him to ravage the lives of other people. That some of the movie's most vivid interaction occurs between Matt and Lorry suggests that Trumbo and the other filmmakers find Matt's abuse of his wife far more contemptible—or at least, far more immediate and tangible—than his abuse of power. Matt's hubris is brought into play when Bob proposes an embezzlement scheme by which he and Matt can steal $12 million.

Following the introduction of the fateful scheme is an exchange that gives viewers a quick snapshot of Matt's machine. The scene begins when Matt is confronted by Stanley Millard (Rhys Williams), a reformer out to bring Matt down—and the brother of the cement business proprietor whom Matt squeezed earlier in the movie.

> STANLEY: I'm going to ruin you, Mr. Brady.... You're a thief and a thug. We have more speakeasies in this city than schools, more gambling dives than churches, and more murders per capita than any city in the country.
> MATT: Uh-huh. What else.
> STANLEY: My daughter isn't safe after nightfall on the streets of the town she was born in. I'm going to see to it that she is safe.
> MATT: I'm all for daughters and safe streets. Especially if they're well-paved. How you going to do all this?
> STANLEY: I'm going to prove to the world that you've been voting 20,000 tombstones in the Third Ward.... We are organizing [to] sweep all those ghost votes of your machine back into the cemetery.
> MATT: Fine. I'm all for it. Put me down for a thousand dollars.

Matt's seething arrogance and contempt—the aside about "well-paved" streets is a reference to his corrupt cement business, and his offer to help pay for Millard's reform effort is like a challenge to a duel—form an allusion to Julius Caesar, in that Matt believes himself impervious to prosecution. In keeping with the Caesar imagery, Matt soon gets his own Brutus. Such allusions to timeless themes, while commonplace in good crime films, help make *The Boss* as much of a morality play as it is an urban drama.

The theme of betrayal, which comes up again and again during Trumbo's blacklist-era films, may have been a particularly poignant one for Trumbo because of how he watched a succession of Hollywood professionals—including former friends and/or co-workers, such as Edward Dmytryk and Edward G. Robinson—turn on their left-wing brothers by naming names before HUAC.

Despite the threat of Millard's reform effort, Matt keeps building his machine by using his influence with politicians, including Governor Beck, to get appointments for friends. He even positions Ernie, whom we're repeatedly told has the strongest morals of any of Matt's friends, as the district's next congressman. One hint of why Matt is tempting fate is presented during a quiet scene involving Matt, Bob, and Elsie. "Trouble is with me, I'm always winning and somebody else walks off with the prize," Matt says, adding that he regards Elsie as such a prize. She retorts that it's time for him to forget the past and pay attention to Lorry. Matt ignores Elsie's advice, then scoffs when informed that he was blackballed at an important political meeting. Instead of taking the news as a cue to lay low, he vindictively uses his power to get a sewer rerouted through the country club at which the meeting took place.

This is a critical moment in the screenplay, because it reveals that Matt's arrogance has made him his own worst enemy. Lorry, ever the cynical voice of reason, prepares him for his impending fall with hard-edged dialogue typical of the film's menacing tone:

> LORRY: I never put very much value on myself. But at least I'm able to see that it's you that's no good. And I'm beginning to understand that I do have value, if only because you have none at all. If you should die alone in this room in the middle of the night, there's not one creature in the whole world that could honestly say that anything had been lost.[23]

In a development reflecting the story's long time span, Matt's problems are compounded when the Great Depression hits, leaving Bob, who has become as crooked as Matt, a half-million dollars in debt. To get himself and Bob out of financial trouble, Matt strikes a deal with his old gangster friend, Johnny Mazia. In exchange for fast cash, Matt promises to open up territories in which it was previously too dangerous for Johnny to operate. This desperate promise represents Matt's hubris taking over, even though his desire to protect a friend reveals the last shred of humanity left in his character. Saving Bob seals Matt's doom, however, because it is an act of mercy by a man who should, given the parameters of his situation, be acting mercilessly. Trumbo establishes this contradiction with uncharacteristic subtlety, so the repercussions of Matt's merciful act provide a fittingly dramatic denouement to the picture.

Once Bob's financial troubles are solved, Matt discovers that his district's U.S. Senate seat has become vacant. He angles to put Ernie into the seat, but Bob says he wants the job. Matt denies the request, thereby betraying his closest friend; soon afterward, he betrays his most dangerous business associate. When one of Johnny's men is implicated in a murder, Matt refuses to help the man. Johnny gets his revenge by kidnapping Bob and threatening to kill the lawyer unless Matt acquiesces to Johnny's various demands. Fearful of losing the man he considers his one true friend, Matt gives Johnny everything he wants: money, protection, and control of the Brady machine. Just as a righteous man can be felled by one sin, so too can a corrupt man be felled by one good deed.

When reformer Stanley Millard finally gathers enough evidence to drag Matt into a courtroom, Matt breezes through the trial with characteristic arrogance until Bob takes the stand. Still seething over the lost Senate seat—and seeing a chance to throw someone else in front of a moving train that's about to run him down—Bob frames Matt for embezzling a million dollar fee from an insurance company. In addition to sealing Matt's fate, the scene conveys that Bob's damnation is as complete as Matt's, and adds the irony that Bob will walk away from the trial unscathed even though he was the person who started Matt down the road of abusing political power.

The picture ends on the downbeat note of the following conversation between Lorry and Matt.

> LORRY: I heard the news. I couldn't believe that Bob had—
> MATT: Don't blame Bob too much. He tried to warn me. He lied, but he could have told the truth about a dozen other things and the answer would have been the same. I've been heading in this direction for a long time. Whatever was wrong in Bob was wrong in me first.
> LORRY: ...Bob was never your friend. Elsie was never your love, and I was never your wife. And the world was never your home. Good-bye, Matt.

Although the ultimate theme of *The Boss*—absolute power corrupts absolutely—is one of the oldest in the world, the vitality with which Trumbo illustrates it makes *The Boss* one of his toughest pictures. It also offers evidence of his versatility. Although many of his pre-blacklist films are broadly moralistic homilies, he excelled at crafting dark parables such as *The Boss, He Ran All the*

Way, *The Prowler*, and *Gun Crazy*, in which people are strangled by their own weaknesses. These two strains of Trumbo's career—rebel heroes fighting to protect their ideals and callow villains suffocated by their lack of ideals—collectively speak to Trumbo's worldview in which men and women are defined by their moral choices. They live and die by honor. Seen in this light, bleak stories such as *The Boss* are as indicative of Trumbo's principles as bright stories along the lines of his next credit, *The Brave One*.

6

Man with a Mission
(1956–1959)

One of only two Trumbo movies to win a writing Oscar, *The Brave One* is almost without precedent among his screenplays. Although he had previously written a film centered around young protagonists (*Our Vines Have Tender Grapes*), *The Brave One* was the only of Trumbo's scripts told entirely from the perspective of a child.[1] The aspect of *The Brave One* that does have ample precedent elsewhere in its writer's *oeuvre* is the film's fairy tale quality. In *The Remarkable Andrew*, *A Guy Named Joe*, and *Roman Holiday*, the stakes of each story are established in brisk introductory sequences (a "Once upon a time" setup), and then elevated when a fantastic or semi-fantastic story element is introduced. The fantastic elements of *Andrew* and *Joe* are obvious, and in *Roman Holiday*, the corresponding contrivance is Princess Ann's ability to move through Rome without being either recognized by members of the public or confronted by representatives of her embassy's staff.

By establishing fairy tale milieus in

such films, Trumbo tacitly prepared viewers for impending homilies, for it followed that if he was using one fairy tale convention (the fantastic plot device), he would likely use another (the denouement as parable). In the most effective such films, Trumbo either subverted the fairy tale structure by preventing the protagonist from achieving a goal or maximized the structure by having the protagonist use extraordinary methods in pursuit of a goal. When Trumbo subverted the structure—by having the lover-protagonists of *A Guy Named Joe* and *Roman Holiday* end up apart, for instance—he made statements through his subversion. But when he told fairy tales without any irony or subtext, he walked a fine line. The artistic failure of *The Remarkable Andrew* stemmed, in part, from Trumbo conjuring a happy ending so false that it dispelled whatever charm preceded; conversely, the sheer entertainment value of *The Brave One* offers proof of what Trumbo could do with fairy tales when he played fair.

Inspired by Trumbo's experiences in Mexico,[2] *The Brave One* adheres to the popular model of a child who bonds with an animal.[3] The picture works on several levels, even though it is among the simplest of Trumbo's entertainments: It works superficially as a travelogue, giving viewers a look at life in Mexico; it works emotionally as a narrative, beginning with the boy's first encounter with his beloved animal and spanning years until the climactic moment of their relationship; and it works spiritually as a comforting fable.

Yet where Trumbo's other family-oriented entertainment, *Our Vines Have Tender Grapes*, feels cloying and manipulative, *The Brave One* operates with such plain-faced sincerity—and, yes, sentimentality—that it's difficult to fault the film for the falsehoods it propagates. As suggested by an over-dramatic metaphor in the scene depicting the boy's first meeting with the bull, the film never tries to be anything but a larger-than-life yarn.

The picture begins with a funeral. Poor Mexican boy Leonardo Rosillo (Michael Ray), walks home from his mother's burial with his grieving father, Rafael (Rodolfo Hoyos), and shortly afterward the family is confronted by Vargas, the unsympathetic boss of the ranch on which Leonardo's family works. Vargas says that the family's cow belongs to the ranch, and that he expects them to surrender the animal the next day. After Vargas leaves, Leonardo asks why his family's property can be so easily appropriated. "After all that we've lost, would you be surprised?" Rafael responds. "All life is a loss." These somber lines set an oppressive mood so that later events will seem lighter by comparison, but they also allude to the iconography of fairy tales. The way the ranch boss oppresses Leonardo's family is similar, for instance, to the manner in which Cinderella was abused by her stepmother and stepsisters.

Next comes a melodramatic sequence set during a nighttime thunderstorm. Leonardo, asleep in his humble room, is awakened not by the sound of thunder but by the pained cries of his family's cow, which is outside in the storm. Leonardo runs through the rain and cold to find the cow trapped beneath a tree that was toppled by a lightning strike. The cow dies, but as Leonardo dejectedly turns to go home, he hears the cry of a newborn calf. Leonardo retrieves the calf and heads home; the next morning, we see Leonardo in bed, cradling the calf like a human baby.

This sequence establishes the nature of the bond between the boy and the bull—both orphans, they are each other's surrogate siblings. And because they share the traumatic experience of losing a mother, their bond runs deeper than friendships born under less dramatic circumstances. That this set-up is predicated upon an animal possessing not only human emotions, but also human cognitive powers, is the element of this picture that is, as necessitated by the norms of the fairy tale structure, elevated to a fantastic level. There are rewards in store for viewers who accept this conceit, because Trumbo tells his story with patience, whimsy, and sense of karmic inevitability.

After convincing his father to let him keep the calf, Leonardo names it Gitano (Spanish for "gypsy"). Leonardo fears that Gitano will someday be taken away from him, so when his school teacher gives a lesson about Mexican president Benito Suarez's benevolence,

Leonardo gets an idea. He has his school teacher write a letter to Don Alejandro Videgray (Carlos Navarro), the owner of the ranch, asking for permanent ownership of Gitano. Meanwhile, Leonardo plays with the calf constantly, at one point pretending to be a matador with a cape; Rafael chides Leonardo for doing so, fearing that the animal will learn the bullfighting routine too well and gore a matador. Despite Leonardo's heartfelt requests that another solution be found, Rafael says that Gitano will have to go into the ring when he is four years old.

And so it goes as the film moves efficiently from one plot point to the next. Even the seemingly gratuitous comic bits, such as when Gitano waits outside Leonardo's school and disturbs the class by knocking over a plant, are functional in that they embellish the playful bond between Leonardo and Gitano.

Although portrayed as a decent man who loves his son, Rafael also has a strong sense of duty to his employers. This storytelling choice is a prudent one, because were Rafael portrayed as more assertive, the valiant actions that Leonardo takes later in the movie would seem unnecessary. In effect, Trumbo emasculates Rafael by making him someone unwilling or unable to overstep his social role. This enables the fairy tale, because it forces Leonardo to overstep his social role, thereby exhibiting greater valor than his father. Because of this dynamic, which is given only minor lip service in the screenplay proper, the picture has a subtext about Leonardo becoming his own man, which is a theme that adults can relate to while children connect with the offbeat tenderness of Leonardo's relationship with Gitano.

Another function that Rafael serves in the screenplay is to offer cynical hom-

ilies such as the curt one he spoke after his wife's funeral. When the inevitable happens and Gitano is taken away from Leonardo—whose letter to Don Alejandro has not yet elicited a response—the boy grows forlorn and asks his father for permission to visit Gitano.

> RAFAEL: Leonardo, my son—it is better that you forget Gitano. The bull will cause you sorrow someday. It is in the nature of things that when loves too much, one loses much. Someday you will understand. But for tonight, you may go.

Soon into Gitano's "exile," though, Leonardo receives a letter from Don Alejandro giving him ownership of his beloved bull. Thereafter, Leonardo continues pressing his father for a way to avoid sending Gitano to the ring, so Rafael finally relents and says that if Gitano passes the upcoming *tienta*, a test of bravery for two-year-old bulls, the animal can be used for stud service. The *tienta* sequence offers a grandiose distraction from scenes set in Leonardo's impoverished home, because Don Alejandro returns from abroad on the occasion of the *tienta*.

Trumbo departs from Leonardo's story for several minutes and uses Don Alejandro's visit as an opportunity to comment on bullfighting. Don Alejandro takes his female companion, American Marion Randall (Joi Lansing), to see a bullfight, and she comments that the sport is cruel. He counters that it is no more so than a fox hunt or a boxing match, then elaborates with an assertion colored by Trumbo's familiarity with Mexican culture.

> DON ALEJANDRO: You Americans wouldn't understand. We Mexicans

are a different and older race. We know there is pain in all of life and that death is never very far away. You people are always outraged by pain. And as for death—I think you may pass a law against it any day.[4]

In addition to offering a suitably romantic justification for bullfighting, Trumbo slips in a bit of mild satire with Don Alejandro's comments about American squeamishness. This is a welcome change of tone, coming as it does midway through an utterly sincere movie. Were one to make a sweeping criticism of *The Brave One*, it might be that the film wants for humor, but the quick answer to that criticism is that satire would not be germane. Quite to the contrary, films such as *The Brave One* are built on a foundation of wide-eyed innocence that would be weakened by irony.

Following the *tienta* sequence—during which Gitano proves to be as brave as expected, therefore ensuring that the animal won't have to fight in the ring—Trumbo develops a handful of subplots, the most important of which is Don Alejandro's auto racing career. When Don Alejandro is killed in a car crash, his estate is declared bankrupt, and his assets are sold at auction. Vargas, the unfeeling ranch boss who tried to claim Gitano's mother at the beginning of the film, announces that Gitano will be sold, because Leonardo has lost the letter proving his ownership of Gitano.

This development precipitates what is probably the most contrived sequence of the film. Up to this point, Trumbo has generated drama either by connecting the story of Leonardo and Gitano to subplots or by finding new ways to challenge Leonardo's ownership of the bull. But at this point in the film, Trumbo pounces on an opportunity for clichéd

outdoor adventure. Leonardo frees Gitano from his pen, and the two run away. That night, while Leonardo sleeps in the woods and Gitano paces around the spot where Leonardo is sleeping, a mountain lion tries to attack the boy. Gitano defends him, killing the mountain lion but sustaining minor injuries in the process. That a bull would feel so protective of a human is at least consistent with the film's main device; that a lion would attack Leonardo during his first night away from home is even more fantastic. The lion attack is the only moment in the picture during which Trumbo defies the logic of his own story to provide a cheap thrill. Luckily for viewers, the moment passes and the picture soon resumes its easy, compelling rhythm.

The remainder of the film is better seen than described because, like the chase scene that dominates the second half of *Lonely Are the Brave*, the long, intercut sequence that concludes *The Brave One* is constructed of repetitious images, false alarms, delays, and ticking-clock tension. This description may make the sequence sound terribly contrived, and in some ways it is. But because it is true to the rest of the movie, the closing sequence is an effective one.

In short, Gitano is sold, inspiring Leonardo to sneak a ride to Mexico City, where the bull is to fight in the ring. Once in Mexico City, Leonardo races to find someone who can prevent Gitano's death. His quest through the city—which serves, like much of the film, the secondary function of providing a travelogue—is intercut with footage of bullfights in Mexico City's Palace de Mexico arena. The idea of the sequence is simple: Leonardo must find a savior before Gitano is killed. What makes the film's denouement work is that after

Leonardo (Michael Ray) enjoys a ride on his pet bull, Gitano, in *The Brave One*. Writing under a pseudonym, Trumbo won an Oscar for this film, in which he put a heartfelt spin on familiar thematic material. (Universal Pictures)

Leonardo gets a letter from Mexico's president requesting mercy for Gitano, he doesn't make it to the arena in time. He then has to watch Gitano fight several rounds in the ring during which the bull is stabbed with six decorative swords that dangle out of its shoulders like bloody epaulets.

Instead of the

for mercy made by the audience after beholding Gitano's bravery. Trumbo introduces the concept of the *indulto* gracefully. As Leonardo sits on the side of the arena, crying because he thinks his beloved Gitano is about to die, the crowd starts chanting "*indulto*," and then a radio commentator explains what the word means. That Trumbo didn't fore-shadow this moment by introducing the *indulto* concept earlier in the film is evidence of two things—the rare restraint with which he crafted the film's conclusion and also the crude grace of the picture.

Despite its strong narrative and handful of well-rendered sequences, *The Brave One* ultimately is pure corn. While Trumbo methodically depicts certain story developments, he plays fast and loose with the introduction and dispatching of Don Alejandro, the business of Leonardo losing a letter that would more believably be secured with his family's most precious possessions, and the central device of Gitano's anthropomorphization. The film, then, is a compromise between the conscientious craftsmanship of Trumbo's pre-blacklist films and the flimflam storytelling of his weakest screenplays.

Even with these shortcomings in mind, *The Brave One* stands alongside *Roman Holiday* as a throwback to the way that Trumbo explored the theme of honor prior to the blacklist—although it's amusing to note that the character in the film who best exemplifies Trumbo's vision of honorable behavior is Gitano, not Leonardo. While the boy is sympathetic for the way he expects adults to behave with integrity, several characters comment on Gitano's bravery with the same admiration one might expect from comments about a noble human being.

That Gitano is ultimately rewarded for his honorable behavior is perhaps the most fantastic contrivance of all, given that Trumbo wrote the picture at a time when he was in exile because of adhering to his principles.

❖ ❖ ❖

After winning an Oscar for *The Brave One*, Trumbo started down the road that eventually led to the end of the blacklist. Because the Robert Rich incident put him back into the public eye, he found it easier to get high-paying jobs, even if many of them were rushed rewrites. By the end of 1957, Trumbo was working with major studios more openly than he had since before the blacklist; by the end of 1958, Kirk Douglas had Trumbo working on a pair of screenplay projects, and was exploring the possibility of returning Trumbo's name to the screen. Meanwhile, Trumbo playfully undermined the blacklist by neither acknowledging nor denying authorship of any film. When his *Brave One* Oscar revealed that blacklisted writers were working underground, journalists asked Trumbo, Michael Wilson, and others to identify which films they had written under pseudonyms or front names. By giving coy answers, Trumbo created the illusion that any film might have been written by a blacklistee— thereby suggesting that the blacklist was a failure.

In the late 1950s, Trumbo was obsessed with finding a way to emerge from the underground, and his main device for achieving this goal was accepting as many jobs as possible. Jean La-Cour Scott, widow of Hollywood Ten member Adrian Scott, recalled this period: "Dalton was working on something like eight scripts at once, on booze and uppers and downers, writing under about four or five pen names to support his family and his penchant for high living."[5]

Trumbo's next screenplay during this frenzied period was *The Green-Eyed Blonde*, on which his front was a woman named Sally Stubblefield. Introduced to Trumbo by Adrian Scott, she was an editor in a studio story department who wanted to become a producer. For the subject of her first (and only) project, she picked the lives of delinquent girls in a juvenile institution, so she took Trumbo to such a place, where he found enough material for his story.[6] That Trumbo twisted the material into a maudlin potboiler reflects the compromises he made to maintain his voluminous blacklist-era output.

The Green-Eyed Blonde is such an unfocused effort that its titular character doesn't even play a pivotal role in the story. Said protagonist, an adolescent girl nicknamed "Greeneyes" (Susan Oliver), is one of several young women living in the MTL Cottage of the Martha Washington School for Girls. When a new inmate, Betsy Abel (Linda Plowman), is incarcerated at the school because she had an illegitimate baby and refused to name the boy's father, the women rally around her. And when one of their number, the appropriately named Cuckoo (Norma Jean Nilsson), kidnaps Betsy's baby from Betsy's parents, the girls find direction by looking after the baby in their cottage for two weeks before their secret is discovered.

One of the film's subplots involves Greeneyes's romance with a lowlife named Cliff Munster (Raymond Foster). When the story begins, Greeneyes is nearly through her term at Washington, and plans to start a new life with Cliff when she gets out. But when her minor part in hiding the baby is discovered, Greeneyes gets extra time put on her sentence. She breaks out and, shortly afterward, gets killed when she and Cliff are involved in a shootout. That the picture is called *The Green-Eyed Blonde*, and framed with saccharine, Greek chorus–type songs that pop up at various intervals to amplify and foreshadow plot developments pertaining to Greeneyes's affair with Cliff, suggests that hers is the central story of the movie, but such is not the case.

Betsy's evolution from an angst-ridden young rebel who couldn't care less about her son's fate to a fledgling nurturer is the main thrust, and vignettes depicting Greeneyes's star-crossed affair are interjected occasionally as a parable from which Betsy and her peers are supposed to learn. Another of the picture's many problems is that it shuns several more provocative tacks on its subject matter—exploring the rigors of the mental illness with which several of the film's characters are seemingly afflicted, exposing abuse of women in such institutions, or even just portraying the realities of institutional life.

Instead, Trumbo presents a contrived yarn about how women can't resist their impulse to become mothers, no matter how extreme or unusual their lifestyles. Still worse, he doesn't even provide a satisfactory ending to Betsy's story—when the picture is over, we don't know if Betsy will be reunited with her son, who is taken away by authorities after the women's secret is discovered. *The Green-Eyed Blonde* doesn't work as story about motherhood, a provocative exposé or m̲ʳ̲d̲l̲i̲

the slag heap of Trumbo's inconsequential blacklist quickies.

Cowboy is atypical of Trumbo's other efforts in the late blacklist era, and for good reason—although it didn't reach theaters until 1958, it was one of the scripts that Trumbo wrote before entering jail almost a decade earlier. And because it was written in the same rush of desperate energy as *Roman Holiday*, *Gun Crazy*, and *The Prowler*, it features the same mixture of assured storytelling and individualistic iconography that distinguishes his other pre-jail scripts. Moreover, Trumbo brought a believable accumulation of detail, jargon, and drama to the script, probably owing to his frontier roots and experience with animal husbandry. *Cowboy*—on which Trumbo was fronted by Edmund H. North—was the kind of taut outdoor adventure at which he excelled.

The picture also features several terrific examples of Trumbo's dialogue writing at its most economical. Because of his terse line delivery, star Glenn Ford was better served by minimal dialogue than verbose speeches, so it worked that Trumbo wrote Ford's character, Tom Reese, as a man of few words.[7] In a larger sense, it was also effective that Trumbo's screenplay as a whole adheres to that most basic screenwriting tenet: "Show, don't tell." Even in sequences that aren't filled with action, per se, Trumbo keeps things lively by having characters interact with props and each other in an active way.

Based on Frank Harris's memoir, *On the Trail: My Reminisces as a Cowboy*, the picture begins when dirty, road-weary cowpoke Paco Mendoza (Victor Manuel Mendoza) struts into the lobby of a posh Chicago hotel and announces that "Mr. Reese" is on his way. The hotel manager tells Paco that the usual rooms will be ready, but unsuspecting clerk Frank Harris (Jack Lemmon) reminds the manager that those rooms are occupied by the Vidal family. The manager says that Reese's party has priority, and Frank is sent to move the Vidals to other quarters.

Outside the Vidals' suite, Frank encounters his inamorata, beautiful young Maria Vidal (Anna Kashfi); the couple chat lovingly until their conversation is interrupted by the entrance of Maria's father, Señor Vidal (Donald Randolph). He is incensed by Frank's designs on his daughter, so when Frank makes the insulting request that the Vidals move to another part of the hotel, Señor Vidal says he's leaving Chicago and returning to Mexico. To ensure that Frank won't try to pursue Maria any further, Señor Vidal offers some curt words: "Good-bye, young man," he says. "And don't think that love can find a way—I know all the ways."

This sequence is typically efficient Trumbo exposition: It sets up the connection between the main plot, Frank's association with Tom Reese, and an important subplot, Frank's romance with Maria. It also reflects an intelligent narrative choice, because using Paco's blustery entrance to foreshadow Tom's first appearance makes viewers curious about why Tom Reese pulls such weight at the hotel. Trumbo also introduces an important idea during Frank's exchange with Señor Vidal, because Frank tells the Mexican patriarch that he intends to make his fortune by getting into the cattle business.

Because so much plot information

is being put across, the picture moves slowly and methodically until Tom makes his first appearance. Trumbo paints him as a classically rough-and-tumble Westerner with no patience for sycophants and artifice. Trumbo crafted playfully artful dialogue for Tom, including the line that Tom barks while disrobing for a bath: "Will you close that door out there? I'm freezin' my wimple tree!"

The picture enjoyably shunts between playful and serious throughout its length, and this split tone is epitomized by the scene in which Frank requests a job on Tom's crew. At the beginning of the scene—when Tom shoots a cockroach off the bathroom wall with his six-shooter—his gruff manner is amusing. But when he sets to debunking Frank's ambition, he turns malicious.

> Tom: You're an idiot. You're a dreamy idiot and that's the worst kind. You know what the trail is really like? Dust storms all day, cloud bursts all night. Man has got to be a fool to want that kind of life.[8]

Later, however, Tom gambles away most of the money he brought to Chicago and then informs Frank, the desk clerk on duty, that he's checking out of the hotel. Frank offers to loan Tom his entire savings, $3,800, in exchange for a stake in Tom's cattle business. A slightly inebriated Tom accepts the offer. After he sobers up, he tries to dismiss Frank by handing him $3,800 plus interest. The men bicker until Frank says that Tom is a liar if he dishonors the arrangement. Paco, standing nearby, asserts that Frank is right. Irritated, Tom barks a question to Paco: "How do you know that?"

"If he wasn't right," Paco answers, "you would h‑‑‑ ‑‑‑‑‑

In addition to providing a satisfying punch line to the scene, Paco's dialogue tells viewers that the narrative will be a matter of life and death. The film then plods through several routine sequences depicting Frank's difficulty in adjusting to life on the trail.

To accomplish the next order of business in the screenplay, Frank's loss of innocence, Trumbo uses the Aristotelian model of three acts by showing three events that collectively break Frank's spirit. The first of them involves two bickering cowboys, Paul (Richard Jaekel) and Charlie (Dick York), who play catch with a live rattler during a dull night around the campfire. As Frank watches in horror, the rattler is accidentally tossed onto the back of a trailhand (Strother Martin), who gets bitten. He quickly succumbs to the snake's poison and dies, at which point Paul tries to steal one of his boots.

Incensed, Frank howls: "You better put it down or I'm gonna bust you wide open!" This line comes as a surprise, because it is the first to imply Frank's capacity for violence. The moment illustrates that, somewhere, in his soul, Frank has the makings of a cowboy as rough-and-tumble as any other. Tom prevents the fight, however, and uses it as an opportunity to try to get rid of Frank. "You don't like what's going on around here, too bad," he says. "Because nobody said you were gonna like it."

Tom then delivers a bitter eulogy over the trailhand's grave: "He was a good man with cattle. He always did the best he knew how. Hope somebody can say the same over me." The eulogy suggests that behind his frontier stoicism, Tom is haunted by thoughts of mortal-

against Frank's innocence when the cattle drive arrives at the Vidal estate, where Frank discovers that Maria is married. When he and the other cowboys attend an exhibition at which Maria's husband, Manuel (Eugene Iglesias), is to put a ring around the horn of a raging bull in a public arena, Frank accepts a challenge in an effort to impress Maria. With Tom's crew and the Vidals watching, Manuel enters the arena on horseback and successfully puts the ring on the bull's horn, but his horse suffers several nasty wounds during the exhibition.

Before Frank can attempt to duplicate the feat, though, Tom announces that he'll enter the ring in Frank's stead. Tom takes bets on his chances, then explains his motivation to Frank. "Getting killed trying to make some money, that's one thing," he says. "Getting killed to impress a female, that's just plain stupid." This line marks an important transition in the screenplay, because it shows that Tom is growing to respect Frank. When he realizes that Frank is willing to risk his life to woo Maria, Tom sees a kindred spirit in the former hotel clerk, then intrudes to protect him. Tom goes into the arena on foot—declaring that he doesn't want to get a horse wounded doing his dirty work—and his dangerous dance with the bull is played for thrills with sped-up camerawork and outrageous stunts. Predictably, Tom succeeds, thereby winning a handful of cash and humiliating Frank.[9]

After the bullring business, Maria steals a private moment with Frank and explains that she can't see him again. The loss of Maria is the second blow to Frank's innocence, and the third follows soon after.

While in Mexico, Charlie angers several men by flirting with their sister. When the cowboys learn of his trouble, however, they choose not to help. Frank, who by now feels a burgeoning camaraderie with the crew, says that even if nobody else will, he's going to help Charlie. Once again, however, Tom protects Frank from his naive impulses, saying: "Man's old enough to get himself in trouble, man's old enough to get himself out of trouble." Frank responds with an outraged speech that prompts Tom to, in effect, describe the main theme of the movie.

> FRANK: You're the most miserable bunch of men I ever saw in my whole life. Not one shred of decency in the lot of you. I never thought life on the trail would be like this—I thought I'd be living with some *men*. Not just a pack of animals.
> TOM: I'm sorry that we don't measure up to your way of thinking. Trouble is, you wanted to play cowboy, [but] you didn't realize the game was going to be rough.

Undeterred, Frank tries to leave the camp so he can help Charlie, but Tom stops him by throwing a crowbar at Frank's legs while Frank's back is turned. Frank hurtles into a brutal brawl that Tom easily wins, thereby preventing Frank from helping Charlie. Frank's loss of innocence is now complete, because he has gone from wanting to be like Tom to utterly despising him.

The morning after the fight, the cowboys learn that Charlie escaped his Mexican troubles with just a broken arm. As the crew heads back onto the trail, Paco tells Tom that Frank is showing, in frontier vernacular, true grit. Tom asks Paco if he's pushing Frank too hard,

One of the most entertaining pictures that Trumbo wrote during the blacklist era was the offbeat western *Cowboy*. In this scene, the veteran rancher played by Glenn Ford (foreground) celebrates a successful cattle drive with his protégé, played by Jack Lemmon. (Columbia Pictures)

and Paco's answer crystallizes the patriarchal imagery that suffuses the film: he draws an analogy between Tom's treatment of Frank and his own childhood. "He always treated me too hard, my father," Paco comments. "But he liked me very much."

Trumbo hammers the patriarchal imagery when Tom tries to make peace by commiserating with Frank about losing Maria; Frank spouts angry comments, then rides away. This exchange sets up tension essential to the next movement of the film, during which Tom's herd is shadowed by a group of Comanche Indians.[10] When Frank realizes that about 40 cows

rides off to collect them, and the Comanches follow Frank. The cowboys realize that Frank's bravery has given them a chance to escape the Comanches, but Tom, obviously smarting with guilt from abusing Frank, tells his crew to stampede the herd in Frank's direction, which he hopes will scare away the Comanches.

By this point, all of the elements of the film's conclusion are in place, and Trumbo moves things along with a minimum of dialogue and a maximum of visual excitement. After the gunfight with the Native Americans, Frank

It shows that Tom pushed Frank too hard, creating a monster instead of a man, and it sets the stage for Frank's comeuppance.

To illustrate how completely Frank has become the man he believed Tom to be, Trumbo inverts several earlier scenes: Frank breaks up a fight between Paul and Charlie (just as Tom broke up a fight between Frank and Paul), then coldly responds to the death of crew member, echoing Tom's heartlessness after the trailhand's demise. Sensing that Frank has grown too callous for his own good, Tom confronts his apprentice.

> TOM: You just don't give a damn, do you?
>
> FRANK: You're a fine one to talk, Reese. I saw you bury a man once. In the long run, it doesn't matter— that's what you said.
>
> TOM: Well, maybe I changed my mind. Maybe watching you made me change it. If you had anything inside you worth saving, I'd beat you till you couldn't stand up, but it wouldn't do any good because you'll never learn. You haven't gotten tough. You've just gotten miserable.

This exchange brings the film nearly full circle by showing that Tom and Frank have traded roles—Tom is now the voice of reason, and Frank is the hard-as-leather cowboy who only cares about bringing in the herd. The clarity with which Trumbo draws the various stages of this evolution reflects his years in the screenwriting game; although the dialogue starts to hit themes "on the nose" toward the end of the picture, most of the character transitions are shown in visual action. More importantly, Trumbo draws these transitions in gradual steps—relying on trustworthy

conventions including the Aristotelian model of three parts being a dramatic whole—which helps keep the changes that occur in Frank's character believable.

The film's final turnabout occurs while Tom and Frank load their cattle onto a train for the last leg of the trip to Chicago. When Frank hears that some of the cattle have fallen over in one of the train cars, he fears they'll be trampled, so he climbs into the car and tries to right the cows, at risk of being trampled himself. One of the cowboys informs Tom what's happening, so Tom follows Frank into the cattle car. Paco asks why Tom is risking his life for a man who hates him. "I'm tired of burying people," Tom barks. This line shows that Tom's inherent decency—the same quality that made him honor his bargain with Frank and prompted him to save Frank from almost-certain death in a Mexican arena—has now risen to the forefront of his character. Viewers' sympathies are fully in Tom's court when he helps Frank right the cows, probably saving Frank's life in the process.

The import of Tom's gesture isn't lost on Frank, and the two men have a short, reconciliatory exchange in the back of the cattle car. Trumbo shows immense faith in the structure of his screenplay by letting this scene be all that's said about Frank's redemption, and it is to his credit that this scene is sufficient. This simple moment of two men working together, bonding, and making peace shows that Frank has been humbled by Tom's example. Along with *Roman Holiday* and *The Brave One*, *Cowboy* represents a throwback to a simpler time in Trumbo's writing; the way that Tom and Frank mature into honorable men by learning from each other closely parallels the way that Andrew Long and Pete Sandige matured in *The Remarkable Andrew* and *A Guy Named Joe*, respectively.

Once the drive crew reaches Chicago, the film returns to the hotel in which it began, and the way that Frank and Tom take equal parts in ordering rooms for the crew pays off the movie's father-son imagery. The picture ends with Frank and Tom in adjoining bathtubs. Mimicking Tom's behavior earlier in the movie, Frank shoots a cockroach off the wall, and the two men laugh, realizing how far they've come. The vaguely homoerotic camaraderie of this scene echoes the pseudoromantic relationships between male protagonists in action movies ranging from *Gunga Din* (1939, RKO) to *Butch Cassidy and the Sundance Kid* (1969, 20th Century–Fox) to *Lethal Weapon* (1987, Warner Bros.), and the only shortcoming of *Cowboy*'s conclusion is that it feels as much like a beginning as an ending—one wonders if the next chapter in these two men's lives might be even more interesting than the one that was just dramatized.

❖ ❖ ❖

Trumbo spent the last months of the blacklist era on a handful of quick rewrites and polish jobs; he also served as a consultant on myriad scripts by other blacklisted writers. His credits in this period include two films for British producer Benedict Bogeaus, who had a special gift for transforming important literary properties into shabby movies. Trumbo wrote an adaptation of Herman Melville's "Typee" for Bogeaus, apparently using film editor James Leicester as a front; it appears th⸻ P⸻

Smith prior to filming it as *Enchanted Island*. Trumbo's next project for Bogeaus was a quick polish of the producer's atrocious adaptation of Jules Verne's *From the Earth to the Moon*.

When considering minor credits such as the Bogeaus pictures, it's amusing to note that far more effort has gone into unraveling the mysteries behind good blacklist-era films than bad ones. While most of the research into the period is well intentioned, it seems that scholars are motivated by the same factors as other movie fans—they want to know who made movies they liked. This goes a long way toward explaining why the authorship of successful films including *Gun Crazy*, *Roman Holiday*, and *The Brave One* is common knowledge, but that of tripe is not.

Even though one must allow for a margin of error when dealing with Trumbo's blacklist-era credits, it appears that Trumbo made substantial contributions to only one more film, *The Young Philadelphians*, between *Enchanted Island* and *Spartacus*. But the credits of *The Young Philadelphians*—a drama starring Paul Newman as a lawyer who rises through Philadelphia society while hiding the fact of his illegitimate birth, a predicament reminiscent of Kitty Foyle's—are typically muddy. Bruce Cook wrote that Trumbo was hired by producer Alec March to rewrite a script based on Richard Pitts Powell's novel, *The Philadelphian*. According to Cook, Ben L. Perry went into an office on the Warner Bros. lot every day for 12 weeks to disguise the fact that the script was, in fact, being written in Trumbo's home. Then, after March and Perry/Trumbo were taken off the proje⸻ N⸻

his own script. Citing other obligations but not betraying his secret, Trumbo refused; James Gunn eventually took the screen credit.[11]

The incestuous nature of Trumbo's working relationships in this period clouds his contributions to various movies. For instance, *The Boss* was a Frank N. Seltzer production for which Trumbo did the screenplay using Perry as a front, while *Terror in a Texas Town* was a Seltzer production for which Perry wrote a screenplay that was in turn rewritten by Trumbo. Trying to make heads or tails of this period of Trumbo's career is very much like trying to assemble a jigsaw puzzle of which all the pieces look identical: the same names pop up again and again, but often with different connotations.

Trumbo, of course, caused much of this confusion. His favorite trick for undermining the blacklist—casting aspersions on movie credits so that no one could be sure whether the names they saw onscreen were true, half true, or utterly false—was an amusing and rather noble effort, and it seems likely that he would be pleased to know that, decades after his death, people are still trying to figure out just what he did or didn't do during the blacklist era.

Putting the credit issue aside, the most significant aspect of Trumbo's last years as a blacklistee is that his skills were being openly solicited by movie industry professionals as visible as Kirk Douglas, whose Bryna Productions began a crucially important relationship with Trumbo in the late 1950s. The mere fact that Trumbo was once again dealing face-to-face with major movie stars, instead of merely making backroom deals with low-budget producers, was an unmistakable omen that, at least for Trumbo, the blacklist would soon be over.

7

The Rebel Hero
(1960)

There are at least three good reasons why *Spartacus* towers high among Trumbo's credits: it's arguably the most famous film upon which he worked; it's among the few instances of Trumbo working with a world class director, even though Stanley Kubrick later disowned *Spartacus*; and, most significantly for the purposes of this study, there is a powerful connection between its intense subject matter and its stature as the first picture in 13 years to bear Trumbo's name. It's essential here to repeat the obvious—that the story of a rebel who defies the social order of his day and becomes a martyr to his cause was written by a man who went to jail on an issue of conscience. *Spartacus* is in every way the zenith of Trumbo's rebel-hero iconography.

The story behind the making of *Spartacus* is filled with politics, egomania, and hostility, all of which add to the picture's angry quality. Douglas and his partner in Bryna productions, Edward Lewis,[1] bought the movie rights to Howard Fast's novel *Spartacus* in the late 1950s.

Trumbo and fellow blacklistee Fast disliked each other immensely, each thinking the other the wrong kind of American communist. Fast was troublesome throughout the production, at one point lecturing the crew about why his ideas on the project mattered more than theirs.

Fast was given the opportunity to write the screenplay mostly out of professional courtesy, but his draft was discarded because it was inactive and talky. Although Douglas said many times that he hired Trumbo out of admiration for the writer's skill and speed, Kubrick biographer John Baxter—not a Trumbo partisan by any stretch—asserted that Trumbo's hiring was a last resort after literary luminaries including Lillian Hellman and Maxwell Anderson turned down the job.[2] Whether his motivation for hiring Trumbo was economic or creative in nature, Douglas quickly realized he made the right choice.

Without Fast's knowing, Dalton was writing at breakneck speed. He was wonderful to work with, never had any hesitancy about rewriting a scene. If you didn't like a scene, he'd just rip it out of the typewriter, crumple it up, throw it in the wastebasket, and start again. He never fought or balked at making changes or taking a different approach. I liked him.

He worked at night, often in the bathtub, the typewriter in front of him on a tray, a cigarette in his mouth (he smoked six packs a day). On his shoulder perched a parrot I had given him, pecking at Dalton's ear while Dalton pecked at the keys.[3]

Just as Trumbo did, Kubrick got the picture as a hand-me-down. Veteran action helmer Anthony Mann, Universal's first choice for the expensive production, was fired by Douglas shortly into production. Because of his magnificent work on the Bryna production *Paths of Glory* (1957, United Artists), Douglas hired Kubrick as Mann's replacement, giving the notorious perfectionist just two days to prepare for the shoot. Although Kubrick made numerous important contributions to the picture—including, for instance, dropping a huge amount of dialogue from the early sequences of the film, greatly adding to the portrayal of Spartacus as a man of action, not words—he determined early on that the picture was more Douglas's and Trumbo's than his, and Kubrick's many hostile comments about *Spartacus* reflect this attitude.[4]

Spartacus tells the real-life story of a Thracian slave, trained by his Roman masters as a gladiator, who breaks free and leads an army of slaves on an exodus that nearly leads them out of Italy and into liberty.[5] Sweeping, filled with battle action, and populated by characters archetypal and complex alike, the picture

played to all of Trumbo's strengths as a storyteller. The violence, scope, and dire stakes of the narrative allowed Trumbo to paint in the broad strokes that characterized much of his best screen work; the picture's long running time allowed him to use systematic methods and long range foreshadowing; and the film's epic nature gave him room to craft eloquent dialogue scenes as a complement to the action. At its most effective, the steady contrasting of intimate moments with larger-than-life goings-on keeps the film from becoming oversized mythology, in effect humanizing abstractions and showing how the freedom to love is one of the prizes for which Spartacus fights. At its least effective, as in contrived scenes involving the characters played by Jean Simmons and Tony Curtis, the insertion of quiet moments seems forced.[6]

Set in 70 B.C., the picture begins violently when Spartacus (Douglas), part of an exhausted slave crew doing back-breaking work at a quarry, saves a fellow slave from crumbling under the weight of a bag of rocks. He then fights with and injures a guard, which gets him chained to a hillside as an example. He is freed when a corpulent nobleman, Lentulus Batiatus (Peter Ustinov), buys Spartacus for his gladiator school. The early scenes of the picture are quick, sharp, and functional, establishing the pervasive violence of the period and the inhuman treatment of slaves. Although the scenes regularly include shots connecting Spartacus to groups of other characters—therefore clearly identifying that he is not unique, but rather representative of a social class—the filmmakers keep the focus strictly on Spartacus and communicate, with a minimum of dialogue, why the Thracian is the center of the story: he seethes with indignation.[7]

Producer-star Kirk Douglas, left, made history when he featured Trumbo's name in the credits of *Spartacus*. Because of the blacklist, his name had not appeared on a screen in 13 The sweeping adventure film was directed by maverick geni~~~ later disowned the picture. (Universal ~~~~~~

The direction in which Trumbo is taking the material becomes clear during the scene depicting Spartacus's first meeting with the love of his life, Varinia (Simmons). She is among several slave women brought in to sleep with the gladiator trainees, and from the moment she and Spartacus meet, they connect as kindred spirits too noble to accept their lots in servitude. The quiet moment the two share is disrupted, though, when it's revealed that Batiatus and a vicious trainer, Marcellus (Charles McGraw), are watching Spartacus and Varinia through a hole in the ceiling of Spartacus's cell. Feeling Varinia's violation as well as his own, Spartacus screams for his masters to leave. "Come, come," Batiatus purrs. "Be generous! We must learn to share our pleasures." This seedy dialogue, the first to hint at the kind of debauchery that will be appear later in the picture, shows two things: first, the wit with which Trumbo crafts the picture's best dialogue, and second, the way that the Romans use their slaves for sport. Both aspects prove highly relevant later in the film, especially when they coincide: the best scenes of *Spartacus* use clever dialogue and surprising turnabouts to show not only how the slaves defy the Romans but that the "higher class" is often such in name only. As suggested by Batiatus's crude request to have Spartacus and Varinia put on a show of lovemaking for him, the real savages in *Spartacus* are not the slaves but the noblemen.

The next several scenes of the film are largely expositional. We see Spartacus and the other trainees learn the deadly craft of the gladiator, and we see Spartacus and Varinia steal private moments amid the oppressive atmosphere of the school. During this stretch of the film, Trumbo identifies the two most important threads of the early part of the story—Spartacus's inherent defiance and, as personified by Varinia, a reason to believe that life holds something better than just slavery—but also provides a travelogue through the school. Kubrick and his collaborators—including cinematographer Russell Metty, production designer Alexander Golitzen, and artist Saul Bass, who crafted the picture's memorable credits sequence and storyboarded several complex scenes—present dynamic training sequences filled with color, motion, and the constant threat of deadly violence.

Trumbo unleashes his sharpest dialogue when Marcus Licinius Crassus (Laurence Olivier) is introduced. Upon hearing the news that Crassus, a powerful Roman senator, is coming to visit his school, the opportunistic Batiatus scrambles to prepare for his important guest. He asks a servant to fetch the "second-best wine," then amends his request to "the best—but small goblets." Ustinov's funny, pathetic portrayal is among the film's greatest pleasures. While Douglas simmers with primal intensity and Olivier burns with ambition, Ustinov and fellow Englishman Charles Laughton—whose character is introduced later—add invaluable humor to the film.[8]

By distributing expositional dialogue among several characters and decorating it with both dramatic and comical touches, Trumbo nimbly puts across an incredible amount of information during the approximately 12 minutes spanning from Crassus's arrival at the school to a climactic duel there. We learn that Crassus is trying to consolidate power in Rome by appointing his brother-in-law, the weak Marcus Publius Glabrus (John Dall, previously in *Gun Crazy*), as commander of the Roman garrison; we learn that Crassus's chief political rival is Batiatus's sponsor, a senator named Lentulus Gracchus (Laughton); and we learn that Crassus is a cold man with little regard for life and a voracious appetite for beauty, as seen by the lust for Varinia that Crassus shows during their first encounter.

Presented parallel to the machinations of the noblemen is a moral conflict among the gladiators, who learn that Crassus has commissioned a duel to the death, something that otherwise never occurs at the school. Spartacus and his fellow slaves realize that two of them will have to face each other, so tension runs underneath the entire sequence—literally. The cell in which the gladiators are kept is situated directly beneath the box occupied by Crassus's party, and Kubrick achieves an effective visual contrast by filming the noblemen in brightness—all marble and flowing white robes—and the slaves in the darkness of their cage.

During the duel, Spartacus is matched against towering Ethiopian Draba (Woody Strode). Draba defeats Spartacus, but instead of killing him, Draba releases Spartacus and attacks Crassus's party, only to be killed before he can inflict any damage.

The fierce emotion in Douglas's acting tells us everything about how Draba's sacrifice affects Spartacus; when Trumbo adds insult to injury by having Spartacus watch Varinia get taken away from the camp because she's been sold to Crassus, it's evident that Spartacus is near his breaking point. And because three is the magic number in screenwriting, Trumbo provides, in short order, the third incident that pushes Spartacus over the edge: After Draba's death and the selling of Varinia, Marcellus taunts and whips Spartacus so coldly that Spartacus

These three incidents reflect the methodical nature of the screenplay; although Trumbo has already spent nearly 40 minutes developing the idea that Spartacus is ready to break free from bondage, when the moment comes for Spartacus to take definitive action, Trumbo summates the information of the preceding scenes with three quick jabs, like salt poured into an open wound. This careful underscoring of Spartacus's motivation proves invaluable later in the screenplay, because the scenes depicting Spartacus as the leader of the slave army quickly give way to larger-than-life iconography. By grounding us in events that we experience with Spartacus on a human level, Trumbo ensures that we don't lose sight of the man inside the hero.

Strangely, Trumbo's clear-headed work gives way to looser writing later in the picture, as if Spartacus's appeal as a character lessened in tandem with his growth as a mythic figure. In some ways, the picture goes downhill after Spartacus kills Marcellus, because in addition to releasing the tension of the early scenes, Spartacus's rebellious act initiates an almost inevitable chain of events leading to his downfall: Spartacus's moment of liberation is the beginning of his story's ending. Specifically, the murder sparks a revolt at the school, wherein the slaves use their gladiatorial skills to slaughter their keepers and escape into the area surrounding the school like a band of runaway convicts.

The picture then makes a dramatic segue to Rome, where we first encounter Crassus's bitter rival for domination of the empire, Gracchus. We first see him assert himself while his fellow senators debate how to contain the slave army led

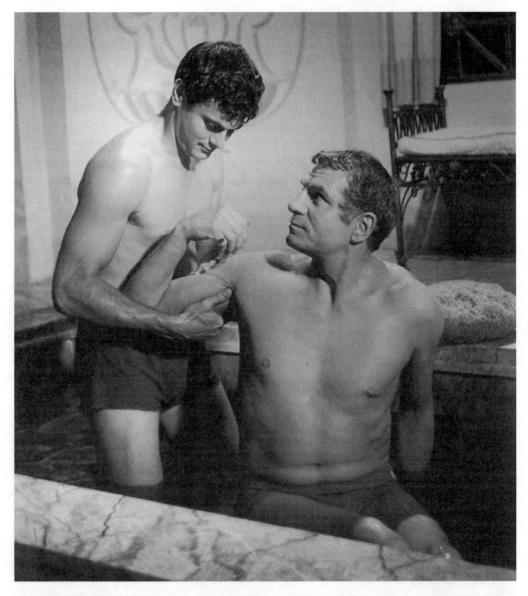

In the most notorious *Spartacus* scene, slave Antoninus (Tony Curtis, standing), massages his manipulative owner, Crassus (Laurence Olivier). Although Trumbo's dialogue for the scene featured no explicit homesexual overtones, the scene was cut by censors. (Universal Pictures)

Italy. Although the responsibility for containing the slaves might rightly fall elsewhere, Gracchus volunteers Crassus's stooge, Glabrus. In an aside as amusing as any of Ustinov's, Gracchus responds to a fellow senator's worry that if Glabrus and the garrison leave Rome, slaves in the city might riot: "Well, I did not say the whole garrison. Six cohorts will more than do the job. The rest can stay in Rome to save you from your housemaids."

This scene indelibly identifies Gracchus as a sophisticate willing to use any means while pursuing a goal. Like a chess player responding to a smart move with a brilliant one, Gracchus undercuts Crassus's installation of Glabrus as the garrison's commander by intimidating Glabrus into volunteering for a fool's errand. Furthermore, Gracchus makes a second move by installing his young charge, Caius Julius Caesar (John Gavin), as Glabrus's temporary replacement. As he does periodically throughout the screenplay, Trumbo inserts cynical commentary at the end of the scene depicting Glabrus's clever parry to Crassus's thrust. As Gracchus and Caesar leave the Senate chamber, Caesar worries that his mentor hasn't done enough to foil Crassus.

> GRACCHUS: Maybe. At least it gives me a chance to separate Glabrus from Crassus for a while. You know, this Republic of ours is something like a rich widow. Most Romans love her as their mother. But Crassus dreams of marrying the old girl—to put it politely.

Trumbo's graphic allusion offers a perfect metaphor for Crassus, because that's really what he is: a seducer. This aspect of Crassus's personality comes up again and again, most perversely in scenes involving the slave played by Tony Curtis. But more than being a metaphor for only one character, the sexual allusion that permeates Trumbo's portrayal of Crassus is a metaphor for entitlement in general. Crassus is a seducer, yes, but behind his seduction is the idea that his would-be lovers—be they human slaves or the sovereign state of Rome—are his to be seduced. The act of seduction is a sham, then, for what Crassus is really doing. Assigning this concept of entitlement to the picture's most repellent

character is among the most potent things that Trumbo does in this screenplay, because it aligns Crassus with contemporary power mongers, therefore helping to ensure that Crassus's machinations resonate with modern audiences.

Temporarily shunted to the periphery of the story, Spartacus spends this stretch of the movie building his army, freeing and then recruiting slaves as he travels through Italy. Back in Rome, Crassus learns of Gracchus's treachery and then acquires a refined, handsome manservant, Antoninus (Curtis). These two developments in Crassus's life amplify the idea of his indiscriminate lust: Even while fixating on an obstacle blocking his quest for power, Crassus grows infatuated with his new slave. That Crassus chooses to seduce Antoninus instead of merely taking him is indicative of Crassus's greatest weakness: vanity. He feels his conquests are unworthy unless won by his cleverness. The various aspects of Crassus's depraved personality are all addressed in a brief monologue that Crassus speaks to Glabrus, and which demonstrates the deft manner in which Trumbo slipped salacious nuances into the movie.

> CRASSUS: One day I shall cleanse this Rome which my fathers bequeathed me. I shall restore all the traditions that made her great. It follows, then, that I cannot come to power, or even defend myself, by an act which betrays the most sacred tradition of them all. I shall not bring my legions within these walls. I shall not violate Rome at the moment of possessing her.

As Sp...

the now-devastated gladiator school and has an epiphany. He sees his compatriots forcing Roman noblemen to fight in the arena, and interrupts the fight to ask the gathered slaves if this was the reward they sought. "We look for wine, when we should be hunting bread," he says. Spartacus conjures a plan wherein the slaves will fight their way out of Italy, freeing every slave they encounter, and looting enough riches to buy passage on ships that will return them all to their respective homelands. And because Spartacus's dream of freedom is entwined with his dream of love, Trumbo arranges for a convenient reunion with Varinia soon after Spartacus and his army embark on their new mission.

Varinia explains that she escaped from Batiatus because he was too fat to chase her when she leapt from his cart and fled. They laugh loudly and joyously, the laughter of free people, and proclaim their love for each other. The idyllic nature of the love scenes between Spartacus and Varinia counters the nefarious machinations of the noblemen and the brutal warfare of the slaves' struggle, but the flowery talk in these scenes doesn't compare favorably to the subtle barbs in scenes featuring Crassus and Gracchus.

Offering a vivid example of the gulf between the witty Rome scenes and the tepid romantic exchanges is the scene immediately following Spartacus's reunion with Varinia. Batiatus, now destitute because his school has been destroyed, petitions Gracchus for help in exacting revenge upon Crassus, whom Batiatus blames for his misfortune. Before they get down to business, though, the two men discuss a particular aspect of Gracchus's personality, and the combination of Trumbo's casual eloquence

and the comfortable performances by Laughton and Ustinov make this one of the most pleasurable scenes in the picture:

> BATIATUS: In spite of your vices, you're the most generous Roman of our time.
> GRACCHUS: Vices?
> BATIATUS: The ladies.
> GRACCHUS: Ladies? Since when are they a vice?
> BATIATUS: Oh, perhaps I used the wrong word. An eccentricity—a foible…. It's well known that even your groom and your butler are women.
> GRACCHUS: I'm the most virtuous man in Rome!
> BATIATUS: Uh—
> GRACCHUS: I keep these women out of my respect for Roman morality. That morality which has made Rome strong enough to steal two-thirds of the world from its rightful owners. Founded on the sanctity of Roman marriage, and the Roman family. I happen to like women. I have a promiscuous nature, and unlike these aristocrats, I will not take a marriage vow which I know that my nature will prevent me from keeping.
> BATIATUS: You have too great a respect for the purity of womankind.
> GRACCHUS: Exactly!

As if the preceding exchange was insufficient to indicate the depths of Roman lechery, the film then offers a notorious scene in which Crassus receives a massage from Antoninus while bathing. This scene, which was extracted from the movie shortly after the picture's initial release because of its implied homosexual content, was restored for the 1991 rerelease.[9]

After these libidinous interludes,

the picture rejoins Spartacus's band, which has swelled to include thousands of liberated slaves. Spartacus is an approachable leader, demanding only that each member of the group pull his or her own weight. A wordless montage that begins with the arrival of a group of new slaves—including Antoninus, who flees Crassus's homosexual advances—draws an intriguingly communistic allusion. In the montage, we see women caring for children, cooking, and knitting, while their men learn to fight. The implication of the montage is that the slaves have formed a harmonious collective in which class has no place and each person's role is defined by the work that they do, not by their heredity. To amplify this point—and to advance the idea that Spartacus's true motivation is love, not hatred—Spartacus directs Antoninus to entertain a group of slaves by singing. "There's a time for fighting and there's a time for singing," he tells Antoninus. "Now you teach us to sing." Antoninus's singing—actually, more of a poetry recital—is featured in the background during the following exchange between Spartacus and Varinia, among the few love scenes in the movie to advance important thematic material.

> SPARTACUS: Who wants to fight? An animal can learn to fight. But to sing beautiful things....
> VARINIA: What are you thinking about?
> SPARTACUS: I'm free. And what do I know? I don't even know how to read.
> VARINIA: You know things that can't be taught.
> SPARTACUS: I know nothing. Nothing! And I want to know....
> VARINIA: K...

falls and a bird doesn't—where the sun goes at night—and why the moon changes shape. I want to know where the wind comes from.
> VARINIA: The wind begins in a cave. Far to the north, a young god sleeps in that cave. He dreams of a girl, and he sighs. And the night wind stirs with his breath.
> SPARTACUS: I want to know all about you. Every line, every curve—I want to know every part of you. Every beat of your heart.

The idyll doesn't last long, however—Spartacus soon learns that Glabrus's soldiers are marching on the slave army's position. Because Glabrus expects only feeble resistance, he doesn't establish proper defenses around his camp, so when Spartacus's army stages a sneak attack, the slaves easily defeat the garrison.

The defeat of Glabrus's soldiers is an important one because it boosts morale among the slaves and hurts Crassus politically. Glabrus is exiled for his incompetence, and Crassus, making a grand display before the senate, announces that he will give up his post because he sponsored Glabrus. Sensing that the senators will implore Crassus to return, Gracchus hastily makes a speech that offers pointed commentary on political posturing.

With Crassus momentarily checked, the film returns to Spartacus and the slaves, now moving steadily across Italy. Varinia reports that she's pregnant, and the future looks bright for Spartacus and his fellow emancipated slaves. During this long middle section of the film, Trumbo effectively diverts viewers' attention from the static, talkative nature

army's progress—by intercutting the two elements. This achieves a dramatic contrast, but it also creates a sense of foreboding, because Rome and the slave army are identified as opposing forces that will inevitably meet. Thus, each cut from Rome to the slave army, or vice versa, is equivalent to one chess board move closer to the endgame.[10]

With the threat of Spartacus's army looming over Rome, Gracchus moves to consolidate his power—and in the process stymie Crassus's attempts to consolidate his—by appointing Caesar as Glabrus's replacement, and ordering two legions to confront Spartacus's army. The legions are handily defeated, so Crassus is forced to seek a new way of reclaiming the senate's favor. He visits Gracchus and offers to take command of Rome's armies and hunt down Spartacus's band—in exchange for nearly absolute political control of Rome's armies and courts. Crassus knows he has the upper hand, because the senate is terrified of Spartacus, but Gracchus initially refuses.

When Crassus leaves their presence, Gracchus reveals to Caesar his own plan for dealing with Spartacus—he has arranged for Spartacus's army to escape Rome without interference from the Roman military. Caesar is suitably incensed, and his mentor's response is a display of pure pragmatism—as well as another in the film's string of jibes at morally compromised politicians.

"So now we deal with pirates," Caesar bleats. "We bargain with criminals!"

"No, don't you be so stiff-necked about it," Gracchus retorts. "Politics is a practical profession. If a criminal has what you want—you do business with him!"

Crassus discovers and undoes Gracchus's scheme, however, thereby ensuring that Spartacus's army will have to fight their way out of Italy. Furthermore, Crassus blocks the most logical alternate route, meaning that instead of pressing down toward the Mediterranean, their only option is a frontal attack on Rome—where the Roman military will have a massive strategic advantage as well as numbers that the slaves can't match. When Spartacus is offered a way to escape the inevitable slaughter, however, he refuses; instead, he gathers his army and announces: "We have no choice but to march against Rome herself and end this war the only way it could've ended. By freeing every slave in Italy!"

In one of the film's most effective devices, Spartacus's most important speech is intercut with an equally crucial oratory by Crassus. The intercutting grounds viewers once more in the players at hand: Spartacus, the rebel, fighting for freedom, and Rome (as represented by Crassus), fighting to protect its oppressive way of life. That Spartacus speaks from atop a craggy hill on a stormy night while Crassus speaks from inside a gleaming temple on a glorious day offers ample visual contrast between the oppressed and the oppressor—and abundant foreshadowing of the reckoning to come. When contrasted with the might and glory of Rome, Spartacus's army looks like cannon fodder, no matter how just its cause.

The battle between the slaves and the Romans is decisive; although many lives are lost on both sides, the slave insurrection is halted and Spartacus's army is defeated. After the battle, however, comes the film's most iconic scene—and, in fact, perhaps the most enduring scene of any Trumbo movie. As Crassus's officers survey the slave survivors, we see Antoninus and Spartacus among the first of dozens of rows of prisoners. A Roman officer says that all of them will be crucified unless the "the body or the living person of the slave called Spartacus" is produced. Spartacus, heavy with the burden of responsibility, slowly stands. But before he can speak, Antoninus stands up next to him and they both say, "I'm Spartacus!" at the same time. Spartacus is dumbfounded as, one by one, each of the slaves stands and yells, "I'm Spartacus!" The climax of the scene is a remarkable close-up of Douglas shedding a tear because Spartacus is moved beyond words that he has engendered such loyalty.

Aside from its dramatic importance in the film, this scene is notable for its perfect representation of Trumbo's vision of personal honor. It involves a rebel hero poised to take responsibility for his actions, and acolytes so moved by his dignity that they offer themselves in sacrifice. Spartacus's soldiers are infected with the sense of honor displayed by their leader. Because Trumbo was ever willing to make grand displays himself—his defiance before HUAC; his model behavior in jail; his principled stands on behalf of unjustly accused individuals; even his controversial "only victims" speech—the moment when the slaves put themselves between death and Spartacus is inspirational on myriad levels. In the context of the movie, it is the scene in which Spartacus's dream of making slaves want freedom comes true; in the context of Trumbo's life, it is the scene in which he most effectively showed the power of noble conduct.

Away from the brave display by the slaves, Cr———— ——d B——————

stead find Varinia, who is guarding her infant son. She tells them Spartacus is dead, but Crassus doesn't believe her; enraged that his quarry has escaped him, Crassus takes the woman and child as his slaves, has Batiatus whipped and sent from the camp, and orders that all the survivors be crucified. A heartbeat after ordering the mass execution, Crassus encounters his own runaway slave, Antoninus, and strongly suspects that the man next to Antoninus might be Spartacus. He orders that these two be killed last.

The series of scenes following the battle are among the most dramatically important—but logically incredible—of the entire film. Relying on a series of coincidences and unlikely events weakens this portion of the picture, and is an indication of why the third acts of Trumbo's films often faltered: he frequently relied on sleight of hand when concluding stories. In this case, he carefully sculpted principal characters and used effective devices including foreshadowing and intercutting to develop two parallel narratives, but when the story reached its final arc, he disregarded his methodical precision and wrote from dramatic need.

The picture needed confrontations between Crassus and Spartacus, so Trumbo provided them even if, in the logic of the story, it's unlikely they would have occurred; Spartacus needed a friend with whom to interact during the last portion of the film, so Antoninus survives the battle despite being a delicate artist among hardened gladiators; Trumbo needed to arrange a fate for Varinia that offered comfort lacking in the resolution of Spartacus's story, so he arranged, in a roundabout way, h—

Trumbo wrote some of his most dextrous dialogue for the politically ambitious characters played by Charles Laughton, left, and Peter Ustinov, center, in *Spartacus*. Here, Laughton's character signs papers freeing Spartacus's wife (Jean Simmons) and child. (Universal Pictures)

benefactor. Although logical lapses of this nature are certainly present in the film's two first acts, they do not become pervasive until the film's final movements. That the same phenomenon affects *Exodus*'s narrative seems to indicate something about Trumbo's ability to tell three-hour stories, but it's interesting to note that *Hawaii*, the other epic that Trumbo wrote in the 1960s, suffers not from a weak third act but rather from a weak first act.[11]

Following his violent expulsion from Crassus's camp, Batiatus visits his old benefactor, Gracchus. Once again, the interplay between Ustinov and Laughton is highly gratifying, even if the languorous rhythms of their conversation slow down the film at a time when it should be speeding toward its denoue-ment. Batiatus explains that Crassus appears to have fallen in love with Varinia, so Gracchus says a fine revenge would be to steal her from Crassus's estate. "I can no longer hurt Crassus in the senate, but I can hurt him where he'll feel it most," Gracchus says. "In his pride."

As if anticipating Gracchus's next treacherous maneuver, Crassus summons Gracchus to the senate chamber, where Crassus reveals that he knows of Gracchus's foiled plan to help Spartacus's army escape Italy. Crassus tells Gracchus that he can avoid punishment by relinquishing his political power and agreeing to serve as Crassus's underling. This dark, understated scene, in which Crassus is presented at his most nefarious, is followed by one showing him at his most ineffectual.

Echoing the manner in which he tried to seduce Antoninus when he could have taken the boy at any time, Crassus tries to seduce Varinia. She defies him, and comments that he appears frightened of Spartacus. Varinia's comment reveals an underlying truth of Crassus's character: he doesn't regard slaves as humans, and therefore can't understand their defiance. Crassus is so drunk with entitlement that he regards "asking" slaves to do things as a game. This moment, when Varinia recognizes Crassus's fear—even though she doesn't articulate its nuances—is an essential one, because it is part of a succession that includes Antoninus's escape from Crassus's estate and the slaves' refusal to identify Spartacus. Because the liberation of slaves is the main theme of *Spartacus*, moments in which supporting characters act willfully are perhaps more important than scenes of Spartacus attacking his captors with a sword; where his actions are immediate and visceral, the actions taken by Antoninus and Varinia reflect a change in thinking. And, as Trumbo proved again and again, a rebellion of the mind is far more dangerous than one of the fist.

The concept of psychological rebellion is also addressed in a quiet scene between Antoninus and Spartacus, the last two rebel slaves left alive. As they await their fate, Antoninus pointedly asks, "Could we have won, Spartacus?" Spartacus's response is, in essence, the film's message:

> SPARTACUS: Well, just by fighting we may have won something. If just one man says, "No, I won't," Rome begins to fear. And if ten thousand should say "no"—that was the wonder of it. To have seen the slaves lift their heads f....

them rise from their knees—to stand tall with a song on their lips....

Now Crassus enters the scene and addresses the two slaves. He calls Spartacus by name, but Spartacus just stares into Crassus's eyes so deeply that his gaze is like a physical assault. Crassus's long-burning frustration explodes, causing him to scream and slap Spartacus—vainly hoping to smite this "lesser" man who is destroying all Crassus holds dear. Seeking one final way to humiliate his opponent, Crassus orders the slaves to fight a duel. Crassus's soldiers form a ring, and the slaves are given swords. Spartacus offers to kill Antoninus quickly, but Antoninus says he'd rather have Spartacus die at the hands of a friend than on the cross. Antoninus is outmatched, though, and the duel ends swiftly with Antoninus's death. Finally stretched to his own breaking point, Spartacus screams at Crassus: "Here's your victory! He'll come back! And he'll be millions!"

Feeling triumphant, Crassus retorts: "I wonder what Spartacus would say if he knew that the woman, Varinia, and her child are slaves in my household." The broken, tearful look on Spartacus's face gives him away, so Crassus, thinking himself fully restored to metaphorical virility, hisses: "Yes—*Spartacus*! Crucify him!"

After ordering the Thracian's death, Crassus speaks with Caesar, who has shifted his alliance from Gracchus. Caesar asks if his new mentor feared Spartacus. "Not when I fought him," Crassus says. "I knew he could be beaten. But now I fear him, even more than I fear you."[12]

the first, Batiatus presents Varinia and her baby—freshly kidnapped from Crassus's estate—to Gracchus, who writes senatorial papers emancipating the woman and child. Because he knows Crassus's men are coming to claim him, Gracchus sends the three travelers on their way and then retires to his bedchamber with a dagger to commit suicide.

In the second scene, the picture ends on the most bittersweet note imaginable. As Batiatus drives a cart taking himself, Varinia, and the baby from Rome, they proceed down the Appian Way, which is lined with the crucified bodies of thousands of slaves. Her eyes growing wide with horror, Varinia sees Spartacus, crucified, a short distance ahead of the cart. She walks over to him and speaks through her tears as Batiatus, terrified of being captured, implores her to return to the cart.

> VARINIA: This is your son. He's free, Spartacus! Free—He'll remember you, Spartacus. Because I'll tell him—I'll tell him who his father was—and what he dreamed of.
> BATIATUS: Varinia—
> VARINIA: Oh, my love, my life—please die. Die, please die, my love. Oh, God, why can't you die?[13]

A towering film filled with intense action and sparkling dialogue exchanges, *Spartacus* was the perfect movie with which to reintroduce Trumbo to the material world. It is the culmination of his rebel-hero iconography, because the film's blend of romanticism and fatalism depicts the price paid for glory. Glory, however, appears to have been the last thing on Douglas's mind when he made his historic decision to put Trumbo's name onscreen. When the credit issue was raised near the end of principal photography, Douglas recalled, options included using Lewis's name or Trumbo's alias, "Sam Jackson." But when Kubrick "horrified" Douglas and Lewis by suggesting that the credit read "Screenplay by Stanley Kubrick," it was the last straw for Douglas:

"The next morning, I called the gate at Universal. 'I'd like to leave a pass for Dalton Trumbo.' The masquerade was over."[14]

Although history books generally concede that Trumbo's credits on *Spartacus* and *Exodus* broke the blacklist, several blacklistees claimed they beat Trumbo to the punch; writer-director Jules Dassin, for one, noted that his caper film *Rififi* (1955, Indus/Pathé) played on American screens, with his real name in the credits, years before Trumbo's epics hit theaters.[15] While such assertions are well documented, they don't diminish the importance of Trumbo's credits on his 1960 epics, because his credits were more symbolic than anything else. Credits such as Dassin's on *Rififi* may have caused a few ripples, but Trumbo's 1960 credits galvanized the nation's opinion makers—and provided a triumphant conclusion to Trumbo's 13-year ordeal.

8

Back in Business
(1960–1961)

As mentioned in the introduction to this book, one factor that mitigates Trumbo's screenwriting accomplishments is that so many of his best films were adaptations. In some cases, such as *Lonely Are the Brave*, Trumbo himself discouraged viewers from overestimating his contributions, because he felt that instead of reinventing the subject matter of his source material, he merely translated it from one medium to another. Even within that context, however, his achievements in the early part of the 1960s are outstanding.

While *Lonely Are the Brave* might be, as Trumbo suggested, merely a translation, *Spartacus* is truly a reinvention. Fast's novel is a mannered, didactic work that deals with the myth of Spartacus, not his life—at the beginning of Fast's novel, Spartacus is already dead, so his adventures are presented in flashback. Moreover, the spectacular dialogue that makes the Roman scenes in the film of *Spartacus* so arresting is nowhere to be found in Fast's novel. Through a long, in-

tensive process of rewrites done in collaboration with Douglas and others, Trumbo crafted not only a linear story, but also a dialogue style that raised Fast's concepts from dry abstractions to pungent realities. Trumbo humanized the novel without diminishing its epic nature.

Trumbo followed *Spartacus* with *Exodus*, Otto Preminger's film on the formation of Israel, and, like its predecessor, *Exodus* had a problematic gestation period. Leon Uris was commissioned by MGM to write a novel that would then become a film, but because Uris was represented by agent Ingo Preminger, the director's brother, Otto Preminger saw Uris's manuscript before it was complete. He bought the project from MGM and set it up at United Artists, but promised Uris a shot at writing the screenplay. As happened with Fast on *Spartacus*, Uris failed to produce a satisfactory script. Preminger fired the author from the project, causing a rift that never healed.

Uris's first replacement was Hollywood Ten member Albert Maltz, but Maltz didn't work at the pace Preminger needed; Trumbo, with his reputation for producing quality work at breakneck speed, was a natural choice as the third person to try adapting *Exodus*. Preminger spent about six weeks working intensely from morning until night with Trumbo until the script was complete,[1] and the close supervision that Preminger did on the project indicates another caveat that must be kept in mind when considering Trumbo's screen output: He had little say in what happened after his scripts were submitted, so his responsibility for the quality of his films varies based on how closely his scripts were followed. Christopher Trumbo noted that *Lonely Are the Brave* was made "almost shot-for-shot" from his father's script, while *The Sandpiper* inflated the simple narrative crafted by his father and Michael Wilson into ridiculous hyperbole.[2]

In the case of *Exodus*, Preminger did much of his tinkering during the writing process and mostly shot what Trumbo gave him; his fidelity to the screenplay made sense, because *Exodus* has a massive story that could have become incoherent without Trumbo's mostly clear-headed road map leading the way. Whereas Uris dealt with literally centuries of history, Trumbo only hinted at the larger historical context. The result was that *Exodus*, the film, is a dramatization of a segment of *Exodus*, the book. That Trumbo often reconstructed source material is the best argument against dismissing his work as mere adaptation—or, as playwright Edward Albee characterized the work of Ernest Lehman, who won an Academy Award for adapting Albee's play, *Who's*

Afraid of Virginia Woolf? (1966, Warner Bros.), "typing."

Notwithstanding the ingenuity that Trumbo showed in crafting the screen story, *Exodus* is in some ways the mirror image of *Spartacus*, because while the latter is filled with action, the former is filled with inaction. *Exodus* starts strongly by introducing a varied cast of characters and presenting several intriguing dialogue scenes, but then it hits a narrative roadblock. The dramatic centerpiece of the story is the heroic escape of a boatload of Jewish refugees from a harbor in Cyprus, but because the means by which the refugees make their escape is not a violent confrontation but rather a passive one, the images comprising the centerpiece are necessarily static.

Furthermore, the film is really two stories spliced together. After the refugees escape Cyprus, the film shifts into a second narrative about the three-way war for control of Palestine involving Jews, Arabs, and the British. Both stories are compelling, but melding them into a single movie seems arbitrary. When compounded by the lack of inspiration that dulls several scenes in the second half of the picture, *Exodus* becomes a cumbersome leviathan.

The picture begins with the introduction of Catherine "Kitty" Fremont (Eva Marie Saint), an American nurse who travels to postwar Cyprus to learn how her photojournalist husband died. The tour guide who drives Kitty around Cyprus is used to deliver exposition about the thousands of Jews who are interred on British-controlled Cyprus: they are European refugees left homeless after World War II and trying to get to Palestine, where Jews are struggling to form a sovereign state. Preminger also uses this sequence to introduce young refugee Karen (Jill Haworth), who figures prominently in the story.

A bracing interlude is provided when one of the refugees, intense young Dov Landau (Sal Mineo), tries to escape his captors. After a lively chase and a brawl with soldiers, Dov falls and suffers serious injuries. He's carted away to the hospital inside the Caraolos interment center, and his stillborn escape attempt offers a microcosm of the Jews' futile struggle to gain liberation from their British "hosts."

To discover her husband's fate, Kitty visits Brigadier General Bruce Sutherland (Ralph Richardson), the man in charge of the British forces on Cyprus. In a long, expositional conversation, we learn that Kitty's foolhardy husband died while taking a picture of an approaching warplane. We also learn that in the year since his death, Kitty miscarried a child and has been listlessly wandering around Europe. Bruce suggests she help in the interment center as a nurse, but Kitty says she feels "strange" among Jews. The expression on Bruce's face suggests that he finds her comment offensive, although he doesn't express any disapproval. But when Bruce's fatuous underling, Major Fred Caldwell (Peter Lawford), startles Kitty by making an anti–Semitic remark, she decides to help at the center after all.

Although there's something to be said for using an outsider as a way into a complicated sociopolitical story, there's something jingoistic about the choice of Kitty as this film's protagonist. Even though Paul Newman gets top billing over Saint, the structure of the story centers around Kitty, not Newman's character. Ari Ben Canaan, it b...

ends with her becoming a fully integrated member of the Jewish independence movement. This narrative choice marginalizes the Jews in their own story, as if their dramatic purpose is to sway America (as represented by Kitty) from indifference to action.

When the movie begins, Kitty regards the Jews' problems as subordinate to her own grief and soul searching; later, social consciousness dominates her personality. We see no such change in any of the Jewish characters, with the possible exception of Karen. When he meets her, Karen is intrigued by the idea of moving to America, but by the end of the picture, she's a committed freedom fighter. What mitigates the significance of Karen's growth is that her function in the narrative is largely to motivate Kitty's evolution. The other Jewish characters exhibit solidarity from the moment we meet them, even though the filmmakers effectively portray the internal schism between the nonviolent activists (the Hagannah) and the bomb-wielding extremists (the Irgun). Jews in the film do not move from one position to another, so the dramatic arc of the story is Kitty's change. Having a character who is essentially a bystander take center stage is distracting.

While working at Caraolos, Kitty encounters characters ranging from the demure to the confrontational: while she's impressed by brilliant Doctor Samuel Odenheim (Martin Miller), she isn't by Dov, who threatens Kitty with a broken bottle until he is put in his place by Karen. Karen's boldness endears her to Kitty.

Simultaneous with Kitty's story, the movie introduces Ari, an insurgent who

plans. Soon after his arrival, he tells a small band of freedom fighters that he wants to liberate the 611 Jews recently transported to Cyprus aboard the *Star of David*—including Dov, Karen, and Odenheim—to show that the Jewish independence movement won't be suppressed. Ari explains that a large, symbolic escape is necessary because the United Nations is scheduled to vote on the Palestine issue—the question of separating Palestine into separate Jewish and Arab states—by the end of its current session.

Meanwhile, Kitty grows closer to Karen. When Kitty asks Bruce for permission to take the internee out for a holiday, Kitty notes that the general seems satisfied with himself. He reveals that he encouraged her to work at the center because he hoped she would be distracted from her grief, and his revelation identifies Bruce as a gentleman eager to honor debts to friends such as Kitty's late husband. Although this exchange sweetly illuminates both characters, it's ultimately trivial to the main thrust of the story, and therefore one of innumerable scenes to reveal the wrongheadedness of building the film around Kitty. When contrasted with the struggle of a people to find a homeland, the story of a widow coming back to life seems petty and boring.

More interesting than Kitty's journey is Ari's intrigue-laden mission. He and his accomplices acquire a dilapidated boat, the *Olympia*, on which the Jews will be transported; prepare a fake British identity for Ari; and get several trucks with which to move the Jews from Caraolos to the *Olympia*. These developments lead to the sharply entertaining scene detailed in the introduction of this book, during which Ari con-

vinces the anti–Semitic Fred to countersign the order releasing the Jews. The rousing adventure of Ari's escape plan is undercut, however, by pedestrian scenes depicting Kitty's quest to become Karen's surrogate mother. The American encounters two major obstacles: the discovery that Karen's father might still be alive, meaning Karen still has ties to Europe; and Karen's relocation to the *Olympia* with the other *Star of David* Jews.

Just when it seems that Ari's plan will succeed, Bruce discovers that Fred was duped and discerns that the *Olympia* is headed for Palestine. The general orders a blockade to prevent the *Olympia* from reaching the open sea; Ari responds by saying that the ship is carrying 200 pounds of dynamite, and that if British soldiers try to board the *Olympia*, he'll destroy it and kill all 611 Jews. Having encountered Hagannah extremism before, Bruce takes the threat seriously and seeks another recourse. He asks Kitty to board the ship, under the auspices of retrieving Karen, and discover if the Jews are being held by force. Once on board, Kitty sees the solidarity of the refugees—and the obstinacy of their leader.

> ARI: Don't expect me to get hysterical over the life of one Jewish child. And don't you get hysterical, either. You're late, lady. You're ten years late. Almost 2 million Jewish children were butchered like animals because nobody wanted them. No country would have them. Not your country or any other country. And nobody wants the ones who survived. Jewish flesh is cheap, lady. It is cheaper than beef—it is cheaper even than herring.

This dialogue, while charged, indicates another of the problems that plague Trumbo's screenplay for *Exodus*: verbosity. The language of the speech is repetitive—excising the phrase, "Not your country or any other country," for instance, wouldn't dull the effect of the speech one whit—and it is alternately bland and obtuse. "Butchered like animals," while accurate, is a tired usage, and drawing an allusion between Jewish flesh and "herring" seems a terribly flip way to put a point across. The same problems that infect this speech infect the rest of the movie.

Preminger loved to film "talking heads" (static shots of people speaking), even if he often dressed up such shots with elaborate widescreen backgrounds and complicated camera movements. Trumbo was a man who loved to hear himself talk. When these two put their heads together, they came up with a bloated movie so filled with repetitive conversation that the potential impact of the story is dulled. The events contained in the narrative—a hunger strike, daring escapes, deadly gunfights—are incredibly exciting, but the manner in which Preminger and Trumbo present those events is not the most dynamic possible.[3]

After Kitty reports that the Jews are not being held by force, Bruce radios Ari and says that the ship will be boarded but cannot leave Cyprus. The freedom fighter then reveals his next plan: a hunger strike. This proposal is met with immediate approval by one of the *Star of David* Jews, diehard racial Lakavitch (Gregory Ratoff). "Now you're beginning to make a little sense," Lakavitch says. "We are going to Palestine, or we're going to die right here." Ari warns his shipmates that a hunger strike is, as the pedantic lan...

itch, charged with idealism, has a quick answer.

> LAKAVITCH: What is so unusual about the Jews dying? Is that anything new? I say right here, there is no excuse for us to go on living unless we start fighting right now. So that every Jew on the face of the earth can start feeling like a human being again. You heard what I said. Fight, not beg. Fight!

Sadly, this intense speech—which attacks the theme of living honorably as voraciously as any of Spartacus's oratories—is undercut by more interminable scenes between Kitty and Bruce. She weakly implores him to let the Jews sail to Palestine on their boat, now re-christened the *Exodus*, but Bruce says his hands are tied. He explains that the British have "an extraordinary talent for troublesome commitments," adding that he can't act until the United Nations makes its decision on Palestine.

This talky scene is followed by several more onboard the *Exodus*, where the Jews hear regular news reports about how their plight relates to other independence efforts across the globe. The hunger strike is shown in laborious detail, as are long conversations between Ari and Kitty, in which he slowly wins her sympathy. "Each person on board this ship is a soldier," he tells her. "The only weapon we have to fight with is our willingness to die." Were that comment the extent of Ari's soapbox posturing, it might have had the power of directness; instead, the comment is part of long-winded scene that makes the same point over and over again.

After what seems like an int...

Trumbo wrote numerous films about rebel heroes, including *Exodus*, director Otto Preminger's epic about the struggle to form an independent Jewish state. Paul Newman (center) plays a freedom fighter who disguises himself as a British officer and encounters harsh anti–Semitism. (United Artists)

part because of Bruce's efforts on their behalf. Had *Exodus* ended here—with the departure from Cyprus to Palestine—the story would have felt like a triumphant parable. But because of Preminger's overwrought approach, there are still nearly two hours of narrative to go.

Once the story reaches Palestine, we're introduced to another set of principal characters, including Barak Ben Canaan (Lee J. Cobb), Ari's father and leader of Gan Dafna, a Jewish youth village; and Ari's childhood friend Taha (John Derek), mukhtar of Abu Yesha, the Arab village that neighbors Gan Dafna. In the talkative spirit of the picture, both characters are introduced not by cleverly conceived dramatic scenes but by long speeches.

Barak and Taha are central to the main conflict of the second half of the picture, which is sparked when the United Nations votes to separate Palestine into Jewish and Arab states. While the first half of the picture was about Jews fighting for freedom from the British—a clear issue of oppression—the second half of the picture deals with the much thornier issue of how religious differences pit brother against brother. The sides of this fraternal conflict are represented by the residents of Gan Dafna (led by Ari) and those of Abu Yesha (led by Taha).

Whereas Uris folded the fundamentally different conflicts depicted in *Exodus* into the larger context of the Jewish struggle for freedom over the course of several centuries, Preminger's choice to splice together two chapters in the Jewish story was a misstep. The lapse in narrative judgment is compounded by the introduction of a romance between Ari and Kitty, which adds yet more dead weight to the story.

Notwithstanding these problems, there are several arresting scenes in the latter portion of the film, most of them involving Ari's radical uncle, Akiva Ben Canaan (David Opatoshu[4]), whom we meet in an effectively indirect fashion. Upon arriving in Palestine, Dov—the hotheaded rebel who suffered injuries while fleeing the British at the beginning of the picture—tries to join the Freedom Fighters of the Irgun, a Jewish underground movement that uses terrorist tactics. Dov is brought before Akiva, who methodically questions Dov about why he wants to become a radical. In a scene that is not only the most tense of the picture but probably Trumbo's hardest-hitting contribution to Uris's narrative, Dov tells Akiva that he learned about demolitions while fighting Nazis in the Warsaw Ghetto. The conversation that ensues is a verbal duel between an overconfident, troubled young man and a brilliant, hardened veteran. At the climax of the long scene, Akiva quizzes Dov about his experiences at Auschwitz. The last part of their exchange has all the energy and weight missing from the worst parts of *Exodus*.

AKIVA: At Auschwitz they had crematoriums only at the last. Before the installation of the ovens, what happened to the bodies?
DOV: They buried them.
AKIVA: How?
DOV: In trenches and holes.
AKIVA: And who dug the holes?

DOV: I don't know.
AKIVA: I ask you again—who dug the graves?
DOV: I don't know—they had demolition squads. At least, ah—sometimes they did. To blow holes in the ground and—and then dump the bodies in.
AKIVA: That is correct. Now, may I tell you something, Dov Landau? At no time did the Jews use dynamite in the Warsaw Ghetto. They had no dynamite. Do you remember better now?
DOV: Maybe.
AKIVA: So it was not possible for you to learn the use of dynamite in the Warsaw Ghetto. You learned about dynamite at Auschwitz making mass graves to receive the dead bodies of your people. True?
DOV: Yes.
AKIVA: Hundreds and hundreds of thousands of them, eh?
DOV: Yes.
AKIVA: And you saved your own life by working in that camp as a Sonderkommando. Correct?
DOV: Yes.
AKIVA: It was the duty of those Jews who became Sonderkommandos to shave the heads of other Jews.
DOV: Yes.
AKIVA: To remove dead bodies from the gas chambers? To collect gold fillings from their teeth?
DOV: [*sobbing*] Yes! Yes. What could I do? What could I do?
AKIVA: We take into consideration that you were less than 13 when you entered Auschwitz. Even so, we must have truth. Is there anything else?
DOV: Yes.
AKIVA: Then tell us.
DOV: No. I won't tell you....
AKIVA: Tell us.
DOV: They used me...

After revealing Dov's shame, Akiva immediately swears him into the Irgun, and the remarkable scene clearly establishes Akiva as a man unwilling to accept compromise, no matter the cost: he's willing to break Dov if that's the only way to get the truth. This makes Akiva yet another in the long string of Trumbo protagonists who live by a strict code of honor; like Andrew Long, Princess Ann, Spartacus, and others before him, Akiva is a personification of moral rectitude. For that reason, his fate is not only poignant but an amplification of Trumbo's vision of how honorable people are treated by the world. Also, that Akiva is an unapologetic terrorist proves that Trumbo's ideas about honor had reached full bloom by 1960. Whereas he previously sanctified one-dimensional heroes, in his latter-day films Trumbo celebrated killers and terrorists—even if he could sometimes be accused of whitewashing his portrayals as a means of engendering audience sympathy.[5]

After Dov joins the Irgun, the group steps up its bombing campaign to put pressure on the British to leave Palestine. The attacks force Ari to confront his uncle and ask if there can't be a compromise between the Hagannah and the Irgun. Ari says that the bombings are hurting the Jews' image in the United Nations, and that what's needed are peaceful protests such as the one staged onboard the *Exodus*.

> ARI: A year ago, we had the respect of the whole world. Now, when they read about us, it's nothing but terror and violence.
> AKIVA: It's not the first time this happens in history. I don't know of one nation—whether existing now or in the past—that was not born in violence. Terror, violence, death. They

are the midwives who bring free nations into this world. Compromisers like the Hagannah produce only abortions.

This bold language is among the most direct and far-reaching in the screenplay, but, like everything else in *Exodus*, it is buried in too much—too much talk, too much didactic posturing, too much repetition. So it's a tremendous relief when, about two hours into the picture, the story veers away from chest thumping and into intense human drama.

One of the significant developments in the second half of the picture is the humanizing of Ari's character, which is achieved by showing his interaction with Akiva and with his father, a righteous man played with tremendous authority by the larger-than-life Cobb. The simple pleasures of these scenes, which range from philosophical arguments to innocuous domestic exchanges, address the movie's themes in a manner more germane to the story than Kitty's character-driven scenes.

The stakes of the film are raised when Dov inadvertently gets Akiva and several other Irgun officials arrested by British soldiers, even though Dov himself escapes capture. The arrests lead to the picture's second major set piece: a daring prison break in which Ari and a team of freedom fighters get Akiva and his colleagues out of jail.

The jailbreak is among several sequences to benefit from Trumbo's methodical style, because vignettes depicting how Ari's operatives sneak parts of explosive devices into the heavily guarded prison create a slow burn leading to the literally explosive climax. This meticulously constructed sequence parallels slow burn scenes in *A Man to Remember* (the influenza epidemic), *Thirty Seconds Over Tokyo* (the bombing run), *The Brave One* (Leonardo's race to save the bull), and other pictures. And because the jailbreak showcases Preminger's underused skill for purely visual storytelling, it is the flip side of the *Olympia* sequence— and therefore filled with the things that the movie desperately lacks elsewhere.

The successful jailbreak is a bittersweet victory, because Akiva dies from wounds sustained during the escape. Ari is also wounded, and when he makes it back to Gan Dafna, Kitty and Ari's Arab friend, Taha, find a secluded place in which to treat his wounds. After a tense scene in which Ari nearly dies during surgery, the film barrels into its last movement as Ari's father, Barak, announces to the throng gathered at Gan Dafna that the United Nations has voted to partition Palestine into separate Jewish and Arab states. The announcement prompts two old friends to discuss their differences in some of the blandest dialogue in the picture, which is disappointing given the import of the scene's content.

> ARI: Taha, what's wrong?
> TAHA: You have won your freedom and I have lost mine.
> ARI: We never had freedom, you or I. All our lives, we've been under British rule. Now we'll be equal citizens in the free state of Israel. The resolution guarantees it.
> TAHA: Guarantees are one thing, realities another. Now that they've made my lands and village part of Israel—
> ARI: But these are still your lands. They always will be.
> TAHA: I'm a minority.
> ARI: We've always been friends in this valley, Taha,

ity—we've proved it makes no difference.
> TAHA: If it makes no difference, why have you fought so hard to bring this about?
> ARI: Because we had hundreds of thousands of people with no other place to go.
> TAHA: And now, where shall my people go?
> ARI: Why should they go anywhere? This is their home as well as ours. Taha, don't you see—we've got to prove to the world that we can get along together. If we don't, then the British are right—we cannot govern ourselves without their help.

Compare the bluntness of this scene with Ari's playful confrontation with Fred or Akiva's interrogation of Dov, and it becomes clear how much momentum the picture has lost; it's as if the film had so many climaxes from which to regroup that Trumbo was as fatigued about facing the next narrative challenge as Ari is about surmounting the obstacles in his path. So when yet another element is thrown into the mix—a Nazi war criminal arrives to help the Arabs of Abu Yesha fight the Jews of Gan Dafna—the movie breaks under the weight of its own narrative.

A pair of unexpected tragedies that occur during the Arab assault on Gan Dafna are used by the filmmakers to connect the various strands of the narrative. After visiting Dov, who is on late night guard duty, Karen is killed by an Arab soldier who leaves her body in the shrubs outside the Jewish village. But before her death is discovered, Ari leads an assault squad into Abu Yesha, only to find it deserted. He then discovers Taha dead, with a Star of David crudely painted on his chest, and Ari

Moments later, Dov finds Karen. Because talk has been the *modus operandi* of the picture, a eulogy that Ari delivers during a dual funeral for Karen and Yaha is used to hammer the picture's message one last time.

> ARI: It is right that these two people shall lie side by side in this grave. Because they will share it in peace. But the dead always share the earth in peace. And that's not enough. It's time for the living to have a turn.

As with many such eloquent passages in *Exodus*, were this eulogy the sole verbose passage amid several action scenes, it would have had more impact; the grace in the eulogy echoes the best parts of this problematic film. But *Exodus* ultimately is more of an endurance test than an epic. It has flashes of utter brilliance; whenever Akiva is on screen, for instance, viewers can sit back and relish Trumbo's cutting wit and intelligent engagement of troubling issues. But the picture on whole is tiresome when it should be thrilling, pedantic when it should be inspiring. The good in the film makes it impossible to dismiss *Exodus* as a failure, but when compared to *Spartacus*—in which Trumbo found an exhilarating middle ground between dialogue and action—the picture pales.

❖ ❖ ❖

Although the artistic and financial success of *Spartacus* could have sparked a long partnership between Trumbo and Kirk Douglas, Trumbo did only a handful of jobs for the iconic actor; less than five years after it began, their collaboration was over, leaving promising projects including *Montezuma*[6] unproduced. While the two major Trumbo-Douglas films, *Spartacus* and *Lonely Are the Brave*, are acknowledged classics, their second full collaboration was a psychologically twisted thriller called *The Last Sunset*—a flop so generally disdained that Trumbo once referred to the film as an "abomination."[7]

In retrospect, though, the picture is hardly a total loss: While burdened by an insufferable second act, *The Last Sunset* has a seedy, writhing story with a great denouement. It is also, like many pictures on Trumbo's résumé, mired in backstage drama. In 1960, Universal was hungry for a film costarring Douglas and rising star Rock Hudson. When *Montezuma* fell through, it was replaced, to the dissatisfaction of many, with an adaptation of Howard Rigsby's novel *Sundown at Crazy Horse*—the project that became *The Last Sunset*.

Along with *Cowboy* and *Lonely Are the Brave*, Trumbo's screenplay for *The Last Sunset* offers proof that the western was a good fit for him. The genre's focus on macho posturing, sweeping outdoors adventure, and fiery story lines driven by vengeance and jealousy allowed Trumbo to use the grandiose devices that seemed to liberate him from the confines of more intimate stories. Although Trumbo appeared to be his most unfettered when writing war films, probably because of his political leanings and strong feelings about the nature of war, westerns had a personal significance because of his frontier heritage. Still, it would be overstating things to say that *The Last Sunset*—or even *Cowboy*, for that matter—belongs among the top ranks of Trumbo's projects.

Both are solid, compelling films with interesting themes, dynamic action, and somewhat offbeat characterizations, but both rely on clichés and spectacle. Whereas some of *Cowboy*'s narrative excesses are germane because they help fuel a focused character study, however, *The Last Sunset* suffers badly for the inclusion of hackneyed material. Tired scenes including a cattle stampede, a barroom brawl, and a campfire fist fight remind viewers that they're watching an example of a genre, not a clever reinvention of it—even when elements including the oddly poetic nature of Douglas's character and a sordid plot twist suggest otherwise.

One particularly interesting aspect of the picture is the manner in which character traits are revealed. Whereas protagonists in his pre–blacklist films were exactly what they seemed (and, in some cases, less), during the blacklist and thereafter Trumbo presented characters in a more circumspect fashion. It's possible that after years in which the blacklist forced Trumbo to play games with the truth—and after seeing truth telling corrupted by HUAC into something more akin to violence than virtue—Trumbo gravitated towards characters who didn't show their hands. Combined with the general darkening of his material that began with his crime films of the late 1940s and early 1950s, this evasive approach to presenting characters underlines that Trumbo's post-blacklist screenplays are more adult in nature than the even the best scripts he wrote before and during World War II.

The Last Sunset opens with black-clad, derringer-toting Brendan O'Malley (Douglas) and earnest-looking Dana Stribling (Rock Hudson) riding through two remote parts of Mexico. By intercutting these two men traveling toward unknown destinations, Trumbo immediately creates a sense of destiny, as if the meeting of th...

fateful. We soon discover that both men are Americans and that Dana has traveled to Mexico looking for Brendan. Early in the story, Brendan arrives at the ranch of John Breckenridge (Joseph Cotten), who is away on business. Strange tension fills the scene when Brendan introduces himself to Breckenridge's wife, Belle (Dorothy Malone), and Belle reacts fearfully when he flirts with her pretty daughter, Melissa "Missy" Breckenridge (Carol Lynley). After Missy impetuously offers Brendan lodging for the night, he casually indicates that he knows Dana is looking for him, but does not reveal why.

In a handful of minutes, Trumbo lays much of the groundwork for the entire movie, establishing Brendan's nonchalance, Dana's determination, and Belle's anxiety over Brendan's presence—the secrets behind which fuel much of the film's drama. This skillful expositional sequence reveals a conundrum that Trumbo faced throughout his career because so many of his scripts were adaptation projects: it's easy to select from source material provocative story elements with which to "tease" viewers at the beginning of the movie, but it's difficult to conjure an interesting ending if one isn't present in the source material. Luckily, Rigsby's novel has a whopper of a climax, so the conclusion of *The Last Sunset* is as heated as its opening sequences are intriguing.

The first hints of the ending are visible barely ten minutes into the movie, when it is revealed that Brendan and Belle were lovers years ago and that she left him after he nearly killed a man for dancing with her. Brendan declares that he's come to claim her, but she says the spark bet...

charms at Missy, who is infatuated with him from the moment they meet. Matters are further complicated when John Breckenridge returns home. A drunken idiot, John is so oblivious to his wife's subtle warnings about Brendan that he hires Brendan as the "gun" on a forthcoming cattle drive from Mexico to Texas. Belle, who keeps her past secret from her husband and daughter, immediately discerns that Brendan is contriving to stay near her and Missy. These various layers of duplicity add a forceful edge to subsequent events, and are compounded by even more lies later in the movie.

Brendan reveals his malicious streak during a scene in which he playfully manipulates John, under the guise of a negotiation. Anticipating that his pursuer, Dana, will soon catch up with him, Brendan persuades John to hire his "friend" as the cattle drive's trail boss. Then Brendan demands ownership of one-fifth of the herd as payment for his services, and tells John that after the cattle drive is over, he's going to try to win Belle's hand. Unable to discern that Brendan's frontier bravado is deadly serious, John accepts Brendan's terms and dares the gunman to court his wife.

When Dana finally arrives at the ranch, he confronts Brendan with a warrant charging that he murdered a man in Texas. A secret plan brewing, Brendan suggests that since he's already headed to Texas with the cattle, why doesn't Dana tag along as trail boss? Wary that he's being manipulated—but swayed by Brendan's promise to surrender peaceably upon arriving in Texas—Dana accepts the proposition. This dramatically changes the dynamic of the picture. Where before it seemed that the picture's romantic triangle involved Bren-

dan, Belle, and John, an instant attraction between Belle and Dana foreshadows a shift in the relationships between the various characters.

Dialogue scenes between Brendan and Missy suggest that, knowingly or not, he is transferring his emotions for Belle to her daughter. This transfer of emotions poignantly speaks to the movie's central theme of redemption: Brendan rode to the Breckenridge ranch with the intent of renewing his relationship with Belle and giving up his rootless life, but because Belle couldn't acknowledge Brendan's ability to evolve, he gravitated toward a woman naive enough to take him at face value. The inference of this plot development—that Brendan's only believer is someone barely removed from childhood—is a saddening one.

By saying that Brendan's search for redemption strikes the adult characters as a sham, the filmmakers imply that violence corrupts violent men beyond redemption—and they make the pseudo–Biblical allusion that violence (personified by Brendan) forever lusts after innocence (personified by Missy), with the intent of corrupting it and thereby destroying the moral contrast that makes violence seem evil. That this juicy thematic material is never directly addressed in the film suggests that Trumbo was either unaware of or uninterested in it, because he rarely ignored opportunities to illuminate thematic material with explanatory dialogue. *The Last Sunset*, then, is a rare case of a Trumbo movie that has more happening beneath the surface than on it.

Trumbo quickly gets back to the business at hand, however, by revealing the reason that Dana traveled so far to bring Brendan to justice—the man Brendan killed was Dana's brother-in-law.

There's more to this backstory, but before Trumbo reveals the bleak details, the story shifts from character drama to spectacle when Brendan, Dana, and the Breckenridge family begin the cattle drive to Texas. This sudden shift, while necessitated by the story's move from one locale to another, signals the beginning of the movie's horrifically bad second act. Excepting a few flashes of the intense interplay that distinguished the opening movements of the film, the middle stretch of *The Last Sunset* is so substandard that it nearly negates the film's virtues.

The interminable macho posturing and clichéd derring-do of the cattle drive is interrupted when the crew makes camp outside a Mexican town. By this point, John has become so ineffectual that he's virtually a nonentity in the story, so it's awkward when the narrative follows his ride into town, which is ostensibly to pick up provisions but really an excuse to get drunk. While drinking in a Mexican bar, John encounters two former Confederate soldiers who recognize him as a deserter; a bar fight ensues in which John is shot dead, despite Brendan's and Dana's efforts to save him.

With John gone, Brendan recommits himself to winning Belle even though Dana declares himself a rival for her affections. Brendan provokes Dana by saying disparaging things about his sister, thus cueing the next cliché to figure prominently in the movie, a brutal campfire brawl that echoes a *Cowboy* scene. Belle breaks up the fight, but Dana bitterly explains why a reckoning is yet to come—after Brendan killed Dana's brother-in-law, Dana's sister killed herself out of grief.

Next comes an uninspired

involving three criminals who join the cattle drive with the undeclared intention of stealing the herd and selling the women, presumably after killing Brendan and Dana. This subplot gets mired with an equally uninteresting story, that of several Native Americans shadowing the herd. Amid these brewing hostilities, Brendan makes his big play for Belle's affections in dialogue so prosaic and maudlin that it could have appeared in Trumbo's screenplay for *A Guy Named Joe*:

> BRENDAN: Don't you know what I've done for you? Something only love could do. I stopped time from touching you. I trapped you in my heart the very first day I saw you and I've never let you change. Oh, Belle, a hundred years from now my eyes could look at you and still see a pretty little girl in a yellow dress.

Trumbo quickly deflates the bloated romanticism of the scene by having Belle issue one of the most stinging and true comments that he ever wrote for a female character.

> BELLE: Oh, you've said it all. Don't you see, Bren? I don't want to be loved as if I were a—a frightened, shivering, innocent little girl. I have to be loved for what I am. I'm a woman with ... the heart the mind and the flesh of a woman! I—I'm not young and I'm not innocent. There's so much more to me—to be loved than just that. But you don't see it. Because you don't want to.

Offering an almost immediate counterpoint to the preceding exchange is a taut scene between Belle and Dana, in which she reiterates her ideas about womanhood and idealization, this time to a more sympathetic

were killed some time ago by marauding Native Americans, and says that after he's brought Brendan to justice, he'll ask Belle for her hand.

But just when the interpersonal relationships of the movie are getting interesting, the story takes an ill-advised detour into frontier action when first the Native Americans and next the three criminals make their moves. These developments, as well as incidents involving a sandstorm and quicksand, are dispatched in perfunctory fashion, and they burden the picture with more clichés than it can bear. Worse, these sequences make viewers impatient for the story's real resolution, the showdown between Brendan and Dana.

After their various tribulations, the drive crew reaches the Rio Grande and decides to have a fiesta before crossing into the United States the next morning. Thankful for the bravery that Brendan showed in protecting the herd and fighting the criminals, Belle urges him to flee from prosecution. But when Missy dresses up for the fiesta by putting on her mother's yellow dress, Brendan gets blinded by lust.

The weird sexual tension created when Brendan sees Missy wearing her mother's dress neatly foreshadows the bombshell that will be dropped in short order; furthermore, the scene in which lifelong wanderer Brendan says that he's found a woman with whom he wants to settle down establishes the stakes of the movie's climactic showdown—in order to start his future, Brendan must first settle accounts with his past. Therefore, Brendan and Dana agree to a showdown at dusk the following day in the border town of Crazy Horse, Texas. These various factors inform a crucial exchange between Brendan and Belle.

BRENDAN: Look, Belle—Missy'll be safe with me. Nothing bad will ever happen to her while I'm with her. I promise that.
BELLE: But it won't last, Bren. She's so young, it can't.
BRENDAN: It will. You see, Missy and I need each other. I don't now how it happened, but—she loves me in a way she'll never love any other man.
BELLE: You don't know what you're saying!
BRENDAN: But I do. I want Missy and she belongs to me. I love her more than I love my life.
BELLE: Don't you know why? Bren, you must! She's your daughter!

Brendan slaps Belle and calls her a liar, but his next action is treated ambiguously. Still unsure if he believes what Belle said, Brendan has brief conversation with Missy at her hotel, then the film dissolves to a shot of Missy lying on her back in a grassy field with Brendan beside her. This setting, combined with the dreamy reverie in Missy's voice, strongly suggests that father and child have just slept together.

This incestuous scene joins the homosexual material in *Spartacus* (Crassus's attempt at seducing Antoninus) and *Exodus* (Dov's description of his rape by Nazis) among the most provocative sexual material in all of Trumbo's movies. Because Trumbo dove deeper and deeper into such dark subject matter as his post-blacklist career progressed, it's interesting to ponder how far down this road he might have traveled had he lived to work in the late 1970s, when cinematic taboos were swept aside by cultural change.

Trumbo had a talent for humanizing evil, and gaining the freedom to speak more frankly about such topics as sexual predators, rape, and incest would

With the worst of their political struggles behind them, Trumbo and his wife, Cleo, enjoyed a comfortable lifestyle in the late 1960s. (Mitzi Trumbo)

have liberated him to comment more openly on the psychology of such behavior. The loosening of restrictions on taboo sexual material, combined with the steady darkening of Trumbo's work that began early in the blacklist era, could easily have made him an edgy contemporary of provocateurs including Paul Schrader and Robert Towne, who addressed taboo subject matter in bold screenplays including, respectively, *Taxi Driver* (1976, Columbia) and *Chinatown* (1974, Paramount).

This is idle speculation, of course— and should not be misinterpreted as a suggestion that sex was becoming a domi-nant theme in Trumbo

which it was not. This assertion is put forth merely to support the argument that, despite having worked in movies since the "innocent" era of the 1930s and 1940s, Trumbo was not out of touch with issues that spoke to modern audiences in the 1960s. The movies were growing up, and Trumbo's screenwriting was growing up right along with them. Trumbo's ability to change with the times had its limits, however, as seen by his and Michael Wilson's doomed attempt to address counterculture-related issues in their screenplay for *The Sandpiper*, which was released four years after *The Last Sunset*

encounter with Missy, he makes a speech about how, after he dies, he wants Missy to find someone else to love. The sudden manner in which Brendan, heretofore a man's man unwilling to display fear, starts talking about his own mortality suggests that on some level, he believes Belle's explanation of Missy's parentage. Furthermore, the scene infers that if what Belle said is true, then Brendan believes he has nothing left for which to live. He has lost Belle and spoiled Missy, so the only salvation that awaits him is the oblivion of death—and if damnation is his destiny, then so be it. His quest for redemption has failed.

So when Brendan shows up for his duel with Dana, he does so with an empty gun. The duel is short and deadly, and although Missy weeps over Brendan while he dies in a Crazy Horse street, it is abundantly clear that the world is better for Brendan's absence.

In moments such as its final ones, *The Last Sunset* feels elegiac and even rather elegant. But because so much of the picture is wasted on stock scenes such as the cattle drive, the quicksand incident, and the imbroglio with the three criminals, its intentions and effect are muted. *The Last Sunset* isn't a great movie by any estimation, but neither is it deserving of the anonymous place it occupies in cinema history—if only because of how Brendan's final sacrifice amplifies the sophisticated way that Trumbo depicted personal honor in his latter-day films. Like the lovers in *Gun Crazy*, Brendan lives and dies by the gun, knowingly paying the price for his sins and, in so doing, clearing the way for those around him to find their own redemptions.

9

The Craftsman at Work
(1962–1969)

Trumbo followed *The Last Sunset* with an adaptation of Edward Abbey's novel *The Brave Cowboy: An Old Tale in a New Time*, and it provided a fitting conclusion for Trumbo's partnership with Douglas—because *Lonely Are the Brave*, as the adaptation was titled, is possibly Trumbo's most exquisite screenplay. It speaks to the central themes of his screen career with poetry and power, and the parable it offers about how a rebel gets trampled by the modern world can easily be seen as a metaphor for the repercussions Trumbo suffered after his HUAC appearance. *Lonely Are the Brave* is a searing story about a man's devotion to his own vision of personal honor, and is probably the most personal movie Trumbo ever wrote, excepting the adaptation of *Johnny Got His Gun*.

"Trumbo was the one and only screenwriter who was right for the novel—what it said, the western background, all of it," Edward Lewis recalled. "His relationship to the material was what made him right for the project."[1]

One issue that is inevitably raised while praising Trumbo's work on *Lonely Are the Brave* is that, like most of his screenplays, it is not Trumbo's creation. Despite his ability to craft memorably original stories, Trumbo flew highest in Hollywood when reimagining the words and ideas of other writers. One way to explain this aspect of his career is to say that he was a craftsman who needed raw materials from which to build his screenplays, but there is also a simpler explanation. Creating original stories involved an element of financial risk, whereas accepting assignments to adapt best-selling books guaranteed a steady income. This compromise didn't prevent Trumbo from employing his gift for provocation, but it makes his accomplishments seem less grand when compared to those of the giants of American screenwriting. Ben Hecht, Joseph Mankiewicz, Preston Sturges, Woody Allen, and other luminaries won their immortality primarily by creating characters whom audiences couldn't forget; Trumbo won his place in cinematic history largely by translating, from one medium to another, characters whom audiences couldn't forget.[2]

Had the circumstances of Trumbo's career not forced him to work with one eye always on the marketplace, it is possible that he might have struck a more even balance between originals and adaptations. But it is equally possible that had he the financial freedom to do so, Trumbo would have made good on his myriad promises to abandon Hollywood entirely and become a novelist. So imagining what might have been is a fool's game that leads to empty theorizing or outright despair. Ultimately, what matters is not what Trumbo might have done, but what he actually did.

In his handful of purely original movie projects,[3] Trumbo's head-on approach to thematic material often led to pedantry, but in his adaptation projects, he often found graceful ways to address thematic material, because he selected the best aspects of his source material and then added elements of his own. Like an instructor who suggests the brush stroke that makes a student's painting come alive, Trumbo discovered the essence of each story that he adapted well—and then put that essence onto movie screens, sometimes with more eloquence than the story's author had shown on the printed page. Trumbo was an interpreter, yes, but, when he was connected with the right projects, he was one of the finest interpreters the movie industry ever had.

At the beginning of *Lonely Are the Brave*, modern-day cowboy Jack W. Burns (Douglas) travels on his horse, Whiskey, to the home of his close friends, Paul and Jerri Bondi. Jerri (Gena Rowlands) tells Jack that Paul was arrested for helping illegal immigrants from Mexico.[4] Jack irritates Jerri by saying that he doesn't understand how Paul's compassionate actions could have been perceived as criminal, and his indignation at what he believes to be an unjust arrest leads Jack to make a speech about how the Establishment has encroached too far into citizens' lives.

> JACK: A Westerner's got to hate fences, and the more fences there are, the more he hates them.... You ever notice how many fences there are getting to be? And the signs they got up: "No Hunting," "No Hiking," "No Trespass," "Private Property," "Closed Area," "Go Away," "Get Lost," "Drop Dead"![5]

Jack's various oratories about freedom stand alongside speeches in *The Remarkable Andrew*, *Spartacus*, *The Fixer*, and other films which feel as if they could have been spoken by Trumbo. Jack's classically antiestablishment rant about fences fits Trumbo's character wonderfully; whether he was campaigning for labor rights, petitioning for the release of prisoners he believed to be unjustly jailed, or blasting the evils of the blacklist era, Trumbo was not shy about telling the powers that be when he thought a law was wrong. Because there is only a fine line between Trumbo's civil disobedience and Jack's lawlessness, it's tantalizing to imagine that Trumbo might have seen Jack as an exaggerated representation of the wild part of his own soul,[6] and the synchronicity between Trumbo and Jack becomes even more tangible in Jerri's response to Jack's tirade.

"I don't understand men anymore," she says. "Paul had a choice and he chose jail instead of his family. Doesn't he need [his family] as much as we need him?" Jack is silent a moment before awkwardly changing the subject, which is a telling detail given that the scene was written by a man who determined a one-year prison sentence preferable to caving to HUAC's demands.

Following the expositional scenes, *Lonely Are the Brave* shifts into adventurous gear for a barroom brawl involving Jack and a one-armed drunk (Bill Raisch), then shifts back to reflective mode when Jack is arrested and thrown into a cell with Paul Bondi (Michael Kane). Trumbo and director David Miller[7] fill the brisk scenes leading to Jack's incarceration with odd peripheral characters, fierce action, and curt dialogue. They also advance the film's anti-establishment theme by introducing a brutish policeman named Guiterrez (George Kennedy), whom Jack imprudently antagonizes upon arriving at the jail. Under cover of night, Guiterrez pulls Jack from his cell and beats him for fun. After taking the beating in stride, Jack asks Paul to join him in a breakout attempt, and their conversation illuminates a difference between the two men.

"Do you think they should have given you two years for what you did?" Jack asks.

"No," Paul answers.

"Then why let 'em win?"

"Nobody's winning. I knew what I was doing and I went right ahead and did it. Now I have a debt to pay off."

In addition to drawing a contrast between hotheaded Jack and pragmatic Paul, the scene offers another allusion to Trumbo's prison experience—and reveals that facets of Trumbo's personality can be seen in characters other than Jack. Like Paul, Trumbo fought his

court battles, but once his recourses were exhausted, Trumbo dutifully reported to the Federal Correctional Institute in Ashland, Kentucky, and was a model prisoner during his ten-month incarceration. So Trumbo was both the unruly rebel determined to subvert the Establishment's power and the urbane activist who fights the system from within.

Acknowledging respect for Paul's decision but not letting it color his own, Jack breaks out of jail and visits Jerri's house to grab his horse, Whiskey, and supplies for what he hopes will be a quick race to the Mexican border and then freedom. The ominous scene at Jerri's house begins with her asking Jack to surrender before he gets into more trouble with the law, then shifts into a darkly romantic mode when she is reminded that it was just this sort of foolishness that made her choose Paul over Jack years ago. Fearing that she won't see him again, Jerri laments that she broke Jack's heart, and the way that he comforts her reveals an intriguing aspect of Jack's noble but lawless character.

> JACK: I didn't want enough. I didn't want a house, didn't want all those pots and pans—I didn't want anything but you. It's God's own blessing I didn't get you.
>
> JERRI: Why?
>
> JACK: 'Cause I'm a loner clear deep down to my very guts. You know what a loner is? He's a born cripple. He's crippled because the only person he can live with is himself. It's his life, the way he wants to live it— it's all for him. Guy like that, he'd kill a woman like you. 'Cause he couldn't love you. Not the way you are loved.

careful transitions from line to line—the repetition of "loner" in the first and second lines in the last passage, and then the reiteration of "cripple" and "crippled." Trumbo builds this speech as systematically as a mathematician composes an equation, ensuring that viewers get from the words just what he's putting into them.[8] And more than just providing a *mea culpa* for a particular character, Trumbo offers a philosophy—he explains a way of life followed by Jack and, one guesses, the millions who share his restlessness but not the eloquence with which to describe their wandering ways. The clarity and power in Trumbo's word choices—"guts" instead of "soul"; "kill" instead of "disappoint"—makes his dialogue soar like music. The words appear with the immediacy and beauty of an epiphany, and the sadness beneath them adds to their impact.

The stretch of the film that follows this scene is largely composed of repetitive action and suspense sequences that work wonderfully on screen but have little that needs to be analyzed here—although Trumbo's taut interpretation of Abbey's story structure is marvelous in the way it throws a net around Jack as assorted policemen pursue him and Whiskey in the New Mexico mountains. During this long, visually driven sequence, Trumbo also finds clever ways to depict the manner in which Jack's main pursuer, Sheriff Johnson (Walter Matthau), grows to admire Jack's tenacity from a safe distance.[9]

Throughout the film's outdoor adventure sequences, Miller and cinematographer Philip H. Lathrop use the underbrush and rocky terrain of the New Mexican landscape to great effect. For his part, Douglas powers through these scenes with a tense physicality that adds expressive nuances to largely nonverbal events. Even more than in *Spartacus*, the combination of Douglas's hot-wired acting and Trumbo's lean screenwriting is combustible.

During the pursuit sequence, Trumbo introduces plot points systematically so that viewers are in step with the development of the story. For instance, when Johnson sends a helicopter to find Jack's hiding place, viewers know that Jack carries a rifle, so when he shoots at the helicopter and causes it to crash, the scene feels germane instead of outlandish.[10]

But Trumbo doesn't use foreshadowing at every turn. An example of an opposite tack involves the brutal policeman Guiterrez, who is sent up to the mountains to hunt Jack. The scene in which Guiterrez sneaks up to the clearing in which Whiskey is standing is a suspenseful one, because it hasn't yet been made clear whether Jack is aware of the policeman's proximity. So when Jack surprises Guiterrez from behind and subdues the thuggish policeman, it provides variety that keeps viewers from growing too confident in their anticipation of the plot developments. Throughout the long and quite compelling chase sequence, Trumbo's screenwriting is so professional and clean that it's virtually invisible.[11]

A repeated trope carried over from Abbey's novel is that of a truck driving toward Duke City. In one of the film's first scenes, we're introduced to the truck's driver, Hinton (Carroll O'Connor), who explains that he's hauling a load of toilets to New Mexico. Thereafter, Miller periodically cuts back to Hinton driving along the highway. These cuts function as intriguing foreshadowing—viewers trust that Hinton is being shown for some salient reason, even if they don't know what it is—and as fodder for the film's bitter irony. Because of the role that Hinton plays in the film's conclusion, the fact of his cargo adds another level to the film's commentary on the disposable nature of modern life.

At the conclusion of the chase sequence, Jack makes it to the other side of the mountain with only one minor injury: a gunshot wound to his ankle. With tenacity, a hunter's patience, and a natural outdoorsman's well-honed instincts, Jack evaded capture and made fools of his pursuers. Even Johnson, otherwise disdainful of Jack's lawlessness, is impressed by his quarry's resourcefulness. "Son of a gun, you did it," Johnson mutters. "Sure did. Crazy fool." But after successfully traversing the mountain, Jack encounters one last obstacle to his quest for freedom: a busy highway like the one he had difficulty coaxing Whiskey across at the beginning of the film. With rain falling, traffic roaring, and Whiskey thoroughly spooked, Jack tries to cross the road—but Whiskey freezes just as Hinton's truck barrels toward the horse and rider. Hinton slams the brakes, which causes the truck to jackknife and slam into Whiskey.

Moments later, as drivers gather on the roadside to stare at Jack, alive but in shock, and Whiskey, dying painfully, Johnson arrives on the scene. As Johnson looks, for the first time, into the face of the man who caused him such trouble, Johnson's deputy puts Whiskey down. Miller accentuates this moment with a closeup of Douglas's face: As rain forms tears that flow from Jack's wide-open eyes and over his quivering features, Jack stiffens at th...

tively conveys that the deputy might just as well have shot Jack.

Soon, an ambulance arrives, and Jack is loaded in on a stretcher, but his fate is left a mystery as Johnson and his deputy go home, their work done. Miller ends the film with the lonely image of Jack's cowboy hat lying by the divider in the middle of the road, with relentless traffic passing by and raindrops pounding the hat. The image is an exquisite metaphor for the film, because it juxtaposes the modern world in which Burns was an outsider—represented by the kind of paved thoroughfare for which he had no use—and the quintessential symbol of the life he led. The image also suggests that these worlds can only collide in violence, not harmony. That is Jack's philosophy in a nutshell, and it's also the haunting theme of *Lonely Are the Brave.*

Douglas later said that *Lonely Are the Brave* is his favorite of all his films, largely due to Trumbo's screenplay. "Of the 75 movies I've acted in, and all the others I've produced, and all the movies I've ever heard of, it's the only time that I know of a writer producing a perfect screenplay: one draft, no revisions," the actor wrote in 1988. "Like a hole-in-one."[12]

Trumbo's credits following the artistic triumph of *Lonely Are the Brave* are erratic and occasionally murky, because many of his latter-day projects were extensive rewrites. In certain cases, his dominant position in the writing credits reflects the nature of movie credit arbitration more than the amount of work

Action, for instance, is highly misleading for reasons that will be discussed later. And just as the credits of his latter-day movies are erratic, so too is the quality of those films. He never wrote another script as poetic as *Lonely Are the Brave*, nor one as grandiose as *Spartacus*; only *The Fixer*, his downbeat drama about a political prisoner, came close. Trumbo didn't lose any of his tremendous skills after the blacklist ended, but he did lose his momentum.

Trumbo attacked screenplay projects in the last years of his blacklisting with as much passion as he had those in the World War II era, because the same phenomenon was at work—Trumbo saw his stock rise every time he wrote something wonderful. So, once he escaped the blacklist and took a well-earned break from screenwriting in the early 1960s, Trumbo probably saw how much he had accomplished and realized that he didn't have to push as hard anymore. His latter-day pictures are often didactic and oppressive, as if he no longer felt compelled to entertain but rather sought opportunities to hammer messages with the piety that plagued pre-blacklist projects such as *We Who Are Young* and *The Remarkable Andrew*.

Without the motivation of having to work twice as hard earn a fraction of his former salary, Trumbo backslid into old habits. But, it must be reiterated, his latter-day films have something that many of his early films lacked: eloquence. Before the blacklist, Trumbo filtered his gorgeous wordplay through a somewhat condescending attitude and through characters who wouldn't believably speak in the same manner as Trumbo; after the blacklist, Trumbo often spoke on the page as articulately as he did in conversation.

Such dialogue is the only saving grace of Trumbo's first credit following *Lonely Are the Brave*. *The Sandpiper*, released by MGM in the summer of 1965, is a boring and utterly false drama that was rightfully panned on its original release and hasn't taken on any new life in the ensuing years. Conceived by producer Martin Ransohoff as an exploration of the gap between the Establishment and the counterculture,[13] the picture became a bloated star vehicle for Elizabeth Taylor and Richard Burton. The couple had appeared onscreen together twice, in *Cleopatra* (1963, 20th Century–Fox) and *The V.I.P.s* (1963, MGM), but because *The Sandpiper* was the first picture made by the couple after their 1964 wedding,[14] Ransohoff hoped to exploit audience curiosity by showing the stars cavorting in a tumultuous romantic drama.

The picture's screenplay was co-written by Trumbo and his old friend Michael Wilson, their only "public" collaboration following the several underground screenplays they wrote together during the blacklist era. The diehard leftists let their politics run wild, particularly when crafting dialogue about civil disobedience for Taylor's character, and the film's closing speech bears the stamp of both writers with its eloquence (Trumbo) and existential nuances (Wilson). Despite such wordplay, the script is among the worst on either writer's résumé. Stiff, inactive, and overwritten, *The Sandpiper* never escapes its roots as a simple polemical comparison because its characters never get to be anything more than artificial constructs.

The Sandpiper is best appreciated as a museum piece that illustrates a historically important generation gap. Trumbo and Wilson belonged to the generation that was losing its hold on the popular consciousness when *The Sandpiper* was made, and it's to their credit that they recognized the inevitability of such a societal shift. Taylor's character represents the youths who cast aside the ideals of Trumbo's generation and sought more individualistic values; one of many reasons this representation doesn't work is that Taylor's persona is inextricably tied to the Hollywood's studio era. She's simply too "Establishment" to be credible as a counterculture icon. The picture's other major shortcoming is Burton's phoned-in performance: he seems tired, bored, and sad through the whole picture.[15]

The filmmakers' intentions are revealed in the first dialogue scene, a conversation between Laura Reynolds (Taylor) and stern Judge Thompson (Torin Thatcher). Laura's young son, Danny (Morgan Mason[16]), killed a deer for sport during the film's opening sequence, so Thompson is deciding how best to discipline the boy.

"What have you taught him about respect for the law?" the judge asks Laura.

"As he grows up," she responds, "he'll learn that there are good ones and bad ones. He'll respect the good ones."

"And disobey the bad ones?"

"At least I hope he does."

This conversation aligns Laura with Trumbo and Wilson, whose blacklist-era defiance matches the dictionary definition of civil disobedience as clearly as Laura's radical attitude. The scene also tells viewers that the film is a platform for a debate about moral relativism, a topic that Trumbo previously addressed in *The Remarkable Andrew, Tender Com-*

tically comments that Laura must believe her life "serene because, like Thoreau, you live in communion with nature." In playing this scene, Thatcher rushes through the impossible dialogue but can't give it credibility; the language is simply too practiced and literary to be convincing as casual speech.

This tendency toward overwriting continues when the Reverend Doctor Edward Hewitt (Burton), headmaster of the San Simeon Episcopalian School, is introduced while disciplining two of his school's young students. "Our English tongue has a long history, and I'm pleased with your interest in its oldest and most ardent words," he tells the boys. "I think it is sad, however, that these ancient expressions should be degraded to a position on a lavatory wall."

If such lines had been relegated to particular moments in which characters would believably have all their wits about them, they would be entertaining and stimulating. But the manner in which the language of the whole picture is elevated to preposterous heights—with the exception of lines spoken by comparatively dull-witted supporting character Ward Hendricks—indicates that Trumbo and Wilson couldn't be bothered with writing accessible dialogue. Instead, they indulged their passions for polemics and polysyllables.[17]

In a weak echo of better Trumbo movies, the expositional sequences of *The Sandpiper* are successful at communicating information but unsuccessful in generating excitement—character traits are presented in such a perfunctory fashion that they don't fascinate or surprise. We learn that Edward is married to docile Claire Hewitt (Eva Marie Saint)

about compromising the school's standards in order to woo donations for its chapel fund.

After Thompson determines that Danny should be sent to San Simeon, Edward visits Laura's home to explain why he believes the school will be a positive environment. During the visit, we see that Edward is immediately attracted to Laura, a painter raising her son alone, and we learn the significance of the film's title: Laura is nursing a wounded sandpiper that she found on the beach outside her home in Big Sur. Edward helps put a splint on the bird's broken wing, then asks why Laura doesn't put the bird in a cage while it recuperates.

"The only way you can tame a bird is to let him fly free—it's the only way you can tame anything," she explains. This line sets up one of the film's many blunt metaphors, because the word "tame" corresponds to Laura's "wild" personality. The twist to this imagery is that it is not Laura's radical thinking that needs to be tamed—but rather Edward's raging emotional conflict. Because this arch metaphor mostly plays out in the film's subtext, it reveals that *The Sandpiper* is far more literary than cinematic.

Shortly after they meet, Edward and Laura begin their inevitable affair, which shifts the focus of the picture to revealing facets of the headmaster's personality. During a bedroom scene, Edward gives Laura a backhanded compliment by saying: "I don't approve of many of your beliefs, but at least you're true to them—I'm just a hypocrite." His bald declaration suggests that he wants a therapist, not a lover, and therapy imagery can be seen in the blocking of many scenes; one of the actors often lays on the floor or ground while the other

actor kneels or sits nearby, a physical dynamic evocative of the way a patient lays on the couch in a psychiatrist's office.

The sandpiper imagery returns during a long montage depicting a romantic weekend. While the lovers lie on the floor of her living room, the sandpiper, whose wing is now healed, sits on Laura's head (an unintentionally funny visual). Edward comments that the bird bonded with Laura because she didn't put it in a cage. "Life always flies back to life, if it isn't penned in," she comments ponderously, adding that the bird will fly away once it's fully recovered. "So will you, my love," she sighs in conclusion. This line identifies the transference of the sandpiper imagery; whereas the bird previously represented Laura, the metaphor now signifies Edward. So when Laura comments that the bird is afraid to leave her house because it is "making his own prison," she is indirectly commenting on Edward's psyche.

The film climaxes when Ward Hendricks (Robert Webber), one of Laura's former lovers and a member of San Simeon's board of directors, publicly reveals Edward's infidelity. The shamed priest determines that the only way to absolve his sins is to leave San Simeon, Laura, and his wife, Claire, behind and go soul searching.

The sandpiper imagery is revisited one last time near the end of the picture. Laura sits on the beach with Danny, who is home on a break from San Simeon. He sees the sandpiper, who is now free, and asks why the bird doesn't stay closer to the cabin where he was nursed to health. "He was healed," Laura says. "He didn't need us anymore." This clunky line offers a pat explanation for why Edward abandoned Laura despite his transforming love for her, thus reiterating the

Known for his ability to produce as many as 40 script pages per day, Trumbo had certain peculiar work habits; as seen here, he enjoyed camping in his bathtub with an endless supply of cigarettes and writing through the night. (Mitzi Trumbo)

therapy allusion but also defining Laura as some kind of spiritual whore.

As a favor to Danny, Laura attends a special service at San Simeon during which Edward makes his farewell speech to the gathered students, parents, and faculty. The speech is quoted in its entirety, because it has the power that is lacking elsewhere in *The Sandpiper*— and because it speaks directly to themes that Trumbo explored throughout his career.

> EDWARD: I've had the privilege of warming myself before the hearth of a generation younger than my own, holding ideas newer than my own, different and—perhaps, to some of us—still strange. I've learned that total adjustment to society is as bad as maladjustment. That principled disobedience of unjust law is more Christian, more truly law-abiding, than unprincipled respect. That only freedom can tame the wild, rebellious, palpitating heart of man. Encagement: never. Life, unfettered, moves toward life; love to love. That in the full blaze of God's cleansing sunlight, men and women are purely innocent and, therefore, most purely beautiful.

The word "disobedience" makes a direct allusion to the loaded phrase "civil disobedience," which, in addition to describing something Trumbo actively practiced, became an essential phrase for describing the student uprisings and civil rights demonstrations that erupted across America in the 1960s. The connection made in the speech between civil disobedience and Christianity draws a heavy-handed parallel between modern-day civil disobedience and the pure martyrdom of Christ; although this may seem outrageously presumptuous, the image drawn in the conclusion of the speech (the symbiotic relationship between innocence and beauty) suggests that Trumbo and Wilson may have been thinking of a time before the Crucifixion. The words "innocence" and "beauty," in the context of a religious homily prompted by a lustful liaison, lead inevitably to the Garden of Eden. So perhaps what the speech is saying is that by

embracing original sin, Edward was cleansed of sin. By returning to the place where man began, he found a new beginning for himself.

Seen in this light, the film's portrayal of the counterculture is totally optimistic, because Trumbo and Wilson may be saying that rebels were bringing humanity back to its original state. Therefore, the only true poetry of this film is that two writers as mired in another era as Trumbo and Wilson found inspiration in a generation that was, to paraphrase Edward's speech, younger than their own.

❖   ❖   ❖

Despite its dismal critical reception, *The Sandpiper* made money for all involved, indicating that for better or worse, Trumbo had fully reclaimed his spot atop the screenwriting heap. And though his output in the late 1960s largely consists of outsized films, a pair of smaller pictures based on his scripts slid into theaters anonymously. The first of these was *The Cavern*, released four months after *The Sandpiper*. Trumbo wrote the script for this character-driven potboiler, about a group of soldiers trapped in a cave with a woman who comes between them, in the 1950s under the pseudonym "Jack Davis." By the time it was made, though, Trumbo had closed the chapter of his life that the picture represented, so he refused to have his real name included in the credits.

The same thing happened when Trumbo's comrades from the blacklist era, the King Brothers, resuscitated a screenplay that Trumbo had written for them in the 1950s. *Heaven With a Gun*, a rather brutal psychological western in the mold of *The Last Sunset* but leaner than the Kirk Douglas-Rock Hudson picture, initially bore the name of Trumbo's front, Robert Presnell, Jr.; when it was released, it bore the name of Richard Carr, the last writer to revise the script. The King Brothers tried to sell the film as a Trumbo original, but he once again refused to let his real name be used. After all he had gone through to reclaim his identity, Trumbo's reluctance to associate himself with B pictures was understandable.[18]

❖ ❖ ❖

It seems that Trumbo found something of a kindred spirit in novelist James A. Michener, an equally verbose and prolific talent from whose massive novel Daniel Taradash and Trumbo adapted *Hawaii.* A sprawling narrative that spans several centuries, Michener's *Hawaii* illustrates how the white men who came to "save" Hawaii from its native citizens virtually destroyed Hawaiian culture. Taradash and Trumbo apparently connected on an instinctive level with Michener's theme of the ugliness of the white man's burden, because in instances where the picture differs from the book, the screenwriters captured Michener's eloquent ire and added to it some of their own.

The history behind this movie is complicated. Fred Zinnemann, who directed *From Here to Eternity* (1953, Columbia) from a Taradash screenplay, spent several years developing *Hawaii* with Taradash. The production went through numerous stops and starts, largely owing to the scope of Michener's novel; eventually a compromise was struck in which the book would be broken into two films.[19] United Artists,

which was financing the picture, doubled back on the decision, however, and the studio's determination that Michener's whole story be told in one film — and on a smaller budget than Zinnemann deemed desirable — prompted him to leave the project. Taradash recalled the film's genesis:

> It was my proposal to Freddie Zinnemann that we do two pictures and sell tickets as a pair — there's no way of doing that whole book even in three hours. United Artists liked the idea and so did [producer] Harold Mirish. We had a big meeting planned ... and Harold was late. He had had a heart attack. It was a bad omen. And I over-researched the picture. I had written 40 pages of screenplay, and I felt I just couldn't do the two pictures in time. I suggested getting Dalton Trumbo in. But they read the 40 pages and they were crazy about them. They said they'd wait.... Well, I got 180 pages of script and I had lunch with Freddie and told him, "Do just the one film and call it a day. I don't know whether any one director would have the stamina to cover this entire thing." He wanted to go all the way, though, and that's when I left. They brought Trumbo in and then [director] George Roy Hill. Freddie could never get the money for two pictures.[20]

The movie begins in 1820, when Yale minister Abner Hale (Max Von Sydow) is moved by the words of a Hawaiian prince, Keoki (Manu Tupou), to become a missionary in Hawaii. Abner is told by his church superiors that he needs to marry before going to Hawaii, so a meeting with sweet Jerusha Bromely (Julie Andrews) is arranged. During the overlong sequence depicting their courtship, we learn that Jerusha was once engaged to a whaler, who left for the sea and, Jerusha believes, never wrote to explain his long absence. The audience is let in on a secret, though: the whaler's letters are hidden from Jerusha by those who determined him an unsatisfactory suitor. Although it contains some mildly useful exposition, the romantic sequence is hampered by the same kind of tortured, over-explicit dialogue that plagued *The Sandpiper*.

Abner and Jerusha marry, and the sequence depicting their troubled sea voyage to Hawaii repeatedly hammers a simple point about Abner's heartiness while providing lackluster spectacle. In fact, had the picture begun with Abner's arrival in Hawaii, the film would likely have been more engaging—and a better showcase for the manner in which Taradash and Trumbo show Abner's rise and fall.

The film gets an infusion of visual energy when the missionaries arrive in the port of Lahaina, a village located on the island of Maui. As Abner and his compatriots watch in disbelief, dozens of topless Hawaiian women swim to the boat as a welcoming gesture. Abner is shocked when Keoki, thus far depicted as a serious seminarian, doffs most of his clothing and swims to greet the boat bringing his mother, Malama (Jocelyn LaGarde), to the missionaries' ship.

Malama is the Alii Nui, sort of a god-like queen, and Abner is appalled by the way she is deified by her subjects. Taradash and Trumbo satirize Abner's arrogance during his first conversation with Malama. Enchanted by Jerusha, Malama announces that Jerusha will stay in Lahaina, even though Abner is assigned to Honolulu, not Maui. When Abner indicates that he doesn't intend to be separated from his wife, Malama shrugs and says: "I'll let you stay, too."

Although this may seem to be a comic aside, it's actually the first part of a classic three-step screenwriting pattern with which Taradash and Trumbo establish how little stature Abner has in Hawaii. Following her blunt comment, Malama slaps Abner to the ground, and the third step in the pattern occurs when Abner tries to destroy a primitive stone icon. He's struck down again, this time by Keoki, who wants to protect his mentor from getting attacked for defiling a holy shrine.

The sequence depicting Abner's first day in Hawaii is filled with dramatic power and rapid fire exposition. For instance, after Abner discovers that Malama is married to her brother, Kelolo (Ted Nobriga), Abner witnesses Keoki's reunion with his sister, Noelani (Elisabeth Logue). The priest learns the siblings are engaged, so he springs into action.

> ABNER: Do you understand that your father expects you to marry this girl and have children by her?
> KEOKI: Uh, yes—I will explain this to her later....
> ABNER: Now, now—make it clear now.
> NOELANI: I understand English, Reverend Hale.
> ABNER: Then you must also understand that your brother is a Christian and any lustful union between you is a damnable sin, and must not take place.

Noelani, confused, asks her brother a question in Hawaiian, and he responds in the same tongue. Noelani gets upset and runs away. Keoki, dropping his usual reserve just a bit, says to Abner: "I wish I had been given just a little more time to prepare her." When seen in succession with the bits depicting Abner's ineffectiveness, this scene of Abner rudely asserting his "power" shows how bitterly his victories will be won: in saving Keoki from Christian damnation, Abner callously breaks Noelani's heart. That this essential thematic point is introduced during Abner's first day in Hawaii is an example of how efficiently the script moves once it reaches its best velocity.

The script then proceeds through a dizzying series of subplots, all of which are depicted in efficient, if occasionally artless, scenes. Jerusha becomes pregnant; Malama is told that she must renounce her incestuous union if she wants to become a Christian; and Jerusha's long lost whaler, Rafer Hoxworth (Richard Harris), runs into her while his ship is docked in Lahaina. In somewhat clichéd fashion, he's depicted as a romantic rogue whose passionate nature defines him as Abner's opposite number. After clarifying that he tried to stay in touch with Jerusha, Rafer says he wants to pick up where they left off. He is appalled to discover that Jerusha is married, and when Abner enters the scene with characteristic arrogance, a skirmish ensues between Jerusha's two loves. She breaks up the fight and sends Rafer away.

Shortly afterward, Jerusha's delivers Abner's first child; the birth is painful and complicated, but Abner rudely refuses to accept help from Hawaiian midwives. After the child is born, director George Roy Hill cuts to black and fades in to Jerusha's ashen face, shown in an iris like an image of a long-dead woman in a cameo necklace. Then the iris opens to reveal the full frame, effectively illustrating the manner in which Jerusha returns to reality after her brush with death. And just when the scene appears to be depicting Abner as a mon-

ster who let his wife suffer, his Hawaiian charge Iliki (Lokelani S. Chicarell) notes quietly: "You know [what] Hawaiians do when baby come out wrong end like that? Number one midwife— she kill the baby. Then she pull him out."

These somber words reveal that despite his crude means, Abner is trying to do something good: to save Hawaiians not from their culture, but from their ignorance. The tragic message is that he ultimately is unable to separate one from the other until it's too late.

The film's climax is a harrowing, overblown sequence centered around Malama's death. By this point in the story, she has emerged as one of the film's most sympathetic characters—particularly because the simplicity of her love for her brother-husband compares favorably to the repression of Abner's relationship with Jerusha. As presaged by Hawaiian fable, the Alii Nui's death is followed by a devastating hurricane that blows away Abner's church with all the force of a fully realized Trumbo metaphor. The death of the Alii Nui also prompts Keoki to acknowledge his obligations as a member of Maui's ruling family, so he casts aside his Christian life and marries Noelani. Abner tries to stop the marriage, but is dragged away and, in one of the picture's most haunting images, screams to heaven for God to smite the heathen backsliders. As if in response, the first child of Keoki's incestuous union is deformed, so Keoki drowns the baby—a development that reiterates the primitivism from which the missionaries hope to save the Hawaiians.

God's blight doesn't end with the death of Keoki's baby, however. A sailor docked in Lahaina brings measles ashore, causing an epidemic among the natives, who don't have a hereditary tolerance to the disease. Scores of Hawaiians die, including Keoki. As his final gesture, Keoki pushes Abner away and howls: "God no longer exists!" This brutal assertion speaks not only to the seeming failure of Abner's attempt to convert the Hawaiians, but also to the inexplicable cruelty of a deity who would wreak such terrible havoc.

The filmmakers deal with the aftermath of Keoki's death in a lengthy exchange between Abner and Jerusha that likely represents Trumbo's biggest contribution to the movie. Trumbo's signature can be seen in the methodical way that the dialogue progresses through logical steps, so that instead of merely nudging Abner from one level of understanding to the next, Jerusha effectively recounts the entire span of his time in Hawaii. This scene, which does not appear in Michener's novel but rather encapsulates ideas that permeate the book, represents Trumbo's footwork at its fanciest.

The most critical reading of the scene finds that Trumbo is, in fact, introducing the idea of Abner's mercy suddenly; although we have seen flashes of Abner's softer side, this is the first time since his arrival in Hawaii that we see Abner express doubt in his own abilities. Therefore, a detractor might say that Trumbo rushes Abner toward a spiritual epiphany instead of drawing the priest's awakening in careful steps placed throughout the narrative. Wriggling free of difficult narrative predicaments was one of Trumbo's most refined skills, so that reading may be a valid one.[21] But an alternate reading, in which Abner's epiphany is the deliverance promised by the aforementioned scenes depicting Abner's softer side, should also be considered.

ABNER: Keoki's dead. He went forth unrepentant into hell.... How could I have known God would scourge them so terribly?

JERUSHA: God had nothing to do with it. It's a disease.

ABNER: But nothing on Earth can happen without God's Consent and Command!

JERUSHA: Abner, do you believe every word in the Bible literally?

ABNER: Believe it? The Bible is God's Holy Word, written exactly as He commanded! I believe it all. I believe in Heaven and Hell and in God's Holy Wrath. If I did not believe, I could not call myself a Christian.

JERUSHA: Then I will no longer call myself a Christian. I don't believe in your God of wrath. I don't believe Keoki's in hell, either. I believe he has found God....

ABNER: But it's impossible for the unbaptized to enter heaven!

JERUSHA: Oh, Abner, I've never seen a people more generous, more loving, more filled with Christian sweetness than these. I will not believe that God has rejected them simply because they haven't been baptized. Not even that lost child whose birth you cursed.

ABNER: These things are God's Will. Not mine. What else but God's wrath has the power to annihilate them?

JERUSHA: Disease. Despair. Our lack of love. Our inability to find them beautiful. Our contempt for their ways. Our lust for their land. Our greed. Our arrogance. That is what kills them, Abner. And that is what you must save them from.

ABNER: They are already lost. I've failed them. I've failed these people.

And God. My ministry here is at an end.

JERUSHA: Your ministry here is not ended. You will stay here in Lahaina and shelter and protect these people. You will win them to a merciful God with bonds of charity so strong they will belong to him forever.

ABNER: How?!!

JERUSHA: By offering what you've always valued most and found it hardest to give—to them and to me. Your love.[22]

Having thus served her purpose in the story—by bringing Abner to a higher level of consciousness in which he understands charity instead of simply speaking of it—Jerusha dies. Her death snuffs much of the vitality from the picture, because she had a hand in many of the film's most important developments. She nudged Abner into proposing marriage; she saved a Hawaiian infant from being killed by a woman superstitious about the baby's birthmark; she convinced Malama to give Abner the land for his church. Jerusha is among the most noble of Trumbo's female characters, so her death is sad within the narrative and without.

The film ends with Abner getting stripped of his ministry by opportunistic church officials who want to steal Lahaina from the Hawaiians. Finally seeing the gulf between the cruelty of the church and God's love, Abner says that he will stay in Lahaina even if he doesn't have the church's support—and even if it means sending his three children to America because he will no longer have an income with which to support them. The stoic manner in which Abner says good-bye to his children is possibly the most effective mo-

ment of Von Sydow's intense performance, and the suppressed emotionalism of the farewell scene provides a crisp setup for the movie's conclusion.

The last scene depicts a sweet young Hawaiian man—the birthmarked baby whom Jerusha saved—offering to work as Abner's assistant. This moment offers an unexpected grace note about two cultures making a step toward harmonious coexistence; that those cultures are represented by a white man who breaks with white culture to preserve the integrity of Hawaiian life and a Hawaiian man dressed in European clothes is the film's final irony.

❖ ❖ ❖

Trumbo followed *Hawaii* with another story of religious persecution. Adapted from Bernard Malamud's Pulitzer Prize–winning novel about a real incident that occurred in 1911 Russia, *The Fixer* offers probably the most direct allegory among Trumbo's movies to his HUAC experiences. Alan Bates stars as Yakov Bok, a provincial, Jewish handyman who travels to a large Russian city seeking work. Upon arriving, he witnesses a rampage by sword-wielding Cossacks, who round up "unregistered" Jews and slaughter several of them. Yakov is saved by a tailor, Latke (David Opatoshu[23]), who notes that because Yakov doesn't look Hasidic, he can pass as a Gentile and seek work outside of the Jewish ghetto.

Yakov's ruse lands him in jail and makes him vulnerable to prosecution when he is framed for the murder of a Gentile boy. His crisis gets exacerbated by his indignation; the more the Russian government pressures him to provide a bogus confession, the more he's driven to defy them. The parallel between Yakov's predicament and the position in which Trumbo found himself when dragged before HUAC is unmistakable, and the result of Trumbo's apparently deep sympathy for the story is that *The Fixer* contains some of his most pungent screenwriting. Yakov's story is told with an almost cold-blooded efficiency, and even when the picture becomes sanctimonious, Trumbo's writing is mostly crisp and powerful.

Given the personal commitment and technical expertise Trumbo brought to the film, it's somewhat surprising that *The Fixer* didn't enjoy a warmer reception—especially considering that the film was released in 1968, when the social unrest on American streets was almost as pervasive as that in tsarist Russia. The picture bombed at the box office, and its only significant recognition during awards season was an Oscar nomination for Bates as Best Actor (he did not win). Most pundits blame the picture's commercial demise on the brutality of its subject matter, but in hindsight, that seems peculiar—just a year later, bleak films including *Easy Rider* (1969, Columbia) and *Midnight Cowboy* (1969, United Artists) enjoyed both critical and commercial success. It's possible that the picture was a year ahead of its time, but it's also possible that MGM, the studio that released *The Fixer*, failed to exploit the connection between Yakov's persecution and the alienation felt by the counterculture. Whatever the reason, the minor historical stature of *The Fixer* is deceptive; while flawed, the film boasts Trumbo's best screenplay in the period between *Lonely Are the Brave* and the end of his career. Every other highlight of this period is muddied by the roles of collaborators or, as in the case of

Johnny Got His Gun, by conflicting intentions.

One reason for the movie's wallop is the clinical camera work and editing of director John Frankenheimer,[24] best known for such controversial, harrowing thrillers as *The Manchurian Candidate* (1962, United Artists) and *Seven Days in May* (1964, Warner Bros.). Frankenheimer literally presses the camera close to the action during the harshest scenes; elsewhere, he uses long shadows, dull earth tones, and pervasive filth to communicate the bleakness of the cell in which Yakov spends nearly three years. More importantly, though, Frankenheimer's pacing is tremendous. By using devices such as dialogue overlaps and jump cuts, Frankenheimer saves *The Fixer* from the problem that plagued many of Trumbo's most ambitious films: oppressive solemnity. *Johnny Got His Gun*, for instance, moves turgidly, as if Trumbo wanted every nuance to sink in before moving to a new idea; *The Fixer* makes its points with the intensity of hammer strikes, then moves on without a backward glance.

The horrific nature of the film is evident from the first major scene, which depicts the Cossack attack. A wordless montage of furious motion and noise, the sequence features a recurring image of a little Jewish boy racing to collect his puppy and find safety; at the end of the sequence, a Cossack rides through the ghetto with the puppy speared on the tip of his sword. Aside from implying that the boy has been killed, the image allows for a grotesque shot of Yakov getting smeared with dog blood when the Cossack inadvertently tosses the animal into Yakov's hiding place.

Once Yakov is pulled to safety by Latke, the tailor gives him a quick sketch of the hostile environment that he has entered. Latke bitterly explains that the Cossacks are trying to suppress the Jewish "revolution," then explains, of course, that there is no such thing. The caustic, combative manner of Latke's next comment sounds like pure Trumbo:

> LATKE: In order to make a revolution, first one must have a country. You name me one Jew who calls this cesspool of a country his own, eh? Pigs! Let them start their own civil disturbances! I wouldn't start a revolution if I could—I wouldn't do them the favor.

Soon after his duplicitous entree into the Christian district, Yakov enters the good graces of wealthy Gentile Lebedev (Hugh Griffith). Yakov takes a job in Lebedev's brickworks as a bookkeeper, and his precise work earns him the distrust of the brickworks's foreman, whose embezzlement Yakov uncovers. Meanwhile, Lebedev's daughter, Zinaida (Elizabeth Hartman), flirts with Yakov and eventually lures him to bed. Partially because of his preoccupation with the wife who abandoned him several months previous and partially because he realizes that Zinaida is menstruating, Yakov leaves her before consummating their flirtation.

These and other incidents connect when Yakov's ruse is discovered and he is arrested. The laborers at the brickworks frame Yakov for their embezzlement, and Zinaida shows her resentment by accusing Yakov of attempted rape. Because Yakov is brought before a sympathetic, rational magistrate named Bibikov (Dirk Bogarde), it seems he'll be exonerated of bogus charges. But then a Gentile boy from the village near the brickworks is killed, and his various detractors pin the murder on Yakov. Thus begins a harsh contest of wills between Yakov's partisan, Bibikov, and a viciously anti–Semitic prosecutor, Grubeshov (Ian Holm).

Using mostly unvarnished dramatic scenes and direct, curt dialogue, Trumbo collapses an enormous amount of narrative material into the sequences leading to Yakov's indictment. There are a few false notes—such as an awkward scene of Yakov talking to himself as he undresses before joining Zinaida in bed—but the brief insertions of voice-over and imagined scenes that viewers have seen by this point are just enough to establish such devices as part of the film's storytelling system. Therefore, when narration and hallucinations become critically important later in the picture, they feel germane. This reasoned way of preparing viewers for what they're about to see is a hallmark of Trumbo's work.

Also, Trumbo briskly establishes the most important relationship in the film, that of Yakov and Bibikov. The visual contrast between the characters is telling—Yakov is a longhair in rags; Bibikov is impeccably groomed and wears perfectly tailored suits—as is the ideological gap between them. Bibikov is a smooth political operative, but his client is utterly nonpolitical. The implication is that Yakov is an ignorant pawn caught in complex political maneuverings, but the truth, as revealed later, goes deeper.

After establishing not only that the Russian government wants to prosecute Yakov as "proof" of Jewish insurgency, but that Yakov is aware of his role in the political game, the film becomes a series of ultraviolent vignettes. Yakov is beaten and threatened with rape by other convicts at Kiev Prison; he's given shoes filled with nails that turn his feet into open wounds; he's repeatedly subjected to invasive physical searches and beaten when he protests.

Offering a sharp contrast to these rugged scenes is a taut dialogue exchange between Bibikov and the Russian minister of justice, lazily elitist Count Odoevsky (David Warner). As he strolls through his palatial offices and receives impeccable service from his silent underlings, Odoevsky casually asserts that he knows Yakov is innocent and that the Tsar's ideas about a Jewish revolution are delusional. But, Odoevsky says, that doesn't mean there isn't a greater good being served by Yakov's persecution.

> ODOEVKSY: There's no Jewish problem in Russia—or anywhere else, for that matter. There's only the problem of human nature.
> BIBIKOV: And is it an extension of human nature to prosecute an innocent man?
> ODOEVKSY: Possibly. It's human nature to be discontented. It's also human nature to react to that discontent with passion rather than wisdom.... To govern men, you must govern their passion. To unite them, you must unify their passion. Since hate is much stronger than love, it follows that men are best united by hate. And best moved to action by a desire to kill what they hate. If our workers and peasants begin to hate the Tsar—as I fear they do—ultimately, they will kill him. Far better they hate and kill the Jew. In fact, it's the only patriotic alternative.

The vicious logic of this scene has numerous parallels in Trumbo's *oeuvre*—Crassus's explanation of why Rome should be his in *Spartacus*; Abner Hale's missionary fervor in *Hawaii*; the terrifying master plan of the assassins in *Ex-ecutive Action*. Because villains with plans for conquering the world—or, worse, simply retaining order—by suppressing or killing innocent people emerged largely in Trumbo's post–HUAC films, it's easy to imply that he saw a parallel between his own persecution and that of others in various periods of history. There is not, however, much evidence to suggest that he saw his own incarceration as commensurate with the horrendous suffering of, say, Jews in tsarist Russia. Instead, Trumbo's off-screen writing suggests that his experiences made him more sympathetic to such suffering. His ability to put himself inside the mind of a Yakov Bok or a Spartacus simply increased once he became the victim of senseless persecution. The quality of the films he wrote after HUAC offers possible verification of this relationship. From the outcast lovers in *Gun Crazy* to the titular character in *Papillon*, Trumbo gravitated toward rebel heroes and rebel anti-heroes not necessarily because he saw their experiences as allegorical to his own, but because his experiences aroused antiestablishment passion. He spoke the language of all stripes of rebel characters, even if the rhetoric changed from movie to movie.

That said, perhaps the major failing of *The Fixer* is that Trumbo did not fully illustrate how Yakov Bok became such a rebel hero. At the beginning of the picture, Yakov is, as the title suggests, a lowly fixer seeking a better life. He describes himself as not dumb but not brilliant, not totally honest but not a deceiver. He is an everyman with enough sophistication to understand his predicament but enough ambition to get himself in trouble. Yet his shift from everyman to heroic martyr is more inferred than illustrated, as if viewers would not believe that a man could suffer the kind of abuse to which Yakov is subjected and not be changed. Trumbo has Yakov say that he was driven to obstinacy and rebellion by hate, and this explanation is provocative in the context of the film and also in how it speaks to Trumbo's career.

Yakov's ideological shift leads to a scene that represents the nadir and apex of the film. The warden of Kiev Prison gives Yakov a yarmulke, a tallith, and other Jewish religious accouterments so the prisoner can "improve" himself. But in a crude affront, the warden gives Yakov a Christian Bible instead of a copy of the Talmud. Making the best of the situation, Yakov studies the Bible intensely until drawing an overstated parallel— that quickly leads to a much more provocative line of thinking.

> YAKOV: A poor carpenter. Sometimes also fixing things with his hands, I bet. The last Jew of the house of David and the first Christian. Did the Christian part of Himself hate the Jewish part? How could that be? All of it was Jewish. And all of it was also Christian. Besides, he was no hater.

At this point, a guard peers into Yakov's cell to inquire what he's talking about. Yakov gets a gleam in his eye when he responds: "I understand something. Who hates the Jew—or any other man— hates Jesus. To be anti–Semitic, you've first got to be anti–Christian."

Yakov's spiritual epiphany leads him to become more devoutly Jewish, much to the consternation of a Christian priest (Murray Melvin) sent to extract a confession from the prisoner. A scene of the priest encountering Yakov—dressed in yarmulke and tallith but clutching the Christian Bible—is one of several arch

moments depicting Yakov's descent into near-derangement toward the end of his long and inhuman imprisonment. He hallucinates that his cell is filling with water; he hallucinates that the floor is rising to the ceiling so he'll be crushed; he hallucinates that the Tsar enters his cell and is Yakov's to subjugate.[25]

Yakov's despair reaches its deepest level in a surreal scene during which he realizes his cell door is open, then ventures into the hallway of the prison. In an adjoining cell, he finds his staunchest champion, Bibikov—hanging dead from the ceiling. The film strongly infers that Bibikov was murdered, which gives Yakov a glimpse of the fate that might await him.

Yakov's "salvation" unexpectedly arrives in the person of Count Odoevsky. The callous, imperious minister strolls into Yakov's cell and says that the Tsar is celebrating the 300th anniversary of his dynasty by giving amnesty to prisoners including Yakov. Yakov shocks Odoevsky by refusing the offer, because to do so would be to "admit" guilt for the murder—which, Yakov has learned, was actually committed by the lover of the Gentile boy's mother. The scene represents the culmination of Yakov's ideological shift.

> ODOEVSKY: I was misinformed about you, Bok. Your dossier is that of a completely unpolitical man.
> YAKOV: There's no such thing as an unpolitical man. Where there's no fight for it, there's no freedom. Spinoza said it best.
> ODOEVSKY: He was a Jew.
> YAKOV: He said you can't stand still and let yourself be destroyed. He said if the state acts in ways that are abhorrent to human nature, then it's the lesser evil to destroy the state.

Yakov is strangely pleased as he utters words that he knows will doom him, because he has finally made his imprisonment his own. Instead of being incarcerated on the government's terms—as an embarrassment to be released when it is politically advantageous to do so—he has decided to accept his fate on his own terms. If he is seen by those outside the prison as a martyr, then he will be one by choice.

This offers yet one more parallel to Trumbo's life. When Trumbo was stripped of his livelihood by HUAC, he turned his persecution against his persecutors by subverting the blacklist and reclaiming a status in the movie industry commensurate to that which he had enjoyed prior to his HUAC appearance—all without the benefit of his valuable name. When the parallels to Yakov are considered alongside the parallels between *Johnny Got His Gun* protagonist Joe Bonham and Trumbo, it becomes clear Trumbo was feeling not only reflective at the end of the 1960s, but also righteous. His detractors interpreted this as sanctimony, and in the worst parts of both *The Fixer* and *Johnny Got His Gun*, that's exactly the trap into which Trumbo's screenwriting fell.

But in the best parts of both films, as well as in those of films made throughout Trumbo's career, the screenwriter did his damnedest to illustrate the price honorable characters pay for living with dignity. Although Trumbo returned to the dominant theme of his screenwriting career again in films such as *Papillon*, *The Fixer* and *Johnny Got His Gun*

represent the apex of Trumbo's depiction of personal honor. Yet the films approach the subject matter from wildly different tacks. Yakov Bok is an unpolitical man who develops principles when forced to by the circumstances of his life; Joe Bonham, the protagonist of *Johnny Got His Gun*, remains an innocent, albeit a haunted one, throughout the picture. So Yakov, ultimately, is a rebel hero in the mold of John Abbott (*A Man to Remember*), Andrew Long (*The Remarkable Andrew*), Spartacus, and other Trumbo characters, while Joe Bonham is a victim of his attempts to do the right thing. Both men are brutalized by the Establishment, but only one of them has the ability to fight back. Joe Bonham's terrible fate is an affront to his personal honor; Yakov Bok's vindication is a celebration of his.

The Fixer ends like a thriller, with a tense scene of the Kiev Prison's inhuman deputy warden (George Murcell) conniving a way to kill Yakov before he's brought to trial. The deputy warden acts on indirect orders from Odoevsky, who fears that Yakov will be acquitted and reveal the Tsar's oppressive tactics. But, in a moment of supreme irony, Yakov is saved by a Cossack—who realizes that the planned "execution" is no more than cold-blooded murder. Yakov lives to get his day in court, and the film's last image is Yakov's pained walk up the stairs of a regal courthouse as he is cheered on by hundreds of supporters. Beaten, humiliated, abused, and imprisoned, Yakov survives his ordeal with his spirit intact.

10

Out of the Past
(1970–1971)

There is so much good, noble, and honest amid the dross of Trumbo's sole directorial effort, *Johnny Got His Gun*, that it can rightly be called the rough draft of a great movie.

While it would provide poetic closure to report that the picture was the triumphant achievement of his career, to do so would unfairly diminish his remarkable accomplishments as a screenwriter. A more fitting way to contextualize *Johnny* is to describe it as by far the most personal of Trumbo's film projects and also the most experimental. But because the story proved so utterly compelling on the page, even with equivalently experimental techniques making it as unusual among novels as the film version is among other movies, the question becomes one of translation: why doesn't the story work as well on film as it did on the page, particularly considering that the same man conceived and executed both versions?

The answer, unfortunately, has to do with Trumbo's lack of directorial discipline. This problem was not necessar-ily the product of a famous writer's narcissistic infatuation with his most important work, however; after failing in several attempts to get the movie made,[1] Trumbo was forced to film *Johnny* on a shoestring, and only the most resourceful filmmakers are able to surmount such a daunting obstacle.

Seen in the most critical light, Trumbo used the picture as a form of therapy, and writing such an indulgent script probably represented a kind of liberation for the veteran screenwriter. After years of working as a hired gun, he was suddenly free to make a film for which he was answerable only to himself. Trumbo's autonomy allowed him to craft a handful of audacious scenes, notably the halting sexual encounter between protagonist Joe Bonham and his sweetheart, and a long, hallucinatory conversation between Joe and Jesus Christ. But the negative repercussions of Trumbo's liberated attitude are felt in repetitive scenes, drab narration, and several pedestrian fantasy sequences.

Its shortcomings thus detailed, it is heartening to catalog elements suggesting that if Trumbo had lived long enough to sharpen his directorial skills, he might have turned into an interesting filmmaker. The film's "present-day" sequences are in black-and-white, while flashbacks are in color, a clever inversion of the cinematic convention of making the past seem less realistic than the present[2]; Christ is integrated into the story with respect, irreverence, and a shattering punch line. Most significantly, the picture features several images that parallel Trumbo's most evocative prose in their telling, literary detail. These images, however, are outnumbered by undramatic visuals—owing less to methodical repetition than to Trumbo's limited camera shot vocabulary and lackluster production values.

After a forceful credit sequence and a quick image of a soldier getting caught directly in the path of an explosion, the picture abruptly fades to black and gives way to the sound of snoring, thus establishing the importance of sound in the movie's representational system. The film's second image, a stark, low-angle shot of three doctors performing an unseen surgical procedure, fades in as the unnamed doctors discuss their patient.

"Curious how they always double up in the fetal position," the first doctor says.

"What's curious about it?" the second doctor retorts. "They're trying to protect their genitals."

"Well, this young man fortunately succeeded," the first doctor says.

The blunt manner in which the doctors discuss their patient's misfortune—and, pointedly, the way that they spin something positive from said misfortune—are signals to the audience that this won't be a gentle picture. Also, the curious coloration of the scene creates an otherworldly sensation fitting the disembodied perspective of the scene. Although the camera is positioned from the patient's viewpoint, we later learn that the patient no longer has sight, making the camera position an odd melding of the character's viewpoint and an omniscient God's eye view.

Next, we're introduced to the military doctor who supervised the surgical procedure, Colonel Tillery[3] (Eduard Franz). He tells the other doctors that he'll personally oversee the patient's progress, adding: "Wouldn't you say ... that it's worth a year of any doctor's life to observe a case like this?" Within minutes of the film's opening, Trumbo has already identified one of his main themes, that of the medical profession's willingness to use patients as guinea pigs for seemingly altruistic, but actually self-serving, reasons.

During a brisk expositional sequence, we discover that the as-yet-unnamed patient is badly injured and that Tillery feels the patient is brain dead even though physically still alive. There's sad poetry in how Tillery describes the case:

> TILLERY: There's no justification for his continued existence unless we learn from him how to help others. Care for him as gently as if he knew what you were doing and would feel the pain if you did it badly.... This young man will be as unfeeling, as unthinking as the dead until the day he joins them.

By now, Trumbo has set up his primary cinematic device: combining voice-over dialogue with images that convey both story information and pure mood. For instance, the end of Tillery's speech

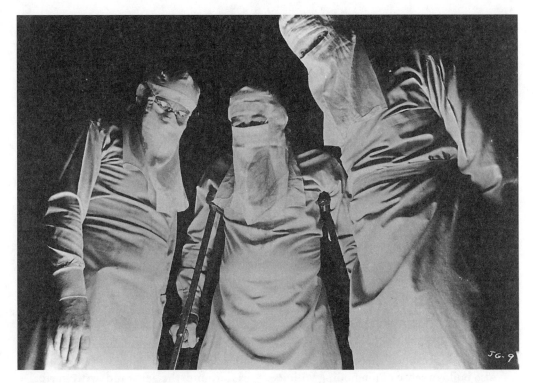

Trumbo's lone directorial effort, an adaptation of his classic novel *Johnny Got His Gun*, was a deeply flawed but often brilliant allegorical drama. In one of the movie's first images, three doctors—seen from a dynamic low angle—survey the extent of a soldier's injuries. (Author's collection)

is played over a shot of a nurse (Marge Redmond) attending the unnamed patient, amplifying his words about the kind of care he feels the patient deserves. Also, Trumbo has established that black—in a characteristic lack of subtlety, the color of death—is a primary visual component. Much of the picture takes place in half-lit hospital rooms so that the patient is, metaphorically, surrounded by death. Trumbo exhausts much of his directorial energy illustrating the irony that, for the patient, death would a salvation, not a tragedy.

After the nurse leaves the patient's room and turns out the light, we hear the protagonist's voice for the first time. "Kareen? Kareen, where am I?" asks Joe Bonham[4] (Timothy Bottoms), whom we hear but don't see. This disembodied query cues the first flashback. In the full-color past, a fresh-faced young Joe is cradling his sweetheart, Kareen (Kathy Fields), in his lap. In between kisses, she expresses anxiety about his imminent departure for boot camp, but they're interrupted by the arrival of Kareen's father, Mike Burkman (Charles McGraw[5]). He sends the young couple into Kareen's bedroom and instructs them to keep at what they're doing, but not illicitly. It is moments such as this one, which convey simple humanity through succinct dialogue and visual action, that are most effectively transposed from the novel. The same is true of the ensuing love scene, one of the most resonant moments in the picture.

The scene begins with a wonderfully framed shot. The camera is positioned behind Kareen's shoulder and looks past it toward the mirror of her vanity. We see three layers of imagery in the mirror: Kareen's ballet slippers, hanging on the mirror, tell us about the little girl she was until this night; Kareen's face, smiling with nervous expectation, tells us about the woman she's going to become; and Joe, standing quietly in the background and reflected in the mirror, shows us the link between these two parts of her life. The tight grouping of these elements conveys tremendous intimacy, and the ritualistic action that follows—in which the youths dance around what they're about to do by engaging in small talk and playing coy about removing their clothes—continues the intimacy of the mirror shot but also builds a sense of foreboding with its quiet movements, dark lighting, and eerie, magical music.

After the love scene, the film progresses briskly through several important developments. In another flashback, Joe recalls being summoned from his job at the Davis Perfection Bakery[6] to rush home because his father just died[7]; in the "present," he awakens and discerns that both of his arms have been amputated. As the realization sinks in, Joe muses in voice-over: "There's a game out there and the stakes are high, and the guy who runs it figures the averages all day long…." This voice-over sets up the first appearance of Jesus Christ (Donald Sutherland[8]), whom we see participating in a card game with several soldiers, including Joe. To establish Trumbo's offbeat portrayal of Christ, the scene includes a bit that begins when one of the soldiers says: "Christ, I sure could do with a shot of whiskey."

"Help yourself," Christ responds. The soldier picks up the glass of liquor that materializes on the table and asks, "How'd you learn that?"

"I used to do it at weddings," Christ says.

The scene also establishes the dream world of the movie, because the soldiers talk about how they're going to die, providing specific dates and events—so they are not actual soldiers but rather soldiers' dreams of their own ghosts. Christ is among them as a chaperone on their journey to eternity.

Back in the "present," Joe discovers that his legs have been amputated as well as his arms, and after pondering in heated voice-over about why doctors would keep a man without arms and legs alive, the film segues into its second dream sequence. Filmed with a Vaseline iris around the lens and with surreal background action, the dream sequence features Trumbo playing the part of a medical director lecturing his colleagues.[9] The distracting background action, of men in white suits holding tennis racquets, appears to suggest that medicine is sport for doctors; it is also the first clue that many of Trumbo's surrealist touches will fall flat. Nonetheless, the monologue that occupies the heart of the scene is potent in its wit, economy, and savagery.

MEDICAL DIRECTOR: War has various meanings to various persons. To the scientist, war means that he has actually been set free to accomplish his most brilliant and most imaginative enterprises. For instance, in previous wars, each injury has resulted in a very serious loss to the taxpayers—the loss of a most expensively trained soldier. Or "fighting unit," as we call them now.

However, in the next war, we shall be able to repair and deliver that same fighting unit to the front line trenches in three weeks or even less. And all because of the radical new techniques which this young man has taught us.

The monologue is filmed in a long, slow zoom that begins with a closeup of the director's face and widens to reveal that Joe's hospital bed is situated at the opposite end of the room; the group to whom the director is making his speech is positioned between him and Joe. This shot is typical of how the most original elements of *Johnny Got His Gun* coexist with the most pedestrian. The concept of the shot, the dialogue, and even Trumbo's delivery are brilliant, but the background action and the Vaseline iris are amateurish. The scene reveals that Trumbo was his own worst enemy once he got into the director's chair.

The next cue that the picture is veering off track comes when Joe has another flashback, this time not to his young adulthood in Los Angeles but to his childhood in Colorado. Although certain elements of the multipart flashback speak to Joe's later fate, several are gratuitous insertions of autobiographical detail indicating that Trumbo's device of using his own upbringing as a model for Joe's led to distraction.

The first bit is a throwback to the kind of heavy-handed irony and foreshadowing that earned Trumbo some of his harshest criticism. As young Joe (Kerry MacLane) speaks in the kitchen with his mother (Marsha Hunt), she says: "Someday those feet are going to get so dirty, they'll never get clean." The line serves no function other than to hammer the tragedy of Joe's amputations. Subsequent bits in the sequence include a shot of young Joe dropping his pants in an outhouse; a shot of Joe attending to a hive of honeybees with his father (Jason Robards, Jr.); and one of Joe fishing in a lake with his father. A generous reading of this sequence would say that the vignettes give viewers a sense of the world from which Joe came—and, by extension, an understanding of the human inside the tragedy—but the details really tell us more about Trumbo than Joe.

The sequence rights itself when it segues to a church scene in which Joe's family, practicing Christian Scientists,[10] listen to a priest delivering a sermon that speaks directly to Joe's later fate: "Spirit is the real and eternal," the priest says. "Spirit is God and man is his image and likeness. Therefore man is not material. He is spiritual." This sermon echoes the next "present-day" narration, in which Joe, thrashing in his hospital bed, howls: "Stop it! I don't want to hear any more about God or I'll begin to hate him!" It's significant that at this point in the story, Joe is still filled with religious belief—he feels wronged by God, not abandoned by Him. The changes in Joe's faith are an important part of the story's thematic makeup.

After this theological detour comes a flashback of young Joe speaking with his father in a shed while the elder Bonham cleans his prized fishing pole. The scene seems awkward at first, because the dialogue is bluntly informative. It soon becomes clear, however, that Trumbo is after something more than exposition. In the following dialogue, note the way that Trumbo veers from realistic conversation to hyperbolic *mea culpas* and back again. As the film drifts deeper into a dream state, even the "real" dialogue of the flashbacks gets infected by Joe's delirium.

Trumbo revisited several scenes from his youth in Colorado and Los Angeles when making the film version of *Johnny Got His Gun*. Jason Robards, Jr. (in hat), played a character based on Trumbo's father, and Timothy Bottoms played the young man destined to suffer horrible injuries in World War I. (Author's collection)

JOE'S FATHER: Nothing I have in this world is really any good, you know. My house is small, my job is small. My salary is also small. Son is small, so is my wife and, when you get right down to it, I'm no giant myself. Everything around me is small, inferior—except this fishing pole. I myself wind it every year with the best silk thread. See this lacquer? Comes from China. No finer lacquer in the world. See those guides? Pure amber. Nobody in town has a fishing pole like this. Not even Mr. Latimer down at the bank. My life is so poor and shoddy that, without this pole, I'd have nothing to set me apart from other men. Nothing to give me distinction. Nothing at all. That's why I love it so much.

YOUNG JOE: Do you love it more than you love me?

JOE'S FATHER: Ha, ha! Of course I do. What is there about you that can give a man distinction? You're not unusual at all.

YOUNG JOE: Yes I am, father.

JOE'S FATHER: How's that?

YOUNG JOE: I may not be unusual now, but I'm going to be.

JOE'S FATHER: Of course you are. Gonna make the world safe for democracy, are you?

YOUNG JOE: What's democracy?

JOE'S FATHER: Well, I was never very clear on that myself. Like every other kind of government, it's got something to do with young men killing each other, I believe....

YOUNG JOE: When it comes my turn—will you want me to go?

JOE'S FATHER: For democracy, any man would sacrifice his only begotten son.

The stilted dialogue of this scene is a means to an end. By having the characters speak to themes directly instead of alluding to themes through artful dialogue, Trumbo is able to make leaps of logic that would otherwise have been impossible. Thus, the conversation stretches from the odd fishing pole allusion to questions of war, responsibility, and mortality. Trumbo is blurring the lines separating hallucination from flashback so that what begins as a scene pulled from memory gets colored by the stream of consciousness running through Joe's head as he sits, helpless, in his hospital bed. Also, the imagery in the last part of the above exchange—that of a father willingly sending his son off to die—connects to the film's many allusions to Christ. Although it is finally defeated by such ambition, *Johnny Got His Gun* is also defined by the kind of narrative ambition visible in this scene. It's certain that any director would have had difficulty putting across the delirious state that Trumbo tried to create, which lessens the sting of his failure to do so.[11]

Once the crucial scene between young Joe and his father is over, all of the devices that figure into the film's narrative have been introduced, and one of the shortcomings of the second half of the picture is that it rather formulaically revisits devices introduced in the first half. Although the narrative is, by definition, advanced each time the picture cuts back to Joe in his hospital bed, the flashbacks to life in Colorado grow steadily more tedious and the hallucinations more didactic. The exception to this is a conversation between Joe and Christ featuring dialogue that exceeds its function in the story and offers the kind of provocative, existential commentary that permeates *Johnny*, the novel.

The long conversation is sparked when Joe realizes that in addition to his other injuries, he no longer has a face.

His horror causes him to imagine himself in a carpenter's workshop, where Christ is building crosses while chatting with Joe. Having Christ build the crosses is among the most effective throwaway touches in the picture, and it provides Sutherland with a great deal of business with which to occupy himself during the long scene. If he's not hammering pieces of wood together or moving a cross from one side of the workshop to the other, he's dealing with a truck driver who enters the room to get Christ's signature authorizing him to leave with a truckload of crosses. We see the truckload of the crosses in the background of several shots, and because they appear modeled after the kind of white crosses that are used to mark soldier's graves, the inference is that while Christ is wasting his time dealing with the problems of one soldier, many more are dying. This speaks to one of the most disturbing assertions of the scene—that despite his extraordinary injuries, Joe's is a commonplace tragedy. The transition into this remarkable scene is made when Joe, alone in his hospital room, asks if Christ knows how to tell the difference between reality and fantasy.

> CHRIST: Maybe the thing to do is police your mind before you go to sleep. Say to yourself: "I'm going to sleep now—and I'm not going to have any nightmares." Could be done, you know—with practice. If you feel yourself getting drowsy—
> JOE: I never feel drowsy. I haven't got anything to feel drowsy with.
> CHRIST: Nothing?... Maybe we should take a different line of attack altogether. Let us begin by assuming that everything is a dream, which, by and large, it is. When we're awake, we have one kind of

dream. When we're asleep, we have another. The difference is that we control our daydreams. And the dream that comes to us at night controls us.

Next, Christ comments on Joe's fear that a rat is feasting on his body while he festers in the hospital bed. Christ tells Joe to knock the rat off his body, saying that if Joe can't do so, then the rat is a dream. But Joe realizes that this experiment won't work, because his living body doesn't have any arms. Christ gets irritated, because all of his suggestions are met with reports of which missing body part makes the particular suggestion moot.

> CHRIST: Since your real life is a greater nightmare than your dreams, it would be cruel to pretend that anyone could help you. What you need is a miracle.
> JOE: No, not a miracle. Just tell me that the rat is real, and the way I am now is a dream.
> CHRIST: Perhaps it would be better for you to go away now. You're a very unlucky young man, and sometimes it rubs off.
> JOE: I'll go, but first tell me just one thing—are you and I really here together, or is this just a dream, too?
> CHRIST: It's a dream.
> JOE: How do you know?
> CHRIST: Because I'm a dream.
> JOE: I don't believe you.
> CHRIST: Nobody does. That's why I'm as unreal as every other dream that didn't come true.

Although marred by atrocious camera placement—Sutherland's face is obscured by his hair during the latter part of the scene, hiding the fact that his character refuses to make eye contact with Joe[12]—this scene is marvel of daring writing. Portraying Christ as an everyman with patience that couldn't by any stretch be described as saintly fuels one of the film's hardest hitting themes: the idea that God has abandoned Joe. This infers that by brutalizing God's creation (Joe's body), the doctors took God's place and thereby assumed responsibility for Joe's soul. That Joe had no say in a decision that defined his existence is the theme most effectively carried over from the novel—Joe belonged to God, and therefore was entitled to God's mercy, until he was stolen from God by presumptuous physicians. That the doctors represent the Establishment ("them") and that Joe is an everyman ("us") positions the movie as Trumbo's most charged attack on man's inhumanity to man. The debate over whether this theme is one that should be retired because of overuse—or one that should be reiterated as often as possible—is one of many that has clouded this film's stature. Some see the picture as a bleeding heart cliché, others as an expression of vital humanism.

The next few plot developments are handled clumsily. Joe discovers that he has enough sensation left in his skin to feel the heat of the sun, meaning that he can determine the passage of day into

After several frustrating attemps to get other directors, including Spanish surrealist Luis Buñuel, to make a film of *Johnny Got His Gun*, Trumbo decided to make his directorial debut at the age of 65. (Mitzi Trumbo)

night and therefore the passage of days into months. Shortly thereafter, Joe has a hallucination in which his dismembered body is the main attraction at a carnival. Trumbo directs the hallucination with a numbing dose of Fellini-esque clichés—a dwarf, exaggerated camera angles, self-consciously satirical dialogue—and it is among the weakest sequences in the picture.

The introduction of an empathetic nurse (Diane Varsi) who seeks a way to communicate with Joe is handled better. The simple relationship between Joe's voice-over and images of the nurse interacting with Joe's body effectively captures the poignancy of his inability to respond to her compassionate gestures. But the clear-headed storytelling of these scenes is undercut by more flashbacks and hallucinations, all of which hammer information put across better in other scenes.

As the picture nears its climax, Joe determines that by tapping his head against his pillow, he can transmit Morse code messages. At first, the compassionate nurse is mystified by Joe's incessant tapping, but when she brings military doctors into Joe's room—including Tillery, now promoted from major to general—they recognize the code. Once it becomes clear that Joe's brain survived his injuries, Tillery receives a dressing-down from his colleagues and leaves Joe's hospital room, realizing that he ignorantly condemned a patient to years of living hell.

The doctors instruct a soldier to tap Morse code messages against Joe's forehead so they can have a two-way conversation. Joe's first request is to be released from the hospital so he can join a carnival. In the novel, this request was Joe's way of trying to reclaim a functional role in society; he thought that admission charged to see him would pay for his upkeep. But in the film, the request comes across as a suggestion that Joe's dreams are blurring his sense of reality, a bad compromise that undermines one of the narrative's most important points: Joe never fully loses touch with reality, even though madness would be a release. Not privy to the unspoken nuances of Joe's request, the doctors dismiss it as a product of delirium. Sensing that he's asked for too much, Joe desperately taps a new message: "If you won't let people see me, then kill me."

Proving that Tillery wasn't the only of their number willing to sacrifice mercy for science, the doctors refuse Joe's request and leave the room. The compassionate nurse, however, remains behind. Fighting back tears and speaking an Act of Contrition, she plugs Joe's breathing tube. In voice-over dialogue, Joe receives her euthanasia like a delivery from the God who seemingly abandoned him—until the doctors return to the room and stop the nurse before she kills Joe. She is dismissed, and Joe is sedated, left to fester in his hospital bed until he meets his natural demise. These last few scenes, in which the hospital story line resumes its prominence over flashbacks and hallucinations, are directed with crisp efficiency, suggesting that had Trumbo gotten out of his own way and simply told his novel's story instead of muddying the waters with autobiography and amateurish surrealism, *Johnny*, the film, could have been as potent as *Johnny*, the novel.

The film ends with a voice-over that repeats, in numbing detail, assertions already made several times elsewhere in the film.

JOE: Well, now I know they'll never let me out. I'll be a secret here till someday when I'm an old, old man.... Inside me, I'm screaming. And howling like a trapped animal.... If I had a voice, I could talk and be some kind of company for myself. I could yell for help, but nobody would help me. Not even God, 'cause there isn't any God. Couldn't be in a place like this....

As the last words of the monologue trail off, suggesting that Joe is condemned to this maddening one-way conversation for the rest of his life, a kettle drum rises on the soundtrack, echoing not only the scene's ominous tone but its unspoken constant, the steady beating of Joe's heart. In one of the film's most effective visual devices, Trumbo begins the monologue scene with a closeup of Joe's bandaged face and then pulls back, eventually revealing the vast darkness surrounding the hospital bed—a simple visual metaphor for the hopelessness of Joe's situation and for his utter solitude. The film's epilogue is a trilogy of epigraphs, the first two of which suit the film by delivering utterly redundant information, and the last of which suits the picture by using esoteric wording meaningful to only the most erudite of viewers.

> War dead since 1914: Over 80,000,000
> Missing or mutilated: Over 150,000,000
> *Dulce Et Decorum Est Pro Patria Mori*

The last epigraph, which translates as "It is sweet and honorable to die for one's country," represents Trumbo's sense of irony at its most bludgeon-like, and the pedantic touch of closing the film not only with a phrase that most viewers won't understand, but with a caustic aside, is the final indulgence of a supremely indulgent film—albeit one featuring a handful of intriguing visual devices, provocative existential and theological musings, and eloquent dialogue passages.[13]

11

Twilight
(1971–1976)

For all its vast influence, Hollywood ultimately is a small town, and proof of that can be found in the production history of Trumbo's penultimate film, *Executive Action*. The project was conceived by Donald Sutherland, who played Christ in *Johnny Got His Gun*, and with whom Trumbo participated in the antiwar revue *F.T.A.*[1] An ardent political activist, Sutherland asked attorney Mark Lane, whose book *Rush to Judgment* questioned the veracity of the Warren Commission's report on the assassination of President John Fitzgerald Kennedy,[2] to collaborate with socially conscious playwright Donald Freed on a screenplay about the assassination. Sutherland tried to set up the project with Edward Lewis, but when financing proved evasive, Lewis succeeded Sutherland as the film's producer. And when he determined the Lane-Freed draft unfilmable, Lewis called in an old friend.

"I've never believed in the conspiracy theory of history," Trumbo recalled. "When Ed Lewis came to me with some material on the assassination and said he wanted me to do a script that suggested conspiracy, I told him I just wasn't his boy." But a perusal of the Warren Commission report and the other literature in the field changed his mind. He was particularly impressed by the home movie shot by Abraham Zapruder during the assassination. As Trumbo put it, "The public has never seen the uncut version of the film, which is a shocking convincer. It clearly shows Kennedy was hit from two different directions. If that's the case, there must have been at least two assassins—hence, a conspiracy."[3]

Trumbo rewrote the Lane-Freed script so heavily that he got sole screenwriting credit, with the original authors demoted to a "story by" credit. Shortly before production, however, the film's producers determined that there were problems with Trumbo's script. Trumbo had grown ill and was unavailable, so Alvah Bessie—a fellow member of the Hollywood Ten—was hired to do a one-week rewrite.[4] Because so many people were involved in the screenplay's conception and execution, it might seem prudent to dismiss *Executive Action* as a minor credit, but several things make it worth exploring in some depth.

Although prominent films such as John Frankenheimer's *Seven Days in May* (1964, Warner Bros.) and Costa-Gavras's *Z* (1969, Reggane) dealt with the issue of assassination in the years following Kennedy's murder, *Executive Action* was the first movie to put forth the argument that a conspiracy led to Kennedy's assassination. While its implications and matter-of-fact tone are haunting, the picture isn't as compelling as its subject matter might suggest; certain of the movie's scenes are as perfunctory as the worst junk that Trumbo wrote during the nadir of the blacklist period.

Despite these shortcomings, the film has several unusual qualities: it has no hero, merely a cabal of cold-blooded villains; it tells its story as much through cleverly selected and edited newsreel footage as it does through new material; and, most interestingly for students of both cinema history and conspiracy theories, it predates Oliver Stone's controversial look at the same subject matter, *JFK* (1991, Warner Bros.), by nearly two decades. Whereas Stone used conspiracy theory as the springboard for a passionate detective story, the makers of *Executive Action* took an approach influenced by documentary filmmaking, so their film is less a thriller than an eerie conversation piece. And while Stone's film is infinitely more sophisticated both in style and content, it is, in a sense, "safer" because it has a hero struggling to expose the conspiracy. *Executive Action* offers no hope that the villains will be brought to justice.

The picture opens on June 5, 1963, when several powerful men, all white, gather at the comfortable Texas estate of Robert Foster (Robert Ryan). The men try to convince an imposing oil tycoon, Harold Ferguson (Will Geer), that the rise of Robert and John Kennedy poses a threat to their way of life. They fear that the Kennedys plan to secure enough political power to win four successive presidential terms—two for John and two for Robert—during which an aggressively left-wing agenda will be enacted. A skeptical Harold counters that the Kennedy clan's patriarch, Joseph, has historically practiced right-wing politics.

"Ancient history, Harold," Robert says. "[John Kennedy] has come out for cuts in the oil-depletion allowance. He's stopping mergers under the antitrust law. He promises to close down 52 domestic and 25 overseas bases."

Robert's words quickly define him as a member of the military-industrial complex identified by many conspiracy theorists as the body behind Kennedy's death. The chilling speeches that the screenwriters provide for Robert and his peers make the persuasive argument that these men of power see themselves not only as unquestionably superior to minorities and the poor, but as entitled to kill if doing so will protect their superiority. In fact, a speech that Robert delivers later in the film draws an connection between the evil designs of the military-industrial complex and the final solution of the Third Reich—suggesting that he's not just entitled to kill Kennedy, but obligated to do so.

In the long but critically important sequence depicting Robert's attempt to involve Harold in the conspiracy, Robert and his peers argue that Kennedy is going to side with blacks in the impending racial struggle, sign a nuclear test ban treaty with Russia, and pull American forces out of Vietnam. Writing from hindsight, the screenwriters found among Kennedy's positions several that would disturb the members of the military-industrial complex, presuming it existed, then took a step back in time to portray such men expressing "prescient" paranoia about Kennedy. Through this pragmatic device, Lane, Freed, and Trumbo used historical facts to ground their historical fiction.

Seeing that the others are not swaying Harold, James Farrington (Burt Lancaster) joins the discussion. At first, he seems to be a faceless master of war like the others in the room, but later it is revealed that James is instead a government-trained operative lured to evil by the promise of extraordinary wealth. James makes an elaborate slide presentation—incidentally, among the most cumbersome of expositional devices—in which he explains the history of assassination attempts against American presidents, concluding that the assassins have historically been lone madmen. The detached manner in which James rates assassination attempts in terms of success and failure is disturbing, but also telling; he speaks as if preparing for a war in which human casualties are justifiable. Therefore, his presentation reveals that there isn't that wide a gulf between governments and conspiracies—both groups are willing to sacrifice individuals for the "greater good" of their international goals.

As the conversation winds down, Robert, James, and the others play their trump card: they explain that the American intelligence community has been in an uproar since the Bay of Pigs fiasco

two years previous. Therefore, they argue, there would be a rush to blame a lone madman for Kennedy's assassination, because to do otherwise would be to admit that intelligence agencies had failed in their duty. Despite these arguments, Harold says he still isn't convinced that Kennedy needs to be killed, but his closing comment proves that he's not objecting on moral grounds:

"Oh, before I took over Trans-Jordanian Oil, my own intelligence man had to eliminate a little local opposition. I understand these things—I just don't like 'em. They're tolerable only if they're necessary and permissible only if they work."

Following the excruciatingly detailed expositional sequence, the picture slides into a second act that is better seen than described, because of its methodical and somewhat repetitive nature. Scenes depicting operatives rehearsing their roles in the assassination plan, for instance, don't so much advance the plot as illuminate the heartlessness of the conspiracy. This suite of procedural scenes leads to the film's longest and murkiest sequence, which argues that the conspirators used stolen intelligence information to learn about Lee Harvey Oswald—the real-life figure arrested for killing Kennedy but never brought to trial—then steered his actions to ensure that Oswald could be credibly framed.

In one of many scenes juxtaposing newsreel footage with reproductions of actual historical documents, James lays out the facts of Oswald's life in another slide presentation, and asserts that Oswald would be susceptible to manipulation. Aside from its integral function in the plot, the scene is essential because it prompts Robert to become introspective about what he, James, and the others are planning.

> ROBERT: The real problem is this, James. In two decades there will be 7 billion human beings on this planet—most of them brown, yellow, or black, all of them hungry, all of them determined to love. They'll swarm out of their breeding grounds into Europe and North America. Hence Vietnam. An all-out effort there will give us control of South Asia for years to come. And with proper planning, we can reduce the population to 550,000,000 by the end of the century. I know. I've seen the data.
>
> JAMES: We sound rather like gods reading the doomsday book, don't we?
>
> ROBERT: Well, someone has to do it. Not only will the nations affected be better off, but the techniques developed there can be used to reduce our own excess population: Puerto Ricans, Mexican Americans, poverty-prone whites and so forth.

To amplify the horrific implications of the speech, the film cuts to newsreel footage of Doctor Martin Luther King, Jr., making his "I Have a Dream" speech during the August 1963 march on Washington. This is a blunt but effective move on the part of the filmmakers; the absence of a hero in the story precludes most conventional means of providing direct counterpoint to the evil being spewed by Robert and his cronies, so the filmmakers let one of the twentieth century's most eloquent speakers do the job. Also, by answering Robert with the words of a civil rights leader slain by an assassin's bullet, the filmmakers amplify that the conspirators are planning to kill more than just one man—they are planning to kill a dream.

The film's disquieting illusion is broken, however, when the picture cuts to a newscast that was obviously faked with an actor on a sound stage, and which features out-of-place right-wing commentary. The ersatz journalist refers to Kennedy's stand on Vietnam as a "suicidal, no-win policy." The fakery in this scene is disappointing, because elsewhere, the filmmakers cleverly intercut actual footage to make points. But to show why Harold finally joins the conspiracy, the filmmakers constructed a newscast that, essentially, says what the conspirators want to hear. This gap in the film's credibility is a substantial one. After Harold joins the conspiracy, the pace of the film accelerates.

As the fateful date of November 22, 1963, draws closer, the film shifts to staccato cuts of newsreel images, shots of the killers preparing, and shots of the conspirators watching events play out on television. During the actual assassination, director David Miller[5] and editors George Grenville and Irving Lerner take the same approach that Oliver Stone took 18 years later—they intercut set-up footage of the gunmen and stand-ins for Kennedy and his entourage with the infamous eight-millimeter footage photographed by Zapruder during the actual assassination. After the killing, the conspirators' operatives slip out of Dallas via a prearranged escape plan.

Executive Action's sleight of hand finally unravels after Oswald is arrested, because the filmmakers suggest that Jack Ruby's murder of Lee Harvey Oswald was a last minute maneuver by the conspirators. After Ruby (Oscar Orcini) is shown in his nightclub, drinking away the shock of Kennedy's assassination, the film shows James's lieutenant, Tim (Colby Chester), heading into Ruby's bar. Even by the dubious standards of conspiracy theory, suggesting that Ruby's action was "part of the plan" seems far-fetched.

The picture ends with Robert and several of his cronies playing pool. Robert receives a phone call, during which he learns of someone's death. With a nonchalance suggesting that he's not surprised by the news, Robert reports the following to his friends: "That was Tim. James Farrington. Heart Attack." And, with what seems like subdued delight at the irony, Robert adds that James died at Parkland Hospital—the same hospital at which Kennedy and Oswald were declared dead. The clear inference is that the conspirators killed James to cover their tracks. Robert casually returns to his pool game, so the last sound of the movie proper is the crack of a cue ball sending another ball in motion, a harsh sonic metaphor for the manner in which Robert and the other conspirators "won" the game.

Executive Action has huge narrative problems. It is never made clear, for instance, why the conspirators need so badly to recruit Harold. Is he the only of their number capable of bankrolling such an operation? Are they concerned that having one of their number free of complicity endangers those whose roles in the conspiracy could be proven? Or is Harold someone whose influence would be useful once a new world order was established in the wake of Kennedy's death? While it is possible that such ambiguity was included in the film by design, it is more likely that the characters were constructs erected to communicate the factual and speculative information that fills the film; because they were not actual characters, the impetus for fleshing them out was not strong.

The most obvious reason why *Papillon* makes a fitting finale for Trumbo's screenwriting career is that it's another example of his rebel-hero iconography. The picture tells the real-life story of Henri "Papillon" Charrière, a French safecracker who was framed for murder and sent to an inhumane prison in French Guyana colloquially known as "Devil's Island." Charrière's real-life escape from the prison makes for rousing adventure, but, as in so many previous films, Trumbo was just one of many writers involved in the picture.

He was hired to rewrite a script by Lorenzo Semple, Jr., because the filmmakers decided late in the game to complement Papillon (Steve McQueen) with a second lead character. Trumbo was charged with integrating the new character, rich counterfeiter Louis Dega (Dustin Hoffman), into all but two major sequences of the picture—while it was being filmed. As he had so many times before, Trumbo made the best of an impossible situation, crafting a handful of artful scenes and disguising the fact that Louis's place in the story was an afterthought.

But partway through the project, Trumbo's age—and probably his incessant cigarette smoking—caught up with him. When he was still about 30 pages shy of completing the script, Trumbo was diagnosed with lung cancer and forced to leave the production. Although he worked on several unproduced screenplays in the last years of his life, his departure from the set of *Papillon* was symbolic of the end of his movie career. In a bit of fateful poetry, though, this ending was also a beginning. By the early 1970s, Trumbo's son was a fledgling screenwriter, so Christopher Trumbo was hired as his father's replacement. Therefore a sense of renewal is present in the film's last scenes, making the picture not Trumbo's epitaph but a glimpse of his legacy.

As directed by Franklin J. Schaffner, a master of action sequences whose credits include *Planet of the Apes* (1968, 20th Century–Fox) and *Patton* (1970, 20th Century–Fox), *Papillon* is a brutal attack on an inhumane prison system. The film is somewhat schizophrenic, however, because it's also an adventure story. In some sequences, Papillon is a passive eyewitness to, or victim of, abuse; in others, he's an active protagonist whose determination to escape stems less from the conditions in French Guyana than from his inherent individualism.

The picture therefore teeters between exposé and myth, echoing the narrative problems Trumbo faced when telling Spartacus's story. Whereas Trumbo found a pleasing balance between visceral detail and larger-than-life drama in *Spartacus*, however, Semple and the Trumbos never fully bridge the gulf between *Papillon*'s conflicting elements— the Trumbos' Louis scenes, Schaffner's vividly filmed outdoor sequences, and Semple's efficient, serialized narrative.

The picture opens with one of Trumbo's few onscreen appearances, an uncredited cameo as the French commandant who addresses prisoners about to be deported from France to Devil's Island. In his short appearance, Trumbo barks out a brief speech with his inimitably nasal tone and crisp enunciation: "As of this moment, you are the property of the penal system of French Guyana.... As for France, the nation has disposed of you. France has rid herself of you altogether. Forget France!"[6]

The graphic tone of the picture becomes clear in *Papillon*'s first dialogue scene. In the steerage chamber of a boat bound for Guyana, Papillon speaks with another inmate, Julot (Don Gordon), while Papillon rolls paper money into tubes that he plans to store in his rectum. "We're really something, aren't we," Papillon muses. "The only animals in the world that shove things up our ass for survival."

Perhaps out of necessity, the scene turns from bracing to perfunctory as Julot cites a gloomy statistic about the survival rate of prisoners sent to Devil's Island. Then the scene's expositional function is broadened when Julot tells Papillon about another prisoner on the boat: the wiry, bespectacled Louis, whom Julot says is a target because he's carrying more money than anybody else.

Seeing an opportunity, Papillon speaks with Louis the next morning and offers protection if the accountant promises to fund Papillon's escape from Devil's Island. Louis initially balks at the offer, but when an inmate in a nearby bunk is killed, he changes his mind. Louis's dialogue reflects Trumbo's verbosity, apparently due to Hoffman's suggestion that Trumbo use himself as a model for the character.[7] "It now seems that until we get to a decent jail with bribable guards," he says, "I may stand in need of rather close physical protection." The humor in the line—referring to a "decent" jail as one with "bribable" guards—indicates the most useful flavor that Trumbo contributed to *Papillon*. Because the story is deadly serious, Trumbo's occasional one-liners offer much-needed variety.

When the prisoners arrive at Devil's Island, they're told that escape attempts will result in years of solitary confinement and that more severe infractions will result in beheading. "Make the best of what we offer you," a warden says cheerlessly, "and you will suffer less than you deserve."

The Louis-Papillon moments interspersed throughout the film's expositional sequences are quick and efficient, and they underline the pragmatic nature of the relationship. Although he shows that the men recognize each other's best qualities (Papillon's indomitable spirit, Louis's wily intelligence), Trumbo doesn't insert any cute interplay, because to do so would break the mood of the film. Trumbo's ability to gracefully slip his material between the building blocks of Semple's screenplay reflects the surgeon-like skill that he developed in his decades of screenwriting.

After several episodes portraying the harshness of the prison, the plot proper gets underway when Papillon meets a trader willing to sell Papillon a boat in which the convict plans to escape Devil's Island. But complications arise. First, Louis has a change of heart. Previously, he explained that his wife was seeking to exonerate him in France, so he didn't plan to attempt escape. But after discovering the brutality of the prison, he decides he does want to flee.

Papillon isn't enthusiastic, and his mood darkens further when he and Louis are assigned to bury an escapee who has just been captured and killed by the prison's two ex-con manhunters. Louis blanches when he realizes the dead man is Julot, the criminal whom Papillon and Louis befriended on the boat from France. When Louis rushes away from the body to vomit, a thuggish sergeant (Victor Tayback) hits Louis, barking, "Stop that, you pig!" The guard steps on Louis's glasses before Papillon, probably acting as much out of indig-

nation as loyalty, tackles the guard, then flees by diving into a nearby river and narrowly avoiding the guards' gunfire. Papillon connects with the trader, but discovers that he's been sold out: the manhunters are waiting by the trader's boat.

His first escape attempt a failure, Papillon is committed to solitary confinement, which cues the picture's most brutal sequence—and the one to which, it appears, Trumbo made the least contributions. During one of several horrific scenes depicting Papillon's sensory deprivation in solitary—where he's not allowed to speak and has no human contact save for the attendants who hand him his daily meal—Papillon's rebel spirit is neatly summarized by a moment in which he leaps from the floor of his cell to grab the cell's iron-bar ceiling and hiss under his breath to a just-out-of-earshot guard: "I'm still here, you bastards!" This succinct, memorable line was written not by Trumbo or Semple, though—it is among the only vestiges of an earlier draft by Oscar-winning screenwriter William Goldman.[8]

Schaffner uses several tricks to make the intrinsically static sequence of Papillon's solitary confinement dynamic. The least effective of the devices is a series of dream scenes in which Papillon hallucinates life outside the cell, and the most effective are shots in which Papillon's activities are seen through a sliver of light. Because Papillon spends six months of his two-year solitary confinement sentence immersed in total darkness save for that sliver of light, the light functions not only as a photographic effect but also as a metaphor for the freedom of which the indefatigable Papillon dreams. Therefore, seeing him use the light as a guide for preparing meals

Although he continued working until his death in 1976, the last feature film to bear Trumbo's name was the 1973 prison drama *Papillon*, starring Steve McQueen (left). Trumbo was hired to write a part for Dustin Hoffman (right) while the movie was being shot. (Allied Artists)

composed of the cockroaches and centipedes in his cell is doubly dispiriting.

In the context of an examination of Trumbo's career, the most interesting thing about the solitary confinement scenes—in which, it should be stressed, Trumbo's participation was likely not very extensive—is how they compare to similar scenes in *Johnny Got His Gun*. Schaffner faced a quandary akin to the one faced by Trumbo when filming Joe Bonham in his hospital room. Both sets of scenes involve static, repetitious images that, for dramatic purposes, need to be on screen extensively and in close succession. It's therefore telling to see how a more experienced and visually minded director attacked the problem.

Schaffner used varied light patterns, focal lengths, and camera positions, so each image of Papillon in his cell is different from the preceding. He created the effect of variety without compromising the narrative significance of the scenes, which was their sameness. So a shot, for instance, of Papillon's face cut from an ink-black background by a tiny point of light is different from a shot of his hands, positioned in the same light, stirring bugs into a bowl of soup.

Admittedly, Schaffner had far more options in terms of movement than Trumbo had when making *Johnny*, but the limited number of camera positions and lighting patterns that Trumbo used to film Joe in his hospital bed reveal that, despite the several interesting images in *Johnny*, Trumbo was an amateur when it came to trying to imagine a scene's visual possibilities. That Schaffner was exactly the opposite is one of the reasons why *Papillon* entertains even as it horrifies and sometimes sickens.

Following Papillon's release from solitary, the movie rushes through the scenes that set up Papillon's next escape attempt. The most important elements are the introduction of gay convict Maturette (Robert Deman) and the indication that Louis will continue to bankroll Papillon's activities. As with the earlier scenes on the ship, the moments between Louis and Papillon immediately following the solitary confinement sequence efficiently portray the growing bond between the two men; moreover, the scenes convey that the quality connecting the two men is integrity. Although this harks back to that hoariest of themes, "honor among thieves," it is nonetheless germane; because Trumbo neatly inserts Louis into almost every significant chapter of Papillon's journey, it's believable that something would grow between them.

The second escape attempt is something of a disaster, but Papillon, Louis, and Maturette nearly reach freedom. Once they reach the shore of Honduras, they are separated and the fates of Louis and Maturette are hidden from viewers as the film plunges into a long, colorful, and spectacular sequence depicting Papillon's adventures away from the prison. But at the end of this vivid detour—notably, another sequence to which Trumbo probably made negligable contributions—Papillon is recaptured and put back into solitary confinement.

Prudently, the picture doesn't revisit the numbing imagery of the earlier solitary confinement sequence; it instead cuts five years ahead to a white-haired Papillon's release from solitary. In an unconvincing coincidence, Maturette is released from solitary the same day as Papillon, and lives long enough to die saying good-bye to his old friend.

After all of its twists and turns, however, the film recovers its sure footing during the closing sequence, which was almost entirely written by Christopher Trumbo after he took over the project from his ailing father. The task that Christopher Trumbo faced was a daunting one, because by separating the two principal characters during the escape, the filmmakers broke the flow of the Papillon-Louis relationship at a crucial point. So the challenge he faced was not only to resolve the relationship between the two men, but in effect to re-create the relationship in microcosm.

In the final sequence, Papillon is sent to a remote island where lifers and ex-cons work as farmers. He discovers that Louis is not only alive, but his neighbor—the last of many incredible contrivances in the film. The filmmakers do wonders with this sequence, because they portray Louis as an old man so defeated by life that he's content feeding his pigs, tending his garden, and planning additions to his tiny house; Louis's wife betrayed him years ago, so he no longer dreams of freedom. These scenes also contain Hoffman's most poignant work in the film. In addition to conveying his character's broken quality, Hoffman communicates the reluctance with which Louis lets Papillon back into his life. Louis is too tired to open his heart again, so the fleeting moments in which Louis shows how deeply Papillon has affected him are touching.

When Papillon suggests one more

escape attempt, though, it feels more comic than inspiring, because of McQueen's ineffective portrayal of old age and because of the audacity of the plan—tossing a bundle of coconuts off a cliff and then jumping into the water, grabbing the bundle, and floating out to sea. Also, after all of the pain and heartbreak that Papillon has suffered, it seems a peculiarly Hollywood assertion that his spirit would be as unbroken when he's an aged veteran of the prison system as it was when he was a newly arrived inmate.[9]

The final scene, in which Papillon and Louis look down from a cliff at the raging water that will either kill them or take them to freedom, is filled with emotion. Louis loses his nerve, so the last exchange between the old friends provides a fitting resolution to their love story—and an indication that Christopher Trumbo, who wrote this scene, brought to the film a style as eloquent as his father's.

> PAPILLON: Ready?
> LOUIS: I must tell you something.
> PAPILLON: Louis—you don't have to say anything.
> LOUIS: I've meant to. I'm sorry.
> PAPILLON: I know.
> LOUIS: You'll be killed. You know that.
> PAPILLON: Maybe.
> LOUIS: Please—don't do it.

But Papillon does it, of course. And, defying all reason and fate, he succeeds—his little bundle of coconuts carries him out to sea. After a heartbreaking shot of Louis watching his last chance for freedom float away on an ocean current, the film cuts to Papillon, reveling in hard-won joy as he leaves Devil's Island behind. Putting all of the story's harrowing hardships aside, the picture closes on a triumphant note with Goldman's line: "Hey, you bastards! I'm still here!"

Given all he went through, the line could just as easily have been spoken by Dalton Trumbo.

In 1975, nearly 20 years after "Robert Rich" won an Oscar for writing the story of *The Brave One,* Trumbo finally was given the statuette. It was one of many accolades that he received in the last years of his life, when colleagues acknowledged the monumental contribution he made to the craft of screenwriting. Trumbo wasn't lauded for being an innovator; instead, he was celebrated for being so proficient that his career survived three decades of political and economic upheaval. While it is true that only a handful of great films appear on his résumé, it is perhaps more significant to note the number of good films that Trumbo wrote. Through a combination of speed, resourcefulness, and tenacity, Trumbo managed to excel in the 1930s, 1940s, 1950s, 1960s, and, arguably, in the 1970s. If only for the sheer number of quality films to which he contributed, Trumbo's output is stunning. "I may not be the best screenwriter in Hollywood," he once humbly quipped, "but I am incomparably the fastest."[10]

Yet it is not the volume of Trumbo's output that is most impressive when one considers his cinematic body of work. It is instead the nobility of his best films that shines. Make no mistake, Trumbo wrote enough junk in his time that it's unsurprising that lofty critics have for decades dismissed him as a hack. It is not difficult to scan Trumbo's credits and find a handful of failed movies in each decade. But it is also not difficult to scan his credits and see a recurring theme, the same theme that has been illustrated again and again throughout this book. Honor is what makes the best of Trumbo's movies loom even larger when considered as part of a body of work.

Look at the protaganists of Trumbo's best screenplays, and see what they share. Matt Ryan of *Fugitives for a Night* learns to think for himself and gains the courage to set aside his shallow dream to pursue a more meaningful one. John Abbott of *A Man to Remember* casts such a long shadow with his unfailingly noble behavior that he shames the men who took him for granted. Kitty Foyle and the heroes of Trumbo's wartime movies all make sacrifices for the betterment of others, and Andrew Long of *The Remarkable Andrew* is the first in the long line of Trumbo's rebel heroes, men who fight for justices both big and small.

But these are just the characters from Trumbo's innocent films. The characters in his films noir represent a different kind of personal honor, in which people live and die by how true they are to themselves. And finally, there are protaganists in his latter-day pictures: Spartacus, Ari Ben Canaan in *Exodus*, Yakov Bok in *The Fixer*, and Papillon. Looking at this gallery of heroes and antiheroes, it is impossible to let the mitigating factors of Trumbo's screen career dull his achievement. Yes, many of these characters were the creations of other writers; yes, the quality of the films in which these characters appeared varies wildly; yes, some of their stories are simple homilies.

What matters, finally, is not who invented the characters or whether their stories were perfect. What matters is that for more than three decades, Trumbo told stories about what he believed to be the most important principles in life. He told stories about people defending freedom of speech, about people fighting persecution, about people taking responsibility for their actions. He told stories about people trying to live honorably.

And from his first great screenplay, *A Man to Remember*, to the script that Kirk Douglas deemed "perfect," *Lonely Are the Brave*, to the unexpectedly experimental adaptation of *Johnny Got His Gun*, Trumbo hit his peaks when the quality of his writing meshed with the quality of his thinking. His best screenwriting was as provocative as his personality.

Still, the eternal question remains—did Trumbo waste his life by spending so much of it writing movies? The lasting impact of *Johnny Got His Gun* would suggest an affirmative answer, but the truth may be more evasive. Trumbo's films reached a wider audience than most novels could, and for nearly 40 years, the American screen was enriched by his work. Even if only some of the socially conscious imagery and doctrine identified in this book made an impression on audiences, his movies served a worthwhile purpose.

And, as many of his friends noted, Trumbo's greatest accomplishment really was being himself—an ornery, pedantic, brilliant man whom fellow blacklistee Paul Jarrico described as "the Mark Twain of my generation."[11] The money that Trumbo made by writing movies allowed him to raise three children and, in his spare time, raise hell. By that measure too, his life was not wasted.

Certainly Trumbo's work has survived. *Johnny Got His Gun* has been printed more than 40 times; the makers of romantic comedies have for decades borrowed from the style of *Roman Holiday*[12]; legendary director Steven Speilberg remade *A Guy Named Joe* as his 1989 film *Always*; *Spartacus* enjoyed a second life when a restored version of the film was released in 1991; *Gun Crazy* was among the first films added to the Library of Congress's National Film Registry.

In a tribute to the strength of his craft, Trumbo's structures have lasted—and so has the enigma of the man who built them. In 1999, when director Elia Kazan's life achievement Oscar caused a controversy because Kazan named names before HUAC, a rush of magazine, newspaper, radio, and television features revisited the facts of the blacklist era to examine the impact that "friendly" witness such as Kazan had on their industry. And in nearly every one of the stories, the name Dalton Trumbo was prominently featured. More than half a century after he testified before Congress, Trumbo is still one of the most visible icons of the blacklist. His defiant spirit is even visible in *Guilty by Suspicion* (1991, Warner Bros.), a drama about HUAC and Hollywood in which the protagonist, a director played by Robert De Niro, makes a spirited demonstration before Congress that would have done the Hollywood Ten proud.

Trumbo died on September 10, 1976, but he was too colorful, too vital, too provocative a figure to be silenced by death. He left behind a characteristically eclectic slate of completed or half-completed screenplay projects, an incomplete novel that was published posthumously, and a life's worth of unpublished prose and unproduced screenplays. We may yet hear from him again.

But in the meantime, we are left with what we make of what he did. And in his prescient, acerbic way, Trumbo wincingly accepted that he would not the be author of his own history.

> The truth is that little by little one grows accustomed to the public picture of oneself. Each newspaper and every book adds something to the portrait. New features emerge from the shadows, the imperfections stand out ever more sharply, the general ugliness acquires perspective and dimension. And there is nothing one can do to stop it…. So one averts his face while the mold cools and the materials harden to their last, irrevocable shape.[13]

It would be a disservice to Trumbo's memory to paint too rosy a picture of his cinematic oeuvre. His movies were sometimes strident and clichéd. But just as often, they were poetic, inspirational, and even moving. And his best movies are infused with his wit, his values, his honor. Despite the often oppressive circumstances of his career, Dalton Trumbo fought the good fight. Because that same fight rages on to this day, it is comforting to have his example leading us into battle.

Filmography

Release dates generally indicate the Los Angeles theatrical premiere date. Cast and crew lists are not inclusive, but rather indicative of the principal participants in each project. Cast members are listed alphabetically, not in billing order. In all references, "DT" stands for Dalton Trumbo.

Road Gang

Alternate title: *Injustice* (British release). Released March 28, 1936 (Warner Bros.). Produced by Brian Foy. Directed by Louis King. Screenplay by DT. Story by Harold Buckley and Abem Finkel. Cinematography by L. William O'Connell. Edited by Jack Killifer. Art direction by Hugh Reticker, Jr. Music by Leo F. Forbstein. B&W; 63 min.

Cast: Harry Cording (Sam Dawson), Joseph Crehan (Sheilds), William B. Davidson (District Attorney Marsden), Joseph King (J.W. Metcalfe), Edward LaSaint (Judge), Marc Lawrence (Pete), Kay Linaker (Barbara Winston), Charles Middleton (Mine Warden), Carlyle Moore, Jr. (Bob Gordon), Henry O'Neill (George Winston), Addison Richards (Warden Parmenter), Eddie Schubert (Buck Draper), Edward Van Sloan (Dudley), Tom Wilson (Bull), Donald Woods (James Larrabie).

Note: Some sources credit Trumbo with writing a picture called *Prison Farm*; in fact, that was the working title of *Road Gang* and not a separate credit.

Love Begins at Twenty

Alternate title: *All One Night* (British release).

Released Sept. 22, 1936 (Warner Bros.). Produced by Brian Foy. Directed by Frank McDonald. Screenplay by Tom Reed and DT. Based on the play *Broken Dishes* by Martin Flavin. Cinematography by George Barnes. Edited by Terry O. Morse. Art direction by Hugh Reticker, Jr. B&W; 58 min.

Cast: Arthur Aylesworth (Justice Felton), Tom Brower (Bert Hanson), Hobart Cavanaugh (Jake Buckley), Patricia Ellis (Lois Gillingwater), Robert Glecker (Mugsy O'Banion/Harold McCauley), Sol Gorss (Jim), Hugh Herbert (Horatio Gillingwater), Warren Hull (Jerry Wayne), Milton Kibbee (Wilbur), Ann Nagel (Miss Perkins), Henry Otho (Lumpy), Mary Treen (Alice Gillingwater), Dorothy Vaughn (Evalina Gillingwater), Max Wagner (Lester), Clarence Wilson (Jonathan Ramp), Tom Wilson (Fred).

Note: Flavin's play was previously filmed as *Too Young to Marry* (1931, Warner Bros.).

Tugboat Princess

Released Nov. 15, 1936 (Columbia). Produced by Kenneth J. Bishop (associate producer). Directed by David Selman. Screenplay by Robert Watson. Story by Isadore Bernstein and DT. Cinematography by William Beckway and William Thompson. Edited by William Austin. B&W; 66 min.

Cast: Emily Booth ("Princess" Judy), Clyde Cook (Steve), Reginald Hincks (Captain Fred Darling), Walter C. Kelly (Captain Zack Livermore), Lester Matthews (Bob Norfolk), Ethel Reese-Burns (Mrs. Price).

The Devil's Playground

Alternate title: *Submarine.*

Released Jan. 24, 1937 (Columbia). Produced by Edward Chodorov. Directed by Erle C. Kenton. Screenplay by Liam O'Flaherty, Jerome Chodorov, and DT. Uncredited screenplay contributions by Edward Chodorov. Story by Norman Springer. Cinematography by Lucien Ballard. Edited by Viola Lawrence. Art direction by Stephen Goosón. Costumes designed by Ernest Dryden. Music by Morris Stoloff. Special camera effects by Ganahl Carson. B&W; 74 min.

Cast: Ward Bond ("Sidecar" Wilson), Dolores del Rio (Carmen), Richard Dix (Jack Dorgan), John Gallaudet (Jones), Francis McDonald (Romano), George McKay (Red Anderson), Chester Morris (Robert Mason), Don Rowan (Reilly), Pierre Watkin (submarine commander).

Notes: This story was previously filmed as *Submarine* (1928, Columbia Pictures) and *Fifty Fathoms Deep* (1931, Columbia Pictures). The working title of this film was *The Depths Below.*

That Man's Here Again

Released April 17, 1937 (Warner Bros.). Produced by Bryan Foy. Directed by Louis King. Screenplay by Lillie Hayward. Screen story by Abem Finkel, Harold Buckley, and DT (uncredited). Based on the story "Young Nowheres" by I.A.R. Wyllie. Cinematography by Warren Lynch. Edited by Harold McLernon. Art direction by Esdras Hartley. B&W; 60 min.

Cast: Arthur Aylesworth (Johnson), Tom Brown (Jimmy Whalen), Teddy Hart (Bud), Hugh Herbert (Thomas J. Jesse), Joseph King (Mr. Murdock), Tetsuo Komai (Wong), Mary Maguire (Nancy Lee), Dorothy Vaughan (Mrs. Matthews).

Note: Wylie's short story was previously filmed as *Young Nowheres* (1929, First National).

Fugitives for a Night

Released Sept. 23, 1938 (RKO). Produced by Lou Lusty. Directed by Leslie Goodwins. Screenplay by DT. Story by Richard Wormser. Cinematography by Frank Redman. Edited by Desmond Marquette. Art direction by Van Nest Polglase. Gowns by Renie. Musical direction by Russell Bennett. Special effects by Vernon L. Walker. B&W; 63 min.

Cast: Frank Albertson (Matt Ryan), Adrienne Ames (Eileen Baker), Paul Guilfoyle (Monks), Jonathan Hale (police captain), Russell Hicks (Maurice Tenwright), Allan Lane (John Nelson), Eleanor Lynn (Ann Wray), Bradley Page (Dennis Poole).

Note: The working title of this film was *Birthday of a Stooge.*

A Man to Remember

Released Oct. 14, 1938 (RKO). Produced by Robert Sisk. Directed by Garson Kanin. Screenplay by DT. Based on the story "Failure" by Katherine Havilland-Taylor. Cinematography by J. Roy Hunt. Edited by Jack Hively. Art direction by Van Nest Polglase. Music by Roy Webb. B&W; 80 min.

Cast: Granvine Bates (George Sykes), Lee Bowman (Dick Abbott as an adult), Harlan Briggs (Homer Ramsey), Edward Ellis (John Abbott), Gilbert Emery (Dr. Robinson), Charles Halton (Perkins), William Henry (Howard Sykes), Dickie Jones (Dick Abbott as a child), Carole Leete (Jean as a child), Anne Shirley (Jean as an adult), Frank M. Thomas (Jode Harkness), John Wray (Johnson).

Notes: Havilland-Taylor's short story was previously filmed as *One Man's Journey* (1933, RKO). The working title of this film was *Country Doctor*.

The Flying Irishman

Released April 7, 1939 (RKO). Produced by Pandro S. Berman. Directed by Leigh Jason. Screenplay by Ernest Pagano and DT. Cinematography by J. Roy Hunt. Edited by Arthur E. Roberts. Music by Roy Webb. Special effects by Vernon L. Walker. B&W; 72 min.

Cast: Dorothy Appleby (Maybelle), Robert Armstrong (Joe Alden), Spencer Charters (Smedley), Joyce Compton (Sally), Douglas Corrigan (Douglas "Wrong Way" Corrigan), Paul Kelly (Butch), J.M. Kerrigan (Clyde Corrigan, Sr.), Knox Manning (commentator), Donald McBride (Thompson), Dorothy Peterson (Mrs. Corrigan), Eddie Quillan (Henry), Gene Reynolds (Clyde Corrigan, Jr. [Doug as a child]), Peggy Ryan (Evelyn Corrigan), Minor Watson (personnel manager), Cora Witherspoon (Mrs. Thompson).

Sorority House

Alternate title: *That Girl from College* (British release).

Released May 5, 1939 (RKO). Produced by Robert Sisk. Directed by John Farrow. Screenplay by DT. Based on the story "Chi House" by Mary Coyle Chase. Cinematography by Nicholas Musuraca. Edited by Harry Marker. Costumes designed by Edward Stevenson. Musical direction by Roy Webb. B&W; 64 min.

Cast: Margaret Armstrong (Mrs. Dawson), Pamela Blake (Merle), Marge Champion (coed), James Ellison (Bill Loomis), Selmer Jackson (Mr. Grant), Doris Jordan (Neva Simpson), J.M. Kerrigan (Lew Fisher), Veronica Lake (coed, credited as Constance Keane), Barbara Reed (Dotty), Elizabeth Risdon (Mrs. Scott), Anne Shirley (Alice Fischer), June Story (Norma Hancock), Chill Wills (Mr. Johnson), Helen Wood (Madame President).

The Kid from Kokomo

Released May 23, 1939 (Warner Bros.). Produced by Samuel Bischoff. Directed by Lewis Seiler. Screenplay by Jerry Wald and Richard Macauley. Uncredited screenplay contributions by Michael Fessier and Ring Lardner, Jr. Based on the story "Broadway Cavalier" by DT. Cinematography by Sidney Hickox. Edited by Jack Killifer. Music by Adolph Deutsch. B&W; 95 min.

Cast: Joan Blondell (Doris Harvey), Ward Bond (Klewicki), Ed Brophy (Eddie Black), Morgan Conway (Louie), Stanely Fields ("Muscles" Malone), Winifred Harris (Mrs. Bronson), Wayne Morris (Homer Baston), Pat O'Brien (William "Square Shooting" Murphy), John Ridgely (Sam), May Robson (Maggie Martin), Maxie Rosenbloom ("Curley" Bender), Sidney Toler (Judge Bronson), Jane Wyman (Marian Bronson).

Five Came Back

Released June 23, 1939 (RKO). Produced by Robert Sisk. Directed by John Farrow. Screenplay by Jerome Cady, DT, and Nathanael West. Story by Richard Carroll. Cinematography by Nicholas Musuraca. Edited by Harry Marker. Art direction by Van Nest Polglase. Costumes designed by Edward Stevenson. Music by Roy Webb. B&W; 75 min.

Cast: Lucille Ball (Peggy Nolan), Wendy Barrie (Alice Melhorne), Joseph Calleia (Vasquez), John Carradine (Crimp), Dick Hogan (Larry), Allen Jenkins (Pete Casey), Casey Johnson (Tommy), Patrick Knowles (Judson Ellis), Chester Morris (Bill), Elisabeth Risdon (Martha Spengler), C. Aubrey Smith (Professor Henry Spengler), Kent Taylor (Joe).

Note: This film was remade, by the same director, as *Back from Eternity* (1956, RKO).

Career

Released July 7, 1939 (RKO). Produced by Robert Sisk. Directed by Leigh Jason.

Screenplay by DT. Screen story by Bert Granet. Based on the novel *Career* by Philip Duffield Strong. Cinematography by Frank Redman. Edited by Arthur E. Redman. Musical direction by Russell Bennett. B&W; 79 min.

Cast: John Archer (Ray Cruthers), Janet Beecher (Amy Cruthers), Hobart Cavanaugh (Jim Bronson), Charles Drake (Rex Chaney), Alice Eden (Merta Krause), Edward Ellis (Stephen Cruthers), Leon Errol (Mudcat), Harrison Greene (Ren Burnett), Raymond Hatton (Deacon), Samuel E. Hinds (Clem Bartholomew), Maurice Murphy (Mel Bartholomew), Anne Shirley (Sylvia Bartholomew).

Notes: This film is unrelated to the 1959 Paramount film of the same name. Certain sources indicate that Trumbo contributed to the screenplay of the latter *Career*—a drama about an actor who, among other things, gets blacklisted for political activities. Reports of Trumbo's role in the 1959 picture are highly dubious, however, so the picture is not included in this book.

Heaven with a Barbed Wire Fence

Released Nov. 3, 1939 (20th Century–Fox). Produced by Sol. M. Wurtzel. Directed by Ricardo Cortez. Screenplay by Leonard Hoffman and Ben Grauman Kohn. Uncredited screenplay contributions by Sam Duncan. Story by DT. Cinematography by Edward Cronjager. Edited by Norman Colbert. Art direction by Richard Day and Chester Gore. Music by Samuel Kaylin. B&W; 61 min.

Cast: Irving Bacon (Sheriff Clem Diggers), Ward Bond (Hunk), Eddie Collins (Bill), Nicholas Conte (Tony Casselli), Glenn Ford (Joe Riley), Marjorie Rambeau (Mamie), Jean Rogers (Anita Santos), Raymond Walburn (Professor Townsend Thayer).

The Lone Wolf Strikes

Released January 26, 1940 (Columbia). Produced by Fred Kohlmar. Directed by Sidney Salkow. Screenplay by Harry Seagall and Albert Duffy. Based on a story by DT and characters created by Louis Joseph Vance. Cinematography by Henry Freulich. Edited by Al Clark. Art direction by Lionel Banks. Costumes designed by Robert Kalloch. Musical direction by Moris Stoloff. B&W; 57 min.

Cast: Astrid Allwyn (Binnie Weldon), Alan Baxter (Jim Ryder), Don Beddoe (Inspector Conroy), Eric Blare (Jamison), Roy Gordon (Phillip Jordan), Montagu Love (Emil Gorlick), Joan Perry (Delia Jordan), Addison Richards (Stanley Young), Harland Tucker (Alberts), Robert Wilcox (Ralph Bolton), Warren William (Michael Lanyard, a.k.a. the Lone Wolf).

Half a Sinner

Released April 5, 1940 (Universal). Produced and directed by Al Christie. Screenplay by Frederick J. Jackson. Based on the story "Lady Takes a Chance" by DT. Cinematography by Charles Van Enger. Edited by Barney Rogan. Musical direction by David Chudnow. B&W; 59 min.

Cast: Heather Angel (Anne Gladden), Clem Bevans (Snuffy), Walter Catlett (station attendant), Constance Collier (Mrs. Jefferson Breckenridge), William B. Davidson (Slick Copescu), Joe Devlin (Steve), Tom Dugan (Red Eagon), Emma Dunn (Grammy Gladden), Robert Elliot (Officer Kelly), Fern Emmett (Margaret Read), John King (Larry Cameron), Wilbur Mack (Mason).

Note: This film is unrelated to a 1934 Universal picture of the same name.

Curtain Call

Released April 26, 1940 (RKO). Produced by Howard Benedict. Directed by Frank Woodruff. Screenplay by DT. Story by Howard J. Green. Cinematography by Russell Metty. Edited by Harry Marker. B&W; 63 min.

Cast: Frank Faylen (Ted Palmer), Ralph Forbes (Leslie Borriville), Tommy Kelly

(Fred Middleton), J.M. Kerrigan (Mr. Middleton), Donald MacBride (Geoffrey Crandall), Alan Mowbray (Donald Avery), Barbara Read (Helen Middleton), Ann Shoemaker (Mrs. Middleton), Helen Vinson (Charlotte Morley).

A Bill of Divorcement

Alternate title: *Never to Love.*

Released May 31, 1940 (RKO). Produced by Robert Sisk. Directed by John Farrow. Screenplay by DT. Based on the play *A Bill of Divorcement* by Clemence Dane (pseudonym for Winifred Ashton). Cinematography by Nicholas Musuraca. Edited by Harry Marker. Costumes designed by Renié. Music by Roy Webb. B&W; 70 min.

Cast: Fay Bainter (Margaret Fairfield), Laurie Beatty (Susan), Kathryn Collier (Basset), Ernest Cossart (Reverend Doctor Pumphrey), Patrick Knowles (John Storm), Herbert Marshall (Gray Meredith), Adolphe Menjou (Hilary Fairfield), Maureen O'Hara (Syndey Fairfield), C. Aubrey Smith (Dr. Alliot), Dame May Whitty (Hester Fairfield).

Note: Dane's play was previously filmed as *A Bill of Divorcement* (1932, RKO).

We Who Are Young

Released July 19, 1940 (MGM). Produced by Seymour Nebenzahl. Directed by Harold S. Bucquet. Screenplay and story by DT. Cinematography by Karl Freund. Edited by Howard O'Neill. Art direction by Cedric Gibbons and Wade B. Rubottom. Costumes designed by Dolly Tree. Music by Bronislau Kaper. B&W; 80 min.

Cast: Henry Armetta (Tony), Truman Bradley (commentator), Jonathan Hale (William Braddock), Charles Lane (Perkins), Gene Lockhart (C.B. Beamis), Grant Mitchell (Jones), Irene Seidner (Mrs. Weinstock), John Shelton (William Brooks), Lana Turner (Margy Brooks), Clarence Wilson (R. Glassford), Shirley Worde (Miss Anderson).

Kitty Foyle: The Natural History of a Woman

Released Dec. 27, 1940 (RKO). Produced by Harry E. Edington (executive producer) and David Hemptstead. Directed by Sam Wood. Screenplay by DT. Additional dialogue by Donald Ogden Stewart. Based on the novel *Kitty Foyle* by Christopher Morley. Cinematography by Robert De-Grasse. Edited by Henry Berman. Art direction by Mark-Lee Kirk and Van Nest Polglase. Costumes designed by Renié. Music by Roy Webb. B&W; 107 min.

Cast: Eduardo Ciannelli (Giono), Gladys Cooper (Mrs. Stratford), Ernest Cossart (Tom Foyle), James Craig (Mark Eisen), Kay Linaker (Veronica Brook Gladwyn), Dennis Morgan (Wynwood Stratford, VI), Odette Myrtil (Delphine Detaille), Richard Nichols (Wyn's boy), Ginger Rogers (Kitty Foyle), Katharine Stevens (Molly), Mary Treen (Pat).

Accent on Love

Released July 11, 1941 (20th Century–Fox). Produced by Ralph Dietrich and Walter Morosco. Directed by Roy McCarey. Screenplay by John Larkin. Story by DT. Cinematography by Charles G. Clarke. Music by Emil Newman. B&W; 61 min.

Cast: Irving Bacon (Mr. Smedley), Stanley Clements (Patrick Henry Lombroso), Leonard Correy (Flowers), Thurston Hall (T.J. Triton), Osa Massen (Osa), George Montgomery (John Worth Hyndman), Jon T. Murray (Wardman), J. Carrol Naish (Manuel Lombroso), Oscar O'Shea (magistrate), Cobina Wright, Jr. (Linda Hyndman), Minerva Urecal (Teresa Lombroso).

You Belong to Me

Alternate title: *Good Morning, Doctor* (British release).

Released Oct. 22, 1941 (Columbia). Produced and directed by Wesley Ruggles. Screenplay by Claude Binyon. Based on the story "The Doctor's Husband" by DT. Cinematography by Joseph Walker. Edited by

Viola Lawrence. Production designed by Lionel Banks. Art direction by Lionel Banks. Costumes designed by Edith Head. Music by Frederick Hollander. B&W; 94 min.

Cast: Edgar Buchanan (Billings), Roger Clark (Vandemer), Melville Cooper (Moody), Ruth Donnelly (Emma), Maude Elburne (Ella), Henry Fonda (Peter Kirk), Ralph Peters (Joseph), Renie Riano (Minnie), Barbara Stanwyck (Doctor Helen Hunt).

Note: This film was remade in 1950, without DT's involvement, as *Emergency Wedding* (see separate entry).

The Remarkable Andrew

Alternate title: *At Good Old Siwash*.

Released March 5, 1942 (Paramount). Produced by Richard Blumenthal. Directed by Stuart Heisler. Screenplay by DT. Based on the novel *The Remarkable Andrew: Being the Chronicle of a Literal Man* by DT. Cinematography by Theodor Sparkuhl. Edited by Archie Marshek. Costumes designed by Edith Head. Music by Victor Young. B&W; 81 min.

Cast: Rod Cameron (Jesse James), Spencer Charters (Doctor Clarence Upjohn), Wallis Clark (City Treasurer R.R. McCall), Jimmy Conlin (Private Henry Bartholomew Smith), Brian Donlevy (General Andrew Jackson), Ellen Drew (Peggy Tobin), Gilbert Emery (Thomas Jefferson), Clyde Fillmore (Mayor Ollie Lancaster), Porter Hall (Chief Clerk Art Slocumb), William Holden (Andrew Long), Brandon Hurst (Chief Justice John Marshall), Montagu Love (General George Washington), Thomas W. Ross (Judge Ormond Krebbs), Minor Watson (District Attorney Orville Beamish), George Watts (Benjamin Franklin), Richard Webb (Randall Stevens).

I Married a Witch

Released Oct. 3, 1942 (Paramount). Produced and directed by René Clair. Screenplay by Robert Pirosh and Marc Connelly. Uncredited screenplay contributions by René Clair, Preston Sturges, and DT. Based on the novel *The Passionate Witch* by Thorne Smith (completed by Norman Matson). Cinematography by Ted Tetzlaff. Music by Roy Webb. B&W; 82 min.

Cast: Robert Benchley (Doctor Dudley White), Susan Hayward (Estelle Masterson), Cecil Kellaway (Daniel), Veronica Lake (Jennifer), Eily Malyon (Tabitha), Frederic March (Wallace Wooley), Elizabeth Patterson (Margaret), Robert Warwick (J.B. Masterson).

A Guy Named Joe

Released Dec. 24, 1943 (MGM). Produced by Everett Riskin. Directed by Victor Fleming. Screenplay by DT. Screen story by Frederick Hazlitt Brennan. Story by David Boehm and Chandler Sprague. Cinematography by George J. Folsey and Karl Freund. Edited by Frank Sullivan. Production designed by Cedric Gibbons and Lyle R. Wheeler. Costumes designed by Irene. Music by Herbert Stothart. Special effects by A. Arnold Gillespie, Donald Jahrus, and Warren Newcombe. B&W; 120 min.

Cast: Lionel Barrymore (the General), Ward Bond (Al Yackey), Don Defore ("Powerhouse" James J. Rourke), Irene Dunne (Dorinda Durston), James Gleason (Lieutenant Colonel "Nails" Kirkpatrick), Van Johnson (Ted Randall), Barry Nelson (Dick Rumney), Henry O'Neill (Colonel Sykes), Addison Richards (Major Corbett), Charles Smith (Sanderson), Spencer Tracy (Pete Sandige), Esther Williams (Ellen Bright).

Note: This film was remade in 1989 as *Always* (see separate entry).

Tender Comrade

Released Dec. 29, 1943 (RKO). Produced by David Hempstead. Directed by Edward Dmytryk. Screenplay and story by DT. Cinematography by Russell Metty. Edited by Roland Gross. Art direction by Albert D'Agostino and Carroll Clark. Costumes designed by Edith Head and Renié. Music by Leigh Harline. B&W; 102 min.

Cast: Mady Christians (Manya Lodge), Patricia Collinge (Helen Stacey), Jane Darwell (Mrs. Henderson), Kim Hunter (Doris

Dumbrowksi), Ruth Hussey (Barbara Thomas), Richard Martin (Mike Dumbrowski), Ginger Rogers (Jo Jones), Robert Ryan (Chris Jones).

Thirty Seconds Over Tokyo

Released Dec. 15, 1944 (MGM). Produced by Sam Zimbalist. Directed by Mervyn LeRoy. Screenplay by DT. Based on the book *Thirty Seconds Over Tokyo* by Captain Ted W. Lawson and Robert Considine. Cinematography by Harold Rosson and Robert Surtees. Edited by Frank Sullivan. Music by Herbert Stothart. Production designed by Cedric Gibbons and Paul Groesse. B&W; 138 min.

Cast: Leon Ames (Lieutenant Jurika), Robert Bice ("Jig" White), Douglas Cowan ("Brick" Holstrom), Donald Curtis (Lieutenant Randall), Don DeFore (Charles McClure), Benson Fong (Doctor Chung, Jr.), Louis Jean Heydt (Lieutenant Miller), Van Johnson (Captain Ted W. Lawson), Doctor Hsin Kung (Doctor Chung, Sr.), Paul Langton (Captain "Ski" York), Ching Wah Lee ("Guerilla Charlie"), Gordon McDonald (Bob Clever), Scott McKay (Davey Jones), Horace McNally ("Doc" White), Robert Mitchum (Bob Gray), Tim Murdock (Dan Davenport), Alan Napier (Mr. Parker), Wm. "Bill" Phillips (Don Smith), John R. Reilly ("Shorty" Manch), Ann Shoemaker (Mrs. Parker), Phillis Thaxter (Ellen Lawson), Spencer Tracy (Lieutenant Colonel James H. Doolittle), Robert Walker (David Thatcher), Bill Williams (Bud Felton).

Our Vines Have Tender Grapes

Released Sept. 28, 1945 (MGM). Produced by Robert Sisk. Directed by Roy Rowland. Screenplay by DT. Based on the novel *Our Vines Have Tender Grapes* by George Victor Martin. Cinematography by Robert Surtees. Edited by Ralph E. Winters. Art direction by Edward Cafagno and Cedric Gibbons. Costumes designed by Kay Carter and Irene. Music by Bronislau Kaper. B&W; 105 min.

Cast: Morris Carnovsky (Bjorn Bjornson), James Craig (Nels "Editor" Halverson), Frances Gifford (Viola Johnson), Sara Haden (Mrs. Bjornson), Jackie "Butch" Jenkins (Arnold Hansen), Agnes Moorehead (Bruna Jacobson), Dorothy Morris (Ingeborg Jensen), Margaret O'Brien (Selma Jacobson), Edward G. Robinson (Martinius Jacobson).

Jealousy

Released Jan. 1, 1946 (Republic). Produced and directed by Gustav Machaty. Screenplay by Arnold Phillips and Gustav Machaty. Story by DT. Cinematography by Henry Sharp. Edited by John F. Link, Sr. Art direction by Frank P. Sylos. Music by Hanns Eilser. Song, "Jealousy," by Rudolf Friml. B&W; 71 min.

Cast: Mary Arden (Nurse), Nils Asther (Peter Urban), Kid Chissell (expressman), Hugo Haas (Hugo Kral), Holmes Herbert (Melvyn Russell), Mauritz Hugo (Bob), Peggy Leon (secretary), John Loder (Doctor David Brent), Michael Mark (shop owner), Karen Morley (Doctor Monica Anderson), Jane Randolph (Janet Urban).

It's a Wonderful Life

Released Dec. 25, 1946 (RKO). Produced and directed by Frank Capra. Screenplay by Frances Goodrich, Albert Hackett, and Frank Capra. Uncredited screenplay contributions by DT, Clifford Odets, Marc Connelly, Joe Swerling, Michael Wilson, and Dorothy Parker. Based on the short story "The Greatest Gift" by Philip Van Doren Stern. Cinematography by Joseph Walker, Joseph Biroc, and Victor Miner (uncredited). Edited by William Hornbeck. Music by Dimitri Tiomkin. B&W; 129 min.

Cast: Frank Albertson (Sam Wainwright), Lionel Barrymore (Mr. Potter), Ward Bond (Bert), Beulah Bondi (Mrs. Bailey), Frank Faylen (Ernie), Gloria Grahame (Violet), Samuel S. Hinds (Pa Bailey), Todd Karns (Harry Bailey), Thomas Mitchell (Uncle Billy), Donna Reed (Mary Hatch), James Stewart (George Bailey), Henry Travers (Clarence), H.B. Warner (Mr. Grover).

The Beautiful Blonde from Bashful Bend

Released in late May, 1949 (Fox). Produced and directed by Preston Sturges. Screenplay by Preston Sturges. Based on the story "The Lady From Laredo" by DT (credited as Earl Felton). Cinematography by Harry Jackson. Edited by Robert Fritch. Art direction by George W. Davis and Lyle Wheeler. Music by Cyril Mockbridge. Color; 77 min.

Cast: Pati Behrs (Roulette), Betty Grable (Freddie Jones), Richard Hale (Mrs. Basserman), Porter Hall (Judge O'Toole), Margaret Hamilton (Elvira O'Toole), Hugh Herbert (doctor), Esther Howard (Mrs. Smidlap), Richard Kean (Doctor Smidlap), and John Farrell MacDonald (Sheriff Sweetzer), Cesar Romero (Blackie Jobero), Olga San Juan (Conchita), Rudy Vallee (Charles Hingleman)

Gun Crazy

Alternate title: *Deadly Is the Female.*
Released Aug. 24, 1949 (United Artists). Produced by Frank King and Maurice King. Directed by Joseph H. Lewis. Screenplay by MacKinlay Kantor and DT (credited as Millard Kaufman). Based on the story "Gun Crazy" by MacKinlay Kantor. Cinematography by Russell Harlan. Edited by Harry Gerstad. Production designed by Gordon Wiles. Costumes designed by Norma. Music by Victor Young. Song, "Mad About You," by Victor Young (music) and Ned Washington (lyric). B&W; 87 min.

Cast: Morris Carnovsky (Judge Willoughby), Peggy Cummins (Annie Laurie Starr), John Dall (Bart Tare), Virginia Farmer (Miss Wynn), Barry Kroeger (Packett), Harry Lewis (Clyde Boston), Stanley Praeger (Bluey-Bluey), Anabel Shaw (Ruby Tare), Russ "Rusty" Tamblyn (Bart Tare, age fourteen), Nedrick Young (Dave Allister).

Emergency Wedding

Released Dec. 16, 1950 (Columbia). Produced by Nat Perrin. Directed by Edward Buzzell. Screenplay by Nat Perrin. Based on the screenplay *You Belong to Me* (see separate entry). Cinematography by Burnett Guffey. Edited by Al Clark. Art direction by Carl Anderson. Music by Werner R. Heyman. B&W; 78 min.

Cast: Jim Backus (Ed Hamley), Irving Bacon (Filbert), Don Beddoe (Forbish), Eduard Franz (Doctor Helmer), Barbara Hale (Doctor Helen Hunt), Una Merkel (Emma), Willard Parker (Vandemer), Larry Parks (Peter Kirk), Alan Reed (Tony).

The Hollywood Ten

Released in 1951. Directed by John Berry.
Note: This black-and-white pseudo-documentary, which runs 15 minutes, features the Hollywood Ten—Alvah Bessie, Herbert Biberman, Lester Cole, Edward Dmytryk, Ring Lardner, Jr., John Howard Lawson, Albert Maltz, Samuel Ornitz, Adrian Scott, and DT—reading prepared statements about HUAC and their legal troubles. It was made as part of their defense campaign.

The Prowler

Alternate title: *The Cost of Living.*
Released June 2, 1951 (United Artists). Produced by Sam Spiegel (credited as S.P. Eagle). Directed by Joseph Losey. Screenplay by DT (credited as Hugo Butler). Screenplay contributions by Hugo Butler. Story by Robert Thoeren and Hans Wilhelm. Cinematography by Arthur C. Miller. Edited by Paul Weathereaux. Art direction by Boris Leven. Costumes designed by Maria P. Donovan. Music by Lyn Murray. B&W; 92 min.

Cast: Madge Blake (Martha Gilvray), Wheaton Chambers (Doctor James), Sherry Hall (John Gilvray), Van Heflin (Webb Garwood), Evelyn Keyes (Susan Gilvray), John Maxwell (Bud Crocker), Robert Osterloh (coroner), Emerson Treacy (William Gilvray), DT (radio voice of John Gilvray), Katherine Warren (Grace Crocker).

He Ran All the Way

Released June 19, 1951 (United Artists). Produced by Bob Roberts. Uncredited production supervision by John Garfield. Directed by John Berry. Screenplay by DT (credited as Guy Endore) and Hugo Butler. Uncredited screenplay contributions by John Berry and Jack Moss. Based on the novel *He Ran All the Way* by Sam Ross. Cinematography by James Wong Howe. Edited by Francis D. Lyon. Production designed by Harry Horner. Costumes designed by Joe King. Music by Franz Waxman. B&W; 77 min.

Cast: Clancy Cooper (Stan), Wallace Ford (Fred Dobbs), John Garfield (Nick Robey), Gladys George (Mrs. Robey), Keith Hetherington (captain of detectives), Bob Hyatt (Tommy Dobbs), Norman Lloyd (Al Molin), Selena Royle (Mrs. Dobbs), Shelley Winters (Peg Dobbs).

Roman Holiday

Released Sept. 30, 1953 (Paramount). Produced and directed by William Wyler. Screenplay by Ian McLellan Hunter and John Dighton. Uncredited screenplay contributions by Ben Hecht. Story by DT (credited as Ian McLellan Hunter). Cinematography by Henri Alekan and Franz Planer. Edited by Robert Swink. Art direction by Hal Pereira and Walter Tyler. Costumes designed by Edith Head. Music by Georges Auric. B&W; 119 min.

Cast: Eddie Albert (Irving Radovich), Paulo Carlini (Mario Delani), Tullio Carminati (General Provno), Claudio Ermelli (Giovanni), Audrey Hepburn (Princess Ann), Gregory Peck (Joe Bradley), Hartley Power (Mr. Hennessy), Margaret Rawlings (Countess Vereberg), Laura Solari (Hennessy's secretary), Harcourt Williams (ambassador).

Note: This film was remade for television in 1987 as *Roman Holiday* (see separate entry).

They Were So Young

Alternate titles: *Mannequin für Rio* (German release), *Adventure in Rio*, *Party Girls for Sale*, *Violated*.

Released Feb. 23, 1954 (Lippert Pictures). Produced and directed by Kurt Neumann. Screenplay by DT and Michael Wilson (collectively credited as Felix Lützkendorf). Based on an outline by Jacques Companéez and "official documents acquired through the cooperation of Interpol, Paris." Cinematography by Ekkehard Kyrath. Edited by Eva Kroll. Art direction by Hans Sohnle. Music by Michael Jary. B&W; 80 min.

Cast: Pero Alexander (Manuel), Hanelore Axman (Vincenta), Erica Beer (Elise), Scott Brady (Lanning), Raymond Burr (Coltos), Joseph Damen (Doctor), Gisela Fackelday (Lanzowa), Gert Froebe (Lobos), Hanita Hallan (Lena), Gordon Howard (Garza), Eduard Linkers (Albert), Johanna Matz (Eve), Katherine Mayberg (Felicia), Kurt Mensl (Pasquale), Ingrid Stenn (Connie), Elizabeth Tanny (Emily), William Trenk-Treblitsch (Bulanso).

Carnival Story

Released April 21, 1954 (RKO). Produced by Frank King and Maurice King. Directed by Kurt Neumann. Screenplay by DT (credited as Marcel Klauber). Screenplay contributions by Kurt Neumann and Hans Jacoby. Cinematography by Ernest Haller. Edited by Ludolf Grisebach and Merrill White. Production designed by Edward S. Haworth. Costumes designed by Ursula Maes. Music by Willy Scmidt-Gentner. Color; 95 min.

Cast: Anne Baxter (Willie), Adi Berber (Groppo), Lyle Bettiger (Frank), Steve Cochran (Joe), Joy C. Flippen (Charley), George Nader (Vines), Helen Stanley (Peggy).

The Boss

Released Oct. 10, 1956 (United Artists). Produced by John Payne and Frank N. Seltzer. Directed by Byron Haskin. Screenplay and story by DT (credited as Ben L. Perry). Screenplay contributions by Ben L. Perry. Cinematography by Hal Mohr. Edited by Ralph Dawson. Music by Albert Glasser. B&W; 88 min.

Cast: Doe Avedon (Elsie Reynolds), William Bishop (Bob Herrick), Harry Cheshire (Governor Beck), Joe Flynn (Ernie Jackson), Alex Frazer (Roy Millard), Gil Lamb (Henry), George Lynn (Tom Masterson), John Mansfield (Lazetti), Gloria McGhee (Lorry Reed), Bob Morgan (Hamhead), Robin Morse (Johnny Mazia), John Payne (Matt Brady), Bill Phips (Stitch), Roy Roberts (Tim Brady), Rhys Williams (Stanley Millard).

The Brave One

Released Oct. 26, 1956 (RKO). Produced by Frank King and Maurice King. Directed by Irving Rapper. Screenplay by DT, Harry Franklin, and Merril G. White. Story by DT (credited as Robert L. Rich). Cinematography by Jack Cardiff. Edited by Merrill G. White. Music by Victor Young. Color/CinemaScope; 100 min.

Cast: Elsa Cardenas (Maria), Rodolfo Hoyos (Rafael Rosillo), Joi Lansing (Marion Randall), Carlos Navarro (Don Alejandro), Michael Ray (Leonardo Rosillo), Fermin Rivera (himself).

Note: This film is sometimes referred to by Trumbo's original title, *The Boy and the Bull.*

Heaven Knows, Mr. Allison

Released March 15, 1957 (20th Century-Fox). Produced by Buddy Adler and Eugene Franke. Directed by John Huston. Screenplay by John Lee Mahin and John Huston. Uncredited screenplay polish/rewrite by DT. Based on the novel *Heaven Knows, Mr. Allison* by Charles Shaw. Cinematography by Oswald Morris. Edited by Russell Lloyd. Art direction by Stephen Grimes. Costumes designed by Elizabeth Hafferden. Music by Georges Auric. Color/CinemaScope; 105 min.

Cast: Deborah Kerr (Sister Angela), Robert Mitchum (Mr. Allison).

No Down Payment

Released Oct. 9, 1957 (20th Century-Fox). Produced by Jerry Wald. Directed by Martin Ritt. Screenplay by Phillip Yordan. Uncredited screenplay consultation and/or contributions by DT. Based on the novel *No Down Payment* by John McPartland. Cinematography by Joseph LaShelle. Edited by Louis Loeffler. Music by Leigh Harline. B&W/CinemaScope; 105 Min.

Cast: Aki Aleong (Iko), Mary Carroll (Mrs. Burnett), Mimi Gibson (Sandra Kreitzer), Robert H. Harris (Markham), Jim Hayward (Mr. Burton), Charles Herbert (Michael Flagg), Pat Hingle (Herman Kreitzer), Jeffrey Hunter (David Martin), Nolan Leary (Reverend), Cameron Mitchell (Troy Boone), Sheree North (Isabelle Flagg), Patricia Owens (Jean Martin), Tony Randall (Jerry Flagg), Barbara Rush (Betty Kreitzer), Donald Towers (Harmon Kreitzer), Joanne Woodward (Leola Boone).

The Green-Eyed Blonde

Alternate title: *The Girl with the Green Eyes.*

Released Dec. 11, 1957 (Warner Bros.). Produced by Martin Melcher and Sally Stubblefield (associate producer). Directed by Bernard Girard. Screenplay by DT (credited as Sally Stubblefield). Cinematography by Ed Fitzgerald. Edited by Thomas Reilly. Art direction by Art Loel. Music by Leith Stevens. Songs by Joe Lubin. B&W; 76 min.

Cast: Olive Blakeney (Miss Vandingham), Margaret Brayton (Mrs. Adams), Raymond Foster (Cliff Munster), Betty Lou Gerson (Mrs. Ferguson), Roy E. Glenn, Sr. (Mr. Budlong), Tom Greenaway (Ed), Jean Inness (Mrs. Nichols), Beverly Long (Ouisie), Juanita Moore (Miss Randall), Tommie Moore (Trixie), Norma Jean Nilsson (Cuckoo), Susan Oliver (Greeneyes), Linda Plowman (Betsy Abel), Stanford Repp (Bill Prell), Evelyn Scott (Helen).

Wild Is the Wind

Released Dec. 13, 1957 (Paramount). Produced by Hal B. Wallis. Directed by George Cukor. Screenplay by Arnold Schulman. Uncredited screenplay contributions by DT, Philip Yordan, Eugene Daniell, and

Stella Linden (credited as Anna Sten). Based on the novel *Furia* by Vittorio Nino Novarese. Cinematography by Charles B. Lang, Jr. Edited by Warren Low. Art direction by Tambi Larsen and Hal Pereira. Music by Dimitri Tiomkin. Song, "Wild Is the Wind," by Dimitri Tiomkin (music) and Ned Washington (lyric). B&W/VistaVision; 114 min.

Cast: Joseph Calleia (Alberto), James Flavin (wool buyer), Anthony Franciosa (Bene), Dolores Hart (Angie), Anna Magnani (Gioia), Anthony Quinn (Gino), Dick Ryan (priest), Lili Valenty (Teresa).

Ten Days to Tulara

Released in 1958 (United Artists). Produced and directed by George Sherman. Screenplay and story by Laurence Mascott. Uncredited screenplay consultation by DT. Cinematography by Alex Phillips. Edited by Carlos Savage. Music by Lou Adomian. Running B&W; 77 min.

Cast: Raphael Alcayde (Colonel), Paco Arenas (Chris), Major M. Badager (Copilot Luis), Milton Bernstein (Teniente), Tony Caravajal (Francisco), Juan Garcia (Piranha), Felix Gonzales (Marco), Barry Grail (Medico), Sterling Hayden (Scotty), Rodolfo Hoyos (Cesar), Carlos Muzquiz (Dario), Jose Pulido (Captain), Grace Raynor (Teresa).

The Two-Headed Spy

Released in 1958 (Columbia Pictures). Produced by Hal E. Chester and Bill Kirby. Directed by André de Toth. Screenplay by Michael Wilson (credited as James O'Donnell) and Alfred Lewis Levitt. Uncredited screenplay consultation by DT. Based on the story "Britain's Two Headed Spy" by J. Alvin Kugelmass. Cinematography by Ted Scaife. Edited by Raymond Poulton. Art direction by Ivan King. Music by Gerard Schurmann. B&W; 93 min.

Cast: Felix Aylmer (Cornaz), Geoffrey Balydon (Dietz), Kenneth Griffith (Adolf Hitler), Jack Hawkins (General Alex Schottland), Walter Hudd (Admiral Canaris), Alexander Knox (Gestapo Leader Mueller), Laurence Naismith (General Hauser), Gia Scala (Lili Geyr), Eric Schumann (Lieutenant Reinisch), Edward Underdown (Kaltenbrunner).

Cowboy

Released March 12, 1958 (Columbia). Produced by Julian Blaustein. Directed by Delmer Daves. Screenplay by DT (credited as Edmund H. North [*see note p. 225*]). Uncredited screenplay contributions by Hugo Butler. Based on the memoir *On the Trail: My Reminisces as a Cowboy* by Frank Harris. Cinematography by Charles Lawton, Jr. Edited by Al Clark and William A. Lyon. Production designed by Cary Odell. Music by George Duning. Title sequence by Saul Bass. Color; 92 min.

Cast: Brian Donlevy (Doc Bender), King Donovan (Joe Capper), Glenn Ford (Tom Reese), Eugene Iglesias (Manuel), Richard Jaekel (Paul Curtis), Anna Kashfi (Maria Vidal), Jack Lemmon (Frank Harris), Strother Martin (trailhand), Victor Manuel Mendoza (Paco Mendoza), Donald Rudolph (Señor Vidal), Dick York (Charlie).

Enchanted Island

Released in early November 1958 (Warner Bros.). Produced by Benedict Bogeaus. Directed by Allan Dwan. Screenplay by DT (credited as James Leicester) and Harold Jacob Smith. Based on the short story "Typee" by Herman Melville. Cinematography by George Stahl. Music by Raul Lavista. Color; 94 min.

Cast: Dana Andrews (Abner Bedford), Ted de Corsia (Captain Vangs), Don Dubbins (Tom), Augustin Fernandes (Kory Kory), Les Hellman (First Mate Moore), Friedrich Ledebur (Mehevi), Jane Powell (Fayaway), Francisco Reiguera (medicine man), Arthur Shields (Jimmy Dooley).

From the Earth to the Moon

Released Nov. 19, 1958 (Warner Bros.). Produced by Benedict Bogeaus. Directed by

Byron Haskin. Screenplay by Robert Blees. Uncredited screenplay polish by DT (credited as James Leicester). Based on the novel *From the Earth to the Moon* by Jules Verne. Cinematography by Edwin DuPar. Edited by James Leicester. Art direction by Hal Wilson Cox. Music by Louis Forbes. Color; 100 min.

Cast: Morris Ankrum (President Ulysses S. Grant), Melville Cooper (Bancroft), Joseph Cotten (Victor Barbicane), Henry Daniell (Morgana), Don Dubbins (Ben Sharpe), Carl Esmond (Jules Verne), Patrick Knowles (Josef Cartier), Debra Paget (Virginia Nicholl), George Sanders (Stuyvesant Nicholl), Ludwig Stosell (Aldo Von Metz).

Terror in a Texas Town

Released Nov. 19, 1958 (United Artists). Produced by Frank N. Seltzer. Directed by Joseph H. Lewis. Screenplay and story by Ben L. Perry. Uncredited screenplay rewrite by DT [*see note p. 225*]. Cinematography by Ray Rennahan. Edited by Stefan Arnsten and Frank Sullivan. Art direction by William Ferrari. Music by Gerald Fried. B&W; 80 min.

Cast: Sebastian Cabot (Ed McNeil), Sterling Hayden (George Hansen), Carol Kelly (Molly), Eugene Martin (Pepe Miranda), Victor Millan (Jose Mirada), Ann Varela (Rosa Miranda), Ned Young (Johnny Crale).

Last Train from Gun Hill

Released July 15, 1959 (Paramount). Produced by Hal B. Wallis, Edward Lewis, and Kirk Douglas. Directed by John Sturges. Screenplay by James Poe. Uncredited screenplay polish by DT. Based on the story "Showdown" by Les Crutchfield. Cinematography by Charles B. Lang, Jr. Art direction by Hal Pereira and Walter Tyler. Music by Dimitri Tiomkin. Color/VistaVision; 98 min.

Cast: Brad Dexter (Beero), Kirk Douglas (Matt Morgan), Earl Holliman (Rick Belden), Brian Hutton (Lee), Carolyn Jones (Linda), Anthony Quinn (Craig Belden), Ziva Rodann (Cahterine Morgan), Bing Russell (Skag).

Note: This film had two working titles: *Showdown at Gun Hill* and *Last Train from Laredo.*

The Young Philadelphians

Alternate title: *The City Jungle* (British release).

Released Aug. 19, 1959 (Warner Bros.). Produced and directed by Vincent Sherman. Screenplay by James Gunn and DT (uncredited). Based on the novel *The Philadelphian* by Richard Pitts Powell. Cinematography by Harry Stradling. Edited by William H. Ziegler. Music by Ernest Gold. B&W; 136 min.

Cast: Diane Brewster (Kate Lawrence), Billie Burke (Mrs. J. Arthur Allen), Brian Keith (Mike Flanagan), Otto Kruger (John Wharton), Paul Newman (Tony Lawrence), Paul Picerni (Louis Donetti), Barbara Rush (Joan Dickinson), Alexis Smith (Carol Wharton), Robert Vaughan (Chester Gwynn), John Williams (Gilbert Dickinson).

Note: The working title of this film was *The Philadelphian*, taken from Powell's novel.

Conspiracy of Hearts

Released in February 1960 (Rank Organization). Produced by Betty E. Box. Directed by Ralph Thomas. Screenplay by Robert Presnell, Jr. Uncredited screenplay contributions by DT. Story by Adrian Scott (credited as Dale Pitt). Cinematography by Ernest Steward. Edited by Alfred Roome. Music by Angelo Francesco Lavagnino. B&W; 113 min.

Cast: Peter Arne (Lieutenant Schmidt), Michael Goodliffe (Father Desmaines), Megs Jenkins (Sister Constance), Ronald Lewis (Major Spoletti), Albert Lieven (Colonel Horsten), Yvonne Mitchell (Sister Gerta), Lili Palmer (Mother Katherine), Nora Swinburne (Sister Tia), Sylvia Syms (Sister Mitya).

Spartacus

Released Oct. 7, 1960; re-released April 28, 1991 (Universal). Produced by Kirk Douglas (executive producer) and Edward

Lewis. Directed by Stanley Kubrick. Opening sequence directed by Anthony Mann. Screenplay by DT. Uncredited screenplay contributions by Calder Willingham. Based on the novel *Spartacus* by Howard Fast. Cinematography by Russell Metty. Additional cinematography by Clifford Stine. Edited by Robert Lawrence. Production designed by Alexander Golitzen and Saul Bass (visual consultant). Costumes designed by Bill Thomas Valles. Music by Alex North. Title sequence by Saul Bass. Color/Super Technirama; 184 minutes (original 1960 release); 198 minutes (1991 restored version). MPAA rating: PG-13 (1991 restored version).

Cast: Tony Curtis (Antoninus), John Dall (Marcus Glabrus), Kirk Douglas (Spartacus), Nina Foch (Helena Glabrus), John Gavin (Caius Julius Caesar), John Ireland (Crixus), Charles Laughton (Lentulus Gracchus), Herbert Lom (Tigranes), Charles McGraw (Marcellus), Laurence Olivier (Marcus Licinius Crassus), Jean Simmons (Varinia), Woody Strode (Draba), Peter Ustinov (Lentulus Batiatus).

Exodus

Released Dec. 22, 1960 (United Artists). Produced and directed by Otto Preminger. Screenplay by DT. Based on the novel *Exodus* by Leon Uris. Cinematography by Sam Leavitt. Edited by Louis R. Loeffler. Costumes designed by Rudi Gerreich, Joe King, Margo Slater, and May Walding. Music by Ernest Gold. Title sequence by Saul Bass. Color/Super Panavision; 212 min.

Cast: Felix Aylmer (Doctor Lieberman), Lee J. Cobb (Barak Ben Canaan), John Derek (Taha), Marius Goring (Von Storch), Hugh Griffith (Mandria), Jill Haworth (Karen), Peter Lawford (Major Fred Caldwell), Martin Miller (Doctor Samuel Odenheim), Sal Mineo (Dov Landau), Paul Newman (Ari Ben Canaan), David Opatoshu (Akiva Ben Canaan), Gregory Ratoff (Lakavitch), Ralph Richardson (Brigadier General Bruce Sutherland), Eva Marie Saint (Catherine "Kitty" Fremont), Paul Stevens (Reuben), Alexandra Stewart (Jordana), Michael Wager (David).

The Last Sunset

Released June 8, 1961 (Universal). Produced by Eugene Frenke and Edward Lewis. Directed by Robert Aldrich. Screenplay by DT. Based on the novel *Sundown at Crazy Horse* by Howard Rigsby. Cinematography by Ernest Laszlo. Edited by Michael Luciano and Edward Mann. Production designed by Joseph Behm. Art direction by Alexander Golitzen and Alfred Sweeney. Costumes designed by Norma Koch. Music by Ernest Gold. Song, "Pretty Little Girl in the Yellow Dress," by Dmitri Tiomkin (music) and Ned Washington (lyric). Color/Panavision; 112 min.

Cast: Neville Brand (Frank Hobbs), Joseph Cotten (John Breckenridge), Margarito De Luna (Jose), Kirk Douglas (Brendan O'Malley), Jack Elam (Ed Hobbs), Red Fulton (Julesburg Kid), Rock Hudson (Dana Stribling), Carol Lynley (Melissa "Missy" Breckenridge), Dorothy Malone (Belle Breckenridge), John Shay (Bowman), Regis Toomey (Milton Wing), Jose Torvay (Rosario), Adam Williams (Calverton).

Note: This film had at least two working titles: *Sundown at Crazy Horse*, taken from Rigsby's novel, and *Day of the Gun*.

Town Without Pity

Released Nov. 17, 1961 (United Artists). Produced by Walter Mirisch and Gottfried Reinhardt. Directed by Gottfried Reinhardt. Screenplay by Silvia Reinhardt and George Hurdalek. Uncredited screenplay polish by DT. Based on the novel *Verdict* by Manfred Gregor. Cinematography by Kurt Hasse. Edited by Walter Boos, Herman Haller, and Werner Preuss. Music by Dimitri Tiomkin. Song, "Town Without Pity," by Dimitri Tiomkin (music) and Ned Washington (lyric). B&W/Panavision; 103 min.

Cast: Robert Blake (Jim), Kirk Douglas (Major Steve Garrett), Alan Gifford (General Steinhof), Karin Hardt (Frau Steinhof), Richard Jaekel (Bidie), Christine Kaufmann

(Karin Steinhof), Gerhard Lippert (Frank Borgmann), E.G. Marshall (Colonel Pakenham), Hans Nielsen (Karl Steinhof), Barbara Rütting (Inge Koerner), Mal Sondock (Joey), Ingrid van Bergen (Trude).

Lonely Are the Brave

Alternate title: *The Last Hero*.

Released June 20, 1962 (Universal). Produced by Edward Lewis. Directed by David Miller. Screenplay by DT. Based on the novel *The Brave Cowboy: An Old Tale in a New Time* by Edward Abbey. Cinematography by Philip H. Lathrop. Edited by Leon Barsha. Music by Jerry Goldsmith. B&W/Panavision; 107 min.

Cast: Kirk Douglas (Jack W. Burns), Michael Kane (Paul Bondi), George Kennedy (Guiterrez), Walter Matthau (Sheriff Johnson), Carroll O'Connor (Hinton), Bill Raisch ("One-Arm"), Gena Rowlands (Jerri Bondi).

The Sandpiper

Released July 14, 1965 (MGM). Produced by John Calley (associate producer), Ben Kadish (executive producer), and Martin Ransohoff. Directed by Vincente Minnelli. Screenplay by DT and Michael Wilson. Story by Martin Ransohoff. Cinematography by Milton R. Krasner. Edited by David Bretherton. Costumes designed by Irene Sharaff. Music by Johnny Mandel. Song, "The Shadow of Your Smile," by Johny Mandel. Color/Panavision; 118 min.

Cast: Charles Bronson (Cos Erickson), Richard Burton (Reverend Doctor Edward Hewitt), Tom Drake (Walter Robinson), James Edwards (Larry Brant), Doug Henderson (Phil Sutcliff), Morgan Mason (Danny Reynolds), Eva Marie Saint (Claire Hewitt), Elizabeth Taylor (Laura Reynolds), Torin Thatcher (Judge Thompson), Robert Webber (Ward Hendricks).

The Cavern

Released in November 1965 (20th Century–Fox). Produced and directed by Edgar G. Ulmer. Screenplay by DT (credited as Jack Davis) and Michael Pertwee. Cinema-

tography by Gábor Pogány. Edited by Renato Cinquini. Music by Carlo Rustichelli. B&W; 83 min.

Cast: Brian Aherne (General Braithwaite), Nino Castelnuovo (Mario), Larry Hagman (Captain Wilson), Joachim Hansen (German soldier), Peter L. Marshall (Lieutenant Peter Carter), John Saxon (Private Joe Kramer), Rosanna Schiaffino (Anna), Hans von Barsady (Hans).

Hawaii

Released Oct. 10, 1966 (United Artists). Produced by Walter Mirisch. Directed by George Roy Hill. Screenplay by Daniel Taradash and DT. Based on the novel *Hawaii* by James Michener. Cinematography by Russell Harlan. Edited by Stuart Gilmore. Production designed by Cary Odell. Costumes designed by Dorothy Jeakins. Music by Elmer Bernstein. Song, "My Wishing Doll," by Elmer Bernstein (music) and Mack David (lyric). Color; 189 min.

Cast: Julie Andrews (Jerusha Bromley), Lou Antonio (Reverend Abraham Hewlett), John David Callum (Reverend Immanuel Quigley), Lokelani S. Chicarell (Iliki), Elizabeth Cole (Abigail Bromley), Robert Crawford, Jr. (Cridland), Gene Hackman (Reverend John Whipple), Richard Harris (Rafer Hoxworth), Jocelyn LaGarde (Queen "Ruth" Malama), Elisabeth Logue (Noelani), Ted Nobriga (Kelolo), Carroll O'Connor (Charles Bromley), Torin Thatcher (Reverend Thorn), Manu Tupou (Keoki), Max Von Sydow (Reverend Abner Hale).

Note: Several shorter versions of this film, with lengths ranging from 151 minutes to 171 minutes, are in circulation on television and on videocassette.

The Fixer

Released Dec. 11, 1968 (MGM). Produced by Edward Lewis. Directed by John Frankenheimer. Screenplay by DT. Based on the novel *The Fixer* by Bernard Malamud. Cinematography by Marcel Grignon. Edited by Henry Berman. Music by Maurice Jarre. Color; 132 min. MPAA rating: PG.

Cast: Alan Bates (Yakov Bok), Dirk Bogarde (Bibikov), Georgia Browne (Mafa Golov), Hugh Griffith (Lebedev), Elizabeth Hartman (Zinaida), Ian Holm (Grubeshov), Murray Melvin (priest), George Murcell (deputy warden), David Opatoshu (Latke), David Warner (Count Odoevsky), Carol White (Raisl).

Heaven with a Gun

Released in May 1969 (MGM). Produced by Frank and Maurice King. Directed by Lee Katzin. Screenplay by Richard Carr and DT. Cinematography by Fred Koenekamp. Edited by Dan Cahn. Music by Johnny Mandel. Song, "A Lonely Place," by Johnny Mandel (music) and Paul Francis Webster (lyric). Color/Panavision; 101 min. MPAA rating: R.

Cast: John Anderson (Asa Beck), Noah Beery (Garvey), William Bryant (Bart Patterson), J.D. Cannon (Mace), David Carradine (Coke Beck), Glenn Ford (Jim Killian), Barbara Hershey (Leloopa), Carolyn Jones (Made McCloud), Harry Townes (Gus Sampson).

Johnny Got His Gun

Released Sept. 15, 1971 (Cinemation). Produced by Bruce Campbell, Tony Monaco (associate producer), and Christopher Trumbo (associate producer). Production supervised by James F. Sommers. Directed by DT. Screenplay by DT. Based on the novel *Johnny Got His Gun* by DT. Cinematography by Jules Brenner. Edited by William P. Dornisch (supervising editor) and Millie Moore (editor). Production design and art direction by Harold Michelson. Costumes designed by Theadora Van Runkle. Music by Jerry Fielding. B&W/color; 111 min. MPAA rating: PG.

Cast: Timothy Bottoms (Joe Bonham), Eric Christmas (Corporal Tilson), Maurice Dallimore (British colonel), Robert Easton (third doctor), Kathy Fields (Kareen), Eduard Franz (Colonel/General Tillery), Edmund Gibert (priest), Ben Hammer (second doctor), Wayne Heffley (Captain), Marsha Hunt (Joe's mother), Joseph Kaufaman (Rudy), Mike Lee (Bill Harper), Kerry MacLane (Joe, age 10), Charles McGraw (Mike Burkman), Byron Morrow (brigadier general), Marge Redmond (first nurse), Jason Robards, Jr. (Joe's father), David Soul (Swede), Donald Sutherland (Jesus Christ), DT (Medical director), Diane Varsi (fourth nurse), Sandy Brown Wyeth (Lucky).

The Horsemen

Released Sept. 22, 1971 (Columbia). Produced by Edward Lewis. Directed by John Frankenheimer. Screenplay by DT. Based on the novel *The Horsemen* by Joseph Kessel. Cinematography by Claude Renoir. Edited by Harold Kress. Production designed by Pierre Thevenet. Music by Georges Delerue. Color/Super Panavision; 109 min. MPAA rating: PG.

Cast: Ishaq Bux (Amjad Kahn), David De (Mukhi), Despo (Uljan), Vernon Dobtcheff (Zam Haiji), Saeed Jaffrey (district chief), Peter Jeffrey (Hayatal), George Murcell (Mizar), Jack Palance (Tursen), Eric Pohlmann (merchant of Kandahar), Mohammed Shamsi (Osman Bey), Omar Sharif (Uraz), Leigh Taylor-Young (Zereh).

F.T.A.

Released July 31, 1972 (American International). Produced by Jane Fonda, Francine Parker, and Donald Sutherland. Directed by Francine Parker. Written by Michael Alaimo, Lou Chandler, Pamela Donegan, Jane Fonda, Ralph Martinson, Ruth Menken, Holly Near, Donald Sutherland, and DT. Music by Aminadav Aloni. Color; 96 min. MPAA rating: R.

Documentary features: Michael Alaimo, Len Chandler, Pamela Donegan, Jane Fonda, Rita Martinson, Paul Mooney, Holly Near, Donald Sutherland, Yale Zimmerman.

Executive Action

Released Nov. 7, 1973 (Warner Bros.). Produced by Edward Lewis. Directed by David Miller. Screenplay by DT. Uncredited screenplay rewrite by Alvah Bessie. Story by

Donald Freed and Mark Lane. Inspired by the book *Rush to Judgment* by Mark Lane. Cinematography by Robert Steadman. Edited by George Grenville and Irving Lerner. Music by Randy Edelman. Color; 91 min. MPAA rating: PG.

Cast: John Anderson (Holliday), Paul Carr (Chris), Colby Chester (Tim), Will Geer (Harold Ferguson), Gilbert Green (Paulitz), Burt Lancaster (James Farrington), Ed Lauter (operation chief, Team "A"), James MacColl (Oswald impersonator [Jim]), Oscar Orcini (Jack Ruby), Robert Ryan (Robert Foster).

Papillon

Released Dec. 19, 1973 (Allied Artists). Produced by Robert Dorfman. Directed by Franklin J. Schaffner. Screenplay by Lorenzo Semple, Jr., and DT. Uncredited screenplay contributions by Robert Benton, David Newman, William Goldman, and Christopher Trumbo. Based on the memoir *Papillon* by Henri Charrière. Cinematography by Fred Koenkamp. Edited by Robert Swink. Production designed by Anthony Masters. Costumes designed by Anthony Powell. Music by Jerry Goldsmith. Color/Panavision; 150 min. MPAA rating: R (later changed to PG).

Cast: Ratna Assan (Zaraima), Val Avery (Pascal), George Colouris (Dr. Chatal), Robert Deman (Maturette), Don Gordon (Julot), Don Hammer (butterfly trader), Dustin Hoffman (Louis Dega), Victor Jory (Indian chief), Steve McQueen (Henri "Papillon" Charrière), Barbara Morrison (Mother Superior), Bill Mumy (Lariot), Woodroy Parfrey (Clusiot), Ron Sable (Santini), Gregory Sierra (Antonio), William Smithers (Warden Barrot), Victor Tayback (sergeant), DT (uncredited cameo as French commandant), Mills Watson (guard), Anthony Zerbe (Toussaint).

Hollywood on Trial

Released in 1976 (October Films). Produced by James C. Gutman and Frank Galvin (associate producer). Directed by David Helpern, Sr. and David Helpern, Jr. Cinematography by Barry Abrams. Edited by

Frank Galvin. Narrated by John Huston. B&W/color; 105 min.

Documentary features: Walter Bernstein, Alvah Bessie, Lester Cole, Gary Cooper, Howard Da Silva, Walt Disney, Edward Dmytryk, Will Geer, Millard Lampell, Ring Lardner, Jr., Albert Maltz, Louis B. Mayer, Joseph McCarthy, Adolphe Menjou, Zero Mostel, Otto Preminger, Ronald Reagan, Martin Ritt, Dore Schary, Gale Sondergaard, Robert Taylor, Leo Townsend, DT, Jack L. Warner.

Ishi: The Last of His Tribe

Telefilm broadcast in 1978. Produced by Edward and Mildred Lewis. Directed by Robert Ellis Miller. Teleplay by Christopher Trumbo and DT. Based on the book *Ishi in Two Worlds: A Biography of the Last Wild Indian in North America* by Theodora Kroeber. Cinematography by Woody Omens. Edited by Argyle Nelson, Jr., and Harold Wilner. Production designed by Mort Rabinowitz. Music by Maurice Jarre. Color; 150 min.

Cast: Eloy Casados (Ishi as an adult), Devon Ericson (Lushi as a teenager), Patricia Ganera (Lushi as a girl), Joaqín Martínez (grandfather), Michael Medina (Ishi as a boy), Joseph Runningfox (Ishi as a teenager), Geno Silva (elder uncle), Dennis Weaver (Professor Benjamin Fuller), Arliene Nofchissey Williams (Mother).

Roman Holiday

Telefilm broadcast on Dec. 28, 1987. Produced by Mel Efros. Directed by Noel Nosseck. Teleplay by Jerrold L. Ludwig. Based on the screenplay *Roman Holiday* (see separate entry). Cinematography by Romana Albani. Edited by Jay Scherberth. Music by Mark Snow. Color; 95 min.

Cast: Patrick Allen (general), Eileen Atkins (countess), Ed Begley, Jr. (Leonard Lupo), Andrew Bickell (squad leader), Tom Conti (Joe Bradley), Paul Daneman (king), Francis Matthews (ambassador), Christopher Munke (Phil), Catherine Oxenberg (Princess Elysa), Shane Rimmer (Hogan), David Rolfe (major-domo).

Always

Released Dec. 22, 1989 (Universal). Produced by Steven Spielberg, Frank Marshall, and Kathleen Kennedy. Directed by Steven Spielberg. Screenplay by Jerry Belson and Diane Thomas. Based on the screenplay *A Guy Named Joe* (see separate entry). Cinematography by Mikael Salomon. Edited by Michael Kahn. Production designed by James Bissell. Music by John Williams. Color; 123 min. MPAA rating: PG.

Cast: Roberts Blossom (Dave), Keith David ("Powerhouse"), Richard Dreyfuss (Pete Sandich), Dale Dye (fire chief), John Goodman (Al Yackey), Marg Helgenberger (Rachel), Audrey Hepburn (Hap), Holly Hunter (Dorinda Durston), Brad Johnson (Ted Baker), Ed Van Nuys ("Nails").

Postscript: In August 2000, after this filmography was completed, the Writers Guild of America issued a slew of corrected blacklist-era credits. Most of the corrections corroborated the research done for this book, but there were two interesting discrepancies. According to the WGA, Trumbo was the sole author of *Terror in a Texas Town*, not merely the rewriter of Ben L. Perry's script.

Also, the WGA gave Edmund H. North half the credit for the screenplay of *Cowboy*, whereas the research for this book determined that North was a front with little or no actual involvement in *Cowboy*. These discrepancies underline the murkiness of blacklist-era credits and amplify that a definitive picture of Trumbo's cinematic output may never emerge.

Notes

Introduction

1. Hereafter, the committee is referred to as HUAC, the standard—albeit inaccurate—acronym. Victor S. Navasky, *Naming Names* (New York: Penguin, 1981), p. vii.

Chapter 1

1. Primary sources of biographical information are Bruce Cook, *Dalton Trumbo* (New York: Scribner, 1977), Dalton Trumbo, *Additional Dialogue: Letters of Dalton Trumbo 1942–1962*, ed. Helen Manfull (New York: Bantam, 1972), and conversations with Trumbo's son, Christopher Trumbo, which took place between mid–1998 and early 2000.

2. Cook, *Dalton Trumbo*, p. 38.

3. Ibid., p. 40.

4. Ibid., p. 53.

5. Ibid., p. 59.

6. Ibid., p. 66.

7. Victor S. Navasky, *Naming Names* (New York: Penguin, 1981), p. 367.

8. Cook, *Dalton Trumbo*, p. 57.

9. Ibid., pp. 71–77.

10. Trumbo, *Additional Dialogue*, pp. 126–127.

11. Cook, *Dalton Trumbo*, p. 86.

12. All quotes in this paragraph: ibid., p. 87.

13. Trumbo, *Additional Dialogue*, p. 211.

14. Quote from Rudy Behlmer, ed., *Inside Warner Bros.* (New York: Viking Penguin, 1985), p. 62. Foy challenged his writers by asking them to imagine ways out of difficult narrative situations, an exercise that showed him whether the writers could conceive story events that utilized exisiting narrative material and production resources. Cook, *Dalton Trumbo*, pp. 88–89.

15. Because an accurate chronology of when Trumbo worked on each of his films is elusive, movies appear in the order in which they were released theatrically. This necessarily results in some breaks in continuity—*Cowboy*, for instance, was written in 1949 or 1950 but released theatrically in 1958. Nonetheless, ordering films by their release dates gives an instructive, if not crystalline, picture of Trumbo's evolution as a screenwriter.

16. Long, of course, was later the model for the ambitious politician in Robert Penn Warren's classic novel, *All the King's Men*.

17. Cook, *Dalton Trumbo*, pp. 93–94.

18. Tom Stempel, *FrameWork: A History*

of Screenwriting in the American Film (New York: Continuum, 1988), pp. 101–102.

19. Metro-Goldwyn-Mayer is hereafter referred to as MGM.

20. Trumbo's only stipulation to his biographer was that Cleo get to read the chapter about her courtship with Trumbo. After scanning the rough pages, she asked for a rewrite by saying: "You don't get the feeling out of this how glad I am I married this crazy man instead of some dull son of a bitch." Cook, *Dalton Trumbo*, p. 120.

21. Former press agent Sisk produced several of Trumbo's important prewar films and was a friend during the blacklist era, by which point Sisk had moved into television production. Sisk's most important collaboration with Trumbo was *A Man to Remember*, on which Trumbo worked closely with noted writer Garson Kanin (see note 1, chapter 2), who made his directorial debut with *A Man to Remember*.

22. This appraisal of the film's merits is not shared by all. "Dalton Trumbo wrote the prosaic, unimaginative screenplay as his first assignment for RKO; it contained not a hint of the narrative excellence that would soon become a Trumbo hallmark." Richard B. Jewell and Vernon Harbin, *The RKO Story* (New York: Arlington House, 1982), p. 122.

Chapter 2

1. After establishing himself on Broadway as an actor and director, Garson Kanin emigrated to Hollywood in 1937 and became friends with Trumbo, who worked in an adjoining office. Their discussions of Trumbo's then-current project—*A Man to Remember*—led Trumbo to suggest that Kanin direct the picture for producer Robert Sisk. Kanin directed only a handful of films prior to joining the military in World War II; later, he and wife Ruth Gordon formed one of the great screenwriting teams, crafting sparkling comedies including *Adam's Rib* (1949, MGM) and *Pat and Mike* (1952,

MGM). His credits as a playwright include *Born Yesterday*. Patrick McGilligan, *Backstory 2: Interviews with Screenwriters of the 1940s and 1950s* (Los Angeles: University of California Press, 1991), pp. 89–91, 96–97.

2. Trumbo used this name for the protaganist of his first novel, *Eclipse*, and later as a blacklist-era alias. Bruce Cook, *Dalton Trumbo* (New York: Scribner, 1977), p. 237.

3. On page 271 of *From Scarface to Scarlett: American Films in the 1930s* (New York: Harcourt Brace Jovanovich, 1981), Roger Dooley writes: "This is the only '30s film other than *The Power and the Glory* (1933 [20th Century–Fox]) to use this narrative structure, so much acclaimed a few years later in *Citizen Kane* [1941], also from RKO." And on page 133 of *The American Film Heritage: Impressions from the American Film Institute Archives* (Washington, D.C.: Acropolis Books, 1972), *I Loved a Woman* (1933, Warner Bros.) is mentioned as another film with a *Kane*-like structure. Incidentally, Trumbo later used a similar flashback structure in *Kitty Foyle*, released by RKO in 1940—and which also bears close similarities to certain aspects of *Kane*.

4. Trumbo's accomplishment is even more impressive when one learns that the screenplay of *A Man to Remember* was written in two weeks. Cook, *Dalton Trumbo*, p. 122.

5. See note 26, chapter 4.

6. Cook, *Dalton Trumbo*, p. 140.

7. "Corrigan [arrived] at Baldonnel Aerodrome, near Dublin, after he had accomplished in 28 hours and 13 minutes the first 'surprise' crossing of the Atlantic. Without official permission, without passport or visa, with no radio and no parachute, he had flown the ocean alone in a 9-year-old, $900 plane which authorities had described as 'not airworthy.'" Cabell Phillips, *From the Crash to the Blitz: 1929–1939* (London: Macmillan, 1969), p. 557.

8. Born Nathan Wallenstein in 1903, West struggled as a screenwriter before using his Hollywood experiences as the basis of his brutal allegorical novel, *The Day of the Locust*, widely considered one of the most

telling portraits of the movie industry in the 1930s. He died in a 1940 car crash at age 37.

9. The most provocative element of the film, the character of Vasquez was among West's most important contributions to the story; another was a memorable dramatic device used in the film's climax. In typical studio fashion, though, West was removed from the project after contributing his first draft. Jerome Cady made negligible contributions, and Trumbo's work consisted of restoring West's ideas and, importantly, discerning that Vasquez was the most interesting character. It was Trumbo who reshaped Vasquez from villain to hero. Jay Martin, *Nathanael West: The Art of His Life* (New York: Farrar, Straus and Giroux, 1970), pp. 284–285.

10. A native Australian noted for his skill with actors, John Farrow came to Hollywood as a technical advisor on war films because of his experience in the British navy. He notched several credits as a screenwriter before embarking on a successful directing career and writing several books. The first husband of actress Maureen O'Sullivan and father of actress Mia Farrow, John Farrow died in 1963.

11. Conversation between Christopher Trumbo and author, January 2000.

12. RKO apparently conceived *Career* as a follow-up to *A Man to Remember*, once again casting Edward Ellis as the most conscientious citizen of a small town. The rushed project did not do well at the box office. Richard B. Jewell and Vernon Harbin, *The RKO Story*, p. 131.

13. Trumbo's "solo" credits are few: *We Who Are Young*, *The Remarkable Andrew*, *Tender Comrade*, *Carnival Story*, *The Boss*, *The Brave One*, *The Green-Eyed Blonde*, and *Johnny Got His Gun*. Looking at this group of titles is instructive, as most of them are heavy-handed parables. But, as Christopher Trumbo noted in a January 2000 conversation with this author, his father's original screenplays need to be viewed through the prism of the marketplace: Except *Johnny*, all of these scripts were written for hire. Chris-

topher Trumbo said that he considers *Roman Holiday* and *The Brave One* to be the most purely original of his father's scripts.

14. Trumbo's mother's maiden name was Tillery, so this is one of many instances of Trumbo winkingly acknowledging his family.

15. Tom Stempel, *FrameWork: A History of Screenwriting in the American Film* (New York: Continuum, 1988), p. 145.

16. Larry Ceplair and Steven Englund, *The Inquisition in Hollywood: Politics in the Film Community, 1930–1960* (Garden City, N.Y.: Anchor, 1980), pp. 299–324.

Chapter 3

1. *Kitty Foyle* was directed by staunch right-winger Sam Wood, with whom Trumbo later quarreled in, among other print media, *The Screen Writer*. Published by the Screen Writers Guild, the magazine debuted in June 1945, and as its founding editor, Trumbo advanced an ardently leftist line.

2. Former blacklistee Jean Rouverol Butler, widow of Trumbo's close friend Hugo Butler, recalled: "I look back and realize that these men were just as chauvinist as anyone. They endowed themselves with a larger-than-life quality, so that [their wives] had to be keepers of the flame and feed into that elevation. They didn't think 'the woman question' applied to them.... The American left male articulated a very good position on women's rights. But he didn't live it in his own domestic relationships. There were very few exceptions." Patrick McGilligan and Paul Buhle, *Tender Comrades: A Backstory of the Hollywood Blacklist* (New York: St. Martin's Press, 1997), p. 164.

3. *Kitty Foyle* was released several months before Orson Welles's towering *Citizen Kane*, which also prominently featured a snow globe as a device used to link disparate time periods. Because both pictures were produced at the same studio, RKO, it's conceivable that the production teams of both movies were aware of each other, and

is therefore conceivable that the writers of one picture borrowed an idea from the writers of the other. Whether Trumbo borrowed from *Kane* cowriters Welles and Herman Mankiewicz—or vice versa—is purely conjecture, though; it is perhaps more likely that the imagery was merely coincidental.

4. In Morley's book, Kitty gets an abortion. The plot development was softened to comply with the Motion Picture Production Code, colloquially known as the "Hays Code," after Motion Picture Producers and Distributors of America president Will H. Hays.

5. Donald Ogden Stewart won for *The Philadelphia Story* (1940, MGM); as noted earlier, he worked on *Kitty Foyle* prior to Trumbo and earned an "additional dialogue" credit on the film.

6. While Trumbo's films seem to contain an old-fashioned view of women in the workplace, he was comparatively progressive in real life. His wife, Cleo, worked as a photographer for much of their marriage, and if his correspondence is any indication, he considered her a full partner in many of his adventures. Also, letters Trumbo wrote to his eldest child, Nikola, show that throughout her college years, he encouraged her to see as much of the world as possible to choose a fulfilling life, whether it involved homemaking or work. Finally, Trumbo's younger daughter, Mitzi, followed her mother by becoming a photographer.

7. The worst of the strikes against the picture is its highly derivative nature. The film's central device, of having a long-dead historical figure magically appear to shepherd a man through a crisis, was previously used to great effect in both Stephen Vincent Benét's short story "The Devil and Daniel Webster" (1937), and *All That Money Can Buy* (a.k.a. *The Devel and Daniel Webster*), RKO's marvelous 1941 film of Benét's story.

8. Stars William Holden and Brian Donlevy had a "serious disagreement" with Heisler and tried to convince *Andrew*'s author to step in as director; Trumbo refused. Bruce Cook, *Dalton Trumbo* (New York: Scribner, 1977), p. 143.

9. This is the first cinematic instance of Trumbo using a fictional city to allude to his hometown, Grand Junction, Colorado. "Shale City" also shows up in *Tender Comrade*.

10. One notable exception to this was the case of HUAC chairman J. Parnell Thomas, with whom Trumbo quarreled during his 1947 testimony. Thomas was later convicted of fraud and sentenced to two years in jail.

11. Trumbo later elaborated on his view of patriotism in a 1956 letter to fellow blacklistee Guy Endore, which features language similar to that in Andrew's speech. Dalton Trumbo, *Additional Dialogue: Letters of Dalton Trumbo 1942–1962*, ed. Helen Manfull (New York: Bantam, 1972), pp. 378–393.

12. Conversation between Christopher Trumbo and author, January 2000.

Chapter 4

1. Background on this movie is from Bruce Cook, *Dalton Trumbo*. (New York: Scribner, 1977), pp. 143–144, and Diane Jacobs, *Christmas in July: The Life and Art of Preston Sturges* (Los Angeles: University of California Press, 1992), p. 266.

2. Cook, *Dalton Trumbo*, p. 145.

3. "I myself have never been a pacificst," Trumbo wrote in 1943. "[World War II is] precisely the kind of war which the maimed hero of *Johnny Got His Gun* had declared to be a good and worthy battle—a war for the liberation of people, a war to make the slogans into realities." Dalton Trumbo, *Additional Dialogue: Letters of Dalton Trumbo 1942–1962*, ed. Helen Manfull (New York: Bantam, 1972), pp. 8, 10–12.

4. One of the children makes a comment explaining the film's title: "In the American armed forces, anyone who's a right chap is a guy named Joe."

5. Everett Riskin produced both *A Guy Named Joe* and *Here Comes Mr. Jordan*.

6. One explanation for this shift in character might be that Ted is emboldened by the flying lessons given him by Pete.

7. Trumbo accepted a life achievement award from the Writers Guild in
March 1970, and during the ceremony made
a notorious speech in which he said there
were no heroes and villains in the blacklist
era; his assertion that there were "only victims" has been widely quoted by both his
partisans and detractors. Some regarded the
speech as a gracious way to put the past behind; others saw it as downright delusional.
One who despised the speech was fellow
Hollywood Ten member Lester Cole, who
described the "only victims" speech as an
"outrageously lofty, ecclesiastical benedic-
tion from 'on high,'" adding that Trumbo
was a victim "of his own rhetoric." The
pedantry in *The Remarkable Andrew* is but
one of many precedents for the "only victims" speech. Lester Cole, *Hollywood Red*
(Berkeley, Calif.: Ramparts Press, 1981), p.
423.

8. See note 9, chapter 3.

9. See note 7, this chapter.

10. Trumbo's "only victims" speech was
not the first time he tried to move beyond
blame with regard to the blacklist. In 1959,
he wrote the following to fellow Hollywood
Ten member Albert Maltz: "[T]here can
never be an *official* end to the blacklist....
Therefore we must *pretend* this is the end
(which it damn near is) and pose not as
angry martyrs, as the persecuted, but as good
winners. In this guise we assume our victory
at last, and carry no grudges forward into
the future." Trumbo, *Additional Dialogue*, p.
498.

11. "As the summer of 1943 was wind-
ing down, I was cast in a picture at RKO
called *Tender Comrade*," Rogers recalled.
"The movie addressed problems related to
the home front, but the story was like a
Valentine out of season. To my great surprise, some of Dalton Trumbo's dialogue had
a communistic turn, which upset me deeply.
I complained to the front office and sent notices to those in authority, including director Edward Dmytryk, that they would have
to make a finer sifting of the script if they
wanted me to continue with the film. In
order to satisfy me, David Hempstead, the

producer, gave the other actors the dialogue,
'Share and share alike,' that I was unhappy
about. I still hold strong feelings against
communism because it is atheistic and anti–
God." Because Rogers indeed says the phrase
"share and share alike" during *Tender Comrade*, her memories of the film should be
considered skeptically. Quote from Ginger
Rogers, *Ginger: My Story* (New York: Harper-
Collins, 1991), p. 257.

12. Dmytryk was the only member of
the Hollywood Ten to "clear" himself before
HUAC by naming names—albeit after serving a jail term for contempt of Congress.
Therefore, blacklist experts often portray
Dmytryk's latter-day comments on *Tender
Comrade* as dubious at best. That said, here
is his side of the story: "*Tender Comrade* was
a somewhat maudlin film, which did moder-
ately well at the box office. It concerned itself with the problems of four working war
wives [whose] motto is 'Share and share
alike,' which sounded quite innocently democratic when we made the film, but which
turned up to haunt me a few years later when
I was instructed that the real motto of democracy is 'Get what you can while you can
and the devil take the hindmost.'" Edward
Dmytryk, *It's a Hell of a Life But Not a Bad
Living* (New York: Times Books, 1978), p.
58.

13. This sudden character shift recalls
similar shifts in *You Belong to Me* (in which
Doctor Helen Hunt abruptly closes her
practice to become a housewife) and *A Guy
Named Joe* (in which flyer Ted Randall inexplicably transforms from a wallflower to a
Casanova).

14. From legendary critic James Agee's
review of *Tender Comrade*: "At the climax,
getting news of her husband's death, she
subjects this defenseless baby to a speech
which lasts 24 hours and five minutes by
my watch and which, in its justifications of
the death, the obligations it clamps on the
child, and its fantastic promises of a better
world to come, is one of the most nauseat-
ing things I have ever sat through. It is terribly pitiful—to choose the mildest word—to
think how much of America this scene and

the picture as a whole are likely to move, console, corroborate, and give eloquence to." James Agee, *Agee on Film: Volume One* (New York: Perigree, 1983), p. 91.

15. Conversation between Christopher Trumbo and author, January 2000.

16. See note 12, this chapter.

17. Larry Ceplair and Steven Englund, *The Inquisition in Hollywood: Politics in the Film Community, 1930–1960* (Garden City, N.Y.: Anchor, 1980), p. 324.

18. Trumbo, *Additional Dialogue*, p. 25.

19. Trumbo makes one of his occasional winking references to his own family during a quiet scene between Ted and Ellen. As Ted works on plans and charts, Ellen dreamily writes possible baby names on a sheet of paper. The second name in the "boy" column is "Christopher," and the last name in the "female" column is "Nickola." These are the names of Trumbo's two oldest children, although the name of Trumbo's eldest child is actually spelled "Nikola."

20. Unity among soldiers was a vaguely socialist theme common to scripts by members of the Hollywood Ten. "While there was nothing particularly Marxist or Stalinist about the radicals' screenplays ... they nevertheless did manage to avoid overemphasizing or overdramatizing the role of the extraordinary individual (the war hero) and instead focused on the teamwork and suffering of average soldiers. Scripts like those for *Sahara* ([John Howard] Lawson), *Thirty Seconds Over Tokyo* (Trumbo), *Objective Burma* ([Alvah] Bessie and [Lester] Cole), or *Pride of the Marines* ([Albert] Maltz) stressed the collective effort of the front-line troops and they presented as authentic a picture of the reality of war as it was possible to do in Hollywood." Ceplair and Englund, *The Inquisition in Hollywood*, pp. 181–182.

21. This scene underscores the points made by Trumbo and historians Larry Ceplair and Steven Englund (included in this book's examination *Tender Comrade*) about leftist screenwriters including humanism in their scripts. While remaining true to the characters, this scene is a refreshing alterna-

tive to the widespread depiction of "Japs" as faceless monsters.

22. For Trumbo's thoughts on pacifism, see note 3, this chapter.

23. Born Emmanuel Goldenberg, legendary screen tough guy Edward G. Robinson was active in Hollywood liberal politics and friendly with Trumbo in the 1940s; he was one of many who loaned Trumbo money at the outset of the HUAC era. Their friendship abruptly ended, however, when Robinson named Trumbo before HUAC. The actor appeared before the committee to clear his name and preserve his employability.

24. It should nonetheless be noted that at the time Trumbo wrote *Our Vines*, he was a member of the Communist Party. He had been associated with the Party since 1936—dating back to his activities with the left wing of the Screen Writers Guild—and formally joined in 1943. He quit in 1946, saying that he didn't have time for meetings, and rejoined briefly in the 1950s, during the blacklist period.

25. The film version of *Johnny Got a Gun* contains a scene with striking similarities to this one. In the *Johnny* scene, a father and son sit in a workshop and discuss democracy and war. While the scenes have wholly different goals, comparing the naiveté of the *Our Vines* scene to the brutal cynicism of the *Johnny* scene is illustrative of how much political discourse was acceptable in two different eras of filmmaking.

26. Trumbo made notable contributions to another 1946 film, one with a substantially higher profile than *Jealousy*. He was the first person to write a script of Philip Van Doren Stern's short story "The Greatest Gift," the basis of Frank Capra's *It's a Wonderful Life*. According to Capra biographer Joseph McBride, the director rejected Trumbo's script because it was too political. "The film shows the influence of Trumbo only in some aspects of George's darker side ... as well as in keeping some of Trumbo's whimsy with the angel, including dialogue for the scene in Nick's Bar in the 'unborn' sequence and the penultimate line about an angel getting his wings every time a bell

rings…. Capra's film retreats from the Marxist implications of Trumbo's view of capitalism, carefully balancing its unfavorable … portrait of an evil businessman (Potter) with a favorable portrait of a good businessman (George)." In an ironic coda to Trumbo's involvement with *It's a Wonderful Life*, Capra crossed paths with Trumbo—albeit unknowingly—during the blacklist period. Capra was the original director of *Roman Holiday*, and developed the project as a vehicle for Cary Grant and Elizabeth Taylor until he quarreled with Paramount over the projected budget. Joseph McBride, *Frank Capra: The Catastrophe of Success* (New York: Simon & Schuster, 1992), pp. 511–522.

Chapter 5

1. Details on Trumbo's HUAC appearance from Dalton Trumbo, *Additional Dialogue: Letters of Dalton Trumbo 1942-1962*, ed. Helen Manfull. (New York: Bantam, 1972), pp. 31–41.

2. Victor S. Navasky, *Naming Names* (New York: Penguin, 1981), p. xv.

3. Trumbo, *Additional Dialogue*, p. 289.

4. Larry Ceplair and Steven Englund, *The Inquisition in Hollywood: Politics in the Film Community, 1930–1960* (Garden City, N.Y., Anchor Press/Doubleday, 1980), pp. 188–189.

5. Patrick McGilligan and Paul Buhle, *Tender Comrades: A Backstory of the Hollywood Blacklist* (New York: St. Martin's Press, 1997), p. 103.

6. Reisz quotes: ibid., pp. 550–551.

7. Throughout this book, Trumbo's films are presented in the order in which they were released (see note 15, chapter 1). This presentation creates some inconsistency in this chapter, because while some of Trumbo's blacklist-era scripts were written just days "ahead of the camera," others sat on shelves for years. When possible, information about the time when projects were written is inserted into discussions of those projects. As it happens, though, the release

order Trumbo's blacklist-era films offers an informative overview of the darkening and maturation of his screenwriting.

8. Diane Jacobs, *Christmas in July: The Life and Art of Preston Sturges* (Los Angeles: University of California Press, 1992), pp. 360–361.

9. Lewis quote and *Gun Crazy* background from Danny Peary, *Cult Movies: The Classics, the Sleepers, the Weird, and the Wonderful* (New York: Grammercy, 1998), pp. 119–120.

10. King and Trumbo quotes from Bruce Cook, *Dalton Trumbo* (New York: Scribner, 1977), pp. 192–193. Additional King Bros. background from Tom Stempel, *FrameWork: A History of Screenwriting in the American Film* (New York: Continuum, 1988), p. 170.

11. Hugo Butler's widow, Jean Rouveral Butler, said her husband's involvement in *The Prowler* was fairly limited, explaining that he went to the set every day to "cover" for Trumbo. "But it was really much more Trumbo than him," she added. McGilligan and Buhle, *Tender Comrades*, p. 165.

12. Incidentally, Losey's assistant director on *The Prowler* was Robert Aldrich—who later directed *The Last Sunset* from a Trumbo script.

13. David Caute, *Joseph Losey: A Revenge on Life* (New York: Oxford University Press, 1994), pp. 91–92.

14. Although John is played by Sherry Hall, his radio voice—as noted earlier—is Trumbo's. Also, the name of John's radio show, "The Cost of Living," is ironic in light of later story events. *The Prowler*'s working title was *The Cost of Living*.

15. McGilligan and Buhle, *Tender Comrades*, p. 73.

16. Navasky, *Naming Names*, p. xix.

17. Shelley Winters recalled: "When I was doing *He Ran All the Way*, at each day's shooting I saw the writers and the director carefully emphasize the fact that the criminal that Garfield played could have been a productive citizen, but, owing to the environment he had been born into—the gangs, the slums, and the crowded schools—his fate

was sealed very early, and he was almost programmed to become an enemy of society. Poverty is Violence." Winters, Shelley. *Shelley II: The Middle of My Century* (New York: Simon & Schuster, 1989), p. 61.

18. Ibid., pp. 63–64.

19. Because of the duplicity necessitated by the blacklist, the Oscar that Hunter accepted for the story of *Roman Holiday* was troubling. "It became a nightmare for me," he remembered. "Nobody likes to get public credit for something he didn't do. I just took the Oscar home and tossed it in a box up in the attic of my New York town house. Looking back, I don't know what else I could do. The blacklist was still very much in effect when *Roman Holiday* was made; at least Dalton got his money. Ironically, I was forced to use fronts myself as the blacklist grew and grew." The story credit on *Roman Holiday* was not corrected until May 1993. Hunter quote from Peter H. Brown and Jim Pinkston, *Oscar Dearest: Six Decades of Scandal, Politics and Greed Behind Hollywood's Academy Awards, 1927–1986* (New York: Harper & Row, 1987), p. 235.

20. Trumbo had nothing to do with this scene. Wyler discovered the "Mouth of Truth" while sightseeing, and developed the action of the scene with Dighton and Peck. The details of who invented what in the scene are somewhat cloudy. "Peck recalls the origin of the 'Mouth of Truth' improvisation somewhat differently [from Wyler]. He says he suggested the idea to Wyler as an old Red Skelton bit: 'Willy said to go ahead and try it, but don't tell Audrey.' Keeping her in the dark is what made the scene work, of course. Her startled look of surprise leaps off the screen.'" Jan Herman, *A Talent for Trouble: The Life of Hollywood's Most Acclaimed Director, William Wyler* (New York: Putnam, 1995), p. 350.

21. Even some of the most sympathetic students of the blacklist period have argued that most of the blacklisted screenwriters were minor talents; Ring Lardner, Jr. generally gets cited as the writer whose absence was felt most deeply by the film industry. But the output of artists including

Trumbo, Waldo Salt, and Michael Wilson reveals that Lardner was not the only genuine talent whose career was compromised by HUAC. Wilson, for instance, was perhaps the only writer to do better work during the blacklist than at any other time in his career; although he stopped writing movies shortly after emerging from the underground, the subsequent revelation of which blacklist-era screenplays contained his work earned him a rightful place among the giants of American screenwriting.

22. Cook, *Dalton Trumbo*, p. 16.

23. The hopelessness in this dialogue echoes themes in Trumbo's other noirs (*Jealousy*, *Gun Crazy*, *The Prowler*, and *He Ran All the Way*), all of which deal on some level with the idea of societal misfits.

Chapter 6

1. *Our Vines* is told both from the perspective of young Selma Jacobson and that of her father, Martinius Jacobson.

2. "Hugo [Butler] was very interested in bullfighting and got Trumbo interested in it, too," Jean Rouverol Butler recalled. "Hugo told him that he couldn't defend it on moral grounds, but that he still thought it was something beautiful. And Trumbo had to admit there was something to that ... although when they started actually going to fights on Sunday afternoons, he and Cleo were very pro-bull. The first time they went, I think, they saw a bad kill and that almost sent them away for good.... [Hugo] got them to come back a couple more times, and then it was fairly soon they got to see the *indulto*, which is pretty rare. We had read about it but hadn't seen one ourselves. And that, of course, made quite an impression." Bruce Cook, *Dalton Trumbo* (New York: Scribner, 1977), pp. 230–231.

3. When Robert L. Rich failed to surface after winning a Best Original Story Oscar for *The Brave One*, several people sued the King Brothers for plagiarism, claiming they conceived the tale. As Trumbo said:

"The story is about as original as *Androcles and the Lion* or *Beautiful Joe* or *Black Beauty* or *The Yearling* or *State Fair. State Fair* is a girl and a sheep; *The Yearling* is a boy and a deer; *The Brave One* is a boy and a bull. What the hell—it was wide open for plagiarism." Victor S. Navasky, *Naming Names* (New York: Penguin, 1981), p. 156.

4. In a 1959 letter to the editor of *The Nation*, Trumbo proposed a series of articles on topics including "the American fear of death," which he found amusing. Dalton Trumbo, *Additional Dialogue: Letters of Dalton Trumbo 1942–1962*, ed. Helen Manfull (New York: Bantam, 1972), pp. 540–541.

5. Patrick McGilligan and Paul Buhle. *Tender Comrades: A Backstory of the Hollywood Blacklist* (New York: St. Martin's Press, 1997), p. 597.

6. Cook, *Dalton Trumbo*, pp. 251–252.

7. As noted earlier, Ford made his screen debut in Trumbo's 1939 film *Heaven with a Barbed Wire Fence*. Ford's character in the earlier film was similar to Lemmon's in *Cowboy*.

8. The use of the word "idiot" recalls how the word was used in *A Guy Named Joe*; both instances are evidence of how Trumbo's misanthropy showed in his movie dialogue.

9. This scene offers a far more simplistic view of bullfighting than *The Brave One*, attributable to the fact that *Cowboy* was written before Trumbo lived in Mexico, and *The Brave One* after.

10. An almost identical plot development shows up in Trumbo's 1961 film, *The Last Sunset*, which bears several coincidental similarities to *Cowboy*. While this could be evidence of Trumbo recycling story ideas from movie to movie, it may simply prove filmmakers' reliance on genre clichés.

11. In a January 2000 conversation between Christopher Trumbo and this author, Trumbo said he doubted the veracity of Cook's story about *The Young Philadelphians* (which appears on pp. 268–269 of *Dalton Trumbo*). Because Cook's book contains several errors pertaining to credits in the blacklist era, it's possible that certain elements of

the *Young Philadelphians* anecdote are false. But because several early drafts of the film are among Trumbo's papers at the University of Wisconsin, it seems likely that he had some level of participation in the project—even if that participation wasn't as laced with intrigue as Cook suggested.

Chapter 7

1. Edward Lewis's career blossomed during his tenure with Bryna; in addition to bringing *Spartacus* to Douglas's attention, Lewis suggested Trumbo write the script of *Lonely Are the Brave*. Lewis's relationship with Trumbo continued long after Trumbo stopped working with Douglas; he produced *The Fixer, The Horsemen, Executive Action*, and the television film *Ishi: The Last of His Tribe* from Trumbo scripts.

2. John Baxter, *Stanley Kubrick: A Biography* (New York: Carroll & Graf, 1997), p. 126.

3. Kirk Douglas, *The Ragman's Son: An Autobiography* (New York: Pocket Books, 1989), pp. 282–283.

4. Part of Kubrick's disdain for the film apparently stems from his desire to make a competing project about Spartacus, the never-filmed United Artists drama *The Gladiators*. Both projects were developed at the same time, part of the complex, three-year drama that Kirk Douglas termed "The Wars of Spartacus." *The Gladiators* was abandoned because *Spartacus* beat it to production.

5. "This historical revolt, which in the film appears to be a mass popular uprising that lasts for years, actually had limited support and was over in two," John Baxter wrote. "[Spartacus] was not the plaster saint of the film. He slaughtered three hundred prisoners as revenge for the killing of his friend Crixus, [and] twice he led his army to the borders of Italy, and could easily have escaped. Each time, however, he turned them back to continue destroying and looting." Baxter argued that Trumbo used Fast's

narrative as the basis for a socialist tract and that Douglas misrepresented Spartacus's historical importance. Although Baxter's points are well taken, they are predicated on a fallacy: that *Spartacus* was conceived as a historical document. Baxter extract from *Stanley Kubrick*, pp. 133–134.

6. There is ample reason why Curtis's character feels shoehorned into the story: Douglas had Trumbo write the role for Curtis, whom Douglas befriended while making *The Vikings* and who owed a picture to Universal.

7. As noted earlier, Trumbo's version had more dialogue in the expositional sequences; while Trumbo certainly contributed vivid visual ideas to many of his projects, the effective changes that Kubrick made to *Spartacus* underline that Trumbo worked best with words, not pictures.

8. Ustinov and Laughton had roles in the drama behind Trumbo's screen credit for *Spartacus*. When word began to slip out that "Sam Jackson" (as production reports listed the film's screenwriter) was actually Trumbo, Ustinov and Laughton visited him, separately, to discuss their characters. Such open meetings fed widespread gossip about Sam Jackson's identity, which led to speculative newspaper items. This publicity contributed to the atmosphere in which Douglas decided to credit Trumbo. Ustinov, who reputedly improvised many of his character's witty asides, won a Best Supporting Actor Oscar for *Spartacus*.

9. Because the soundtrack of the scene had been lost in the interim, Curtis rerecorded his dialogue and Oscar-winning English actor Anthony Hopkins used convincing mimicry to read the lines that were originally spoken by the late Olivier.

10. Trumbo's sure hand can be felt throughout the film, and not just because of the detailed camera directions that he put into the screenplay. After viewing a rough cut of *Spartacus*, Trumbo legendarily wrote an 80-page memo dissecting what he perceived to be the picture's problems. Douglas, who described the memo as "the most brilliant analysis of movie-making that

I have ever read," called for extensive re-shoots and followed many of Trumbo's directions; the memo is one of the reasons that Kubrick never considered *Spartacus* a "Kubrick film." Douglas, *The Ragman's Son*, p. 297.

11. This is understandable, because *Hawaii* was structured not by Trumbo but by screenwriter Daniel Taradash.

12. In these surprising lines, Trumbo foreshadows a story beyond this one, that of Caesar's reign. The function of the dialogue is not merely to make a winking nod to history, however; it is to make a comment about how the son destroys the father. Although Gracchus molded Caesar into a political being, the speed with which Caesar changed his allegiance shows that he is very much a child of Crassus's generation. Raised on power, subjugation, and opportunism, Caesar promises to become more of a monster than either of his masters, and Crassus's sad line about fearing him reveals that all he loves is lost—even though he has "saved" Rome from the slaves, he can't save Rome from itself. It is important to note that Caesar was not a character in Fast's book.

13. This scene contains a glaring error. Varinia's earlier dialogue about a "young god" whose sighs become the night wind suggests that she's polytheistic, while her comment upon seeing Spartacus crucified—"Oh, God, why can't you die"—suggests she's monotheistic.

14. Douglas, *The Ragman's Son*, p. 296.

15. Patrick McGilligan and Paul Buhle, *Tender Comrades: A Backstory of the Hollywood Blacklist* (New York: St. Martin's Press, 1997), p. 219.

Chapter 8

1. Background on *Exodus* from Otto Preminger, *Preminger: An Autobiography* (Garden City, N.Y.: Doubleday, 1977), pp. 165–172.

2. Conversation between Christopher Trumbo and author, January 2000.

3. When Trumbo and Preminger worked together on a draft of *Bunny Lake Is Missing* (1965, Columbia), Trumbo noted the problem of writing talky movies: "Examine our individual scenes," Trumbo wrote about the *Bunny Lake* draft. "There is not a cinema scene among them. They are nothing but talk, each torrent of dialogue conducted against a static set." Trumbo convinced Preminger to discard this version of *Bunny Lake*, and the version the director filmed was written by John and Penelope Mortimer. Dalton Trumbo, *Additional Dialogue: Letters of Dalton Trumbo, 1942–1962*, ed. Helen Manfull (New York: Bantam, 1972), pp. 580–582.

4. A New York City–born actor who began his career in the Yiddish theater, David Opatoshu also appeared in *The Fixer*. His two appearances in Trumbo movies distinguished him as one of the finest interpreters of Trumbo's dialogue; while Spencer Tracy personified the lovable rascal of Trumbo's war movies and Kirk Douglas was the most powerful vessel for Trumbo's rebel-hero iconography, Opatoshu invested his *Exodus* and *Fixer* roles with a weary, knowing passion that fit Trumbo's mix of cynicism and optimism.

5. See note 5, chapter 7.

6. By all reports, this drama about the relationship between sixteenth-century Spanish conquistador Hernando Cortés and the Aztec ruler he vanquished, Montezuma, was the best of Trumbo's unproduced screenplays. John Huston was to direct.

7. Trumbo, *Additional Dialogue*, p. 539.

Chapter 9

1. Bruce Cook, *Dalton Trumbo* (New York: Scribner, 1977), p. 270.

2. Trumbo is hardly the only major screenwriter who didn't invent most of his stories; other notables whose output is filled with adaptations include Billy Wilder, Ernest Lehman, Horton Foote, and Francis Ford Coppola.

3. See note 13, chapter 2.

4. In Abbey's book, Paul's crime is draft dodging.

5. Abbey described his reactions to Trumbo's script: "It's very good—the dialogue is much livelier, heartier, wittier than my own. More authenticity in the jail and truck scenes. Swift pace, no drag. Follows the original in all essentials. I'm delighted." Edward Abbey, *Confessions of a Barbarian: Selections From the Journals of Edward Abbey, 1951–1969* (New York: Little, Brown, 1994), p. 174.

6. Trumbo wrote to Douglas: "Once in while when God smiles and the table is tilted just slightly in our favor, something happens. It comes from inside and reveals what we really are. I think it happened with you in [*Lonely Are the Brave*]. I think they are going to leave the theatre saying, 'That is what I really am. Or at least it is what I want to be in my finest hour.' You showed the heart of a man." Dalton Trumbo, *Additional Dialogue: Letters of Dalton Trumbo 1942–1962*, ed. Helen Manfull. (New York: Bantam, 1972), p. 602.

7. A New Jersey native who started his film career in 1930 as an editor, David Miller is generally regarded as a journeyman whose craft peaked with *Lonely Are the Brave*; he later reteamed with Trumbo on *Executive Action*.

8. When Trumbo used a similar technique in *Exodus*, he often overstated the steps in layered lines, which may owe to director Otto Preminger's close supervision of Trumbo's work on that picture, as Preminger's films often featured overwrought dialogue.

9. Trumbo's biographer noted similarities between Johnson and Trumbo's grandfather, frontier sheriff Millard F. Tillery. Cook, *Dalton Trumbo*, p. 48.

10. Legendary critic Pauline Kael criticized Trumbo's use of foreshadowing in a 1967 essay about cinematic story construction. "In *Lonely Are the Brave*, the whole movie [is] preparation for the final collision. In life there were accidents; in art, it was assumed, there had to be reasons, and fates

were explained by character and circumstance. Hack writers and directors showed
their hand, forcing each plot creakingly into
place." In a separate 1967 essay, she cited
Lonely Are the Brave among interesting recent westerns, but wrote: "Despite the inge-
nious and entertaining performance by Walter Matthau and the excellent performance
by Kirk Douglas, the Dalton Trumbo script
gives the film that awful messagey self-right-
eousness of *High Noon* and *The Gunfighter*
and a fake iconic tragedy, an O. Henry
finish." Kael's dislike for Trumbo's approach
echoes concerns about Trumbo's pedantry
that permeate this book, and parallel the disdain in Lester Cole's reaction to Trumbo's
"only victims" speech (see note 7, chapter 4).
Pauline Kael, *For Keeps: 30 Years at the
Movies* (New York: Plume, 1994), p. 104, 136.

11. Much of this action is echoed during a sequence of the Sylvester Stallone adventure film *First Blood* (1982, Caralco)—
another story about a rebel in conflict with
"unjust" law. *First Blood* novelist David Mor-
rell has cited *Lonely* as an influence.

12. Kirk Douglas, *The Ragman's Son:
An Autobiography* (New York: Pocket Books,
1989), p. 310.

13. Although the word "counterculture" did not enter common usage until
about 1968, it is used here as a loose reference to the societal elements that later con-
gealed as the counterculture.

14. Taylor and Burton divorced in the
early 1970s, then remarried in 1975, only to
divorce again in 1976.

15. Taylor and Burton openly acknowledged that they did *The Sandpiper* for
money. Taylor got $1 million, Burton half
that. "'The film was so bad it nearly broke up
our marriage,' said Richard a few years
later.... As for Elizabeth, she later heard the
news of a good review for her performance
in *The Sandpiper*, and she replied that she
intended to sue for libel: she was surprised
that anyone could find the film remotely interesting, let alone intelligent or laced with
human feeling." Donald Spoto, *A Passion for
Life: The Biography of Elizabeth Taylor* (New
York: HarperCollins, 1995), pp. 219–220.

16. The son of actor James Mason,
Morgan Mason shifted from acting to producing when he became an adult; his credits include coproducing the provocative
drama *sex, lies, and videotape* (1989, Miramax).

17. Taylor and Burton reportedly did a
great deal of ad-libbing during the production, so they may share some of the blame for
the picture's fatuous dialogue.

18. Background on *The Cavern* and
Heaven with a Gun from Cook, *Dalton
Trumbo*, p. 244.

19. The second film was eventually
made—by the same producer but without
Taradash or Trumbo—as *The Hawaiians*
(1970, United Artists). It flopped.

20. Patrick McGilligan, *Backstory 2:
Interviews with Screenwriters of the 1940s and
1950s* (Los Angeles: University of California
Press, 1991), p. 325.

21. On projects such as *Hawaii*, which
are repeatedly reconcieved during laborious
development processes, screenwriters often
have to scramble to both introduce and resolve thematic material that got lost in the
shuffle of drafts and rewrites. A parallel to
the way Abner's softening is treated in this
scene with Jerusha can be found in the last
segment of *Papillon*. In that film, two characters who have been separated for years are
reunited, so the screenwriting challenge is
to re-establish and then resolve the characters' relationship in a minimum of screen
time. That the *Papillon* sequence was written not by Dalton Trumbo, but by his son,
Christopher Trumbo, indicates that Dalton
Trumbo passed on his gift for finding creative solutions to narrative problems.

22. In the aforementioned 1959 letter
to the editor of *The Nation* (see note 4, chapter 6), Trumbo pitches an article about the
inhumanity of the American penal system.
The language of the letter echoes Jerusha's
dialogue: "What in our national character
makes us so ferocious? Lack of faith? Lack
of love? Lack of respect for man himself?"
Trumbo, *Additional Dialogue*, pg. 538–539.

23. See note 4, chapter 8.

24. Trumbo reteamed with Frankenheimer for another brutal drama, 1971's *The

Horsemen. The picture, which enjoyed neither critical nor commercial success, was the only of Trumbo's major films unavailable for review in this book, hence its seemingly dismissive treatment.

25. Trumbo apparently wrote several more hallucinations that were shot but then excised by Frankenheimer; while Trumbo biographer Bruce Cook argues that these scenes would have made the film less oppressive, a look at the rampant and distracting hallucinations in *Johnny Got His Gun* suggests that Frankenheimer was right to make the cuts. The film has a powerful flow that would have been slowed by such intrusions, and it seems odd to suggest that a true story about imprisonment should be softened by heartening vignettes. Cook, *Dalton Trumbo*, pp. 290–291.

Chapter 10

1. In 1940, *Johnny Got His Gun* was performed as a one-hour radio drama starring Jimmy Cagney as Joe Bonham; in the late '40s, John Garfield considered playing the character in a film. (Garfield's final film, ironically, was the partially Trumbo-penned *He Ran All the Way*.) Finally, celebrated Spanish director Luis Buñuel nearly helmed an adaptation of the book in the mid-'60s; when plans for that version fell apart, Trumbo made the decision to become a first-time director at age 65. Bruce Cook, *Dalton Trumbo* (New York: Scribner, 1977), p. 300.

2. Christopher Trumbo, who associate produced *Johnny Got His Gun*, noted that the film's color scheme actually has a third element—albeit one that is lost on those who view the picture via the poor-quality print often shown on television and featured on the only widely available videotape. The third level of the color scheme involves the fantasy sequences, all of which are in color but treated in some peculiar way. Some have obvious filter effects, while others have a desaturated, surreal quality. Conversation between Christopher Trumbo and author, January 2000.

3. As he did in *We Who Are Young* (see note 14, chapter 2), Trumbo used his mother's maiden name, Tillery, for a character.

4. Trumbo's father's name was Orus Bonham Trumbo.

5. A New York City–born character actor who played regularly in films and television from the early '40s to the late '70s, McGraw made another memorable appearance in a Trumbo film: in *Spartacus*, he played the brutal guard Marcellus, whose murder is the event that begins Spartacus's revolution against Rome.

6. Trumbo used the real name of his onetime employer as Joe's employer.

7. Actress Marsha Hunt, the former blacklistee who played Joe's mother, recalled this about the production: "Such a long story, that movie. We had to shoot the death scene in the very room in downtown L.A. where Dalton's own father had died. No reason on earth for us to do it there, to drag the lights and cameras up those narrow stairs. But for Dalton it was such a subjective venture. He was so bound up in his own statement." Patrick McGilligan and Paul Buhle, *Tender Comrades: A Backstory of the Hollywood Blacklist* (New York: St. Martin's Press, 1997), p. 318.

8. Sutherland was also involved in the Trumbo films *F.T.A.* and *Executive Action* (see chapter 11).

9. Trumbo played this role because the actor who was to play the medical director was disqualified by the Screen Actors Guild on such short notice that a replacement could not be hired. Bruce Cook, *Dalton Trumbo*, photo caption.

10. As noted in chapter 1, Trumbo's parents were Christian Scientists. In a January 2000 conversation with the author, Christopher Trumbo noted that certain elements of Christian Science philosophy appear in some of his father's films, including *A Guy Named Joe*. That Dalton Trumbo spoke to a religion that he did not practice as an adult is indicative of how deeply his personality colored his work; it also echoes

the significance of parallels between Trumbo's politics and those of his movie characters.

11. See note 25, chapter 4.

12. Christopher Trumbo said the film's technical shortcomings should be considered in the context of the production's limitations. All of Sutherland's scenes, for instance, were shot in two days; moreover, time was lost on Sutherland's first day because the crew had to build a camera dolly. Conversation between Christopher Trumbo and author, January 2000.

13. Critical opinion on *Johnny Got His Gun*, which won awards including the *Prix spécial du Jury* at the 1971 Cannes Film Festival, was split, but its champions included Pulitzer Prize–winning critic Roger Ebert. "Trumbo has taken the most difficult sort of material ... and handled it, strange to say, in a way that's not so much anti-war as pro-life," Ebert wrote. "Perhaps that's why I admire it. Instead of belaboring ironic points about the 'war to end war,' Trumbo remains stubbornly on the human level. He lets his ideology grow out of his characters, instead of imposing it from above." Roger Ebert, *Roger Ebert's Video Companion: 1998 Edition* (Kansas City: Andrews McMeel, 1997), p. 412.

Chapter 11

1. Notorious anti–Vietnam War activist Jane Fonda gathered several friends in a performance troupe called F.T.A. (billed in ads as "Free the Army," but taken from the colloquialism "Fuck the Army"). Director Francine Parker filmed several of the troupe's performances, and these vignettes were put together as a film titled *F.T.A.* Trumbo was among several writers who contributed to sketches featured in the documentary. Owing to controversy surrounding Fonda's antiwar activities, the picture received limited distribution—as well as lukewarm reviews. George Haddad-Garcia, *The Films of Jane Fonda* (Secaucus, N.J.: Citadel Press, 1981), pp. 162–164.

2. Trumbo admired Kennedy for many reasons, among them the president's decision to cross, accompanied by his brother Robert, a Catholic War Veterans picket line at a screening of *Spartacus*. After seeing the film—which right-wingers protested because of Trumbo's politics—Kennedy gave a complimentary quote to the press.

3. Background on *Executive Action* and Trumbo quote from Gary Fishgall, *Against Type: The Biography of Burt Lancaster* (New York: Scribner, 1995), pp. 291–292.

4. Patrick McGilligan and Paul Buhle, *Tender Comrades: A Backstory of the Hollywood Blacklist* (New York: St. Martin's Press, 1997), pg. 111.

5. See note 7, chapter 9.

6. Although it would be exaggerating to say, based on his appearances in *Johnny Got His Gun* and *Papillon*, that Trumbo had a screen career ahead of him, his commanding air and alacrity with language could have been put to use in character parts; the acting careers of directors including Martin Scorsese, Sydney Pollack, and Barry Levinson come to mind as precedents. Certainly, the baggage that Trumbo brought with him was almost sufficient to make him an interesting screen presence.

7. Hoffman once described Trumbo this way: "He's a real feisty man, and he's got a combination of toughness and sophistication and integrity that I felt were right for Dega." Bruce Cook, *Dalton Trumbo* (New York: Scribner, 1977), p. 4.

8. Information on Goldman's contribution from William Goldman, *Adventures in the Screen Trade: A Personal View of Hollywood and Screenwriting* (New York: Warner Books, 1984), p. 133. In a January 2000 phone conversation with the author, Christopher Trumbo recalled that the team of Robert Benton and David Newman did a treatment that began the long development process of *Papillon*; in order, they were succeeded by Goldman, Semple, Dalton Trumbo, and Christopher Trumbo.

9. While the facts of Charrière's life may suggest that his spirit was indeed indomitable, the oversized heroism of the

finale parallels the portayal of other real-life characters in Trumbo films, including *The Flying Irishman*, *Thirty Seconds Over Tokyo*, and *Spartacus*. Even though Dalton and Christopher Trumbo tried to ground Papillon's story in reality, a certain amount of Tinseltown gloss was still required to put over some aspects of the movie.

10. Cook, *Dalton Trumbo*, p. 4.

11. McGilligan and Buhle, *Tender Comrades*, pp. 328–329.

12. *Roman Holiday* was remade for television in 1987 (see Filmography), and a verbatim reference to *Roman Holiday*'s Mouth of Truth sequence appears in the 1994 film *Only You* (Columbia).

13. Dalton Trumbo, *Additional Dialogue: Letters of Dalton Trumbo, 1942–1962*, ed. Helen Manfull (New York: Bantam, 1972), p. 411.

Bibliography

Abbey, Edward. *The Brave Cowboy: An Old Tale in a New Time*. New York: Dodd, Mead (1956).

_____. *Confessions of a Barbarian: Selections From the Journals of Edward Abbey, 1951–1969*. New York: Little, Brown (1994).

Adams, Les, and Buck Rainey. *Shoot-Em-Ups: The Complete Reference Guide to Westerns of the Sound Era*. New Rochelle, N.Y.: Arlington House (1978).

Agee, James. *Agee on Film: Volume One*. New York: Perigree (1983).

Baxter, John. *Stanley Kubrick: A Biography*. New York: Carroll & Graf (1997).

Behlmer, Rudy, ed. *Inside Warner Bros. (1935-1951)*. New York: Viking (1985).

Brown, Peter H., and Jim Pinkston. *Oscar Dearest: Six Decades of Scandal, Politics and Greed Behind Hollywood's Academy Awards, 1927–1986*. New York: Harper & Row (1987).

Caute, David. *Joseph Losey: A Revenge on Life*. New York: Oxford University Press (1994).

Ceplair, Larry, and Steven Englund. *The Inquisition in Hollywood: Politics in the Film Community, 1930–1960*. Garden City, N.Y.: Anchor Press/Doubleday (1980).

Cole, Lester. *Hollywood Red*. Berkeley, Calif.: Ramparts Press (1981).

Connors, Martin, and Jim Craddock, eds. *VideoHound's Golden Movie Retriever*, 1998 edition. Detroit: Visible Ink (1997).

Cook, Bruce. *Dalton Trumbo*. New York: Scribner (1977).

Dimmitt, Richard Bertrand. *A Title Guide to the Talkies*. New York: Scarecrow (1965).

Dmytryk, Edward. *It's a Hell of a Life But Not a Bad Living: A Hollywood Memoir*. New York: Times Books (1978).

Dooley, Roger. *From Scarface to Scarlett: American Films in the 1930s*. New York: Harcort Brace Jovanovich (1981).

Douglas, Kirk. *The Ragman's Son: An Autobiography*. New York: Pocket Books (1989). [Originally published in 1988 by Simon & Schuster.]

Drabble, Margaret, ed. *The Oxford Companion to English Literature*, fifth edition. New York: Oxford University Press (1985).

Ebert, Roger. *Roger Ebert's Video Companion: 1998 Edition*. Kansas City, Mo.: Andrews McMeel (1997).

Fishgall, Gary. *Against Type: The Biography of Burt Lancaster*. New York: Scribner (1995).

Goldman, William. *Adventures in the Screen Trade: A Personal View of Hollywood and Screenwriting*. New York: Warner Books (1984). [Originally published in 1983 by Warner.]

Haddad-Garcia, George. *The Films of Jane Fonda*. Secaucus, N.J.: Citadel (1981).

Halliwell, Leslie. *Halliwell's Film Guide*, 1996 edition. Edited by John Walker. New York: HarperCollins (1995).

243

Herman, Jan. *A Talent for Trouble: The Life of Hollywood's Most Acclaimed Director, William Wyler*. New York: Putnam (1995).

Hirsch, E.D. Jr., Joseph F. Kett, and James Trefil. *The Dictionary of Cultural Literacy*, second editon. Boston: Houghton Mifflin (1993).

Jacobs, Diane. *Christmas in July: The Life and Art of Preston Sturges*. Los Angeles: University of California Press (1992).

Jewell, Richard B., and Vernon Harbin. *The RKO Story*. New York: Arlington House (1982).

Kael, Pauline. *For Keeps: 30 Years at the Movies*. New York: Plume (1994).

Katz, Ephraim. *The Film Encyclopedia*, third edition, revised by Fred Klein and Ronald Dean Nolen. New York: HarperCollins (1998).

LoBrutto, Vincent. *Stanley Kubrick: A Biography*. New York: Donald I. Fine (1997).

Magill, Frank N. *Magill's Survey of Cinema: English Language Films* (Second Series). Englewood Cliffs, N.J.: Salem Press (1981).

Martin, Jay. *Nathanael West: The Art of His Life*. New York: Farrar, Straus and Giroux (1970).

McBride, Joseph. *Frank Capra: The Catastrophe of Success*. New York: Simon & Schuster (1992).

McGilligan, Patrick. *Backstory 2: Interviews with Screenwriters of the 1940s and 1950s*. Los Angeles: University of California Press (1991).

_____, and Paul Buhle. *Tender Comrades: A Backstory of the Hollywood Blacklist*. New York: St. Martin's (1997).

Michener, James A. *Hawaii*. New York: Random House (1959).

Morley, Christopher. *Kitty Foyle*. Philadelphia: Lippincot (1959). [Originally published in 1939.]

Munden, Kenneth W., ed. *The American Film Institute Catalog of Motion Pictures Produced in the United States: Feature Films 1931–1940*. Berkeley: University of California Press (1993).

Nash, Jay Robert, and Stanley Ralph Ross, eds. *The Motion Picture Guide*. Chicago: Cinebooks (1986).

Navasky, Victor S. *Naming Names*. New York: Penguin (1981). [Originally published in 1980 by The Viking Press.]

Peary, Danny. *Cult Movies: The Classics, the Sleepers, the Weird, and the Wonderful*. New York: Grammercy Books (1998). [Originally published in 1981 by Dell.]

Phillips, Cabell. *From the Crash to the Blitz: 1929–1939*. London: Macmillan (1969).

Preminger, Otto. *Preminger: An Autobiography*. Garden City, N.Y.: Doubleday. 1977.

Rogers, Ginger. *Ginger: My Story*. New York: HarperCollins (1991).

Salo, Matti. *Hiljaiset sankarit: Käsikirjoitksen tekijät Hollywoodin mustalla listalla* (*The Silent Heroes [The Brave Ones]: Screenwriters on the Hollywood Blacklist*). Helsinki: Painatuskeskus (1994).

Shales, Tom, et al. *The American Film Heritage: Impressions from the American Film Institute Archives*. Washington, D.C.: Acropolis Books (1972).

Spoto, Donald. *A Passion for Life: The Biography of Elizabeth Taylor*. New York: HarperCollins (1995).

Stempel, Tom. *FrameWork: A History of Screenwriting in the American Film*. New York: Continuum (1988).

Trumbo, Dalton. *Johnny Got His Gun*. New York: Bantam (1989). [Originally published in 1939 by Lippincot.]

_____. *Additional Dialogue: Letters of Dalton Trumbo 1942–1962*, ed. Helen Manfull. New York: Bantam (1972). [Originally published in 1970 by M. Evans.]

Uris, Leon. *Exodus*. New York: Bantam (1986). [Originally published in 1958 by Doubleday.]

Winters, Shelley. *Shelley II: The Middle of My Century*. New York: Simon & Schuster (1989).

Television shows

Backstory: Roman Holiday. American Movie Classics. May 4, 1999.

"Honor or Betrayal?" *Nightline*. ABC. March 19, 1999.

Online resources

All-Movie Guide. www.allmovie.com. September 1998–August 1999.

Internet Movie Data Base. www.imdb.com. September 1998–August 1999.

Index